PRAISE FOR
TORPEDO JUNCTION

"Score . . . equally . . . to reopning . . . its . . . to . . . both
lovers of the sea and military historians . . . It brings a
very readable focus about . . . that one chapter of the U-boat
war."
    —Book Review, Oakland, Cal.)

"A ROUSING SEA STORY . . . a worthy tribute to the
brave seamen who fought at Torpedo Junction . . ."
    —Union News/Springfield Republican

"Hickam puts the readers right in the midst of a deadly
war waged by German submarines at America's
step."
    —The Record (N.J.)

"DRAMA . . . AND SUSPENSE . . . Detail . . . it reads
interestingly . . . That's The Torpedo . . . No truck is . . .
    —Evening Bulletin (Philadelphia, Miss.)

"EMINENTLY READABLE . . . captures the reality, the
very essence of what it was like to contend with the U-boat
onslaught in America, particularly in World War . . . U.S.
— . . . Davis, author of Mr. Roosevelt's . . ."

*Books by Homer Hickam*

OCTOBER SKY

BACK TO THE MOON

THE COALWOOD WAY

TORPEDO JUNCTION

# HOMER H. HICKAM

# TORPEDO JUNCTION

## U-boat War Off America's East Coast, 1942

A Dell Book

Published by
Dell Publishing
a division of
Random House, Inc.
1540 Broadway
New York, New York 10036

ISBN: 0-440-21027-5

Reprinted by arrangement with the United States Naval Institute, Annapolis, Maryland

Printed in the United States of America
Published simultaneously in Canada

May 1991

OPM  16  15  14  13  12  11  10

To the United States Coast Guard Cutter *Dione* (WPC 107). Wherever she is, may she be happy in the knowledge that she served her country well.

The massacre which the U-boats were able to "enjoy" along the Atlantic coast in 1942 was as great a national disaster as if saboteurs had blown up half a dozen of our biggest munitions factories.

SAMUEL ELIOT MORISON

I will show that the U-boat alone can win the war . . . nothing is impossible to us!

ADMIRAL KARL DOENITZ

The only thing that ever really frightened me during the war was the U-boat peril . . . the U-boat attack was our worst evil. It would have been wise for the Germans to stake all upon it.

WINSTON CHURCHILL

# Contents

# Foreword

This thoroughly documented and detailed account of the 1942 slaughter of ships by U-boats off the East and Gulf Coasts of the United States is by far the best that I have read covering that black episode in our naval history. During the first six months of 1942, foreign invaders dominated our coastal waters for the first time since the War of 1812. While the navy's attention was riveted on the far Pacific and the Japanese Combined Fleet, arguably the best navy in the world at that time, the Allied merchant marine was being decimated on our Atlantic doorstep. When midyear arrived, more tonnage had been sunk by a handful of U-boats than had been put down in the Pacific by the entire Japanese Navy from Pearl Harbor to Midway! Painful though the losses were, they might have proven terminal except for the intervention of Hitler, who refused to release more U-boats from his own intuitive projects. As a result, there were never more than a dozen U-boats manned by 500 or so men on the American station at any time, and the first did not arrive until weeks after war was declared. That such a small force could inflict such damage was a damning indictment of both our readiness and our priorities.

As we read this fascinating account, it seems incredible

that we were so unprepared after having observed for two years the U-boats and their performance against the British. The often amateurish efforts of our forces in the early months is not remarkable; such is usual at the onset of war. These were the same men who two years later as seasoned combat veterans were sweeping the seas. But the absence of ASW ships, doctrine, and training; the refusal to set up convoys; the employment of the few available warships in solo sweeping and patrol operations twenty-five years after it had been proven to be a useless tactic against submarines; and the refusal to employ fleet destroyers against an enemy running amuck only a few miles away defies logic. One answer seems to lie in the orientation and dogmatic personality of Admiral Ernest J. King, COMINCH, and his Pacific-first outlook. Despite the repeated urging of the British Admiralty, for which King had little use, the intervention of President Roosevelt was required to start convoys and provide adequate forces to escort them. In fairness to King, he had tried two years before to push a program of escort construction, but it was turned down by Roosevelt. When escorted convoys were finally implemented, the U-boats were quickly forced into the less heavily defended Caribbean and Gulf, and finally back to the North Atlantic, where the massive and decisive Battle of the Convoys was fought out in the "Bloody Winter" of 1942–43. After their defeat in that battle, the wolfpacks withdrew, and with them went Germany's last chance to avoid final defeat.

Oddly enough, the author of this definitive account of our home-front naval battle of World War II is a decorated *army* combat officer who served with the Fourth Infantry Division in Vietnam in 1967–68. But the nearly forgotten battle of 1942 has held a long-time fascination for him, so much so that he even dived down to examine numerous wrecks of that era. This included dives to the *U-352* and the *U-85* to verify the damage suffered during their final fights, a bit of research above and beyond the call of duty for most writers. He does not content himself with a description of the actions, which in view of the large number of ships sunk could become repetitious, but also deals with the personalities and people who manned the ships and U-boats, as well as those who controlled their destinies from the command hierarchy. This provides interesting insights and welcome relief from the slaughter.

This book should also give us a greater appreciation of the hard life of the "small boys" in this coastal war. At the time, many of us on the big Atlantic convoys, often engaged in pitched battles with up to thirty combatants involved, were prone to assign second-class status to the coastal fighting. But the seas were as rough off Hatteras as off Iceland, the escort ships were much smaller and more uncomfortable, and the losses were horrifying. Most of the ASW vessels were slower than the U-boats, less experienced, and outgunned. It is surprising that more were not destroyed by U-boat gun action. Yet *Icarus* and *Thetis*, small 165-foot cutters, were able to successfully attack and sink the larger *U-352* and *U-157*. One of their sister cutters, the *Dione*, is used by the author to represent all of the small ASW vessels out on that lonely and deadly sea. He returns often to her and follows her as she fights from tragedy to triumph.

The lessons of this book should not be overlooked by naval officers today. Only a few submarines were able to inflict shocking damage on us just a few miles from our shoreline. What would have been the result had Germany been aware of the pending Pearl Harbor attack and been able to pre-position twenty or thirty boats, including minelayers? The slaughter would have been much greater, and the East Coast would in all likelihood have been completely shut down.

There are today two important differences from 1942, and neither is in our favor. First, the Russian submarine fleet is far larger and more imposing than was the German. In the event of war, these boats would surely be deployed ahead of time on our shipping lanes. Many have minelaying capabilities, while our minesweeping resources are minimal. In the 1942 debacle, fleet escorts were withheld to protect the heavy units rather than fight the U-boats. Would future hostilities see a similar scenario, with most of the available escorts protecting the carrier battle groups? The second difference is that the American merchant marine is a mere shadow of its 1942 size. Today, losses such as we suffered in 1942 would completely destroy our sea-cargo-carrying capacity in six months!

This book is good reading for sea history buffs, but it also
should be required reading for professional officers responsible for antisubmarine warfare and the protection of our maritime defense zone. The mistakes are all right here to read
about. Let us not make them again.

                                        John M. Waters
                                        Captain, USCG (Retired)

# Preface

**P**erhaps I will never know why or how I came to write this book. I do know it began as an adventure in that most beautiful but treacherous sea off North Carolina known as the Graveyard of the Atlantic. There, I found not only danger and excitement but also a mystery. Why were there German U-boat wrecks there? And why were there so many tankers and freighters lying dead with great torpedo wounds in their sides on that white, sandy bottom? I had to find out. As I searched out the truth for more than a decade, it gradually dawned on me that I was not only solving a mystery but unveiling a wonderful story. But before that story could be told, there would have to be many people who would have to help me. I will never be able to name them all, but there are a few who stand out in my memory.

First there were the divers who accompanied and led me to the great wrecks. John Harkins, Ed Huff, Cliff McClure, Dave Todd, "Buddy" Stokes, Lucy Fuller, Carl Spurlock, Bruce Hutson, "Doogie" Pledger, Bob Eastep, Jim Bunch, John Smathers, and Art Lepage were just some of the colorful crew of scuba divers and boat captains who helped me survive those deep, dark, and often deadly waters.

While diving created my interest, only the memories and

reflections of the men who fought the battle they called "Torpedo Junction" could give me the insight and information to write about what happened. The names of those individuals who took the time from their still busy lives to help me can be found in the primary source bibliography of this book, but special mention has to be made of the kind and careful assistance given me by Major Harold "Swede" Larson, USMC (Retired), and Rear Admiral James Alger, Jr., USCG (Retired), of the USCGC *Dione*; Harry Heyman, Bill Mouquin, and Rear Admiral Hamilton W. Howe, USN (Retired), of the USS *Roper*; and John Bruce of the USCGC *Icarus*.

My research into the archival documentation was also assisted by many over the years. They include Mrs. Lucile B. Portlock of the Norfolk Public Library System, Ms. Sally Ripatti of the Knoxville-Knox County Public Library, Dr. D. C. Allard and Mr. Bernard Cavalcante of the Naval Historical Center, Dr. Jürgen Rohwer of the Bibliothek Für Zeitgeschichte, Ms. Charlotte Valentine of The Mariner's Museum, and the entire staff of the Huntsville, Alabama, Public Library.

To the staff of the Naval Institute Press, who have worked so hard to make *Torpedo Junction* a reality, I offer my thanks, especially to Ms. Deborah Estes and Ms. Carol Swartz, attentive editors to a new writer, and Ms. Linda Cullen, who found, on her own, many of the photographs in this book.

And, finally, on a personal note, my thanks must include Ms. Mary Lou Shunk, who read the first draft, and Ms. Linda Terry, who encouraged and helped me to keep going and accomplished the artwork on the charts found in this book. I would also thank my parents, who gave me the perspective to not only appreciate an adventure but to try to make it a positive accomplishment as well.

# Introduction

This is the story of a World War II naval battle that began soon after Pearl Harbor when German U-boats arrived off the American Atlantic coast and began to decimate merchant shipping. Before the battle ended, the U-boats would inflict terrible damage and suffering not only on the Allied merchant marine but also on the small force of obsolete warships sent against them. The bloodiest of the battle's many bull's-eyes was the sea off North Carolina, known for centuries as the "Graveyard of the Atlantic." This was the patrol area assigned to the United States Coast Guard Cutter *Dione*. She was always there, grappling with an often unseen but always deadly enemy, fighting a battle that had to be won but was in doubt almost to the end. This book, then, is the story of all who were in this battle—but especially it is the story of the brave men of the *Dione* who fought what they called "The Battle of Torpedo Junction."

# 1

# Paukenschlag

f lines were to be drawn on a map from Cape Race, Newfoundland, down the east coast of the North American continent and into the Gulf of Mexico and the Caribbean, they would coincide with perhaps the most congested sea lanes in the world. When the United States entered World War II, the industrial cities of the eastern seaboard were particularly vulnerable to the disruption of these lanes. Fuel was required to keep those cities from freezing during the winter, and most of that fuel was provided by ships hauling it from Curaçao and Aruba in the Netherlands West Indies, from Venezuelan oil fields, and from the Gulf of Mexico ports of Corpus Christi, Houston, and Port Arthur, Texas. The United States military was also vulnerable. The oil reserves of the United States were simply not large enough to meet the sustained, high demands of world conflict. To cut her supply lines along the Atlantic coast and to the south would be, in effect, to defeat the United States, to freeze much of her population, and force her out of the war. In January 1942, five German Type IX U-boats set forth to accomplish all that.

Although Admiral Karl Doenitz, commander of the German U-boat fleet, was surprised by Pearl Harbor and the entry of the United States into the war, he quickly improvised a plan for an attack across the Atlantic. Sensing a great opportunity, he proposed sending twelve U-boats to American waters, six of which were to be the new Type IXs, which had greater fuel and armaments than the standard Type VIIs.[1] Doenitz called this operation *Paukenschlag*, the word meaning "drumroll." The admiral's bold plan, however, was turned down. The Mediterranean and Norwegian fronts, he was told, were of first priority for his U-boats, and not some risky adventure across the Atlantic. Doenitz was disappointed but not surprised by the denial. It was simply a continuation of the bureaucratic battle he had fought for what he considered to be the proper operation of his U-boats since the beginning of the war.

Admiral Doenitz was an intense, studious man who had spent much of the years after World War I planning a huge force of submarines that would lay waste to convoys in the Atlantic. But on the day Britain declared hostilities against Germany, the *Kriegsmarine* had in its inventory only twenty-two U-boats large enough to operate in the open ocean.[2] Ordered to blockade the British Isles and pin down the Royal Navy, Doenitz knew that all he could actually do while waiting for a promised increase in the numbers of his U-boats was to inflict a few wounds here and there using "hit and run" tactics. Still, his fiercely loyal commanders were able to spring several surprises on the Royal Navy, the most spectacular being the sinking of the battleship *Royal Oak* inside the British fleet anchorage at Scapa Flow. This success, perhaps more than any other, was the one that established the U-boat myth of reckless daring and made a hero of the *U-47*'s commander, Günther Prien. Doenitz did not mind the adulation given to one of his commanders. If it helped in his struggle to wage U-boat warfare and get more U-boats built, he minded nothing.

The first of what U-boat sailors would come to refer to as their "Happy Time" would be in the summer of 1940. The British had gone to the convoy system to defend their merchant ships as they brought vital supplies from the United States and Canada. This system had worked well during World War I and, it was assumed, would be just as effective in

World War II, especially with the new ASDIC "pinging" equipment that would allow defending destroyers to locate intruding submarines. Doenitz, however, had studied the convoy system and thought that he had found a way to defeat it. His tactic was to send his U-boats out singly but with orders to immediately radio command headquarters the moment a convoy was sighted. When this was done, other U-boats would be routed into the area and ordered to wait until night, surface, and attack. Doenitz reasoned that ASDIC would not be able to locate the U-boats on the surface and that night would allow them to get in close without being spotted by lookouts. To the dismay of the Royal Navy, this simple tactic worked spectacularly. In June, 284,000 tons of shipping were sunk, followed by 196,000 in July, 268,000 in August, 295,000 in September, and a stunning 352,000 tons sent to the bottom of the ocean in October.[3] This was the time of the U-boat aces, of Prien and Endrass and Kretschmer and Schepke. Still, despite all their swashbuckling successes, the U-boat commanders were never lone wolves. Doenitz had them all very much in control, requiring them to check in with him daily so that he could route them efficiently and effectively.

The "Happy Time" did not last long. For one thing, Doenitz still did not have very many U-boats available. For another, the British started to install radar on their ships and gradually learned to fight at night. Using carefully coordinated air and ship operations, the Royal Navy was soon able to reestablish control over the convoy routes and, by January 1941, had reduced U-boat sinkings to 127,000 tons for that month.[4] Doenitz's response was to call for a fleet of bigger and faster submarines. He could knock the British out of the war, he was certain of it, if only his recommendations were followed. The German government considered his proposals but decided against them. More submarines, primarily the old Type VIIs, would be produced, but the focus of the war would remain on the ground and in the air.

Doenitz knew that tenacity counted as much in bureaucratic battles as anything. After the initial denial of his proposed American attack, he reviewed the ninety-one U-boats then operational. Thirty-three were in the dockyards for re-

pairs and maintenance and twenty en route to or from operations. Thirty-three more were on battle station, twenty-three
in the Mediterranean, six off Gibraltar, and four off Norway.
He could not touch any of these. But there were five U-boats,
fortunately the long-range Type IXs, that had no assignment
and were ready to sail.[5] Could these be used? Doenitz badgered
his superiors again for *Paukenschlag*. He was granted his request but only on the condition that the U-boats be immediately recalled if required for the Norwegian campaign.
Doenitz eagerly agreed and called in the commanders of the
five *Unterseeboote*, briefed them, and wished them luck. He had
no idea of the reception they would receive in American waters, but the commanders—the veterans Hardegen (*U-123*),
Kals (*U-130*), Zapp (*U-66*), Bleichrodt (*U-109*), and Folkers
(*U-125*)—were supremely confident. Between December 16th
and 25th, the five U-boats left their French ports to cross the
Atlantic. To ensure surprise, Doenitz ordered them to keep
out of sight between Newfoundland and the American east
coast unless a worthwhile target—ships of over 10,000 tons—
presented itself. The operational area was to be the coast between the St. Lawrence and Cape Hatteras.[6]

Despite Doenitz's caution, the United States was aware
that the U-boats were probably coming. The moment they left
occupied France, British agents warned London, which, in
turn, passed on the information to Washington. Since the coast
guard had come under the Department of the Navy's command early in 1941, the responsibility for the defense of the
Atlantic coast had been given to 62-year-old Rear Admiral
Adolphus Andrews, known to his friends as "Dolly." When
this huge undertaking was given him, Admiral Andrews had
already been on the active list for forty-one years, with a varied career that had made him one of the best-known flag officers in the navy. An '01 graduate of the Naval Academy,
Andrews had, among many other assignments, been the commander of the presidential yacht *Mayflower*, the naval aide to
President Coolidge, and the American representative to the
Geneva Conference of 1927. A Texan, he liked to do everything on a grand scale. His large staff reflected his enthusiasm.
They included Captain Thomas R. Kurtz (chief of staff), Cap-

tain S. B. Bunting (assistant chief of staff), Captain John T. G. Stapler (operations), Captains Harry E. Shoemaker and Stephan B. Robinson (convoy and routing), Captain Ralph Hungerford (antisubmarine warfare), Captain Henry M. Mullinnix (air), and Lieutenant Commander Harry H. Hess (submarine tracking). Before the war began, Admiral Andrews set up his headquarters in New York City, in the old Federal Building on 90 Church Street, and packed it with a communications center and plotting room from which he planned to manage American coastal defense. All he had to manage, however, were twenty ships, some of them no more than barges and the largest a 165-foot coast guard cutter, plus 103 obsolete aircraft, most of them down for repairs.[7] This pitiful force was supposed to guard the First, Third, Fourth, and Fifth Naval Districts—over 1,500 miles of rugged coastline from the Canadian border to South Carolina!

Admiral Andrews hoped that the commander in chief of the U.S. Fleet, Admiral Ernest J. King, would eventually agree to his request for assistance from the rest of the navy. An entire fleet of battleships, cruisers, destroyers, aircraft carriers, and submarines operated out of Hampton Roads and Norfolk, Virginia. Admiral Andrews believed that those forces should be used in coastal defense, but King and his fleet admirals wanted to ensure that their ships were ready to do battle with the German surface fleet (at that time completely bottled up by the British) or be available to steam to the Pacific to fight the Japanese. In a complaint to King, Admiral Andrews pointed out that of the ships he had available, ". . . there is not a vessel . . . that an enemy submarine could not outdistance when operating on the surface. In most cases, the guns of these vessels would be outranged by those of the submarines."[8] King told him to do what he could with what he had, so Andrews assigned his tiny floating force to patrols around important harbors and convinced the army to send planes from Mitchell Field and Langley Field on two daily sweeps over the ocean. He was aware that the army pilots had virtually no chance of spotting anything and, even if they did, would probably not be able to distinguish a German U-boat from an American submarine, but it was a beginning

in what he hoped would be a continuing close cooperation
between his command and the army air forces. The one con-
cession made by Admiral King was to order fleet minelayers to
mine the approaches to New York, Boston, and Portland
harbors as well as the approaches to the Chesapeake Bay. Otherwise, Admiral Andrews was on his own.

According to the *North Atlantic Naval Coastal Frontier War
Diary*, the first indication of the coming disaster began on 31
December 1941 with a dispatch from the First Naval District
that a periscope had been spotted by fishing boats between
Cushing and Ram Islands in Portland Channel. A week later,
an army plane spotted a fleet of unidentified "destroyers and
cruisers" 50 miles east of Cape May headed for the coast. No
further word was received, and the fleet was written off as
"probably fishermen." The next day, however, a "large, black
submarine with a long conning tower and gun forward" was
seen on the surface moving slowly northeast. It submerged
when it was spotted by the plane. Admiral Andrews took this
report seriously and asked for stepped-up surveillance. On the
same day, 7 January 1942, the admiral received an intelligence
report that "there are strong indications that 16 German submarines are proceeding to the area off the southeast
coast of Newfoundland. The object of this operation is not
understood." On the night of 11 January, the *Cyclops*, a large
freighter, was sunk, apparently by torpedoes or mines about
300 miles off Cape Cod. Admiral Andrews rushed off to meet
with Admiral King to again request assistance. King flatly
turned him down. The navy would keep up routine patrols as
always, but the bulk of the fleet would be kept ready for surface action. Frustrated, Andrews sent the army's First Bomber
Command a memorandum that stated, "Submarines may be
expected off our coast at any time. At least four are known to
be about 300 miles east of Nantucket Light on 12 January, and
are probably proceeding westward." On 14 January, Andrews's worst fears were confirmed with the report of a torpedo attack on the freighter *Norness* just 60 miles southeast of
Montauk Point.

The U-boats had arrived.

# 2

# Hatteras

---

A huge winter storm swept the North Atlantic as the *Paukenschlag* U-boats battled their way toward America. Unable to spend much time submerged due to the limitations of their batteries, the U-boats were forced to stay on the surface, taking the blows of massive waves and hurricane-force winds. Only when the batteries were fully charged and the crew close to madness would a commander finally give the order to dive for a brief respite. But the U-boats were too slow underwater and soon they were back on the surface, fighting westward.

There were others also out on that frightening sea. Frantic distress signals were received from dozens of damaged or lost Allied ships torn from their convoys. Following the orders given them by BdU (*Befehlshaber der Unterseeboote* (Commander U-boats)), the U-boats ignored the easy prey.[1] This was a secret operation, not to commence until Admiral Doenitz determined the time to be right. In the *BdU War Diary*, Doenitz wrote his hopes for *Paukenschlag*. "The entrance of America into the war has provided the commanders with areas which are not hemmed in by defenses and which offer much better chances for success." He still harbored doubts, however. "In retrospect," he wrote, "the defenses of these areas are un-

known." Doenitz knew he had gambled much of his prestige
on the operation. It had to work. Finally, when the U-boats
were near the mid-point in their crossing, Doenitz sent the
signal: *"Paukenschlag* will take effect January 13."[2]

Perhaps the most ambitious and aggressive of the five commanders was Kapitänleutnant Reinhard Hardegen of the
*U-123.* Hardegen was considered something of a braggart by
his fellow U-boat commanders, easy to get started talking but
difficult to stop. He had also been thought a coward by some,
but after a serious aircraft accident, it seemed he had been
transformed into a courageous and determined leader.[3] Whatever the merit of these opinions, Doenitz obviously had respect for him, having given him a lead position in *Paukenschlag.*

Hardegen managed to be the first across, arriving off Newfoundland on the night of 11 January.[4] While traveling south
on the surface, one of his lookouts spotted smoke. Kaleun (ab-
breviated, affectionate term for Kapitänleutnant) Hardegen
moved his U-boat toward the sighting and then submerged
when a big freighter appeared over the horizon. He decided to
attack her even if Doenitz had said to wait until the 13th to
begin the American operation. Perhaps, Hardegen reasoned,
he was still out far enough to sink the ship without alerting
coastal forces.[5]

The freighter, the 9,076-ton British steamship *Cyclops,* was
struck by two of Hardegen's torpedoes. The first one stopped
her, the second broke her in two, and she sank quickly. The
*U-123* submerged and kept heading west while most of the
crewmen of the *Cyclops* drowned in the cold Atlantic. Only 82
of the 181-man crew would survive.[6]

Coming in behind Hardegen the next day, Kapitänleutnant Ernst Kals of the *U-130* officially opened *Paukenschlag* by
sinking two small freighters off Newfoundland.[7] Kals had
been ordered to that area to catch commercial traffic going in
and coming out of the St. Lawrence and also to attack out-
bound American convoys. He would obey those orders and
stay put. Hardegen, however, was heading south. On the night
of the 14th, he took the *U-123* into Rhode Island Sound and
was amazed at the sight that confronted him. The American
shore seemed a fairyland of glowing lights and street signs

compared with blacked-out Europe. Automobile headlights moved up and down the coast, a coast clearly marked by dozens of bobbing, well-lit marker buoys. "It's unbelievable," he breathed to the lookouts on the conning tower with him. "I have a feeling the Americans are going to be very surprised . . ."[8]

One of the lookouts hissed a warning. He had seen the Panamanian tanker *Norness*. Hardegen maneuvered until he had the tanker between him and the lights on shore and then sent two torpedoes streaking into her side. The radioman sent up a report. The tanker had identified herself and believed she had struck a mine. Hardegen was surprised. "You're certain they're saying a mine?"

"Yes, sir. They're sending it in the clear."[9]

Hardegen just couldn't believe it. "A mine!" he exploded. "Nobody seems to be expecting any German U-boats around here!"[10] Unable to resist making a little speech, he turned to the voice tube. "Listen to me, everyone! We're here like a wolf in the middle of a flock of sheep. We've just sunk a tanker, and the Americans still haven't realized that there's a submarine in the area. So much the better for us. Let's take advantage of the situation."[11]

Hardegen waited for the *Norness* to sink, but she stubbornly remained afloat. His radioman reported that she was also continuously signaling for help. Another torpedo was sent into the listing tanker, and this time she broke in two, her stern sinking and her bow settling. Satisfied, Hardegen took the *U-123* down and spent the rest of the night running south until he was opposite Long Island, almost at the mouth of New York harbor. "We could make out many lights," he would write in his log, "probably a suburb of New York . . . Distance to downtown approximately 30 miles. Depth approximately 33 feet. Cannot get any shallower or the topside bridge will not be submerged when diving." Early on the morning of 15 January, he caught the British tanker *Coimbra* all alone and sent two torpedoes into her side.[12] The *Coimbra* buckled and then blew up. "The effect was amazing," Hardegen wrote, "strong detonation, fire column reaching 200 meters and the whole sky was illuminated . . . Quite a bonfire we leave be-

hind for the Yankees as navigational help . . ." There were no
other ships or airplanes visible, and the shore lights continued
burning placidly as if nothing unusual were happening. Hardegen found himself no longer being very cautious. He stayed
on the surface and kept moving south.[13]

When word of Hardegen's successes reached New York,
Admiral Andrews ordered everything under his command to
sea, including some ships never designed for anything beyond
harbor traffic.[14] Typical of these was the *YP 49*, a small,
wooden-hulled ship used for twenty-three years by the coast
guard to patrol the Philadelphia Naval Shipyard. By adding
two 300-pound depth charges, the navy had made her into an
official subchaser. On 16 January 1942, navy Ensign Lee E.
O'Neill was ordered to take charge of the *YP 49* and sail her to
Barnegat Bay on an antisubmarine patrol. O'Neill did as he
was told, and the next day found the "Yippy 49" pitching and
wallowing on a gray sea passing dozens of small coastal ships
hugging the coast. After turning north for the return leg, the
*YP 49*'s engine, clogged by sludge in the fuel tanks, caught fire
and one of the enlisted men was badly burned. O'Neill had no
choice but to head sputteringly for the coast guard base in
Atlantic City for assistance. Even though barely able to move,
O'Neill conscientiously kept looking through his salt-smeared
binoculars for U-boats. None was seen. One, however, saw
him. Kaleun Hardegen watched with disinterest as the small
patrol craft passed. It was the ship behind that he had his eye
on.

O'Neill was standing on the dock watching the coast
guard mechanics when he felt a shock. When he looked up, he
saw a small freighter no more than 1,000 yards away shudder-
ing from the impact of a torpedo. She quickly sank upright,
her masts showing in the shallow water. The coast guard
abandoned their service-station chores and launched a small
unarmed boat to go out and rescue the crew of what proved to
be the freighter *San José*. Hardegen came to the surface in clear
view of the Americans on shore to observe the damage he had
done and then moved slowly away, still on the surface. All
Ensign O'Neill could do was watch helplessly.[15] It was all Ad-

miral Andrews back in his New York headquarters could do as
well.

While Hardegen was battering the Americans, Fregattenkapitän Richard Zapp and his *U-66* had ignored all shipping and gone straight to Cape Hatteras. Admiral Doenitz had
assigned Zapp to perhaps the best area to find freighters and
tankers. Hundreds of ships used the wide, warm Gulf Stream
that swerved near Cape Hatteras to sail north to the ports of
North America and Europe. Southbound ships, not wanting
to sail against the Gulf Stream or swing too far out into the
open ocean, were forced near the jutting North Carolina coast.
It was a natural choke point. On the morning of 18 January,
the *U-66* was in position, waiting. A lookout called Zapp's
attention to a light on the southwestern horizon. The light
was rising, turning into two lights, then three and more, red
and green and white lights all over the deck of an approaching
ship. "Recognize tanker with 3 masts, narrow medium-high
funnel," Zapp wrote in his log. "Tanker is heavily loaded . . .
did not tack."

Zapp was careful with his torpedoes, stalking the tanker
for four hours until he was in position.[16] The tanker was the
*Allan Jackson*, bound for New York with a cargo of 72,870 barrels of crude oil. Second Mate Melvin A. Rand was on the
bridge when he happened to look to starboard and saw the
wake of something coming toward the ship. Although he
found it difficult to believe, he thought it looked like a torpedo.
"Hard to port!" he yelled at Seaman Randy Larson at the
wheel, but it was too late. The torpedo struck the tanker in the
nearly empty forward tank on the starboard side. A second
torpedo was close behind, this one exploding between two full
oil tanks. The *Allan Jackson*, engulfed in flames, began to break
apart. Rand and Larson leaped from the bridge into the sea.

The *Allan Jackson*'s master, Captain Felix W. Kretchmer,
was thrown out of his bunk and all the way across his cabin by
the second torpedo. Trapped by fire, he was only able to get
out of his cabin by squeezing through a tiny porthole. He
headed toward the bridge but the tanker suddenly tore in two,
the sea rushing up and sweeping him away. Boatswain Rolf

Clausen had been playing cards in the messroom on the port side aft when the torpedoes struck. He and his companions rushed out on deck, lowered a lifeboat, and pushed it toward the stern where it seemed to be clear of flames. It was only at the last that they realized the reason for the clearing was because the tanker's huge propeller was still turning, creating a backwash. The propeller struck the boat and would have torn it to bits, but the *Allan Jackson* settled a little and the propeller dropped farther down into the water. In doing so, it also flushed out a clear lane through the burning oil. Someone prayed aloud as the lifeboat entered the fiery corridor. Heat blistered their faces and singed their hair but they kept going until, finally, the flames were behind. Almost instantly, the burning oil closed in, sealing the narrow escape route. Looking back, Clausen saw a man on fire leap from the ship.[1~]

The *U-66* eased to a stop while Zapp assessed the damage he had caused. He tried to identify the tanker with his searchlight but could not. It was too badly torn up to make an identification by silhouette, and burning oil had spread for almost a half a mile around the ship. No matter. Undoubtedly, the Americans would announce on the radio the next day what tanker it was. He took the *U-66* down.[18]

Clausen and his fellow survivors kept rowing away. A shout led them to the radio operator, Stephen Verbonich, just before he went under. Three hours later, one of the men aboard the lifeboat spotted a bluish light to the east. Hoping it wasn't the U-boat, Clausen used a flashlight and turned it against the sail and blinked an SOS signal. Shortly before daylight, Clausen saw with relief that it was an American destroyer. He sent up two distress flares and the ship turned in their direction. It was the American destroyer *Roe* on normal patrol. The *Roe*, which had already picked up three *Allan Jackson* survivors, including Larson and Rand, took Clausen and his mates aboard, and then moved forward carefully. There were bodies floating in the water. A *Roe* lookout yelled that he thought he had seen one of them move. He had. Drenched in oil, Captain Felix W. Kretchmer climbed aboard the destroyer and stood straight on the polished deck. He had been in the water for over seven hours. He wasn't certain what had happened, he reported, but he thought his ship had perhaps hit a mine. Twenty-two men had lost their lives.[19]

While the *Roe* returned to Norfolk with the *Allan Jackson*'s survivors, Zapp continued his hunt, moving the *U-66* out to sea a little, dropping down to the bottom for a day of rest, and then surfacing just as the Canadian passenger liner *Lady Hawkins* hove into view. The big ship was blacked out and tacking but made a perfect silhouette against the lit-up American shore. After six hours of stalking, Zapp sent two torpedoes after the fast liner. On the *Lady Hawkins*, the terrified passengers rushed for the lifeboats, but only three of the boats would get away before their ship sank. Three hundred passengers and crew would go into the water that night. Only ninety-six would survive after a torturous five days with little food or water.[20]

Although Zapp and the *U-66* were enjoying being first off the North Carolina capes, Hardegen and the *U-123* had sunk four ships while moving south.[21] Four ships! Hardegen pondered that fact. Where were the defenses? Where was the American navy? Except for O'Neill's tiny "Yippy," he had not encountered a single warship or airplane. The opportunities for success gave Hardegen no time to puzzle for long. On 19 January, he was at a position off Cape Hatteras despite the fact that BdU had assigned him only the New York and New Jersey coasts. Hardegen had no intention of allowing Zapp to have the exclusive rights to such an obvious killing zone as Hatteras. Besides, he believed that once a U-boat was at sea, a commander should always use his initiative and find the best spot for killing ships no matter what the orders. In this, he had the blessings of Admiral Doenitz.[22] At 0207 (unless otherwise specified, all times given are Eastern War Time (EWT)), a big freighter was spotted. Hardegen backed off to get her between him and the bright lights of shore and then loosed two torpedoes.[23]

It was the American *City of Atlanta*. After the torpedoes struck, the crew panicked. Men milled and yelled and frantically clawed at the lifeboats, trying to push them overboard. One, with eighteen men, was finally dropped but it immedi-

ately capsized, spilling the men into the sea. Hardegen was on
the bridge and ordered a searchlight turned on. He had been
surprised that the freighter had sunk so fast and had not seen
anyone get off. He ordered one of his men to call out to see if
there were any survivors. Again and again, the man called
"*Kamerade! Kamerade!*", but there was no reply and Hardegen
soon gave up, taking the *U-123* down. The next morning, the
freighter *Seatrain Texas* would find only three survivors of the
*City of Atlanta.* Forty-three men had been lost.[24]

But Hardegen and the *U-123* were not finished for the
night. At 0430, one of the lookouts whispered he could see
another light, this one a white mast light coming up over the
horizon to the north. Hardegen alerted the bow torpedo room
to prepare for a salvo. More reports came from the lookouts.
Three more ships could be seen coming up over the horizon.
Hardegen decided, however, to concentrate on his original target. At 0500, the ship, moving very slowly and festooned with
lights, sailed into Hardegen's cross-hairs.[25]

The *Ciltvaira*, a Latvian ship, was the small freighter moving slowly in front of Hardegen. She was on her way to Savan-
nah from Norfolk with a mixed crew of thirty-two Finns,
Danes, Estonians, Dutch, Swedes, Romanians, and even a few
Latvians aboard. There was also a ship's cat named Briskis and
a puppy, Pluskis. Captain Karl Skerbergs had heard about
German U-boats operating off the Atlantic coast but had dismissed it as fantastic. In any case, he believed the *Ciltvaira* was
much too unimportant a target for a U-boat. They would be
after bigger game, that much Skerbergs knew.

It was still dark outside when Captain Skerbergs was
awakened by a loud "thump." He leaped out of bed. He
thought his ship had hit a shoal, but the shouts of his crewmen
outside his cabin quickly dispelled this theory. An explosion!
Skerbergs guessed that the *Ciltvaira* had struck a mine. He
grabbed his clothes and made for the bridge. The ship had
stopped and was drifting. He looked out to port, thought he
saw a light, but what light could it be? To starboard, he could
see the light of a buoy. Which one? He found the bridge deserted except for the mess boy who was standing in a corner,
looking very frightened. He calmed the boy and asked where

the mates were. Just then, the first mate appeared and together, he and Captain Skerbergs tried to determine where they were. For some reason, none of the charts made any sense. Skerbergs suddenly felt his ship lurch. Was she sinking? He heard the sound of a lifeboat being released. He made his way out on deck with the first mate and saw that almost all of his crew had left the ship in the large standard lifeboat. They yelled at the captain to get off, that the ship was sinking. Skerbergs yelled back at them to return, but when he saw that they had taken Briskis and Pluskis with them, he knew they would not come back. Reluctantly, he gathered the remaining crewmen and told them to get the wounded and follow him into the other, smaller lifeboat. He was told then that two of the firemen had been killed by the explosion, whatever it was, but that no one else had been seriously injured. Captain Skerbergs ordered the two bodies wrapped in blankets and brought with them. Soon, the captain and the others found themselves adrift while the sun rose placidly and brilliantly over a flat, calm sea.[26]

Hardegen, through with the *Ciltvaira*, turned after the other ships his lookouts had spotted. The three that had been there had disappeared, running in to shore, but five more had appeared, apparently unaware of the killing ahead of them. Believing that the closest tanker was too small to waste a torpedo on, Hardegen decided to use his deck gun.[27] His second-in-command, Von Schroeter, was skeptical of the idea. "Attack while running up astern of them?" he questioned. "Can't be done, sir. For one thing they'd be bound to see us before we had fired the first shot and then we'd get it in the neck."[28]

Hardegen reddened. "I don't give a shit!" he snapped. "Guns are not in my line but I have a hunch it will work . . . The bolder you are, the more likely your bluff will be successful."[29]

Hardegen demanded full speed and, with a puff of black diesel smoke, the *U-123* pushed ahead, closing on the tanker. The deck gun fired once, then again. There was a spout of flame on the tanker's deck and then a huge boil of fire and smoke. The lookouts reported that the other ships had turned off their lights and were running away, so Hardegen decided to stay with the burning tanker. He ordered his *Obermas-chinistmaat* to maintain maximum speed, but just as he did, the port diesel clanked to a stop with a broken cooling-water pump. A cursing Hardegen was forced to suspend the chase.

While the *U-123*'s machinists worked on the engine, the radioman brought Hardegen a message sent by the tanker. "Tanker *Malay* on fire after being shelled by U-boat," it read. "Please inform nearest naval command. Fire under control. Am making for Norfolk." The radioman added, "The *Malay* is 8,206 tons, herr Kaleun."

"Good God, I had no idea she was so big!" Hardegen exclaimed. He decided to catch her no matter what it took.[30]

The *U-123* strained ahead, her one good engine giving her barely 15 knots. The smoke from the *Malay* was still visible and gave Hardegen something to chase. An hour later, the *Malay* could be seen. The fires were out. "It aggravated me that the tanker was OK again," Hardegen wrote, "and I intended to spoil their success." The *U-123*'s last torpedo hit the *Malay* in an empty compartment, flooding it. Three panicky crew members of the tanker attempted to launch a lifeboat while the ship was still steaming full ahead, but the instant the boat hit the water, it overturned and the men in it were lost. After the *Malay* came to a stop, another lifeboat, this one with fourteen men in it, was successfully dropped to the sea. An hour later, however, the *Malay*'s master, John Dodge, ordered the lifeboat back. The *Malay* could still make way. Hardegen, thinking that he had sunk the tanker, had already left to chase another ship. Amazingly, the *Malay* would yet manage to limp into Norfolk the next day.[31]

The *Ciltvaira* was also still afloat. After her crew had abandoned her, a tanker, the *Socony-Vacuum*, happened upon the scene and took aboard the crew. Captain Skerbergs had barely gotten on the tanker when he looked back and saw the *Ciltvaira* about a mile away. He could see no discernible damage besides a slight tilt. Perhaps he could yet save his ship. He called for volunteers, got eight, and climbed back into the small lifeboat. Soon, he and the men were scrambling back aboard their freighter while the *Socony-Vacuum* motored on toward Charleston, South Carolina, with the rest of the crew,

including Briskis and Pluskis. Carefully, Skerbergs climbed
down toward the fireroom. He heard much gurgling even before he got there but he still had hope. Once there, however,
he was disappointed. The *Ciltvaira* was broken open in the
middle and was filling fast. Skerbergs scrambled back to the
deck and ordered the lifeboat launched again. Another ship
appeared, this one the Brazilian freighter *Bury*. Soon, Skerbergs was on his way to New York while behind him, his little
ship kept filling with water. She was still afloat when Skerbergs, from the stern of the *Bury*, sadly watched her disappear
below the horizon.[32]

There was no sadness aboard the *U-123*. Quite the opposite. A general celebration was going on. The cook was called
to fix the best meal he could. It was apparent to the crew of the
U-boat that they and their commander had become something
special. They were all aces. They had sunk six ships, believed
it to be eight, without so much as an answering firecracker
from the hapless Americans. "The night of the long knives is
over," Hardegen wrote. "A drum roll for 8 ships, among them
3 tankers, with a total of 53,860 GRT. What a pity that when I
was positioned off New York we didn't have two additional
mine-laying U-boats closing everything down and 10–20 boats
tonight in addition to ours. I believe each one of them would
have been able to get her limit." More than ships had been
sunk, too. He noted in his log that, as a result of his activities
". . . the entire telegram communications of Jews across the
sea has stopped completely." He made a report to BdU announcing his success and Doenitz promptly replied: "To
'Drummer' Hardegen. Bravo! You drummed very well."
Shortly afterwards, Doenitz also awarded Hardegen the
Knight's Cross. A ceremony was held in the control room of
the *U-123*, the crew presenting their commander with a home-
made version of the decoration. Even though the *U-123* was
out of torpedoes, Hardegen's glorious patrol wasn't over. On
the way back to France, he would use his deck gun to sink two
more ships.[33]

After the initial losses in January, a worried Admiral Andrews ordered a review by his staff to see if any pattern to the

U-boat attacks could be discerned. Cape Hatteras seemed to be the U-boat's favorite hunting grounds, that was clear. Also, the U-boats were working primarily alone. This surprised Andrews. Why were they not using the famous "wolfpack" tactics he had heard so much about? His staff had no answer for that, but it was clear that the U-boats were being given easy shots because the merchant ships were keeping their running lights on at night. It was also believed that city lights were being used by the U-boat commanders to silhouette their targets.

Admiral Andrews's task was to convince Admiral King of his needs. He began to make a series of trips back and forth to Washington to argue his case. First, Andrews told King, he wanted more ships and airplanes for patrol duty. Next, he wanted the president to order a complete blackout along the eastern shore. He had sent a member of his staff, a Captain McFall, down the coast to observe the light intensity. McFall had come back and reported, "It is possible for a submarine to select either the bow or stern of a ship as his target by the glare of lights." The people would understand, Andrews earnestly explained, if they knew their lights were causing the deaths of men at sea. Finally, Andrews wanted to move the commercial sea lanes 60 miles out to sea around Cape Hatteras. This would spread the traffic out and make it harder for the U-boats to find targets.[34]

King and Andrews could speak plainly to each other. Both were from the same Naval Academy class and had climbed up through the rungs of command of a small navy. The officers of such a force invariably form a society of their own, and the peacetime United States Navy had been no different. King and Andrews had crossed paths often. Both men were ambitious but had different styles. Where Andrews recognized his own limitations and that of other men, King was completely unsparing of himself and all others. King had finally climbed to the position of Commander in Chief, U.S. Fleet on 20 December 1941. Three months later, he would also take on the additional duties of the chief of naval operations.[35]

King turned down the first two requests Andrews made with the explanation that he still intended to keep his fleet

intact and there were scientific instruments being designed
that would take care of the U-boat problem. He did, however,
allow a temporary movement of the shipping lanes, at least
through the month. Recognizing King's intransigence on the
subject, Andrews accepted the decision but then made an attempt to educate King a bit on the mathematics of submarine
warfare. From his studies of the British battle against the
U-boats, Andrews said, he had determined that nothing mat-
tered so much as having as many ships and planes arranged
against the submarines as possible. The British had succeeded
only because they had put everything they had to sea, including converted trawlers. They had, Admiral Andrews told his
dubious commander, actually defeated the U-boats in the
North Atlantic, although it had hardly been recognized. The
United States could do the same by following their example.
What Andrews really needed, he said, were destroyers. Admiral King replied that this was not possible. He would have no
destroyers to spare for the east coast, not now, probably not
ever. He reminded Admiral Andrews that he had a war to
fight in the Pacific as well. As far as King was concerned, the
subject was closed.[36]

Although Hardegen was heading back to France, Zapp
and his *U-66* were still off Hatteras, determined to use the last
of their torpedoes. Since sinking the *Lady Hawkins*, the *U-66*
had sunk the American freighter *Norvana* and its cargo of
sugar on the morning of January 22. Nothing was ever heard
of the ship or its crew of twenty-nine again. Zapp had used
two stern torpedoes on the diminutive freighter, ensuring its
doom. "Steamer breaks apart midships and sinks within one
minute," Zapp logged. He estimated it at 7,500 tons and 400
feet in length. The *Norvana* was, in fact, only 2,677 tons and
253 feet long.[37]

The *Venore*, loaded with 22,700 tons of iron ore from Chile,
was to be the *U-66*'s last victim of *Paukenschlag*. The *Venore*'s
captain, Fritz Dourloo, had heard rumors of German U-boat
activity all the way back at the Panama Canal. In fact, his
second cook had been told by soldiers at the canal that four
ships had been sunk right off Cape Hatteras. But the *Venore*

was bound for Baltimore, so Dourloo had no choice but to sail
up the east coast of the United States. The night of 23 January
1942, found her 80 miles off Hatteras, heading almost due
north. Dourloo had decided to stay out that far, reasoning that
if there were any U-boats, they would probably be working in
closer. Lookouts had spotted another ship behind them earlier
in the day and as the day wore on, the ship, the British tanker
*Empire Gem*, began to catch up. At twilight, the tanker was
only a mile off the starboard quarter. Ahead lay Diamond
Shoals. Dourloo ordered only the dimmed sidelights turned on
and proceeded forward through the darkness at 10 knots. The
*Empire Gem* was still a little behind, her running lights fully
on. Peter Karlson, the quartermaster, was at the wheel of the
*Venore* with the captain beside him. Ahead of them, they saw a
light blinking. Dourloo read the code. It was the Diamond
Shoals Lightship and it was messaging for them to come
nearer. Perhaps they were going to be ordered into a safe harbor for the night. After several minutes of running toward the
light, it suddenly went out. Dourloo ordered Karlson back on
his original course. Neither man said anything but both
thought it. *Trap.*

If Zapp had, in fact, lured the *Venore* in closer, he made no
mention of it in his log. He had, however, been wrestling with
the problem of which ship to attack first. He had decided to go
after the *Venore* because she appeared to be bigger, but just as
he lined up, the *Empire Gem* suddenly changed course, running
right in front of the *U-66*'s tubes.

The *Venore* was just beginning a turn when a terrific shock
wave knocked everyone on the bridge to their knees. A column of fire climbed 500 feet into the night sky where the
*Empire Gem* had been. Dourloo turned the *Venore* away from
the burning tanker and pointed her bow directly toward
shore. It was their only chance. Better to hit the shoals than
take a torpedo. Dourloo looked back. The U-boat was following.[38] He ordered his radioman to call the coast guard station
at Ocracoke and alert them to the *Venore*'s situation. The radioman, Vernon Minzey, did so, adding the plaintive comment,
*Think Swimming Soon.*[39]

While the *Venore* raced for shore, many of her confused

crew prepared to lower the lifeboats. No orders had come to them, but after seeing the *Empire Gem* explode, they were all certain the *Venore* was next. Before a boat could be swung out, however, there was a slight concussion aft. Just then, a man erupted from somewhere below and ran screaming all the way to the stern and jumped off. Two lifeboats were swung out, dozens of panicky men climbing aboard. The *Venore* was still grinding on at full speed. As soon as the boats hit the sea, they were torn apart, planks and bodies smashing against the side of the ship. It happened so quickly not a single whimper was heard from the crewmen. A third boat was dropped, this one with only two men aboard. Somehow, it avoided hitting the *Venore* and was seen swirling away into the darkness.

Since the *U-66* had torpedoed the *Empire Gem*, Zapp had busily tried to cut off the speeding *Venore*. From 1,000 meters, he had sent two bow torpedoes after her with one hit. Disappointingly, however, the "iron ore freighter," as Zapp referred to the *Venore* in his log, had kept going. Although the *U-66* was in hot pursuit, Zapp saw that he was going to lose the race and decided to fire another torpedo even though he was more than a mile behind. To hit the fleeing freighter would take an extraordinary shot.

Third Mate Andy Jackson was on the bridge when the torpedo plunged into the Number 9 ballast tank of the *Venore*. Zapp had made his shot. The ship listed sharply to port, the deck going completely under. When she righted, a huge torrent of water, thrown high into the air by the torpedo, cascaded down to wash across the decks. Captain Dourloo went outside and unleashed a liferaft and threw it overboard for any men who might be in the water. He told Jackson to go to the remaining lifeboat. Jackson complied, finding Minzey, the radio operator, along the way. Together, they made their way to the lifeboat station only to find that the boat had already been lowered under the direction of Chief Mate Mulligan. Mulligan yelled up at them to come down the falls. Jackson got tangled in the ropes and fell headlong into the boat. Minzey, who only had one arm, also lost his grip but missed the boat and fell into the sea. He did not come up. Three days later, the twenty-one survivors in the lifeboat were found by the tanker *Tennessee*.

The remaining twenty-two crewmen, including Captain Dourloo, remained missing forever.[40]

As for Fregattenkapitän Zapp and the crew of the *U-66*, they had at last used all their torpedoes. They were triumphantly sailing for France, while Kals in the *U-130* and Folkers in the *U-125*, unsuccessful in finding targets farther north, moved into the Hatteras killing grounds. In quick succession, the *U-130* sank the *Veranger*, the *Francis E. Powell*, and severely damaged the tanker *Halo*.[41] The *U-125* found Hatteras to be profitable as well, running the tanker *Olney* aground and sinking the freighter *West Ivis*.[42] Cape Hatteras, the Graveyard of the Atlantic, was starting to be called a new name by the freighter and tanker crews: Torpedo Junction.[43]

On 25 January 1942, Admiral Andrews was given a message from Admiral King. It read "Atlantic Fleet aircraft within limits your respective coastal frontiers hereby made available to you to assist actively in combatting enemy sub actions."[44]

Admiral Andrews reacted with satisfaction. His battle was finally being recognized! He immediately relayed the message to his staff and commanders at sea. On the same day, three utility planes from the Atlantic fleet pool were assigned to the airfield at Elizabeth City, North Carolina, the first addition to the small force of unarmed coast guard airplanes stationed there. Cape Hatteras would be their patrol area. On 27 January, Andrews assigned twelve more planes there for patrolling. The next day, he attempted to provide for Elizabeth City in a different way. In a letter to Admiral King, he wrote, "It is understood that there are approximately twenty PBY-5s belonging to the Royal Air Force now at Elizabeth City, N.C., and that due to lack of crews these aircraft are not all in transit. In view of the immediate demand for long-range patrol planes, it is suggested that arrangements might be made for temporary assignment for six of the PBY's . . . until such time as suitable replacements can be furnished." Admiral King's reply was negative but not abruptly so. "Shortage of patrol type aircraft for specific duty under Naval Coastal Frontier Commanders is recognized," his letter to Andrews said, ". . . provision is made in the current aircraft program for patrol squadrons which will be allocated to the Naval Coastal Frontier Commands."[45] Admiral Andrews now felt he had the attention of his commander. But he would keep asking and pushing even if it made him the most unpopular officer in the navy. He only had to check his teletype machines each morning to see the obvious. There was a battle being fought for which he was responsible, and it was a battle that was being lost. He was going to fight back with whatever he could.

While Admiral Andrews wrestled with the problems of his command, Admiral Doenitz was beginning to realize the success of his. In his private office, Doenitz nervously ruffled through the papers on his desk as Kapitänleutnant Hardegen concluded his report. Nodding approval, the admiral waved Hardegen to a chair and then slowly made his own assessment. It was obvious, he said, that the combat conditions off the American coast should be exploited. But there was a problem. The High Command. Always the High Command. Doenitz was as angry as Hardegen had ever seen him. "Can anyone tell me," he said in his high-pitched voice, "what good tanks and trucks and airplanes are if the enemy doesn't have fuel for them? Once again, I've tried to explain this simple fact to them . . . our sole mission should be to sink as much tonnage as possible, as quickly as possible, and in the place where we can do it most efficiently." Doenitz clasped his hands so tightly his knuckles whitened. His lips were tightly pursed. "Well, gentlemen, I've received an answer . . . 'You are over-simplifying,' they say. It seems to me that these fine gentlemen have forgotten what Napoleon said: 'War is a simple art and consists entirely in performance.' "[46]

*Paukenschlag*, then, would continue, but at nothing like the level Doenitz wished. In fact, just as six more U-boats were gathered to cross the Atlantic, Hitler himself diverted them to the Norwegian fjords to stop a British invasion he intuitively believed was coming.[47] Doenitz protested, but the Fuhrer's order was law. Admiral Andrews had no way of knowing it, but Adolf Hitler had given him at least a little more time to gather what resources he could to stop the U-boats.

# 3

# The *Dione*

When the U-boats took up their stations off Cape Hatteras in January 1942, only one large antisubmarine
ship was there to oppose them. That was the United
States Coast Guard Cutter *Dione*, responsible for patrolling
from Norfolk, Virginia, to Morehead City, North Carolina,
and making mail runs to the lightships along the Outer Banks
of North Carolina.[1] Most of the men who served aboard the
cutter were local "Bankers," born and raised in the little fishing towns on the islands and strips of sand that defined the
Banks. Many had relatives who worked on the lightships, so
there was often a reunion of sorts while mail was delivered
and picked up. The lightship men would try to keep the *Dione*
tied up as they were lonely and bored, but she never stayed
long. Her duty was patrol, which meant covering as much of
the sea lanes as possible, even well out into the Gulf Stream.
There, even in winter, the sea was blue and clear. Tropical fish
swam below, blue angels and crevalle jacks and big barracuda.
Often, the sea would be as flat as a mountain lake, and the
*Dione* would leave behind her a great, white phosphorescent
trail. Then, her off-duty men would come out to the rails just
to think about the same things all off-duty men think about
and unconsciously savor the beauty that surrounded them.

The cook of the *Dione* especially liked to come out on the fan-tail and feed the seagulls. It usually produced quite a show. A crowd of gulls would quickly collect around the stern of the cutter to swoop in one at a time to the cook's outstretched hand for a piece of stale bread and then wheel off, with the next gull moving in to fill the position. A lot of the men liked to throw pieces of bread as high as they could and watch the gulls catch them in mid-air. Sometimes the birds would add in a little extra for their appreciative audience, doing barrel-rolls and flips in mid-air catching the bread.

Even those crewmen who were not locals found them-selves falling in love with the Banks. Whenever the *Dione* moved in close to shore, they could see the great white dunes, festooned with waving sea oats and girdled by the blue sea shimmering in the sun. At night, the sun set behind these dunes, turning them golden and soft against the red-stained sky. It was well known, of course, how treacherous the sea off North Carolina could be. It was called, after all, the "Grave-yard of the Atlantic" because of the hundreds of wrecks left there by the combination of violent weather and shifting shoals.[2] Still, as the winter of 1941–42 began, there was what appeared to be a respite from the turmoil that had sunk so many ships. The winds were gentle and from the south. It was a sea of incredible beauty and peace and the *Dione* was home.

But everything for the *Dione* and her crew changed when the U-boats arrived.

The *Dione,* part of Admiral Andrews's force, was first or-dered to maintain her patrol but to keep a sharp lookout for U-boats. When Zapp and Hardegen started to destroy ship-ping off the Banks, the *Dione* was further ordered to provide assistance to torpedoed ships. The commander of the *Dione,* Lieutenant (j.g.) Nelson C. McCormick, a Texan, was a capa-ble, serious young man with such high personal standards and ability that he tended, without being much aware of it, to intimidate his crew, officers and men alike. His response to the orders given him was typical of the man—he intended to carry them out with all the vigor and intelligence he could bring forth from himself, his crew, and his ship. When the tankers and freighters started blowing up all over his patrol area, Mc-

Cormick's first response was to race the cutter toward every reported attack, but it seemed he was always too far away. By the time the *Dione* would get anywhere near the area of the attack, it would all be over, the ship sunk or limping off, the survivors rescued or drifted away. After days of this kind of frustration, McCormick gave the matter some thought and deduced that the *Dione* would be more effective as a killer than a rescuer. The *Dione* was, after all, a warship, not a hospital barge. But if McCormick was going to have any chance at sinking a U-boat, he was going to have to surprise one. Using the limited information available to him, he determined that the U-boats were primarily attacking at night and presumably resting during the day. If that were true, grid pattern searches might find one while it was asleep. It would take some luck but it was worth a try. Since he had no specific orders other than to patrol, he abandoned his routine and began to make extensive daytime searches using sonar and sound-detection gear. He ordered dozens of depth-charge runs on what turned out to be bottom rocks or schools of fish or shipwrecks. It was frustratingly difficult for his soundmen to tell the difference between them and a submarine. The crew also had difficulty at first in just dropping their depth charges. Because of peacetime austerity, the *Dione* had rarely been allowed to drop live depth charges. On the very first run the cutter made on a suspected U-boat, the men at the racks had forgotten to pull the safety pins. After that had been corrected, the charges had been accidentally set to explode at only 50 feet deep during a slow pass on the target. Instead of the U-boat or whatever was below, the *Dione* had nearly blown herself out of the water.

A particularly frustrating event had occurred when McCormick had been maneuvering the *Dione* approximately 20 miles off Oregon Inlet. His sonar man had yelled back that an "underwater object" was just ahead. McCormick had made a fast attack, dropping six depth charges, and then two airplanes had showed up and sniffed around, making several runs on a spreading oil slick. McCormick asked the pilots to let him know if they could make out the size and shape of the target. Their reports were enthusiastic. It was long and narrow. They were certain it was a U-boat! That was all McCormick needed to hear. The *Dione*'s crew hung on. Because the sea was so shallow, every depth-charge blast badly shook the cutter, but McCormick kept going until, finally, something recognizable came up. It was an oar and a boat hook, strange implements for a U-boat. When brought aboard, they were found to have the identification *Francis E. Powell*. It was the tanker sunk by the *U-130* on 27 January 1942. The object of the *Dione*'s attack had been long all right, about twice as long as any German U-boat, and certainly a lot wider. The pilots had reported what they had wanted to see and, McCormick had to admit, what he had wanted to hear. He and the *Dione* had succeeded only in blasting a dead ship.

But McCormick kept trying. He believed his only chance in killing a U-boat was to be as aggressive as possible. In January 1942, the *Dione* would drop more depth charges than any other ship along the Atlantic coast.³ As she cut across the sea, the *Dione* was no longer accompanied by her usual friendly flock of sea gulls. The activity of the men at the depth-charge racks had brought them in close several times in the hope of being fed. Instead, they had become the victims of depth-charge blasts, their mangled bodies left behind in the cutter's wake. The men still tried to feed them when there was time, coming up to wave pieces of bread, but the gulls hung back, too frightened to try. Instead of food and life, the *Dione* had become to them a ship of pain and death.

In early February, McCormick received orders to take the *Dione* back into the Little Creek Section Base of Norfolk to pick up a new skipper for the cutter. McCormick accepted the news that he was being replaced (but to be left aboard as the executive officer) with a mask of unconcern. The coast guard rarely gave reasons for its assignments so there was little he could do about it, in any case. Instead, he spent the week before going in to work out a new tactic he had invented, that of night drift-hunting. If a ship was silently drifting at night rather than running its engines and charging about near suspected U-boat positions, he had theorized, it might better hear a U-boat's propellers. Then all that would be needed would be a good sonar echo and a proper depth-charge run to chalk up one dead U-boat. If the *Dione* and a dozen other ships would

drift-hunt at night off Hatteras, McCormick was certain a
U-boat would be found and sunk. Before he had left on patrol,
he had tried to interest his superiors in his innovation but they
had not thought much of it. To drift blacked out in one of the
busiest shipping lanes in the world was to invite disaster, they
told him. Better to keep on the move. Although nothing had
come of McCormick's experiments, he hadn't been run over,
either. He was still certain his plan would work.

The *Dione*'s new skipper was Lieutenant James "Jimmy"
Alger. As would become clear very quickly, his assignment
was no reflection on McCormick. It was the result of Alger's
pulling a few strings back in Washington. A very competent
staff officer, he had still wanted to get away from a desk and
into the war. The *Dione* was allowed to have a full lieutenant
as commander, so Alger was eligible for the assignment and he
had gone after it. He knew the *Dione* to be one of a class of 165-
foot cutters the coast guard had built to combat the smugglers
of the Prohibition era. Alger had served in an old World War
I-era four-stacker destroyer during Prohibition, going out to
keep the fast "booze carriers" from rendezvousing with the
mother ships. The 165-footers, however, had been much better
at that job, being more maneuverable and able to enter shallow waters in hot pursuit. Alger had always admired them and
finally had one of his own. As he boarded the *Dione*, he
thought of his wife and son back in Washington, D.C. He was
painfully aware at that moment that he could have stayed in
Washington with them probably for the entire war. But ashore
was no place for an officer of the coast guard. His wife was
coast guard, just as he. She would cope.

Alger wasted no time in taking the *Dione* back to sea, going
out the next morning after coming aboard. It was not the first
time an Alger of Virginia had commanded a United States
Coast Guard vessel. In fact, Lieutenant Alger's father had
been witness to one of the strangest episodes in the Graveyard
of the Atlantic's long, destructive history. As commander of
the coast guard cutter *Manning*, the elder Alger had gone to
the rescue of the *Carol A. Deering* on a stormy winter's night in
1921. The *Deering*, a five-masted schooner, had fetched up on a
shoal and been spotted by observers on the beach. When the

coast guardsmen went aboard her, she was found to be completely abandoned. Food was still on the table, charts were laid out to be read, everything was normal . . . except there was no crew. Their fate remained one of the Graveyard's greatest mysteries.[4] Such was the sea, Alger had learned from his father, and such was the United States Coast Guard, too. Standing out of Little Creek, Alger turned the gray cutter down Thimble Shoals Channel toward the Chesapeake Bay Entrance. His destination: Torpedo Junction.

# 4

# The American Shooting Gallery

In February 1942, Admiral King officially gave Admiral Andrews command of the Eastern Sea Frontier created from the old North Atlantic Naval Coastal Frontier and Southern Atlantic Naval Coastal Frontier.[1] This, in effect, gave Admiral Andrews complete control over all coastal naval vessels and aircraft from Maine to Florida and also any army air forces and civil units that might be available for U-boat defense duties. Despite this promising development, a page of the navy's *Enemy Action Diary* for one typical 24-hour period on the Atlantic coast illustrated the "constant tension that existed almost every hour of every day." U-boats seemed to be everywhere. If they weren't actually sinking ships, they were chasing them, disrupting routing and generally causing confusion all up and down the coast. There were "bursts of light" and "gunfire" and "suspicious ships" being reported by everyone on the ocean, it seemed.[2] There were good analysts on Admiral Andrews's staff, however, who could glean the truth from this jumble of reports. It was clear to them that the habits of the U-boats had changed little from their first arrival. They were attacking mostly at night and were now also using gunfire "remarkable for its accuracy" to supplement their torpedoes.[3]

The *Eastern Sea Frontier War Diary* for February also reported that Admiral Andrews's search for forces "was not very gratifying . . . the negotiations carried on during the past month between the various commands at times looked much like robbing Peter of a promissory note so that Paul could be paid for it." Availability of air support also "was not entirely satisfactory because the duty was an 'emergency' measure and admittedly temporary. Also use of the planes could not be permitted to interfere with regular duty with the Fleet." In fact, hopes that the situation might be improved were dashed by Admiral King's assurance to his Fleet admirals that the Eastern Sea Frontier would not be provided with more planes until Fleet squadrons were brought up to strength. "Thus," it was gloomily written, "the month began without much promise that the situation in the air could be improved in the immediate future." In fact, the situation as February 1942 began was much the same as it had been from the moment the first U-boats had arrived. There was simply not enough of anything to stop the Germans.

But still the freighters and tankers would sail . . .

And still they would die.

No merchantman seemed safe. On 2 February 1942, one of the largest and fastest freighters in the world, the Swedish *Amerikaland*, was assaulted by two U-boats off Cape Hatteras. Kapitänleutnant Walter Schug had brought his *U-86*, a Type VIIB, into American waters in mid-January off Nova Scotia and had immediately attacked a big tanker, the *Toorak*.[4] Since then, he had not spotted anything worthwhile and had decided to move south where he had heard that Hardegen and others were doing very well. Kapitänleutnant Herman Rasch and his *U-106*, a Type IXB, had been in American waters for only a few days but had already sunk the tanker *Rochester* just a few miles off Norfolk, practically within sight of the American fleet.[5] As soon as it was dark, the two U-boats surfaced and began to move south, hoping to pick up a ship as it rounded Hatteras. They had not gone far before they were rewarded by the sight of a huge freighter, lit up from bow to stern, coming straight at them. The ship, as yet unidentified, had no one escorting her. She was a perfect target. Rasch and his U-106 would attack first.

Captain Ragnar Schutz of the *Amerikaland* had just gotten into bed when he felt the torpedo thud into his ship somewhere far below. He had heard that sound before. In 1917, he had been aboard a freighter in the North Atlantic that had been sunk by a German torpedo. He had gone into the frigid water naked and it had been 19 hours before he had been picked up.[6]

Waiting for their chance, Kaleun Schug and the men on the conning tower of the U-86 observed the torpedo attack of the U-106. Almost instantly, the freighter stopped, lights flickering, dimming, and then coming back on just as brightly as before. Schug could see movement on deck, the crew rushing to the lifeboats. He ordered the U-86 closer. As soon as the crew was off, he would finish the kill.

Captain Schutz sadly got aboard the last lifeboat being let down. Two other lifeboats had already been launched. He made a quick count. Twelve sailors besides himself. One of them was hurt and bleeding badly. After the lifeboat was a hundred yards away from the freighter, a torpedo spewed across the lifeboat's bow and slammed into the *Amerikaland*. Already listing, the freighter rolled heavily toward her new wound and sank. The U-86 inspected the lifeboat containing Captain Schutz and then submerged. Just before the water ran out two days later, the wounded seaman, who had been screaming and delirious, suddenly subsided as if he had finally fallen asleep. Schutz had gone to him, to try to make him more comfortable. When he took the man's hand, it was as cold as the frigid sea. Although he had just died, his shrunken corpse was that of a man who had been dead for days. Many of the men had come close to breaking then. Some of them had to be forcibly restrained from jumping overboard. "I have gone through this before—naked!," Schutz screamed at them. He would get them through, he promised, if only they would not give up. Schutz did as he promised but it would be three and a half days before rescue came from a passing freighter. No trace was ever found of the twenty-seven men in the two other lifeboats of the *Amerikaland*.[7]

\* \* \*

By the end of his first day in command of the *Dione*, Lieutenant Alger had repeatedly drilled his men and had been impressed by their skill. Lieutenant McCormick, trying to fit in, watched Alger as carefully as any junior officer dares to watch the commander of a warship at sea. Alger, for his part, had noted McCormick's fine seamanship and had been content to allow his exec to continue to command the helm when intricate maneuvers were required. Still, it was clear that Alger had taken command. He was about to call a General Quarters drill when the sonar operator called out an echo. Alger ordered the *Dione* in hot pursuit of the target, whatever it was. Nothing was found, but later in the afternoon a better contact was made and Alger ordered the *Dione* to General Quarters and maneuvered to drop depth charges. A single depth charge was dropped and immediately a spew of oil bubbled to the surface and then spread into a large, rainbow-hued stain on the calm surface. Alger ordered two liferafts into the water to secure oil samples, waited patiently for them to return, and then dropped another depth charge. More oil came up, this time in thick globules. Alger had gotten his first taste of the frustration McCormick had already experienced. He had doubtless been attacking a sunken tanker.

Later that night, a dispatch was received. Drifting lifeboats had been spotted just north of the *Dione*'s position. Speeding to the scene, Alger and McCormick peered from the bridge into the darkness. First one, then two more empty lifeboats floated by. McCormick went down on deck and helped the crew bring them alongside. Provisions on board identified them as English but there were no other identifying symbols. The boats could have been adrift for hours or weeks, there was no way to tell. The next morning, with Ensign Richard Welton at the helm, the sonar again picked up an excellent echo. Alger and McCormick came up. Alger ordered both engines stopped and the *Dione* drifted over the target. The sonar operator listened intently to the bouncing pulse from his set. It was solid but it was also all over the place. That meant it was big, very big. Another wreck. That night, the U.S. Navy destroyer *Roe* came into view and signals were exchanged. The

*Roe* was on standard patrol duty and not looking for submarines so she continued on to Norfolk, leaving the *Dione* wallowing in her wake. Alger was beginning to feel very alone on
a very dangerous ocean.

On the same day the *Amerikaland* was sunk, the *U-103*, destined to be one of the most successful U-boats in American
waters, finished its transatlantic voyage. More U-boats, anxious to get in on what was rapidly becoming known among
the U-boat captains as the "American Shooting Gallery," were
making the journey, and the *U-103*, a Type IXB, was part of
this new wave. Kapitänleutnant Werner Winter, the *U-103*'s
commander, was tough, aggressive, and ambitious. He wished
to prove his worth to Doenitz with the one thing that seemed
to impress the admiral the most—tonnage sunk. Winter got
his bearings by triangulating on American radio stations and
then prepared to begin his campaign. He did not wait until
night to make his first kill. The 6,182-ton tanker *W. L. Steed*
was caught about 100 miles off Ocean City, Maryland. It was a
bitterly cold day with rough seas. Rising at the sound of rum-
bling engines, Winter dismissed any possibility of attack from
the Americans and began to stalk the tanker. The *W. L. Steed*
was seen plunging into great gray waves, her engines groaning against them, plumes of white foam pouring over her
decks and streaming off her stern. Winter turned the *U-103*
broadside to the waves, and a mound of water crashed against
the side of the conning tower. The submariners on the bridge
gasped as some of them were swept off their feet, only the
safety harnesses keeping them from being thrown into the sea.
Winter, undaunted and ignoring the cries of his men, braced
himself against the tower fairing, his eyes glued to the torpedo
aimer. When he had the tanker in his sights, he sent a single
torpedo leaping from a bow tube. The seas were too rough for
Winter to track the torpedo even with binoculars so he
watched the tanker instead. Less than a minute passed before
there was a flash of light and then a satisfying rumble as the
tanker exploded in a billowing hell of smoke and flame.[8]

On the *W. L. Steed*, thirty-eight-year-old Seaman Louis
Hartz was in the chartroom with Captain Harold G.

McAvenia when the torpedo struck. Hartz and the captain were flung against a bulkhead, and then a dark brown, sulfurous smoke enveloped them. Gasping for breath, Hartz staggered out of the chartroom into the bitter cold. He tried to find the captain but it was impossible in the thick, oily smoke. From memory, he was able to get to the main deck and there helped launch a lifeboat. Hartz looked around and saw three other lifeboats. Captain McAvenia was not aboard any of them. He thought about going back to the tanker to search for him, but his attention was diverted by the sudden appearance of the U-103. Silently, the tanker crewmen watched the big black submarine sweep past them, six men at the deck gun and two on the conning tower. One of the conn crew had binoculars and seemed to be studying them carefully. "We're in for it now," Hartz heard one of the other men say, and he was suddenly very afraid.

Winter apparently was determined to make certain the tanker was destroyed. The Americans were known to be geniuses at repairing ships, so the U-boat commanders felt that damaging a ship wasn't enough. It had to be sunk. Taking the time to be certain the lifeboats were clear, Winter began to fire the 88-mm gun at the tanker. Finally, after forty minutes of shelling, the *W. L. Steed* suddenly exploded, the flash of heat causing the German gun crew to throw up their arms for protection. Winter hastily ordered them below and backed the U-103 off. It was snowing. He looked around and saw the four lifeboats filled with men. He had no room for them. But it was the middle of the day and a huge plume of smoke marked their location. They had a chance. Winter ordered the U-103 below.

Hartz and the rest of the crew of the *W. L. Steed* watched the U-boat disappear. At first, men in the four lifeboats yelled back and forth, but the sea worsened and the boats drifted apart. By the next day, two men in Hartz's boat had frozen to death and were dropped over the side. Another day would pass before the HMCS *Alcantara* would find Hartz and the other two men, delirious with pain and severely frost-bitten. They were, however, very lucky. The #2 lifeboat, holding fifteen survivors, would drift for four days and when found by the British SS *Hartlepool*, only two men would be still alive.

Lifeboat #4 with fourteen men aboard would not be found until 12 February by the British SS *Raby Castle* 100 miles farther out to sea. Only one man was still alive, the second engineer, and he would die three days later. The #1 boat with four men aboard was never found.[9]

Winter moved his U-boat farther south. On the morning of 4 February, the 3,598-ton Panamanian-registered freighter *San Gil*, carrying a load of bananas from Honduras, was sailing off Virginia under a bright moon. The sea was unseasonably calm. When the sea is flat and the air is clear, sometimes sound will carry for incredible distances. Some of the crew of the *San Gil* were certain they heard the torpedoes from the moment they were launched. The captain of the freighter, Walter W. Koch, heard nothing but the explosion that rocked his vessel shortly after midnight. In the engine room, the side of the ship suddenly buckled and an incredible burst of smoke and fire and seawater erupted. Two of the engine crew were blown apart, their limbs and torsos and body fragments strewn around the room and over the other stunned crewmen. As the water steadily rose behind them, the survivors of the engine-room crew made their way upward, some of them limping and bleeding from wounds.

Left behind was young Hildebrand Hall, just turned nineteen, who was still confused by the explosion. He found himself under one of the step grates, pressed up against it by the rising water. Finally, nothing could be seen of him but his fingers twisted in the grating and his nose jammed up between two steel bars. The third mate, Franklin W. Adams, twenty-four, came below to check on the damage and almost stepped on Hall's fingers before he saw them and the boy's nose. An opening in the grate was only three feet away so Adams got down on his hands and knees and screamed at Hall to move. Hall's response was to tighten his grip on the grate. Finally, Adams was able to reach through and pull Hall through the opening and together the two young men ran up the steps while the sea closed in behind them.

Above, Radioman Robert S. Thorp had rigged an emergency antenna to replace the original that had been brought down by the shock of the torpedo. Continuously, he radioed his position alternating with an SOS. Finally, Koch ordered him aboard a lifeboat. Three lifeboats, filled with forty-one men, pulled away from the drifting, silent ship. Koch turned at a sound and saw a submarine, not more than a thousand feet away, rise to the surface, men racing to a deck gun.[10]

It was the *U-103*. Winter ordered his men to shell the listing freighter after the lifeboats had pushed off. It was common practice for U-boat commanders to listen in on the radio traffic of a ship attacked, and Thorp's frantic signals could be bringing in airplanes. Winter would want as little evidence of his location as possible and that meant sinking the freighter quickly.

Captain Koch saw the U-boat turn its bow toward him and realized his lifeboat was between the gun and the *San Gil*. Winter waited patiently, however, until Koch and his madly rowing crew moved out of the way. He then ordered continual shelling until the freighter was sunk. Fifteen 88-mm rounds were fired, eleven of them on target. The *San Gil*'s deck was devastated, but still the small freighter remained stubbornly afloat. Ordering his gun crew below, Winter moved the *U-103* until it was on the other side of the ship from the lifeboats. Aiming quickly, he sent another torpedo into the side of the freighter. The *San Gil* rocked once and then plunged out of sight. Six hours later, as the sun rose bright and golden over the men of the *San Gil*, they found themselves floating in a sea of bananas, their cargo a huge yellow signal to any rescuers. An hour later, they were picked up by another freighter.[11]

The next night, Winter found the American tanker *India Arrow* sailing north about 20 miles southeast of Cape May, New Jersey. The *India Arrow*, out of Corpus Christi, was loaded with diesel fuel bound for Carteret, New Jersey. Winter waited on the surface until the tanker had moved between him and the lights of Atlantic City. He launched a single torpedo. There was a satisfying flash well astern the starboard side and then a huge, spewing explosion of flaming diesel fuel. So hot was the explosion that Winter ordered the *U-103* backed away. Several of his men were allowed topside to see the results. What they saw must have sickened some of them.

The *India Arrow* was engulfed with flames and men were burning.[12]

The *Dione* was squarely in the middle of the Hatteras shipping lane, blacked out and engines off. Lieutenant Alger had liked McCormick's idea of drifting and listening. Inside the darkened radio room, the only sound was that of the almost silent pulses of the signals being received. All night, Radioman Harold "Swede" Larson had picked up the signals. *SSSS*, they had said over and over—*Submarine—Submarine—Submarine—Submarine*—and then, almost without fail, *SOS—SOS—SOS*. The U-boat had attacked. Swede had dutifully relayed each report to the bridge and then bent back over his radio. It was all coming over 500 kc, the international calling and distress frequency. Swede turned as his fellow radioman clambered into the room after yet another visit to the rail. Ever since the *Dione* had gone after the U-boats, the big, muscular farm boy from somewhere in the Midwest had been miserably seasick. The latest tactic of wallowing in the shipping lanes had been particularly hard on him. As Swede did his best not to watch, the radioman found a bucket and began to worship it on his knees. Something would have to be done, Swede thought, or the boy was going to die. It was hard enough on everybody else. Continuous calls to General Quarters with nothing to show for it had left every man on board tired and frustrated. Even off-duty hours gave no respite. At night, the crew were packed below in the Glory Hole with no ventilation so that the *Dione* would be completely blacked out. Moreover, the *Dione* had no capability for making fresh water so the crew were always grubby, their work clothes caked with salt and grime. The *Dione* had become hard duty, but no one aboard her had complained. The men of the *Dione* were willing to endure whatever came their way if they could find and kill a U-boat.

Everybody except Swede's fellow radioman, that is. Swede heard the farm boy groan and fall heavily on the deck. More signals were coming in. Ships were dying out there, and all the *Dione* could do was listen helplessly. The farm boy got up and slipped and fell, crawling finally outside. *SSSS*, the signals begged. *SOS, SOS, SOS, SOS.* The *Dione* was too far away . . . too far away.[13]

At 1108 on the morning of 5 February, Kaleun Winter and his *U-103* continued their successes by ambushing the 8,403-ton Socony-Vacuum Oil Company *China Arrow*, which was trying to get past Cape Hatteras 20 miles out. Two torpedoes crashed into the big tanker, blowing off the main deck and setting the cargo of fuel oil ablaze. Although a steam smothering system, a recent invention, was used to put out the oil fires, Winter surfaced and finished the tanker off with his deck gun.[14]

On 7 February, the Type IXB *U-108*, commanded by Korvettenkapitän Klaus Scholtz, sighted the Chesapeake Light Vessel and then moved north to try to catch traffic bound in and out of the Chesapeake Bay. The weather was favorable, only a slight wind out of the northwest, with the seas calm. Scholtz grounded his U-boat in the sandy mud of the ocean floor during the day and allowed his crew to rest. Later that night under a bright moon, the *U-108* rose, hissing and groaning like a great sea monster. For the *Ocean Venture*, she was to be a monster, indeed. That vessel, in ballast and heading south, would receive two of Scholtz's torpedoes. Survivors of the *Ocean Venture* observed the *U-108* inspecting her kill and thought it almost certainly to be an Italian submarine of the Benditto Brin type and reported it as such.[15]

The *U-108* moved a little south, caught the small steamer *Tolosa* bound from Jamaica to Chester, Pennsylvania, and sank her with a single torpedo with all hands lost.[16] Scholtz then moved back north in time to spot on the night of 11 February the Norwegian freighter *Blink* 160 miles off Cape Hatteras. The *U-108*'s first torpedo, fired from the surface, struck the *Blink*'s port side, passing completely through the vessel without exploding. Scholtz maneuvered some more and then sent two more torpedoes speeding toward his target. This time, his efforts were rewarded with two explosions. The ship sank in less than ten minutes. Scholtz moved in closer, playing his searchlight on the ship to identify her and then moved away, heading toward the east.

Of the *Blink*'s thirty crewmen, there would be only six survivors, even though seventeen of them managed to get aboard a lifeboat. One by one, the men of the *Blink* went mad. Several of them jumped overboard and were taken by sharks, but most simply died while raving. The survivors, a knot of desperate, incoherent men huddled in the bottom of a sinking lifeboat, were finally picked up three days after the sinking by a passing freighter.[17]

# 5

# The Battle Expands

The *Dione* had a contact! Lieutenant Alger was on the bridge with Ensign J. V. B. Metts when a young sonar operator came bounding to the bridge. It was dusk, 12 February 1942. Alger noted the boy's wide eyes and then followed his outstretched arm and finger. *There! A periscope! Just off the port beam!* Alger didn't see anything except the sea, which had been building all day. The operator retreated back to his set and called excitedly that the U-boat was maneuvering. Alger ordered General Quarters. Depth charges from both the rack and the Y-gun were dropped, some of them set to go off at 100 feet, others at 50 feet. The *Dione* was still accelerating when they went off, shaking the cutter and lifting her props out of the water. All over the ship, lights and electrical equipment went dead. On the bridge, the gyros, compass, and sound gear shut down, leaving the ship directionless and blind, all in one moment. Swede Larson hung on to his radio set, cursed as he ineffectively flicked its switch to get it started up, and then headed below to find the breakers to reset them. The sonar operator raced back to the bridge to peer anxiously through the window. Alger ordered the engines stopped and the *Dione* slid forward on the depth-charge wave. Swede plunged deeper into the *Dione*, still cursing as he cracked his knee on a brace.

Finally, his weak flashlight found the box and he was able to
reset the breakers. Immediately, the *Dione* came back to life to
the cheers of her crew. Alger ordered silence. The *Dione* was
turning, her bow facing the still spreading wake of the depth
charges. Nothing was heard. The U-boat, if there had been
one, was gone, lost while the *Dione* was blinded by her own
depth charges. Swede clambered back to the deck and Alger
turned to him with an idea. As part of the General Quarters
drill, why not insert wooden wedges between the circuit
breakers? Maybe then the depth charges wouldn't knock them
out.

Swede thought about it. It might just work! He went off to
find one of the engineers to make the wedges.

After a night of maneuvering, Alger decided to return to
the scene of the periscope sighting and make another search
of the area. He spent the day making fruitless search patterns
on the sea. But just as darkness approached, a wake was spotted in the water ahead. It could have been a periscope, so Alger ordered the *Dione* cautiously forward. Suddenly, the cutter
was in a huge oil slick that stretched from horizon to horizon.
Currituck's lighted buoy blinked nearby as Alger maneuvered
to get out of the slick. The sonar was picking up nothing.
Where had the slick come from? How far had it drifted? Who
had died? Try as he might, Alger could find no answers except
one. The oil slick was there, tangible evidence of his and the
*Dione*'s continuing failure.

Kaleun Heinz-Otto Schultze brought his *U-432*, a Type
VIIC, into the battle area on 14 February. He was 20 miles off
Currituck Inlet, just south of the huge American naval bases at
Norfolk and Hampton Roads. He waited until after dark to
surface and spotted a masthead light to the south. It was big,
whatever it was, and completely lit up from bow to stern.
Very soon the ship, apparently a passenger liner or large
freighter, was moving directly into his crosshairs.[1]

Captain Juan J. Moura of the 5,142-ton Brazilian
passenger-cargo ship *Buarque* had a reason for keeping his
lights on. Brazil was neutral and thus far in the war no Brazilian ship had been attacked by a German U-boat. Accordingly,

he had ordered a spotlight to be shown on the Brazilian flag on his masthead at all times. Brazil was not at war even if the rest of the world was. Everything was safe and warm aboard the *Buarque*.

It was just before midnight when the *Buarque* began to die. Cyniaco Sfrippini, the chief radio operator, was in his cabin when a torpedo from the *U-432* struck the starboard bow. The *Buarque* shuddered its length and then plunged forward as if it had been smashed by a gigantic wave. Sfrippini hurried to the deck where he was hailed by Captain Moura and ordered to the radio room to send SOS signals. Sfrippini left at a run and was soon at his console, steadily tapping out the emergency signal, all the while feeling the sickening sensation of the ship sinking beneath him. In one of the after cabins, a passenger, Mrs. Adrin Ferreira of Newark, New Jersey, sat up in bed at the moment of the torpedo impact. She switched on the cabin lights and looked at her sleeping son, five-year-old Freddie Ferreira. She did not hesitate a moment. Cradling him in her arms, she took little Freddie, still in his pajamas, out on the frigid deck just as the lights went out all over the ship. Crewmen rushed past her, frantically shouting in Portuguese something she couldn't understand. Calmly, she spoke to two of the crewmen and they led her to a lifeboat. Barefoot and still holding the now-whimpering Freddie, Mrs. Ferreira patiently waited in a howling, bitter wind.

In another cabin, passengers John B. Dunn and Walter F. Shivers, both Pan-American Airways employees, were knocked from their berths by the shock of the torpedo and were just climbing to their feet when the lights blinked once and then went completely off. Groping in the dark, the two men tried to find warm clothing before they braved the cold outside. After finding his shirt and pants, Shivers found the closet and took his overcoat off a hanger. As he did, he knocked the hanger to the floor. Immediately, he fell to his knees and felt all about until he found and replaced the hanger back on the hook. Only then did he follow Dunn to the deck, where he found one of the passengers he recognized to be Mrs. Ferreira standing near a lifeboat with her son in her arms. The two men offered to take the tiny, crying boy, but Mrs. Ferreira only smiled and shook her head. Neither man noticed that she was wearing only her nightdress and the boy only his pajamas. The crewmen were swearing loudly in Portuguese and were having difficulty launching the lifeboat, but finally it swung free and Dunn and Shivers and Mrs. Ferreira and Freddie got aboard. As soon as the lifeboat touched the water, the lines parted and they were swept out into the darkness. The Brazilian sailors began to call out and other voices in the night answered them. All the lifeboats had been launched. Only the captain remained aboard. One of the lifeboats was still near the *Buarque* when Captain Moura appeared and slid down a fall line. Quickly, the boat moved to him and dragged him aboard. Huge waves were tossing the lifeboats about, and most of the passengers and even the crew were sick. Soon, the floorboards of the lifeboats were slick and foul with vomit.

The *U-432* was not bothered by the churning sea. Schultze edged in closer to see if he could identify his target. A lifeboat swept past him but he ignored it. Turning on his spotlight, he moved it down the length of the vessel but its identification still eluded him. It also appeared that the ship had stopped sinking. Schultze studied it for a moment longer, assured himself that it had been completely abandoned, and ordered another torpedo fired. This one hit amidships, exploding a boiler. Almost immediately, the *Buarque* went down. Walter Shivers, not very far away, watched the death dive of the *Buarque* and then heard a sound he would never forget, a "scream like the voice of a human being," as the *Buarque* disappeared forever beneath the sea.

The weather was getting worse. Schultze swept his spotlight around once, saw nothing, and ordered his U-boat submerged. As he clanged the hatch shut, he may have briefly thought of the poor survivors above, still in the raging storm, but a U-boat commander's first concern always had to be his boat and his crew. Schultze needed to get away from the area just in case American forces were anywhere in the vicinity. His concern was not warranted. The *Buarque*'s frantic signals had not been picked up. The four lifeboats were on their own.

On lifeboat #4, the one with the four Americans plus several Brazilian crewmen, everyone was soaked and freezing.

Little Freddie Ferreira could not stop vomiting. Ice kept forming on his face and Mrs. Ferreira frantically scraped at it to allow him to breathe. Finally, one of the men noticed that the woman and her son were practically naked and covered them with a blanket. All night long, the lifeboat pitched up and down and rocked back and forth while the sea slammed into it, threatening with each wave to turn them completely over. Freddie, still ill, smiled when Dunn asked him how he was doing. Choking out the words, Freddie asked Dunn if he had brought along his phonograph records. Freddie had loved to listen to them. Laughing, Dunn said he had forgotten them, but as soon as they got to shore, he would buy new ones and play them for Freddie as often as he liked. At daybreak, several ships spotted the drifting lifeboats. Incredibly, only one person, a woman passenger, had died during the freezing night. Mrs. Ferreira, Freddie, Dunn, and Shivers were all safely delivered to Norfolk.[2]

Kaleun Schultze kept moving the *U-432* north. Perhaps reasoning that the sinking of the *Buarque* would bring hordes of American destroyers and cutters, he had decided to leave the area off Norfolk and take up a new position just north of Chesapeake Bay. For two days, no worthwhile targets presented themselves for execution until noon on 18 February; another Brazilian ship, the *Olinda*, loaded with cocoa and castor beans, appeared. Schultze holed her with gunfire and then ordered the captain and the radio operator out of their lifeboats and into his U-boat for questioning. The two Brazilians, frightened that Schultze meant to shoot them, were relieved when he only politely asked in perfect English for the ship's papers (which had been left aboard) and then inquired as to the cargo, the loading port, and destination. It did not apparently bother Schultze that he had attacked a Brazilian ship. This was a war zone, he told the captain. All ships here were his prey. He let the two men go and then continued to pummel the freighter with his deck gun, stopping only when a United States Navy airplane came into view. Ordering the *U-432* submerged, he was completely under well before the airplane arrived. Later in the day, the *Olinda*'s crew were picked up by the USS *Dallas* while the *U-432* continued north.[1]

Schultze made an inventory of his remaining supplies and decided to head for France. That night, he happened upon the small steamer *Miraflores*, sank her, and then kept going.[4] During their short stay in American waters, Schultze and the *U-432* had managed to sink three merchant vessels without interference from a single warship belonging to the enemy.

The *Dione* was back on the open sea on 16 February, maneuvering during the day and drifting at night. Swede stayed at his radio, logging the frantic signals for help from freighters and tankers. His fellow radioman, the farm boy, had still not been cured of his seasickness. He had tried everything, including the Bible, but there was nothing that helped. This meant that Swede often had to pull a double watch, but he preferred that to being awakened by the retching sounds of the boy as he lurched to the rail. Lieutenant Alger had not been informed of the boy's condition and Swede wondered if he should be the one to do it. Before he could think about it, however, a call came through. It concerned the *Paramount*, a navy minesweeper. She had run aground inside Ocracoke Inlet. The *Dione* was the closest vessel to her with the possible exception of a German U-boat that had been spotted that morning. Alger ordered the *Dione* about and then full ahead. A grounded ship in these shoal-ridden waters was bad enough, but with the Germans around . . . was it a trap that waited for the *Dione*? It didn't matter. It was her duty. Full ahead.

All night long, the *Dione* droned south. Dispatches concerning the *Paramount* were coming in. She seemed to be in no immediate danger, but the *Dione* was still needed. The next day, as the cutter approached Ocracoke, Alger was startled to hear the cry "Man overboard!" McCormick had the helm and immediately turned the *Dione* about. Alger went outside with his binoculars to try to spot the man. After a moment, he saw him but, oddly, he seemed to be swimming away from the *Dione*. McCormick began to maneuver, turning port and then starboard as the swimming figure turned as well. The wind was blowing into their faces as members of the crew crowded up on the bow to watch. McCormick finally maneuvered the ship alongside the sailor, but still he swam straight ahead. Swede came up on deck and then turned away as, finally, two of the ship's crew hung down and grabbed the swimmer. He was still struggling and crying in a choked voice when forced below. Swede went to his radio room and slumped heavily into his chair. He looked at the bucket nearby. He was pretty certain his farm-boy friend wouldn't have to use it much longer. That was something, at least.

The *Dione* found the *Paramount* aground at the entrance to Ocracoke Inlet. She was anchored and not hard aground but bouncing on the sand. After hailing her, Alger realized she had been abandoned. He called the coast guard lifeboat station on Ocracoke to let them know the minesweeper appeared to be in no immediate danger except that she was obviously somewhat flooded. The weather was also a consideration, as it did not look good for a long tow around Lookout Shoals. The lifeboat station answered that the crew of the *Paramount* was lodged with them. They had been caught in a bad northwester off Cape Hatteras and had managed to get lost with most of the hands seasick. They had been lucky, Alger thought. They could have ended up on Diamond Shoals and would have been finished there. Alger decided to wait a day and let the weather clear before attempting to salvage the minesweeper. Patience was always wise in the Graveyard. When the weather is bad there, it usually gets worse before getting better.

The *Dione* spent the night in a raging gale, but by morning the skies had cleared and the winds dropped. Alger got on the radio and ordered the crew of the *Paramount* back out to their ship. It made an interesting scene to the coast guardsmen to see the personnel of the *Paramount* reluctantly return. They were all in their dress blues, flat hats, and peacoats. The skipper was naval reserve, an old fisherman-type. Obviously, he and his crew had left without planning to return. Alger shepherded them aboard, anyway, and sent over a party to assist in pumping. Soon, the minesweeper was off the shoal and the tow began. It was an awkward one since the *Paramount* was partially flooded, but the *Dione* managed to get her into Morehead City. It wasn't long, with the aid of fire-engine pumpers, that the *Paramount* was dry and her own generating plant functioning. Alger immediately took the *Dione* back to sea. He had lost two days in his search for U-boats.[5]

As early as February, some U-boats had already scouted the southern end of the Eastern Sea Frontier. On 19 February, the *U-128*, a Type IXC commanded by Korvettenkapitän Ulrich Heyse, was maneuvering off Jacksonville, Florida, when he spotted a big tanker looming over the horizon. It was broad daylight, but Heyse was too tempted by the size of his target to resist. The tanker he had spotted was the *Pan Massachusetts*, an 8,201-ton American ship owned by National Bulk Carriers, Inc., and completely topped off with a cargo of gasoline and fuel oil. Heyse decided to attack submerged so he backed off a bit and waited until the tanker was between him and the shore and loosed a pair of torpedoes. Both of them ran true and hit the *Pan Massachusetts* amidships, causing the vessel to be showered with flaming gasoline. Since all of the bunkers were completely filled, the tanker did not explode, but fire instantly engulfed her decks incinerating many of her crew. The rest of the men clustered on the bow until one of the bunkers let go with a mighty spew of burning gasoline. There were agonized screams and then the whimpers of dying, horribly burned men. Quickly, a heavy mooring line was secured to the end of the bow and men began to use it to slide down into the sea. Upon reaching the sea, each man found himself among islands of burning gasoline. To get away required swimming underwater to patches of clear sea. Several of the men weren't able to hold their breath long enough and surfaced in the middle of the flames. Still, the men kept going down the line. Behind them, men were burning. The sea at least offered a chance of survival.

Paddling around in the water, the captain of the tanker, Robert E. Christie, was certain he was a dead man. Fifteen-foot seas were running and a cold rain was falling. If the rest of the oil and gasoline on the water didn't catch on fire and burn him to death, he was certain he would drown in any case. Suddenly, he looked up and saw another ship, the British tanker *Elizabeth Massey*, heaving into view. He had passed the

*Massey* five miles back, but never expected the extremely vulnerable tanker to turn around and come to his aid. The *Massey* lowered a lifeboat just as the U.S. Coast Guard Cutter *Forward* arrived. The *Forward* took the lifeboat in tow and began to go around the wreckage, picking up survivors and dead bodies. Twenty of the *Pan Massachusetts*'s crew were dead. The third officer, H. L. Dodge, drifted until he was 2 miles from his blazing tanker. Finally, two navy planes passed over him, waggled their wings, and then buzzed the *Massey*. An hour later, with sharks circling him ever closer, Dodge gratefully reached up to the helping hands of the crewmen of the *Elizabeth Massey*.[6]

The Type IXC *U-504* commanded by Fregattenkapitän Fritz Poske also found the waters off Florida to be lucrative. After sinking the tanker *Republic* and holing an unidentified freighter, Poske found on the night of 22 February the American tanker *W. D. Anderson* loitering 12 miles northeast of Jupiter Light. Poske's torpedo into her side was reportedly heard as far away as Miami. Only one crewman would survive the holocaust. He had been drinking a cup of coffee on deck with a friend and, incredibly, had spotted the torpedo coming right at him. Without hesitation, he dived overboard, swam under the torpedo, and kept going when, behind him, the *Anderson* literally disintegrated into a massive spewing volcano of fire. While the survivor swam about, trying to avoid being seen by the U-boat, Poske slammed three more of his torpedoes into the drifting hulk until the tanker groaned and went down. In an hour, navy planes were circling the ship. The radio operator aboard the freighter *Walter Jennings*, coming in behind the *Anderson*, picked up a clear transmission in perfect English but with a Germanic accent. "You are next," it said. Frightened, the captain of the *Jennings* sped in close to shore, intending to spend the rest of the night in a safe harbor. The lone survivor of the *Anderson* drifted through the night until he was picked up by a small fishing boat. A coast guard boat also appeared and took the survivor aboard only to be pinned down by a bright searchlight. The coast guard vessel headed toward shore but was chased by the searchlight-wielding craft for thirty minutes before it dropped away. It had been a harrowing night for all Americans off the Florida coast.[7] As for Poske and the *U-504*, they had moved north to sink the Dutch tanker *Mamura* off the Georgia coast before turning east in triumph for home.[8]

The *Paramount* operation completed, the *Dione* returned on patrol on 20 February. Almost immediately, there was a sonar contact and Alger ordered a series of depth charges dropped. Again, the *Dione* was shaken and again Swede made his journey into the darkness. The breakers had held with the wooden wedges, but the shallow water had caused the concussion to be so bad that even the insulators had shattered. The *Dione* moved south all day and then Alger turned her north and cut all engines to drift. After a while, the sonar operator called out a clear contact. A depth charge was dropped and then the *Dione* drifted some more. Suddenly, a loud spewing noise was heard. Alger turned toward the noise, half expecting to see a fully armed Nazi U-boat hauling up to do battle. Instead, he saw the back of a whale break the surface and then sink out of sight. Alger allowed himself a small grin and then ordered the *Dione* ahead again. He was pleased. If his sonar crew could pick up a solitary whale, they could certainly hear a U-boat. That was something, at least.

Later that evening, Alger found himself amidst almost a fleet of freighters and tankers heading north. They formed no convoy but were proceeding individually. He maneuvered through the giant ships, aware that he could be crushed by any one of them if rammed. They seemed oblivious to the *Dione* and everything else in their headlong rush to get past the capes and into safer waters. Another day was spent maneuvering around Diamond Shoals, and then Alger ordered the *Dione* in. The ship needed food and fuel. To the disappointment of her tired crew, the *Dione* would stay in Norfolk for less than twelve hours. Alger and McCormick were two alike in that regard. They wanted to be at sea. That was their place.

Night and day the *Dione* maneuvered, stopping to drift occasionally, and then operating the engines again to check out any suspicious sounds. The weather was bad and a squall could come out of nowhere at any time. One moment, the sea would be flat and calm, the next it would be crashing all around, trying its best to put the *Dione* down with all the other wrecks. Late on 27 February, Swede received a signal that the freighter *North Sea* was being attacked by a German U-boat. Lieutenant Alger checked his charts, determined a course, and set off through a wild, spewing sea toward Cape Henry to try to assist. By morning, the *Dione* had found the freighter. She had been shelled by a U-boat and had been saved only by the storm that had apparently tossed the U-boat around and spoiled its aim. The freighter had lost its steering control and required a tow, so Alger had McCormick maneuver the *Dione* to set it up. By the end of the day, the *North Sea* was safe, tied up at Little Creek. The U-boat that had shelled her had gotten away, but she had at least been frustrated in her attack. Alger felt for the first time that perhaps he and the *Dione* were doing some good. He had not sunk a U-boat, but at least he had managed to help frustrate one. That was something at least!

On 26 February 1942, just as she had done so often before, the *R. P. Resor*, commanded by Captain Fred Marcus, was steaming steadily off New Jersey toward her destination—Fall River, Massachusetts. She carried with her 78,729 barrels of fuel oil and a merchant crew of forty-one officers and men. Also aboard was a naval ensign and eight navy gunners for protection. She was totally blacked out, zigzagging, and following navy routing instructions. She had lookouts posted with the gunners maintaining watch twenty-four hours a day. Her radios were sealed. The *R. P. Resor* was doing everything right to avoid the U-boats, but she was still about to die in the most horrendous disaster yet to strike the American merchant fleet.

Captain Marcus was in the wheelhouse when Able Seaman John J. Forsdal was relieved from his duty at the wheel. Forsdal had enjoyed his watch and was almost sorry to leave the bridge. The night had been clear with only a light northwesterly breeze and a long, moderate, lazy easterly swell. The moon was half full and since the night was cloudless, it shone brightly off the almost ripple-free waters. Looking to the west, Forsdal could easily see the lights of the New Jersey coast. It was a beautiful night even though it was very cold. Forsdal was wearing a heavy coat and ear muffs as he left the blacked-out bridge and made his way to the foc'sle. He stopped along the way and admired the view. As he did, he thought he saw a dark object lying low in the water. He looked again, blinked, and still thought he could see something. Turning aft, he walked toward the bridge to report what he had seen. Before he had taken more than a few steps, however, the object, whatever it was, suddenly turned on what appeared to be navigational lights. A white light was above green and red lights. Forsdal assumed it must be a fishing vessel of some kind that had turned on its lights to avoid the *Resor*. Nevertheless, Forsdal found a phone and rang the bridge. "Small vessel about two points on your port bow, sir," he reported. Captain Marcus replied "Aye! Aye!" and hung up.

Forsdal began to walk forward, still watching the lights. Suddenly, the lights were switched off and Forsdal lost sight of the craft. Certain that he had seen only a fishing boat since a U-boat would not dare get so close to shore, Forsdal went forward to be a lookout. He had not taken his station for more than a minute before there was a deafening roar and the *Resor* reared up and fell heavily on her left side. Forsdal was thrown high into the air and then slammed onto the deck. Huge flaming chunks of the tanker were coming down all around him and he had to crawl under a platform that had been built for a deck gun but never used. When it seemed safe, he got up and went down to the foredeck. He found himself cut off by huge boils of orange flame. He began to shout for help but no one answered him. He shielded his face from the flames and backed to the rail. Turning, he looked out and saw, clearly visible in the light of the burning tanker, a U-boat not more than 400 yards away. It was heading toward the New Jersey coast. Forsdal turned and shouted for help again but still no one answered. It was as if the *Resor* had instantly turned into a ghost ship. Forsdal decided to take off his heavy overcoat. He had been wearing a life belt and this he cinched around his waist again and then ran ahead, still expecting to see someone. There were only more flames. When he noticed fuel oil running across the deck toward his feet, he seized a liferaft, threw

it into the water and followed it. The sea was icy cold and
Forsdal couldn't find the raft so he began to swim away from
the ship. It was as if he were swimming in molasses. When he
was able to think, he realized he was swimming in a huge layer
of oil.

It seemed to take forever for Forsdal to put any distance
between himself and the *Resor*, but finally he turned and saw
that he was at least 50 yards away. Just as he started to swim
again, the *Resor* suddenly exploded. Forsdal swam as hard as he
could for at least twenty minutes while the patch of oil he was
in drifted toward the burning tanker. Finally, he broke free of
the oil and heard someone call his name. It was the radio operator, Clarence Armstrong, in a liferaft. Forsdal was covered
with oil, making it difficult for him to move at all. Just as he
reached Armstrong, another man, one of the navy guards,
swam up and grabbed hold of the liferaft as well. All night, the
men drifted in the raft while the sea burned.

At first light, a huge funeral pyre marked the still burning
*R. P. Resor*, attracting the attention of a small coast guard
picket boat. Spotting a raft, the boat moved alongside and
tossed a life ring down. It landed on Forsdal, who slipped it
under his arms. He was so heavy from the oil, however, that
two men could not lift him. A swell dragged him out of the
raft and then he slid out of the ring. Slowly, agonizingly, he
swam back to the raft and climbed aboard. This time, four
men were used to pull Forsdal aboard. Forsdal kept talking to
Armstrong, encouraging him. The coast guardsmen brought
the navy guard on board next and then reached down and
dragged Armstrong to the deck. Forsdal crawled over to him.
"We made it, Sparks," he gasped, a blob of oil draining from
his mouth. One of the coast guardsmen turned the radioman
over. Only sightless eyes stared back at Forsdal. Armstrong
was dead.[9]

The *R. P. Resor* was to burn for two days before she finally
capsized and sank. She was clearly visible to crowds along the
New Jersey coast. Besides Forsdal, Armstrong, and the navy
guard, no other crewman of the *Resor*, dead or alive, was ever
found even though dozens of ships and planes scoured the area
of the sinking. The U-boat that sank her, the Type VIIC

*U-578*, commanded by Korvettenkapitän Ernst-August Reh-winkel, briefly observed the destruction of the *Resor* and then moved out to sea to wait for another victim. The *U-578*'s first kill on this patrol had been a spectacularly bloody one. The next would establish once and for all the complete domination of American waters during the winter of 1942 by the National Socialist government of Germany.

# 6

# The Jacob Jones

Since *Paukenschlag* had begun, the British Admiralty had noted with increasing apprehension that the American navy seemed unwilling or unable to do anything to stop the slaughter along the American coast. The ships that were being sunk were, after all, carrying the fuel and supplies Britain needed to survive. The Trade Division of the Admiralty, responsible for convoys, complained that it found it "quite incomprehensible" that so little was being done. After Admiral King had curtly replied to the British suggestion for a coastal convoy system, the Trade Division's director, Captain B. B. Schofield, "found it extremely difficult to be polite about it." Admiral Pound, the first sea lord, cabled King and firmly stated that the only way the U-boats were going to be stopped in American waters was by using a convoy system and that he would be willing to help out with twenty-four Royal Navy trawlers.[1]

King's reply was frosty. He detested the British, distrusted their motives, and believed them to be haughty and arrogant.[2] The British admirals, in turn, had little love for Admiral Ernest J. King. A member of Churchill's staff would later say that he was "blunt and stand-offish, almost to the point of rudeness . . . he was intolerant and suspicious of all things

British, especially the Royal Navy . . ."[3] Even General
Dwight D. Eisenhower would say of his fellow American officer: "He is an arbitrary stubborn type, with not too much
brains and a tendency toward bullying his juniors. One thing
that might help win this war is to shoot King."[4]

But Eisenhower and the British were of a like mind. They
wanted to defeat Nazi Germany above all else. The Japanese
were secondary. Admiral King, however, had spent a lifetime
studying and planning for a war against the Japanese. That
was his focus, deepened to bedrock by the horrible navy defeat
at Pearl Harbor. In the Pacific was a real admiral's war, a war
of fast carriers, slugging cruisers, and big battleships. The war
with Germany was a nuisance requiring the nursemaiding of a
bunch of fat freighters and tankers. All King wanted out of
the British was for them to bomb the U-boat pens into rubble
and for Eisenhower and his army to go in and make certain
none of them would ever sail again. That was his solution to
the U-boat problem, not with the use of his warships on plodding convoy duty.[5]

As the end of February 1942 approached, the *Eastern Sea
Frontier War Diary* reflected the fact that, despite King, Admiral Pound had at least gone ahead with his promise: "In the
middle of the month . . ." the *Diary* read, ". . . 24 trawlers
. . . were being lent to CinC U.S. Fleet for A/S [anti-subma-
rine] operations on East Coast North America . . . None of
them actually [arrived] during the month and it is recognized
that when they do, their usefulness will be limited by their
capabilities. They are not equipped to operate in southern cli-
mates, they contain not so much as a small pipe-threading tool
with which to make repairs, and with two exceptions, they are
coal burners requiring a very high grade of coal. Of needed
assistance, they certainly will be but as Commander, Eastern
Sea Frontier [Admiral Andrews] said on February 26, 'it is not
considered that these vessels would be satisfactory escort
units.' " Still, any assistance was appreciated.

"Of more importance," the *Diary* continued, "were the destroyers assigned from the Fleet." During the month of February, eleven different destroyers were made available to Admiral Andrews but only on temporary duty. To stress this

unsatisfactory situation, the *Diary* added a statement from the commander of the Fifth Naval District. "Upon arrival [of the destroyers], it is usually found that the vessels need fuel, provision, stores, and repairs. Each time a change is made, there is considerable loss of time occasioned by supplying the needs of the vessel. Also [there is] frequent confusion of orders. New vessels have to get local orders, communication plans, special information, and indoctrination. The result is that there is a great deal of lost motion and considerable loss in effectiveness of anti-submarine patrols." Finally it was written, "The most obvious remedy for this unsatisfactory condition lay in the permanent assignment of destroyers to duty with the Frontier." This, however, was not to be. King still insisted that destroyers were only to be lent to Andrews for short periods. One of them was to be the *Jacob Jones*.

On 27 February 1942, the captain of the United States Navy destroyer *Jacob Jones*, Hugh David "Dubie" Black, reported to Headquarters, Eastern Sea Frontier in New York City for assignment. In a February press conference, Admiral Andrews had been unmercifully grilled by reporters demanding to know the truth about the U-boat operations. He had snapped "untrue" to the report of "five or six" ships being sunk off New Jersey but finally had to concede he was not entirely satisfied with the battle against the U-boats.[6] Andrews needed a success. He hoped the *Jacob Jones*, a World War I-era "4-piper" known affectionately throughout the fleet as the "Jakie," would provide it.

Andrews met Black and then turned him over to Captain Stapler and Lieutenant Commander Farley. Stapler chatted with Black for a while and then let Farley take the young skipper into the conference room. Farley used a pointer to advise Black of the U-boat situation off the Atlantic coast. He then told Black to take the *Jacob Jones* and patrol the area between Barnegat and Five Fathom Bank Lighted Buoy off New Jersey. By day, Black was to keep his ship at least 40 miles offshore, running along the 100-fathom curve. At night, he was to come in closer to search 5 or so miles off the line of

lighted buoys that ran along the coast. Black was then dismissed to ready his ship for action.[7]

The orders to "Dubie" Black had been very carefully
thought out by Eastern Sea Frontier. Intelligence reports had
shown three key facts about the U-boat operations off the
American coast:

First, the U-boats undoubtedly preferred to attack at
night.

Second, there was invariably a lighted buoy near the site of
an attack.

And third, most reports of U-boats and sinkings during
the day seemed to be out in deeper water. Any at night were
in closer.

After analyzing these facts, the staff at Eastern Sea Frontier felt they had discerned the U-boat's operational tactics.
Obviously, the preference for attacking at night was probably
due to the camouflage darkness provided for the low-silhou-
etted U-boats. It also allowed them to easily spot freighter and
tanker traffic, either by the ships' own lights (which were invariably staying on no matter how many orders Admiral Andrews put out to extinguish them) or by the glow of city lights
on the horizon (which also seemed to be outside Admiral Andrews's power to shut down). As for the lighted buoys being
nearby during many attacks, it was believed the U-boat commanders were near them because that was where the merchantmen were likely to be. The masters of the freighters and
tankers that ran up and down the American coast were a hard-
headed bunch, independent and resentful of any regimenta-
tion the navy might try to place on them. Since the war had
begun, they all seemed to have their own pet method of running the U-boat gauntlet. Many of them had determined
through some strange reasoning that traveling at night was
the safest for them, especially if they ran near the shore. Perhaps they believed the U-boats could not operate in such shallow water. Whatever the reasoning had been, it had proved
false, as tons of wreckage on the shallow sea bottom up and
down the coast could attest. This shallow water was too dangerous for the U-boats to remain in during the day, however,
so apparently they were going out into deeper water to either

rest or wait for stray ships. With the timing involved, the Eastern Sea Frontier staff thought the U-boats could not go out
much farther than the 100-fathom curve. Beyond that, it
would take them too long to sneak in at night to set up station
at one buoy or another.

It was this analysis that had created the *Jacob Jones*'s orders
and the reason Andrews and his staff believed there was a
good chance that the old destroyer just might bag herself a
U-boat. Considering the lack of any other success, it was
worth a try.

On the same morning he had been briefed, Lieutenant
Commander Black confidently took his ship out. It was not the
first time an American destroyer named *Jacob Jones* had sailed
against German submarines. Black's ship was named after a
destroyer that had been sunk by a German U-boat in World
War I. When it had gone down, the depth charges on the destroyer had gone off. Only a handful of the crew from the first
*Jacob Jones* would survive that horrible day. The present *Jacob
Jones* had been in construction when the catastrophe had happened and was given the name of her lost sister.[8]

The *Jacob Jones* proceeded into the Atlantic after receiving
salutes from several tugs and trawlers. The destroyer acknowledged and kept going. The men on board had a good feeling
about this cruise. Their "Jakie" was going after the marauding
U-boats and would not rest until the seas were cleared. Accordingly, Black ordered every depth charge armed. When
they caught up with a U-boat, he meant to be ready.

Several miles out at sea, the destroyer USS *Dickerson*, part
of the same division (DD 47) as the *Jacob Jones*, caught up with
Black. Admiral Andrews had sent word that the two destroyers were to patrol together, using the same tactics. As they
neared the Delaware capes, smoke could be seen on the horizon. It was the burning hull of the freighter, *R. P. Resor*. The
men of the two destroyers crowded against the rails to get a
look. Wreckage was floating all about.

After a short consultation between captains, the *Dickerson*
went on while the *Jacob Jones* stayed behind, circling the wreck
and looking for survivors. None were found. Three hours
later, when it became too dark to look further, Black radioed

Admiral Andrews that he was going back on patrol. The *Jacob Jones*, completely darkened with neither running nor navigational lights showing, droned south on a straight course through the night. There was a light wind, but the seas were exceptionally smooth. Overhead, wisps of clouds blew across a bright, full moon. A full one-third of her crew were on alert, ready for anything. Black had posted one crewman in the crow's nest and several men on each side of the galley deckhouse with instructions to call the bridge if anything suspicious was sighted. The *Jacob Jones* kept going straight ahead at a constant 15 knots.

At 0500 the next morning, the first streaks of false dawn began to slash across the eastern horizon. The moon began to fade. Ahead of the *Jacob Jones*, the *U-578*, surfaced, sat waiting. Korvettenkapitän Rehwinkel, fresh from the spectacular destruction of the *R. P. Resor*, watched the destroyer coming toward him with interest. He had obviously not been spotted. The warship was going steadily south, apparently heading for some rendezvous. Rehwinkel was an experienced commander who had been in combat since 1939. He knew what to do.

No one aboard the *Jacob Jones* saw the two torpedoes. When they struck, it was in rapid succession. One of them detonated beneath the ship's magazine, which exploded in a horrendous fireball, totally destroying the bridge and the officers' quarters. The other torpedo struck 40 feet forward of the fantail, tearing off everything above the keel plates and shafts and destroying the crew's quarters. The *Jacob Jones* went completely and almost instantaneously dead in the water, her broken stern swirling away into the darkness while bodies and pieces of bodies rained like bloody meteors into the calm, dark sea.

Fireman Third Class George Edward Pantell was on watch in the No. 2 fireroom when the torpedoes struck. He was sent flying against a bulkhead and then slammed to the deck. Scrambling up on buckled floor plates, Pantell grabbed a life preserver. He noticed the other men on the watch. Some of them were just standing around, as if in shock. The water tender, Carl Smith, looked at the gauges. "Down to fifty pounds," he said, almost routinely. "All right, boys, go ahead up through the hatch." He smiled at Pantell and indicated for him to go, too. Pantell didn't hesitate. He could feel the *Jacob Jones* listing. He knew she was going down.

Apprentice Seaman Adolph Storm was stationed on the starboard side of the "Jakie," one of the special watch atop the galley deckhouse, when the torpedoes hit. He had been trying his best to stay awake during the long, boring night. Suddenly, there had been a tremendous concussion and a flash of flame behind him. Storm grabbed for the rail, almost going over. He hung on, and the next thing he knew he was lying down. He dragged himself up by the splinter shield of one of the 3-inch guns just as there was another explosion, this one forward on the starboard side, knocking him down again. There Storm remained for a few minutes, barely conscious, while it seemed to him the entire world blew up. There was hideous noise, the sound of shrieking steam amidst the deep thunder of burning oil all around him. Finally, he blinked back to reality and stumbled to the ladder that led to the main deck. He didn't know where he was. Everything was in chaos. He heard choking screams from below. He saw several men working at one of the lifeboats and went over to help. They seemed totally confused. Nothing seemed to work. Everything was so strange, so wrong. "What happened?" somebody kept asking. "What happened?"

Out of the hell below, one rating, "Dusty" Rhodes, appeared, his skin blackened by soot. He looked around and saw that everything forward was a mass of tangled steel. There was no bridge at all. Lieutenant Commander Black and all of his officers had apparently been blown to bits in the initial explosions. The number one stack was also gone, with number two lying over against the galley deckhouse. The deck over the No. 1 fireroom was rolled up like a carpet against the galley house as was the deck over the forward compartments. It was obvious to Rhodes that the *Jacob Jones* was finished. He found some of the crew working futilely at trying to launch a lifeboat. It was jammed against the skids. There was oil running over the decks as well, making footing treacherous. Rhodes ordered the men away from the boat and told them to get liferafts, instead. Some were found and soon the men were

going overboard with them or with lifejackets. Suddenly, from
the spurting flames of where the bridge had once been, an
ensign, burned almost beyond recognition, appeared. Bab-
bling incoherently, he collapsed at Rhodes's feet. Rhodes
picked him up and passed him down to one of the liferafts. As
the liferaft pushed off, the young officer began to scream in
agony.

Seaman Thomas R. Moody climbed to the deck and braced
himself to leap into the cold sea. The more he looked, the less
he liked the idea. He found a lifeboat dangling from its lines
and tried to release it, but it was completely entangled. The
wind was picking up and it blew a frigid spray into his face.
Moody left the deck and made his way into the galley. A big
pot of coffee was still on the stove. He searched around but
couldn't find an unbroken cup. Finally, he found a soup ladle
and used it to dip out some of the hot coffee. Then he went to a
locker that had had its door blown off. The heavy underwear
that had been stored there had spilled out on the floor. Moody
could hear the sea gurgling under his feet but he took the time
to don three sets of the underwear. Only then did Tom Moody
climb back up on deck. He spotted a raft and got into it. Warm
inside and out, Moody pushed away from the *Jacob Jones*.

George Pantell had gotten away on one of the first liferafts
but something, against all reason, forced him to swim back to
the ship. Oil ran in rivulets around his ankles as he searched
the wreckage for survivors. He went to the steamfitters' room
and found a man standing at the door. He started to help the
man but was shrugged away. "When the ship starts to go, I'll
tell you," the man said. Pantell stood quietly with the man
while the *Jacob Jones* groaned and shuddered. "The ship is going down," the man whispered. Pantell left and jumped overboard. He spotted one of the liferafts, the one with the screaming ensign aboard. He swam toward it but found that it
already had fourteen men either in or hanging on it. There
was no room for him.

The overloaded liferaft was very close to the "Jakie" as she
slipped down into the ocean. Seconds later, one of the men in
the raft saw a sheet of flame flash beneath them. It spread out
like a gigantic, fiery fan and then closed. A jar was felt by

those aboard the raft and then a column of water, a hundred feet high, smashed up and then fell down on them. Just as it had happened to her namesake during World War I, the depth charges of the *Jacob Jones* were going off under her men as she sank. Some of the men began to scream.

There seemed to be no end to the chain of explosions that erupted in the dark depths beneath the struggling crew of the "Jakie." As each depth charge went off, a massive shock wave smashed through the water and through the bodies of the crew, exploding their internal organs. Their own ship was killing them as she had been killed.

Somehow, even after several of the depth charges had gone off beneath him, George Pantell found himself alive. He was very tired and didn't think he could stay afloat much longer. He looked up one last time and saw that the liferaft that had been overloaded was floating just a few feet away. It was almost empty now. He crawled up on the side of it and hung on while the sea erupted all around him. He burrowed his face into the fabric, gripping the side of the raft tightly. Somebody was yelling something but it seemed very far away. George Pantell hung on. "Dusty" Rhodes had also found himself a liferaft. With him was Adolph Storm, Tom Moody, and four bodies they had pulled aboard.

"What happened?" Storm wondered.

"They just died one at a time, that's all," Rhodes answered quietly, "just one at a time."

It was quiet now. The "Jakie" had disappeared forever beneath the sea, the last of her explosives spent. It was 0610, just barely more than an hour since the *U-578*'s torpedoes had struck. Rehwinkel had not stayed around. He knew he had sunk an American warship and that retaliatory forces would be coming to the rescue. Such forces did not, however, exist. It would be two more hours before a small observation plane, out on routine patrol, spotted the liferafts. The only help the pilot could contact was the tiny USS *Eagle 56*, a wooden coast guard patrol boat. The *Eagle 56* changed course, knowing only that there were liferafts on the sea ahead and that also a marauding U-boat was probably there as well. An hour later, an empty lifeboat was spotted and then a few minutes later the

liferaft carrying Rhodes and Storm. The wind was picking up
so the three survivors were hurriedly brought aboard and the
raft and the dead crewmen taken in tow. The *Eagle 56* clawed
her way into the rising sea, desperately searching for more
survivors. Nine were found, including Carl Smith, the water
tender who had been so calm in the face of disaster. Finally,
the captain of the *Eagle 56* had to turn back. The sea had gone
mad, giant waves rolling over the deck of the tiny craft. The
survivors that had been picked up were obviously in poor condition. There seemed to be no hope of finding anyone else. All
the *Eagle 56* could do was run. On the way back, Carl Smith
died. For two days, the navy would search for survivors of the
*Jacob Jones* with no success. Of her crew of nearly two hundred, only the eleven men the *Eagle 56* picked up had survived.[9]

   The morning after the sinking there was shocked silence at
90 Church Street in New York City. It had only been the day
before that "Dubie" Black had been dispatched with such high
hopes. That afternoon, a young ensign sought out Lieutenant
Commander Farley and told him that he had been on forty-
eight hours' leave to get married and wanted to report back to
his ship.

   "Which ship?" Farley asked.

   "The *Jacob Jones*, sir," the ensign replied.[10]

   On 2 March 1942, Admiral A. W. Watson, commandant,
Fourth Naval District, signed a letter covering a secret packet
of documents destined for Admiral King. Furiously, Watson
scribbled his name and pushed the packet across his desk to
the courier, glad to get it out of his sight. Inside the packet was
a secret intelligence report concerning the sinking of the *Jacob
Jones*. In eight blood-chilling single-spaced pages, the report
told how the "Jakie" had died. What it did not say, however,
was that what Admiral Andrews had been saying all along had
come true. The American Atlantic coast no longer belonged to
the Americans. It quite literally had become the safe hunting
grounds for the U-boats of Nazi Germany. A destroyer of the
United States Navy's Atlantic Fleet had been—worse than
sunk—smashed, swept from the sea like a paltry nuisance by
the black knights of Admiral Doenitz's U-boat flotilla.

# 7

# The Friday the 13th Patrol

With the destruction of the *Jacob Jones*, Admiral Andrews was faced with the unpalatable task of going to Admiral King and requesting another destroyer to replace her. King agreed to do so but only on the same temporary basis that the *Jacob Jones* had originally been assigned. Clearly, the destruction of the destroyer had not changed King's belief that Andrews's battle was temporary as well, one that would simply go away as the war was taken to the German homeland. General Marshall was already pushing for an invasion of the Continent in 1942. Admiral Andrews agreed that an invasion might relieve pressure along the American coast, but there was no assurance when such an invasion might actually take place. In the meantime, could the Allied merchant marine survive the U-boat assault without better protection? Andrews thought not, but since King had given Andrews all the support he meant to give, events would have to unfold to determine if this support was sufficient. Those events would be recorded, of course, in sunken tonnage and blood. March 1942 would be the months that would prove either King or Andrews correct.[1]

As March began, the U-boats had begun to be routinely replaced as others ran out of fuel or torpedoes. In the Eastern

Sea Frontier area, eight ships went down during the first week
of March but none in the bulls-eye area off the North Carolina
capes.[2]

This was corrected on 7 March by the *U-155* commanded
by Kapitänleutnant Adolf Piening. Piening found the 7,878-
ton Brazilian freighter *Arabutan* running alone on a sunny afternoon off Cape Hatteras and slammed a single torpedo into
her starboard side. After the *Arabutan* went down, Piening
ordered the *U-155* to the surface. He looked over the lifeboats
until a yelled alarm sent him and his men clambering inside
for a crash dive. For the first time since the U-boats had come
to American shores, United States Navy planes arrived as a
result of a call for help soon enough to at least give the Germans a scare. The survivors of the *Arabutan* were picked up by
the coast guard cutter *Calypso*. Interestingly enough, the *U-155*
would suffer the first loss of a German sailor in American
waters during the battle. It was not, however, the U.S. Navy
that caused the casualty but the Graveyard of the Atlantic,
continuing its relentless, destructive career. During a violent
storm on 10 March, an officer named Oentrop was washed
overboard and drowned.[3]

It appeared that the Brazilians were becoming a preferred
target of the U-boats. After the *Buarque, Blink,* and the *Arabutan,* the 5,152-ton Brazilian cargo-passenger liner *Cayrú* was
next. She was just off Ambrose Light, New Jersey, on the
night of 8 March when the *U-94,* commanded by Kapitänleutnant Otto Ites, holed her with a dud torpedo. Captain Torger
Olsen, 56, of Port Arthur, Texas, ordered evacuation, and four
lifeboats were lowered. Ites moved his U-boat through the lifeboats until he found the lifeboat that contained Captain Olsen.
Politely, he inquired as to the health of the passengers and
crew and then asked the name and destination of the ship.
Before Olsen could say anything, everyone on the boat
shouted back the answers. Ites smiled and thanked them and
then asked if everyone had gotten off the liner. When the answer was affirmative, Ites showed his appreciation by sending
a second torpedo into the *Cayrú*, this one breaking the ship in
two. Without another word to the survivors in the lifeboats,
Ites took his U-boat below. A howling gale had come up in the

meantime and, before long, the lifeboats were separated. Of the four lifeboats containing eighty-five passengers and crew, only one, the lifeboat containing Captain Olsen and twenty-six survivors, would be found and its passengers rescued.[4] After the *Cayrú*, Ites moved south to the Delaware capes and on 10 March made a savage two-torpedo attack on the small Norwegian merchant ship *Hvosleff.* The freighter blew up and sank within 90 seconds. Ites, who had expended all but his reserve torpedoes, turned his *U-94*, completely unscathed, toward home.[5]

Just after midnight on 11 March, Kapitänleutnant Erich Rostin and his *U-158* arrived in American waters off Cape Lookout. He was just in time to catch the *Caribsea*, a small American freighter carrying a load of manganese, creeping down toward Cape Hatteras. Only seven crewmen managed to get off the freighter before she sank. They were to spend a nervous night hanging on to a small raft while the *U-158* circled them, occasionally flashing an amber light in their direction. At daybreak, the *U-158* finally submerged. Passing freighters soon picked up the seven survivors of the *Caribsea.* Twenty-one men had died.[6]

One of the men who had died was Jim Baum Gaskill, a sailor from the North Carolina Outer Banks. The story is still told along the Banks that the day after the sinking, his father, Bill Gaskill, was cleaning up after a gale that had just passed. It had been a violent storm, but Outer Bankers are used to them and always there is the inevitable work to do afterwards. Gaskill went down to his pier to inspect it for damage and to see how well his and the other boats tied up to it had weathered the storm. Once there, he noticed a large plank beating against the weather piling. Fearful that the heavy board might inflict further damage to his pier, Gaskill used a boathook to push it away. As soon as the board had cleared the reach of the boathook, however, it returned to the piling where it began to beat insistently once more against the slender supports. Gaskill, exasperated, again used the boathook to push the offending board away, but as soon as he had lifted the hook, the board returned as if propelled by some unseen force, beating even harder against the pier.

Finally, Gaskill used the hook to bring up one end of the
board. He grabbed it and dragged the entire thing up on the
dock. As he did, the side that had been underwater was turned
up and to Gaskill's incredulous and horrified eyes, the large
gilt letters *Caribsea* glittered in the sunlight. Later that night,
the word would come to the Outer Banks that Jim Baum Gaskill had died. It would be no surprise.[7]

It was Friday, 13 March, when Lieutenant Alger again
took his fully provisioned *Dione* to sea. The men of the coast
guard cutter were intensely aware that it was Friday the 13th,
the worst possible day for a sailor to begin a journey. The
consensus was that the *Dione* was in for trouble because of it.
Alger was aware of the murmurings among the crew but had
no time for such things. The *Dione*'s patrol area had become a
killing ground, and he felt almost responsible for every
torpedoed ship. All of his and McCormick's tactics and innovations had done no good. He felt that the *Dione* had probably
scared a lurking U-boat or two away, but he also knew they
had probably come right back after the *Dione* had left the area.
Alger didn't care if it was Friday the 13th or not. The *Dione*
belonged at sea, and Alger was going to keep her out there as
much as he could.

It was beginning to get dark when the *Dione* emerged on
the open sea after several hours of maneuvering down Lynnhaven Roads and past the False Cape lighted whistle buoy.
There was only a light southerly wind and the temperature
was unseasonably warm. The men on deck were treated to a
spectacular sunset, a burst of reds and oranges with spokes of
pale pink. If it was to be an unlucky voyage, it was at least
beginning with an auspicious view. Alger scanned the horizon
with his binoculars, trying to decide where he should go,
where the U-boats might be. South, he finally decided. South
to Hatteras.

At about the same time the *Dione* was beginning her patrol, the *U-158* was moving closer to Cape Fear to ambush any
ships before they reached Hatteras. It was also Friday the 13th
for the *U-158* when she rose to the surface 20 miles off Cape

Fear, but there was nothing unlucky about it for Kapitänleut-nant Rostin and his crew. Immediately, the tanker *John D. Gill*, laden with a cargo of Texas crude oil, was spotted moving majestically past. On board the *Gill* were forty-two crew members and seven navy guards. The navy men assigned to the tankers and freighters had adopted a fatalistic view of their assignments. Modifying the famous "Sighted Sub—Sank Same" message, they had taken as their motto "Sighted Sub—Glub, Glub."[8]

Lookouts had been posted, but the night was dark and the *U-158* was not seen. Ensign Robert B. Hutchins, United States Naval Reserve, commander of the gun crew and twenty-six years old, was in his bunk reading when the torpedo struck. The blast knocked Hutchins to the floor, but he got up and ran to his gun and tried to spot the U-boat. Nothing could be seen. While Hutchins peered into the dark, a crewman came on deck with a lifering in his hand. Almost casually, Hutchins watched the man pitch the lifering into the sea. It drifted down, down. When it hit, an automatic carbide light came on and with a whoosh the oil that had leaked out of the *Gill* caught fire. A wall of flames rushed toward the guards, forcing them to hurl themselves overboard. Hutchins and four of his men landed in the clear, but two of the navy men fell screaming into a burning patch of oil. Hutchins tried to help but was beaten back by the scorching heat. When a patch of burning oil enveloped two more of his men, they begged him to save them. He could do nothing but watch them burn. Of the forty-nine men of the *John D. Gill*, there were to be only twenty-six survivors, most of them badly burned.[9]

It was early evening on 14 March when Lieutenant Alger took the *Dione* into Hatteras Bight. He decided to turn off his engines and drift for a while to see if the sonar could detect anything. After a few minutes, a lookout spotted a drifting lifeboat and Ensign Dunton, on the bridge, moved the cutter over for a look. The empty boat was from the *Caribsea*. Dunton relayed the news to Alger and then had several of the men stave in the boat's bottom to sink it. Alger came up to stand watch on the port wing of the bridge for a while and then

moved over to the starboard wing for a while longer. Dusk
and dawn were the most dangerous times, Alger believed, and,
though he trusted his lookouts, he just wanted to be certain.
Down below, the off-watches turned to supper—baked beans
and corn bread with a slice of dried beef thrown on top.
Swede Larson, like all the *Dione*'s crew, never relished the
food on board but ate it anyway. A boy had to keep up his
strength, after all. The corn bread and biscuits the cook made
weren't bad, in any case. They were courtesy of the jokers
who had slopped a bucket of sea-water on the commercial
bread locker. Otherwise, the cook would have fed them stale
white bread to the end. It was almost part of the routine now
to slip up and douse the bread locker after a couple of days at
sea. Somehow, the cooks never caught on or, if they did, never
made any comment.

Swede sat down at a long table with his mates and prepared for the type of combat sailors always seem to make of
eating. Meals reminded him of fighting a many-armed monster
crab. As soon as the food was brought out, arms reached across
tables, down tables, length-wise, cross-wise, from underneath,
passing by, etc., etc. Somehow, among all of the uncultured,
Swede got his fair portion as well. Swede was unique in the
crew in a couple of ways. Not only was he one of the few who
was not from the Outer Banks, but he also had not managed to
get a tattoo. Almost all of the *Dione*'s crew had a tattoo—some
big, some little, but all either patriotic or effusively sentimen-
tal. The coast guard emblem, or a dagger through a heart with
*Death Before Dishonor* inscribed beneath it, or a gravestone with
*Mother* on it were three favorites. When he had first arrived,
Swede, in an attempt to be friendly, noticed one large and
hairy coast guardsman with the *Mother* tombstone on his
shoulder and asked him how long it had been since his mother
had died. The man, a cigarette dangling from his lower lip,
stopped painting red lead only long enough to growl, "She
ain't dead yet, bub." Swede didn't ask about tattoos too much
after that.

An all-wave receiver radio was also nearly always blaring
on the mess deck. Usually, it was tuned to the broadcast band,
and the sweet music of Harry James, Artie Shaw, Benny

Goodman, and Guy Lombardo drifted across the undercurrent of conversation, raucous laughter, burps, and other exhalations. One of the men on board had confessed to catching venereal disease during the *Dione*'s last port call, and this had made him an instant celebrity, with much rowdy cheering and general congratulations. The young sailor had only been allowed to go on shore to pick up the mail, a chore that had taken no more than fifteen minutes. Quiet and withdrawn before, the boy, crimson with pride, was now recognized as a true leader among men. Swede joined in with the general commotion. God, these were good men and he was proud to be part of them. Hell, since they had only been out for two days, most of them didn't even smell bad yet—not the ones who had taken a bath while they were in port, anyway.

While the *Dione* searched around Hatteras without success, the *U-124*, commanded by Kapitänleutnant Johann Mohr, slid past Bermuda after two weeks at sea. Mohr was heading right at the *Dione*. He had heard that the best chance of success lay near Cape Hatteras and saw no reason to come into American waters to the north and then travel all the way down the coast as so many of his brethren had done. Mohr was a direct man. He meant to go straight to where the ships were. It was the eighth war cruise for his Type IXB U-boat, the previous seven making her one of the most successful U-boats in the war. With her famous edelweiss painted on her conning tower, the *U-124* had been the scourge of the British merchant fleet, having sunk twenty-five freighters and tankers for a total of 102,412 tons since the war began.[10] First under Kaleun Wilhelm Schulz and then under Mohr, the *U-124* seemed to be a charmed boat, always just out of reach of the angry torrents of depth charges sent down on top of her after every success. Johann Mohr, for that matter, seemed a charmed man. One of Admiral Doenitz's favorites, he was an exceptional leader and a clever, intuitive commander who seemed to always know what the enemy was going to do. The U-boat men had a name for his talents—*Fingerspitzengefuhl*—the sure touch.

It was not Mohr's intention to call attention to himself or his submarine before reaching American waters, but on the

evening of 14 March, one of his lookouts sang out and Mohr
raced to the bridge to see the *British Resource*, a medium-sized
tanker, come up over the horizon. He couldn't resist and sent
three torpedoes into the tanker, which exploded in an im-
mense fireball. Mohr waited around until he got what he
wanted, the identity of his victim. He would need that so as to
add the correct total to the *U-124*'s tonnage. He was a meticulous man in that regard. The last thing he heard before he
clamped down the tower hatch was the rumble of oil and the
screams of men on fire. They were not his concern. Ahead lay
the Americans and even more glory.[11]

The night of 14 March would prove to be a busy one at
Torpedo Junction. Fifteen miles south of Cape Lookout, the
*U-158* rose after a day of lying on the sandy bottom and
headed out toward the Gulf Stream. Kaleun Rostin had not
moved far before he spotted the *Olean*, an American tanker
owned by the Socony-Vacuum Oil Company. The tanker was
heading south. Rostin knew that meant the tanker was probably empty, but a kill was a kill so he began to stalk her. The
*Olean*, completely blacked out, had a number of lookouts on
duty, including some navy gunners. One of them thought he
saw a bobbing light off the port quarter about 300 feet away
and reported it to the bridge. It was too late. Two torpedoes
struck the *Olean*, the first disabling the tanker's steering, the
second slamming through a lifeboat being lowered, disinte-
grating it and the six men in it, and punching a fatal hole into
the tanker's side. Rostin took the *U-158* down, but after an
hour came back up, almost directly underneath the lifeboat
carrying the *Olean*'s captain. Rostin looked over the sullen
men in the lifeboat and then again took the *U-158* down. Days
later, the *Olean* would be found drifting and abandoned. In a
few months, she would be repaired and returned to service as
the SS *Sweep*.[12]

Rostin was not finished. After his attack on the *Olean*, he
spotted the 6,952-ton tanker *Ario*, also owned by Socony-Vacuum, ten miles southwest of Cape Lookout Buoy. Bringing up
a red light, Rostin blinked it on and off, emulating a buoy. He
was hoping the tanker would come closer to investigate. In-

stead, the *Ario* swerved away and then increased her speed, heading southwesterly, all the while sending SOS signals in the clear. Rostin was not deterred. The Americans had so far proved incapable of coming to the rescue of anything. He gave chase for an hour and a half, finally crossing in front of the tanker in an attempt to slow her, only to lose her again when the *Ario* made several desperate zigzags and then churned away. Finally, Rostin got the tanker in range, fired two flares to illuminate her, and then sent a torpedo into her side. Running low on torpedoes, he ordered his gun crew topside to finish the job. Thirty rounds were pumped into the ship while her harried crew tried to launch the lifeboats. One of the lifeboats was struck squarely with a shell and five men killed. The remainder of the crew were able to take to the sea while Rostin moved in closer and layed in ten more rounds. Still, the *Ario* floated. To the east, the deep red glow of sunrise began to illuminate the smoking tanker, and Rostin decided he had chanced enough. He took his U-boat down. After an hour, the *Ario*'s crew rowed back to their ship and went aboard only to have to take to the boats again when she suddenly began to sink. Within minutes, she was gone. The SOS of the previous night had, however, done some good. The U.S. Navy destroyer *DuPont* soon arrived and rescued the survivors.[13] Of the combined crews of the *Olean* and the *Ario*, the *U-158* had killed this night fourteen out of seventy-four.[14]

The early morning hours of 15 March found the *Dione* moving generally southwest toward Cape Lookout. All night long, Swede Larson had been up and down, monitoring the frantic signals of sinking ships. But where were they? The lookouts had not reported anything. Half-dozing, Swede could hear the CW codes from the radio shack coming down through the ventilators as he lay in his bunk. It was supposed to be four hours on and eight hours off, but it never seemed to work out that way for the radiomen. Lieutenants Alger and McCormick were up most of the night as well. Things were happening all around them, but so far nothing had been spotted. Although the sonar operators stayed hunched over their set, nothing was seen or heard. Alger kept going out on the

wings of the bridge to look over the sea. He ached to see just
one thing that would lead him to a U-boat.

As the sun rose, Alger spotted something lying low in the
water. McCormick supervised the maneuvers necessary to
bring the *Dione* up to it. It was a grounded tanker, its bow
shoved into a shoal. The *Dione* swung around it, looking for a
name. It was the *Olean*. After hailing it several times and getting no response, Alger assumed it had been abandoned. A big
hole in her side told the story. The *Olean* had probably been
one of the ships calling for help the night before. Alger could
do nothing for the tanker except alert headquarters to the
navigational hazard it represented. After doing so, he moved
the *Dione* slowly back out to sea, carefully zigzagging. It
seemed a strong possibility that the U-boat that had done the
torpedoing of the *Olean* might also use it as a decoy. For the
remainder of the day, the *Dione* patrolled around the derelict
tanker, alerting traffic in the area to the danger and presenting
herself as a tempting target. To the frustration of Alger and
the rest of his officers and men, however, all remained quiet
with not a single interesting echo returned.

On the afternoon of 16 March, Swede sent up an electrify-
ing message. The American tanker *Australia* was being attacked by a U-boat only 20 miles away! Alger sent the *Dione*
flying to the rescue. Within two hours, the cutter found the
tanker with her stern down but her bow still afloat. There
were no signs of survivors. The freighter *William J. Salman*
and the USS *Ruby* had already picked them up. The tanker had
been struck by a single torpedo launched from the *U-332* commanded by Kapitänleutnant Johannes Liebe.[15] Three days before, the *U-332* had successfully attacked the small Chilean
freighter *Tolten* and sunk her with only one survivor out of a
crew of twenty-one.[16] Liebe's attack on the *Australia* had not
been so clean, however. The tanker, even though she was fully
loaded, had not immediately sunk and none of her cargo tanks
were ruptured. Perhaps Liebe had been considering a follow-
up torpedo and that was why he was still nearby when the
*Dione* arrived. Within minutes, he was found.

The sonar operator yelled up to the bridge. Contact! Alger
called General Quarters and instantly the *Dione* became

primed and cocked for action. Alger commenced tracking, careful not to overrun his excited sonar operator's equipment. The water was very shallow, Alger knew. The U-boat would have little room to maneuver. Maybe the *Dione*'s chance had finally come. Three depth charges were dropped and then two charges from the Y-gun. The sea exploded and the *Dione* rattled. Dark brown mud boiled up and then spread across the sea. Alger maneuvered around the stain, looking for the telltale sign of oil or diesel fuel or pieces of decking. There was nothing. He kept maneuvering, but his sonar operator was now getting nothing but "mush." Alger stayed in the area for several more hours, but nothing else was heard. The *U-332* had gotten away. Finally, and reluctantly, Alger secured from General Quarters. Maybe next time . . .

Since the sinking of the *British Resource*, Kaleun Mohr had moved his *U-124* steadily west. At 2000 on 16 March, he was only 90 miles east of Cape Hatteras. The sea was calm, winds gentle and easterly, visibility good. An alert from his lookouts brought him to the conning-tower bridge. He followed their point and saw a small freighter proceeding north at about 12 knots. The freighter, the *Ceiba*, owned by the Standard Fruit Company, had a full load of bananas bound for New York. All of her lights were on. Her master had reasoned no U-boat would bother with such a small ship, so he might as well advertise to the world that the *Ceiba* was just an inoffensive banana boat. Perhaps if Mohr had recognized her as such, he would have let her go. He thought her a larger freighter, however, and sent a torpedo after her. It struck under the bridge on the port side, almost turning the small ship over. Righting herself, the *Ceiba* stayed afloat only long enough for the crew, predominantly Honduran, including some wives and children, to get aboard two lifeboats and several rafts.

Mohr brought the *U-124* alongside to inquire the identity of his kill and was at first surprised and then irritated when told the name and nature of the ship he had sunk. What a waste of a torpedo! One of the liferafts contained two women and a seven-year-old boy. It was almost swamped by the big submarine when it broke the surface. The women in the raft

were crying and so was the small boy, but if Mohr noted their
difficulty, he made no comment. He was more interested in
properly recording the tonnage of his victim. After the captain of the *Ceiba* told him it was 1,500 tons, Mohr disputed him
and called down for a check of the Lloyd's Registry of Shipping. After a moment, Mohr told the captain the tonnage of
his vessel was exactly 1,698 tons. The *Ceiba*'s captain thanked
Mohr for this now completely useless information and
watched with consternation as the *U-124* abruptly submerged,
leaving nothing behind but a surge of bubbles and foam and
the raft with the boy and the women spinning around.

The phosphorescent shape of the U-boat sped off seaward
and then cut sharply across where the *Ceiba* had gone down.
From below, first one banana and then another and then a
thousand more came floating up. The third mate, Timothy C.
O'Brien, was on one of the liferafts. At least, he thought as he
slumped down, we won't starve. Shortly afterwards, however,
the bananas, the rafts, and the boats were separated by a cold
wind out of the north. All night long, O'Brien and five others
drifted on their tiny yellow raft. The first night was not so bad
as there was plenty of water and food, but by morning rain
was falling and the sea getting rough. It would be another day,
after a harrowing ride in the raft through a bitter winter
storm, before the men were picked up by a passing freighter.
Forty-four members of the *Ceiba*'s crew and families were
never found, including three women, two girls, and the seven-
year-old boy, victims of Mohr's bloody hunt for tonnage.[17]

It was not only the *U-124* that was active that night. About
30 miles south of where the crew of the *Ceiba* were drifting,
the *U-404*, commanded by Korvettenkapitän Otto von Bülow,
attacked and sank the 8,073-ton tanker *San Demetrio* with two
torpedoes. Although the *U-404* inspected the lifeboats, no attempt at communication was made by von Bülow, who soon
decided to submerge. The men in the lifeboats watched the
submarine pass beneath them and then head out to sea. Later,
they thought they could see the U-boat's searchlight again,
winking on and off as if signaling. Despite two answers from
shore in response to the *San Demetrio*'s distress calls, the survivors would drift for two days before rescue.[18]

* * *

While the *Ceiba* and the *San Demetrio* were being attacked, the *Dione*, unaware of their plight, was drifting in a night fog off Ocracoke Inlet. The cutter had been tracking a U-boat and had stayed with it until it had suddenly cut its engines and dropped to the shallow bottom. Alger had decided to secure engines, observe absolute quiet, and wait out the sub until it started moving again. Ensign J. Van B. Metts, Jr., was the officer on deck. He was peering into the gloom when a lookout on the port wing suddenly yelled that he could see something big—*and it was coming right at them!* The first indication that anything was wrong to Lieutenant Alger was the sound of the engine telegraph frantically ringing over his head. When he opened the starboard door of his cabin, he saw the bow of a huge freighter bearing down. He turned and ran out the port door and up to the bridge. Just as he arrived, the freighter slammed into the *Dione*, its bow swinging across and catching the cutter's depth-charge rack. With a sickening crunch, part of the rack pulled loose and depth charges rolled across the deck, with two of them going over the side. Alger could do nothing while the freighter continued to grind on. Finally, the two ships broke loose. Alger grabbed a megaphone and strode out on the starboard wing and hailed the freighter, identifying himself and demanding an explanation. There was a moment of silence before a weak voice answered. It was the *Ardmore*, the voice said. The *Dione* had been mistaken for a U-boat and the *Ardmore*'s master had decided to ram it. Coldly, Alger asked if the master was in the habit of running over everything that was smaller than his freighter on the outside chance it might be a U-boat. The ship's company would hear from coast guard headquarters, he continued. The master would be lucky to keep his license.

After a few more words, the *Ardmore* continued on while the officers and men of the *Dione* returned to their duties or bed. Alger, however, would not sleep. He worked with his soundmen, urging them to continue to listen for any indication of the U-boat. They heard nothing. Whether it escaped while the *Dione* was entangled with the *Ardmore*, Alger would never know. Before dawn, the depth-charge racks were re-

paired and the huge scrape down the starboard side caulked,
sanded, and painted. No one asked Alger if he intended to take
the *Dione* into Norfolk for further repairs. No one had to. The
cutter still had plenty of fuel and depth charges. She was staying.

As the sun rose, Swede Larson received a signal for help. It
was the tanker *Gulf Dawn*. Fearing the U-boats, the tanker had
come so close to the coast she had run up on Diamond Shoals
and was completely stuck, a perfect target.

Alger sent the *Dione* running toward the stricken ship. In
less than an hour, he could make out the tanker and told Mc-
Cormick to begin maneuvering through the shallows toward
it. Moments later, the sonar picked up something metallic
moving just off the *Dione*'s port bow. Alger wanted to attack
the target but reluctantly decided the *Gulf Dawn* came first.
From the look of the tides, the freighter was being forced
deeper into the shoal. Alger ordered Swede to put out a call
for assistance, and an hour later the navy destroyer USS *Dickerson* appeared and began a screening operation. The tug
*Margot Moran* was also spotted passing by and requested to
assist as well. Although strong currents swirled around the
freighter, men of the *Dione* got into a liferaft and carried over a
hawser. The *Margot Moran* also managed to get a line on the
freighter's bow and the rescue began. As the two ships pulled
in unison, the *Dione*'s starboard engine died completely. The
shaking from depth charges combined with the collision by
the *Ardmore* had finally done it in. At last, with the *Gulf
Dawn*'s engines at full power, the freighter broke free. Her
master relayed his compliments and thanks and then asked the
*Dione* to please accompany him past the rest of the shoals. Alger had no choice but to comply. His duties were more than
hunting U-boats. He had to assist commercial shipping in any
way he could. The *Dione* took up station beside the freighter
and the *Dickerson* fell in line.

Kapitänleutnant Mohr and the *U-124* had made it. Cape
Hatteras! Mohr could see the Diamond Shoals Buoy blinking
its lonely warning, and then he saw a ship and then another
and another and another. He had come up in the middle of

what appeared to be a convoy! Mohr was surprised. He had heard that the Americans did not believe in convoys along their coast, but this one held not only three merchant vessels but also apparently two escorting American warships. Mohr took his U-boat down and started to maneuver ahead. He had no way of knowing, of course, that the "convoy" was in fact only a coincidence, the converging of three tankers—the *Acme*, the *Kassandra Louloudis*, and the *Gulf Dawn*. The apparently escorting warships were the *Dione*, still assisting the *Gulf Dawn*, and the *Dickerson*, providing an impromptu screen to seaward. Both the *Dione* and the *Dickerson* were as surprised as Mohr to find themselves in a highly vulnerable tanker convoy. Mohr maneuvered for about an hour, getting the *U-124* into position and then waited at periscope depth for the first tanker, the *Acme*, to pass by.

Captain Sigmund Schultz of the *Acme* was pleased. It had been just luck that the other tankers and the *Dione* and *Dickerson* had been brought together, but it was about as safe a way he knew to pass Diamond Shoals. The weather was good as well. There was a haze in the air, but it wasn't thick enough to stop him from keeping an eye on the other ships. Astern was the Greek tanker *Kassandra Louloudis*. The other ships he could not identify, but he had made contact with the *Dione* and the *Dickerson* and had been advised that they meant to screen them all the way past the shoals. Schultz was looking aft toward some of his crew on the stern when the first torpedo struck. When the smoke cleared, all the men were gone and the *Acme*'s stern awash. A report came from below. The *Acme* had been struck by a torpedo or a mine that had blasted up through the engine room, completely destroying it. Schultz ordered an emergency distress call put out and then ordered the ship abandoned. "Get the lifeboats down, Jim," he calmly said to James J. Galvani, the third mate, "and count as many heads as you can. Take care, now, and we'll get out of this."

As Galvani hurried off the bridge, two navy airplanes whooshed overhead. A cheer involuntarily leapt from his throat when he saw one of them wheel and drop a depth charge. The sea erupted in a welter of blue and white. "Get him!" Galvani cried. "Get him! Oh God! Get him!"

The *Dione* was on her way. Her frustrated sonar operators were getting no echoes, but Alger figured his first task, in any case, was to rescue the crewmen of the sinking tanker. McCormick went down on deck to supervise from there. He looked up to see the navy planes fly over and each drop a depth charge about a mile seaward of the stricken tanker. Then he turned his attentions to the survivors, all of whom were crammed in a single lifeboat. Captain Schultz reported to McCormick that eleven of his crew had been lost at the moment of the torpedo explosion and that he had four injured, one seriously. That was crewman Leo Bojarski, 23, who had both of his legs broken in the torpedo explosion. Ensign David Oliver was the "medical officer" because he had once taken a first-aid course. He, along with a pharmacist's mate, laid Bojarski on a mess table and gave him some morphine. Bojarski quietened, but every breath was still ragged and came through the clenched teeth of terrible pain. A bone protruded from one leg and the other was broken in two places. The pharmacist's mate took one look and covered Bojarski's legs with a blanket. There was nothing he could do.

The *U-124*'s crew were crammed in the bow of their submarine, trying with their weight to help their boat dive quicker. It had been only at the last moment that Mohr had spotted the two bombers, both of them out of the sun and dropping down to practically skim the waves as they made their attack. Mohr had screamed the alarm and started a crash dive. The *U-124* hesitated at a thermocline and then pushed through, dropping rapidly. A depth charge had exploded close by, its shock wave heeling the *U-124* over and then slamming it against the sandy bottom. Mohr sat down on the cushioned bench behind the navigation table while some of the crew, going back to their assigned stations, passed by. Each man as he filed past looked at their commander closely. What was he going to do? Would he run away? Mohr answered their unasked questions by ordering the *U-124* to periscope depth.

Captain Themistokles Mitlas, master of the *Kassandra Louloudis*, was looking directly at the *Acme* when she suddenly shook and then stopped, smoke pluming up her side. Then the planes had flown over. Mitlas rang the engine room. The

*Louloudis* must zigzag, he ordered, and he must have full power. To seaward, the American destroyer seemed to be turning this way and then that, as if it was chasing after something. Mitlas turned to look back at the *Acme* and saw a black object suddenly push up out of the sea. Mitlas had never seen one but he had no doubt about what he was seeing. A periscope! Before he could say or do anything, there was an ominous series of splashes coming in his direction. Behind the first splashes came more. Mitlas guessed correctly that two torpedoes had been fired at his ship. He looked down. Almost all of his crew were out on deck, some of them gesticulating at the approaching torpedoes. They were a mixed bag of gentlemen—Arabs, Hindus, a little of everything out of the Middle East. Mitlas had no idea how they were going to react. A zigzag took care of the first torpedo but there was no way to avoid the second. It struck an empty hold about three feet below the waterline, leaving a huge hole and tons of water rushing in. Mitlas ordered the ship abandoned and was the last one in the second of two boats launched. All of his men, he proudly noted, were safe, even though the *Louloudis* was definitely sinking.

Mohr again ordered his boat to crash dive and soon the *U-124* was sliding along the shallow bottom while the ominous swish-swish of the *Dickerson*'s propellers passed overhead. A little later, there was the rumble of depth charges far away. The crew of the *U-124* smiled at each other. The Americans had better improve their aim if they wished to fight the likes of them![19]

There was controlled chaos on board the *Dione*. Lieutenant McCormick tried to keep the *Louloudis*'s survivors moving, out of the lifeboats, onto the deck, and then below. *"Pronto! Pronto!"* he urged everyone, even though few of them spoke any Spanish. Men with turbans and loin cloths were part of the survivors of the Greek tanker, and it seemed as if they and everyone else coming aboard spoke another language. But McCormick was from Texas and it seemed natural to assume that anyone foreign would speak Spanish. The tough coast guardsmen watched incredulously as several of the Hindus dropped to their knees before their saviors, kow-towing and chattering their thanks.

There were now more survivors on board the *Dione* than crew. They were everywhere, below, on deck, some of them even accidentally barging in on the bridge. A lot of them were seasick and weren't bothering to use the rail. Captain Alger looked down and watched his men trying to go about their duties in the crowd. Two men in turbans were even sitting on one of the depth-charge racks. Alger briefly considered turning immediately for a safe port and then, as always, decided to stay at sea. The *Dione* had only one place in this battle, and it didn't matter if she were covered with Hottentots or wild men from Borneo!

McCormick came to the bridge and reported that twenty men of the *Acme* and thirty-five from the *Kassandra Louloudis* had been saved. Alger complimented McCormick for his good work and ordered the *Dione* ahead. He reminded his sonar operators to keep listening. He had no idea how many U-boats he faced, but he was almost certain it was more than one. Below, Captains Schultz and Mitlas received the word. They were asked to make themselves and their men as comfortable as possible, but the *Dione* wasn't going directly in to port. She was going sub-hunting, instead. The *Dickerson* was heading south. Alger went north. Luck, that's what was needed as much as anything. Luck!

The luck, however, was running for Mohr and his *Fingerspitzengefuhl*. Seven hours after the *Kassandra Louloudis* had gone under, the *E. M. Clark*, a 9,647-ton tanker owned by Standard Oil of New Jersey, sailed on a course required to take her safely past the deadly shoals marked by the Diamond Shoals Lighted Buoy. The *Clark*, droning at a steady 10 knots and blacked out, was completely unaware of the fate of the *Acme* and *Louloudis*, both wrecks now only a few miles away. With darkness had come a sudden Hatteras-style thunderstorm. Brilliant flashes of lightning revealed at intervals to Mohr the rain-drenched hull and superstructure of the fully loaded tanker as she plowed north through the choppy sea. The *U-124* had spent a few hours avoiding both the *Dione* and the *Dickerson* before turning back for the lighted buoy that seemed to be attracting big tankers like a magnet. This maneuver was rewarded by the sight of the big *E. M. Clark*.

The *E. M. Clark* was captained by Hubert L. Hassel, an experienced master. Hassel was in bed when he heard a loud thump forward. He jumped up, dressed, and hurried to the bridge. Reports from below told of a gaping hole on the port side. Hassel left the bridge, bound for the radio room. An emergency signal had to be sent out immediately.

Radio Operator Earle J. Schlarb arrived at the radio room at the same time as Captain Hassel. The main antenna was found to be broken so temporary repairs were attempted, but before anything could be tested, there was a dull, heavy explosion forward. Torpedoed again! The impact jammed open the ship's whistle and it started a continuous cry. Broken steam lines hissed loudly. Below, there was a groan as if a great bear had awakened. The *U-124*'s second torpedo had penetrated deep before exploding, and it spelled death for the *E. M. Clark*. Radioman Schlarb thought it was still raining but what felt like rain on his face was not water. It was heating oil, falling in a fine spray. Captain Hassel had no choice but to order the ship abandoned.

Below, many men were working their way toward the top deck. Storekeeper Jack Gray had slept through the first torpedo explosion. One of his shipmates had awakened him and told him the ship had been torpedoed. "What of it?" Gray had replied and gone back to sleep. Likewise, an all-night poker party had heard the first explosion and kept playing. The second torpedo convinced everyone that something serious had happened. All the cards and money were left behind and Jack Gray made it topside so fast he didn't even remember how he got there.

Captain Hassel collected his ship's documents and threw the secret codes overboard in a weighted canvas bag and then took leave of his ship in a lifeboat. It did not get far, however, before a seaman yelled and pointed to a man standing at the ship's rail. Captain Hassel ordered the lifeboat back and shouted to the man to jump. It was a scene from the worst seaman's nightmare. A huge chain of lightning lit up the sea, revealing the rapidly sinking tanker and the terrified man at

the rail. Ringing in every man's ears was also the banshee cry
of the *Clark*'s still madly shrieking whistle. Finally, the man,
Wiper Glen Barnhart, jumped. Barnhart weighed 240 pounds
and, like most of the crew, didn't know how to swim. He sank
like a stone and then came back up, flailing and sputtering. A
wave picked him up and neatly tossed him inside the lifeboat
on top of radioman Schlarb. While Schlarb crawled out from
beneath him, Barnhart lay on the bottom of the boat, breathing deeply. A flashlight revealed a big grin on his face.

Hassel's attention was called to a yellow light moving on
the water. Hassel was certain it was the U-boat, looking for
survivors to murder. Suddenly, the *E. M. Clark*'s stern lifted
high and the tanker plunged forward and down. Just before
the smokestack disappeared under the surface, the whistle
stopped for a moment and then began again. Finally, there
was a great bubbling noise and the *E. M. Clark* slid smoothly
beneath the waves, stilling her whistle forever. As the first
gray streaks of dawn crept over the sea, several ships were
spotted. One of them was a destroyer. Hassel shot two red
flares and it changed course and ran over to them. It was the
*Dickerson*, still looking for the killer U-boat but finding, instead, only its victims.[20]

The long night of 17–18 March was over for the men of the
*E. M. Clark* and also for the men of the *Dickerson* and *Dione*. It
was clear that the U-boat or U-boats had gotten cleanly away.
Lieutenant Alger heard the *Dickerson*'s report and reluctantly
took his cutter in to drop off his passengers and reprovision.
All night long, he had maneuvered the *Dione*, stopped, listened, maneuvered some more, all with negative results. He
had not even been aware of the *E. M. Clark*'s peril. If only the
tanker had gotten off a signal, the *Dione* could have charged
over, maybe caught the U-boat on the surface. *If only* . . .
The *Dione*'s Friday the 13th patrol was over. Within her assigned area during the patrol, fourteen freighters and tankers
for a total of 90,460 tons had been sunk.[21]

# 8

# The USS *Dickerson*

On 6 March 1942, the United States destroyer *Dickerson*, on loan to Admiral Andrews, came steaming by herself down the coast of New Jersey, heading for "Torpedo Junction." Lieutenant Commander John K. Reybold, on the bridge, carefully scanned the sea ahead. Enough had already happened to convince him that the Germans were out to kill anything that moved off the American Atlantic coast—his destroyer included. He had to respect these German submariners. They were audacious and skilled, a deadly combination. His respect for them was tempered by only one thing and that was his own confidence. He could and would bring his ship through even if he had to work himself and his men 24 hours a day. Not only would he get them through, he was also confident of one thing: the *Dickerson* would gain a kill.

The executive officer, Lieutenant F. E. Wilson, had been briefed by Reybold as to what was expected throughout the cruise and had made plans accordingly. The ship was to have a General Quarters drill every morning one hour before sunrise and again at night one-half hour after sunset. One-third of the crew was to be on watch at all times, water-tight integrity was to be maintained constantly below decks, and the sonar and radar were to be operational at all times. Reybold had a strong affection for his old four-stacker, but he knew she was limited. It would take maximum alertness to keep her safe. The *Dickerson*'s crew did not entirely share their captain's attitude. The *Dickerson* had already undergone some very difficult convoy duties in the North Atlantic. It seemed to many of the crew that running up and down the coast of Virginia and North Carolina would be something of a lark, the fate of the *Jacob Jones* being considered a fluke.[1]

Throughout the day, the *Dickerson* droned steadily southward until she was off Delaware Bay. Almost immediately she was in a sea covered with oil. A U-boat had been at its deadly work and close by. The sonar operator called out a target and Reybold turned the *Dickerson* around and began a series of search patterns, culminating in the dropping of several depth charges. He was rewarded by a froth of oil, cork, and wood springing to the surface. There were cheers on deck that Reybold ordered immediately silenced. He knew the truth. The *Dickerson* had only depth-charged a U-boat victim far below. He turned the *Dickerson* south again. To starboard, within sight, was the shoreline of the United States of America, but he felt as if he were inside enemy lines. This was a situation that would have to be turned around.[2]

After a refueling stop in Norfolk, Reybold again took the *Dickerson* out and headed toward Hatteras. On the way, he found wandering merchantmen and organized them into impromptu convoys. For more than a week, the *Dickerson* swarmed all over Torpedo Junction, trying to be either everywhere or heading in that direction. Perhaps as a result of her frantic activity, no ships were sunk during that time.[3]

After refueling again, Reybold eagerly ordered the *Dickerson* back out for more patrolling. Sweeping down to Cape Lookout, he poked his destroyer around, found nothing suspicious, and headed back toward Diamond Shoals. That day and night, he was caught up in the madness that saw the *U-124* sink the *Acme*, the *Kassandra Louloudis*, and the *E. M. Clark*. By nightfall, the exhausted and frustrated crew of the *Dickerson* strained into the dusky sky, still looking for the unseen enemy that had caused so much carnage within sight of them. All day, Reybold had ordered the *Dickerson* to and fro, but nothing had been found. Not even a depth charge had been dropped. Finally, after midnight, some red flares were sighted. The U-boats signaling to each other, Reybold guessed. Exhausted himself, Reybold still ordered the *Dickerson* toward the flares. Instead of the enemy, however, he found the poor remnants of the torpedoed *E. M. Clark*.

There were fourteen survivors. After transferring them to a coast guard vessel, Reybold ordered the *Dickerson* on. The U-boats were out there. Patience. That was the key. Patience.

Patience was one of Kapitänleutnant Johann Mohr's virtues as well. After his spectacular successes of 17–18 March, he took his boat out to sea and settled down near the 60-meter line for a day of crew rest. He could hear ship traffic near him all day long, but he resisted attacking. Better to check things out. The *U-124* had been shaken by the depth-charge dropped by the airplane, and the chief wanted an opportunity to do some maintenance. As night fell, Mohr took the *U-124* up and sent some signals to BdU confirming the previous day's kills and making certain he received credit for the tonnage sunk. He also included a little poem meant for Doenitz:

> The new-moon night is black as ink
> Off Hatteras the tankers sink
> While sadly Roosevelt counts the score—
> Some fifty thousand tons—by

> MOHR[4]

Mohr received what he was hoping for—a personal reply and congratulations from Doenitz. He was also told that the *U-332* was nearby. He could, if he liked, work in coordination with Kapitänleutnant Liebe. Mohr signaled Liebe and the two U-boats moved closer. Mohr then moved in toward shallower waters, all the way to the 20-meter line. He marveled at the sweep of the bright spotlight of the Cape Lookout Lighthouse, guiding friend and enemy alike. He could even see an occasional automobile driving down the Outer Banks. Considering the reputation of the North Carolina capes, Mohr could not

complain about the weather. The skies were perfectly clear
and the seas only moderately rough. All the *U-124* had to do
was to loll on the surface and wait. As the night deepened, a
ship came in sight, heading south. Mohr quietly ordered his
U-boat forward and then turned out to sea, all the while making his firing calculations.

The night of 18–19 March was going to be a bloody one.
The first ship to die was the *Papoose*, a 5,939-ton tanker in
ballast, en route from Providence, Rhode Island, to Port Arthur, Texas, with a crew of thirty-four. Her captain, Raymond
Zalnick, had ordered his ship blacked out but was not zigzagging. He just wanted to get past Cape Lookout as fast as he
could. The first of Mohr's torpedoes caught the *Papoose* on the
port side and entered the fuel compartment. The engine room
and fire room were instantly flooded with oil and water. The
engines were stopped and the *Papoose* helplessly drifted. Two
men were dead, drowned in the engine room. Zalnick sent out
an SOS and received an answer from a shore station.[5]

Mohr, aboard the *U-124*, heard both messages as well.
"We'd better sink her quick," he told his executive officer,
"and get out of here while we can."[6]

Zalnick ordered his men to abandon ship. He fully expected to get torpedoed again. Once the lifeboats were
launched, they pulled away from the settling *Papoose*. Before
they got very far, a phosphorescent shape flashed beneath
them. Torpedo! Again, the *Papoose* shuddered under the impact of one of the *U-124*'s MK VII torpedoes. A hole was torn
near the waterline and the *Papoose* rolled toward it. Mohr had
his searchlight turned on and flashed it at the tanker and then
at her crew. There was no doubt about it. The tanker was
going down. It had been a good kill. He ordered his U-boat
down and out to deeper water. Then he headed south on the
surface. An hour later, a lookout reported seeing another
tanker. It was the *W. E. Hutton* loaded with 65,000 barrels of
heating oil, en route to Marcus Hook, Pennsylvania.

Mohr chose to fire from the surface. A lookout on the
bridge of the *Hutton* spotted the torpedo but could not give a
warning in time. The torpedo's blast caved in the bow, flooded
the forward tanks, and carried away the anchors. A fire started

but quickly flickered out. Captain Carl Flaathen immediately had a distress signal sent and an acknowledgment came back. Once more, the *U-124*'s signalman picked up the emergency traffic and relayed the news to Mohr. Mohr turned for another run on the stationary target.

A terrific explosion buckled the decks and overturned the pilothouse. This time, the *Hutton*'s crew ran out of luck as the fuel oil caught fire. There was a raging inferno throughout the ship in seconds. Walter Clark, an oiler who had spent most of his life at sea, was caught in his bunk when the first torpedo struck and had just made it topside when the second torpedo set the tanker on fire. Flaming oil was raining straight down on top of him as he rolled off the deck into the sea. Nearby, Able Seaman James H. Cosgrove was on lookout duty and was thrown high into the air, cartwheeling over and over all the way down to the ocean. All of his clothes except for a jacket were blown off. He found a liferaft and crawled aboard. When he looked up, he saw a man, completely on fire, running to and fro on the deck. Another man, also on fire, dropped off the tanker and hit the sea with a spewing hiss of steam and bubbles. Cosgrove turned away. By daybreak, he saw that there were two lifeboats and several rafts drifting in a great pool of oil. After they had all transferred to a single lifeboat, the survivors of the *W. E. Hutton* began to pull toward shore. Shortly afterwards, they were picked up by the British freighter MV *Port Halifax*. The crew of the *Papoose*, still rowing their lifeboats to shore, were provided an unexpected torch to light their way—the spewing, burning *W. E. Hutton*.[7]

Lieutenant Commander John K. Reybold and the USS *Dickerson* were coming. The *Dickerson* had received signals from Norfolk to proceed immediately to the Cape Lookout Lighted Buoy area where two unidentified ships were in distress. The U-boat that had attacked them was reported to be loitering in that area, attacking any ship that dared try to pass. Reybold had called for General Quarters. He was at least 30 miles north of Cape Lookout, but the old *Dickerson* was, if nothing else, fast. He would be on station within a couple of hours. He could only hope the U-boat would still be there, brazenly thumbing its nose at the United States Navy. If so, Reybold was certain the Nazis were going to be surprised. His *Dickerson* was primed and ready.

The *Liberator*, a medium-sized freighter of 7,720 tons, was a nervous ship. As she warily approached Cape Lookout, her officers on the bridge had been presented with a horrifying sight. A big tanker was burning, its spewing fuel oil sending flames hundreds of feet into the sky. The sea was lit up all around for miles and the *Liberator*'s captain seriously considered turning about. Instead, he called down and made certain that the navy gun crew aboard was prepared for action. Routing instructions from the navy had ordered him to pass Cape Lookout that night, and he felt he had little choice but to comply. Still, he meant to be ready for anything. The coxswain in charge of the gun crew saw to the loading of their gun and set lookouts. He and his men had also seen the burning tanker and knew that a U-boat was certain to be about. They all peered into the darkness. Reports had filtered in that the U-boats often attacked from the surface. Maybe the coxswain could get off a round before a torpedo was launched. That was why he was on board, in any case, and all he could do was try. On the bridge, the captain of the *Liberator* rang down to the engine room. He wanted maximum rpm's while going past Cape Lookout.

At 0230, the *Dickerson* made a radar contact. It was a fast-moving target headed north and was about 14,000 yards away. The sea was calm but the sky overcast. The night had started clear but, typical for the North Carolina capes, had suddenly clouded over. Captain Reybold decided to move in closer to check the contact. He didn't want to fire on a friendly ship, but he felt the target was moving faster than the ordinary freighter or tanker. He had to be certain, and the only way to do that was to get close enough to see the target. It took almost 40 minutes for the *Dickerson* to close. Lookouts reported back. It appeared to be a freighter. Disappointed, Reybold gave the order to turn to port and clear the area. Reybold was in the chartroom where the radar and sonar gear were located. A signalman was operating the radar while a sonar operator listened. A light had shown several times from the target ship, as if a door were opening and closing.

Quartermaster Victor M. Merchant, Jr., started to make a comment about the apparent carelessness aboard the ship when suddenly there was a flash of light and an explosion. Merchant was lifted up and slammed against the Polaris stand and then fell to the deck. Darkness covered him. When he came to and looked around, he saw only wounded and dead. The bridge of the *Dickerson* was a shambles. The sound operator and the radar operator were both dead, their blood streaming across the deck. The radio was shattered and the flag locker smashed open. Flag bags had broken open, the colorful pennants strewn about. In the radio room, Captain Reybold was sprawled out, his legs shattered, numerous shrapnel wounds all over his body. Glassy-eyed, he stared upwards.

Merchant got to his feet just as another round came whistling over the after stack. A third round was also high, flying over the mainmast. The *Dickerson* was still in a turn. Merchant, disoriented, began to look around, into the pilot-house, out to the port wing, back to the pilot-house. Had the *Dickerson* been abandoned? It was very quiet and dark. He put his hand up to turn on the General Alarm and another hand closed over his. It was the officer of the deck. He had been out on the starboard wing and had survived the attack. Shortly, Lieutenant Wilson was on the bridge. He knelt beside Reybold, the captain murmuring something. He was telling Wilson to get his ship, his beloved *Dickerson*, home safe.

Wilson immediately set a course for Norfolk, but about fifteen minutes later he checked the master compass and found the repeaters were completely out of step with the gyro and that the *Dickerson* had actually been steaming south. Cursing, he turned the destroyer about, following the magnetic compass. The *Dickerson* had a doctor aboard, and Wilson ordered him to take the dead and wounded below. Shortly, a message came up from Reybold. It was word to proceed at 27 knots, maximum speed, to Norfolk. Wilson sent word back that he would comply, and soon the *Dickerson* was speeding across the sea—her wake a furious, spewing trail of phosphoresence.

Quartermaster Victor Merchant had cleared the cobwebs

from his brain and had not stopped working since he had
regained consciousness. As the *Dickerson* plowed north, he
brought his notebook up-to-date and helped with the repair of
the repeaters. His left leg was getting stiff, but he put it down
to being slammed against the Polaris stand when the ship was
hit. He also had water in his shoe, he believed, although he
couldn't remember the *Dickerson* taking aboard any water.
When his watch was over, he went below to change and found
his shoe full of blood. He checked in with the doctor and
found a piece of shrapnel had gone completely through his left
calf.

Captain Reybold kept sending messages to Wilson, inquir-
ing as to how well the ship was doing, the condition of the
crew, the estimated time of arrival at Norfolk, what equipment had been damaged, etc. Wilson had ordered one of the
other lieutenants to establish communications, but it was not
until the *Dickerson* was within sight of Cape Henry that the
damaged radio worked. Even in the channel, Wilson kept
the *Dickerson* going with all four boilers lit. Along the way, the
destroyer USS *Roper* was passed. The *Roper*, on her way to sea,
blinked a greeting but Wilson had no time to reply. The doctor had advised that Captain Reybold's injuries were extremely serious. As the *Dickerson* finally entered the Norfolk
Navy Yard, ambulances and doctors were waiting for her. Wilson hurried below to see to Captain Reybold. As he entered,
the doctor turned and shook his head. Reybold had just died,
conscious to the end.[8]

At about the same moment, the sulphur-laden freighter
*Liberator* was 3 miles west of Diamond Shoals heading east
toward deeper water. Suddenly, an explosion shook her, the
result of a torpedo from Liebe's *U-332*. An effort was made by
the crew to enter the engine room, but sulphur fumes pre-
vented it. Shortly, the *Liberator* filled with black and bluish
smoke and began to list. The engines went dead and then all
power was lost. An SOS was sent out but there was no answer. The seas were empty. Soon the remaining crew of the
*Liberator*, plus her navy gun crew, took to the lifeboats. In a
matter of minutes, the *Liberator* sank. An hour later, the USS
*Umpqua* picked up all of the survivors. Besides the story of the

sinking, the coxswain of the navy gun crew had quite a tale to tell the rescuers. Before being sunk, the *Liberator* had been attacked by another U-boat, but the coxswain and his gun crew had replied with a well-placed four-inch round. The U-boat had not only been hit, the coxswain said, but had rolled completely over. He claimed a sinking.[9] There is no record of when, or if, he was ever informed that the U-boat he had attacked had been, in fact, the USS *Dickerson*.

# 9

# On the Sea
# of Death

For the U-boat commanders, March 1942 had turned into their "Second Happy Time."[1] Of all the U-boat commanders off the American coast, perhaps Kaleun Johann Mohr was the happiest. He had not only mauled the American merchant fleet, but a recent observation had convinced him that he would have no trouble finding more targets for his remaining torpedoes. The American freighters and tankers had begun sailing close to shore, practically steaming over the buoys that marked the dangerous shoals off the capes of North Carolina. Mohr believed there could only be one reason for this foolhardiness. The merchant masters must believe that the U-boats could not operate in such shallow water. If it had been the coast of the British Isles, Mohr knew this might be sound reasoning. The U-boats needed depth to maneuver and hide when the Royal Navy was around. But the American Navy? Mohr only needed 30 feet of water, perhaps less, because he and the rest of the U-boat commanders were willing to attack from the surface in American waters. That meant all they had to do was go to a buoy and wait.[2]

It was 21 March, just after midnight, when Mohr and his *U-124* again saw a target that interested them. They were just south of Frying Pan Buoy. Lookouts on the conn had spotted the blinking light of the buoy and some jest had been made of it, Mohr laughingly thanking the Americans for leaving their navigational lights on for "the tourists."[3] Shortly afterwards, a lookout announced a rapidly moving shadow against the lights from shore. Whatever the ship, it was several miles away and it looked big. Mohr aimed the *U-124* for an intercept. Big and fast . . . it had to be a tanker!

Mohr was correct. She was the *Esso Nashville*, loaded with a full cargo of 78,000 barrels of fuel oil. As she neared Frying Pan Shoals, there was no moon and a drizzle of cold rain was falling. Captain Edward V. Peters had retired to his quarters, confident that he had done everything he could to pass Cape Hatteras without trouble from the U-boats. His ship was blacked out and was moving as fast as he dared. He had also repeatedly drilled his men in launching the lifeboats, often calling the drills without warning. Someone very wise had told him years before that the best way to avoid trouble was to prepare for it. Captain Edwards was prepared as best he could be. He was also alone at night on the bull's-eye of Torpedo Junction.

The *U-124* shuddered slightly as the first torpedo jumped from her bow tube. The men on the conn stared after it while the chief counted the seconds below. Mohr strained to see through his binoculars. But nothing happened. A dud!

Captain Peters jerked his head off his pillow. He had heard a thud far below, as if his ship had brushed against a buoy or some wreckage. He got to his feet and headed for the bridge. Chief Mate Christian A. Hansen also felt something hit the ship on the starboard side. Third Assistant Engineer Henry H. Garig, going off watch at midnight, was heading for the petty officers' messroom with Oiler Tom Hemphill and Fireman-Watertender Austin Wolfe when they also felt it. Garig turned to the others and said, "Well, we got it!" Garig met the chief engineer, Aloysius J. Kist, coming out of his room. Kist wanted to know what was going on.

"I think we've just been torpedoed," Garig answered. The two men decided to go to the engine room to prepare for additional steam if needed. They would barely have time to get there. Mohr had launched a second torpedo. The *Esso Nashville*,

fully loaded, and with 13,000 deadweight tons, was suddenly
picked up and slammed down on her starboard side. A massive
shock wave flashed across the water and through the sleeping
rookeries of gulls and pelicans on the near banks. The birds
cried and wheeled in confusion as a fireball rose from the sea.
Mohr watched it all through his periscope. Success!

Captain Peters gave the order to abandon ship and, because of his drills, an orderly evacuation began. There was a
supply of the new lifesaving suits on board, rubber pullovers
designed to protect against cold water, and most of the men
were wearing them. One of the men who wasn't was Oiler
Leonard Mills, 56, a navy veteran and a retiree from the Ak-
ron, Ohio, fire department who, for patriotic reasons, had
gone back to sea. He had not been able to find one of the new
suits in the confusion but had, at least, put on a life preserver.
When one of the younger men yelled that he couldn't find a
life preserver, Mills took his off and threw it to the man. Garig
called to Mills. "You'll need that, Leonard."

"I'll be OK," was Mills' reply. "I can swim. He can't."

It was starting to rain harder and the wind was frigid.
Garig found his lifeboat was too full. With every wave, water
sloshed in and it appeared it might sink at any moment. "All
men with rubber suits into the water!" he ordered. The first
man in was Leonard Mills, clad only in trunks. Garig ordered
him back into the boat but he refused. Seeing the nearly naked, older man in the water was enough for the men in rubber
suits. They followed him. Mills and the others would remain
in the freezing water for four hours before daybreak and a
calming of the sea.[4]

Mohr and his crew had not allowed themselves any sort of
a victory celebration. Another tanker had been found. With
the *Nashville* just below the horizon, the tanker did not know
of the previous attack. Unconcerned, she ran right up to the
*U-124*. Mohr, however, was having problems lining up the
fast-moving ship. He screamed down to his chief to give him
more power. He wanted this tanker! Mohr kept chasing but an
hour later was no closer. Frustrated, he decided to try a long-
distance shot and sent two torpedoes speeding away. Three
minutes and twenty-one seconds passed before there was a

bright flash on the tanker's side and a rewarding rumble across the sea. A hit! But the tanker was still speeding north, too fast for Mohr to catch her, so he reluctantly stopped chasing. Captain Montague of the *Atlantic Sun* was indeed heading out of the area. As soon as the torpedo hit, he called in an SSSS and veered toward shore, entering the harbor at Beaufort, North Carolina. He would not venture out again that night.[5]

While the *Atlantic Sun* was running for her life, the survivors of the *Esso Nashville* were rowing toward shore. On the settling tanker, however, one man remained. Captain Peters, given up for lost by his crew, was still aboard and very much alive although suffering a broken left leg. The next morning, the first survivors of the *Esso Nashville* arrived in Norfolk. They reported that all the crew had managed to get off except the captain, who had bravely died trying to rescue secret documents. They were certain their ship had gone to the bottom of the Atlantic since it had been completely broken in two. At that moment, however, Captain Peters was waving in the destroyer *McKean* and the coast guard cutters *Agassiz* and *Tallapossa*. He was taken off and the stern of his tanker towed in behind him. In one year, the *Esso Nashville* would be completely rebuilt and back in service. She would deliver oil for the remainder of the war all over the world. Captain Peters would be given the American Legion Medal for outstanding heroism and made master of another Esso tanker. As for the crew, all would go back to sea, most of them on other tankers. In fact, Oiler Leonard Mills, the heroic fire department retiree, would die aboard the torpedoed tanker *R. W. Gallagher* just four months later.[6]

The *Dione* was too far north to pick up either the sound or the fury of Mohr's attacks. She was drifting again, just south of Hatteras and only a mile off the beach. Lieutenant Alger had covered the area the day before, dropping several series of depth charges on good echoes. But only the brown sand of the shoals had been turned up. The next day, Alger ordered his cutter south toward reported sinkings. No sign of the marauding U-boats was found, so the *Dione* spent the night drifting, listening, maneuvering, stopping to listen again, moving again.

On 22 March, Alger took the *Dione* into Morehead City, North Carolina, to pick up some supplies and to undergo degaussing. Demagnetized and with a full load of depth charges, the cutter headed toward Cape Lookout. That night, Ensign Dunton had the bridge when word crackled across the radio. There had been another attack on a tanker about 20 miles north. There might be survivors. Alger called up Lieutenant McCormick to take the bridge while he plotted the course. Up ahead, a lookout called that he could see something. Alger and McCormick peered ahead. There was a spew of flames on the horizon. It looked like a volcano. Still miles away, the men of the *Dione* could almost feel the heat. Could anyone survive such a disaster?

Swede Larson left his radio for a few minutes to look ahead. This was going to be a gruesome chore, he sensed. He looked back toward the bridge. McCormick was grimly maintaining course while Alger made the preparations for rescue. Depth charges were primed and ready as well. Perhaps the U-boat was planning a trap.

The furiously burning vessel the *Dione* was heading toward was the tanker *Naeco*, another victim of Kaleun Mohr and the *U-124*. Mohr had spent the previous day resting his crew and going over his two remaining torpedoes. He wanted no more duds. During the early morning of 23 March, he crept up toward Cape Lookout on a flat sea. Soon, his lookouts reported a shadow ahead. Mohr maneuvered the *U-124* and saw that it was a tanker. He launched a torpedo and then peered anxiously ahead, watching the big ship move across his bow unscathed. Another dud! He bitterly ordered the last torpedo readied. Was this one also to be defective? It didn't matter. Mohr was going to have this tanker if he had to ram it![17]

Emil Engelbrecht, the master of the *Naeco*, was unaware of the *U-124*. He kept his tanker straight ahead, on course off the deadly shoals of Cape Lookout. Garland Henderson, the boatswain, was in his bunk. Work on a tanker is always hard work, and rest, when it could be gained, was welcome. He had no idea of the hell heading his way. At 0315, the *U-124*'s last torpedo struck the *Naeco* on her starboard side. Instantly, the tanker's cargo of fuel oil and gasoline ignited in a mighty firestorm that swept the entire midship house and almost melted the bridge. Captain Engelbrecht was burned alive as was the rest of the watch. Running to the deck, Henderson saw men on fire jumping off the ship. Below, Chief Engineer Martin Walczak struggled to shut down the engines and turn on the steam smothering system. But it was too late. The *Naeco* was burning out of control.

Walszak ran topside and saw a lifeboat being lowered and jumped in it. Garland Henderson was aboard. The men pushed away from the groaning tanker, skirting patches of burning oil and gasoline. But the lifeboat was overloaded and it suddenly overturned and sank, sending all on board gasping into the water. Henderson and Walczak swam away and were soon picked up by a lifeboat commanded by the quartermaster, John Oberer. There were ten men aboard. The *Naeco* blew again, and a hot sheet of flames burst into the sky. The men aboard the lifeboat pulled as hard as they could as a blast of superheated air swept over them, sucking the breath out of their lungs. They kept rowing, desperate to get away from the funeral pyre of the *Naeco*. Men were screaming and begging all around them, but none could be seen to be picked up.[8]

Kaleun Mohr was ecstatic. What a success! He immediately sent a message to Doenitz with news of his latest victory and then directed the *U-124* to assume an easterly course. Toward home and glory! In fact, his crew would confer the glory before home was reached. They had prepared a Knight's Cross made from metal taken from the *U-124*. When the orders came in over the wireless, the crew surrounded their famous commander while the cook brought in a huge cake. It was decorated with a Knight's Cross in icing with the words, *Der Mohr hat seiner Schuldigkeit getan*, a quote from the famous signal Doenitz had sent to Mohr at the end of his first patrol: "Mohr has done his duty." Although Mohr would later receive the decoration personally from Doenitz, the Knight's Cross he would always wear would be the one made of U-boat steel.[9]

Behind the *U-124* and her jubilant, victorious crew, the men of the *Naeco* died. Their bodies charred, they drifted on a

sea covered with oil and gasoline while sharks bumped and bit
at them. Horrified, Garland Henderson watched from the one
floating lifeboat as the sun peeked over the horizon. Suddenly,
he was overwhelmed by the destruction and death. He dived
into the sea and swam past the bobbing dead until he reached
the *Naeco*, now a smoking hulk. Climbing aboard, he made his
way through the groaning, gurgling tanker until he reached
his quarters. He pulled his sea chest out of the debris and flung
open the top. What he was looking for was still there. Holding
it to his chest, Henderson staggered to the tilted deck. The
*Naeco* had broken in two, the stern and the bow sticking skyward. Henderson snaked his way up the deck of the bow,
jumped across a great gash that fell all the way to the sea, and
then clambered up the remaining struts and bars of the bow
railing. There, he rested until he saw something in the distance, an indistinct shape. He blinked and looked again. The
U-boat! It was coming in to finish the *Naeco* off. Henderson
unfolded his package and looked around. He found a broken
steel bar. It was perfect. He jammed the bar into the railing
and defiantly raised the American flag.[10]

On the *Dione*, lookouts were straining to see through the
choking, noxious fumes that enveloped them. When they finally began to make out the *Naeco*, they could see something
moving on the bow. Alger went out on the wing to see for
himself. As the *Dione* came nearer, he could see what it was.
An American flag was flying and what appeared to be a crewman hanging on the railing beneath it. The lookouts began to
call out other sightings. There were bodies everywhere. Suddenly, the fumes became stronger. The *Dione* was motoring on
a layer of volatile gasoline and oil. One spark and it could all
go up. The men of the black gang, down in the din of their hot
engines, were having trouble breathing. The heat became ex-
cruciating and all oxygen seemed to escape the air. The sweet
odor of gasoline permeated everything. Some of the men
looked up longingly toward the comparative safety of the
deck. Panic was near in the engine room, but not one man
moved. All was outwardly calm and quiet aboard the *Dione*.
She sailed forward to do her duty, but those aboard her had

lost forever their cocky confidence. The *Dione* and her crew were trapped on a sea of death.

Miles west of the *Dione*, the destroyer *Roper* also found herself steaming in the midst of an oil slick. The sun had risen blood-red through a layer of heavy smoke on the horizon. There was a stricken tanker out there, likely the source of the smoke. The *Roper*'s captain, Lieutenant Commander Hamilton Howe, ordered the *Roper* to follow up the slick and reluctantly kept his tired men at their guns. An hour later, the *Roper* found the *Dione* beside the *Naeco*. Two small converted yachts, the *Osprey* and the *Umpqua*, were also standing by. It was a grisly scene. Charred bodies were floating everywhere. Not fifteen minutes after arrival, the *Naeco*'s bow suddenly sank, taking with it a proudly fluttering American flag. The crewman who had apparently raised it had clambered down the anchor chain and then had dropped into the sea and disappeared. All the *Roper* could do was to provide a screen to the rescue. She was too big to conduct the kind of careful picking through the remaining wreckage that needed to be done.[11]

Lieutenant Alger ordered the *Dione* to approach a raft that held four men. McCormick eased the cutter over to it, carefully skirting drifting wreckage. Strangely, the men aboard the raft made no move to help themselves. They sat stiffly upright. Clambering over the side, several coast guardsmen stuck out their hands to help. The *Naeco* crewmen did not respond. One of the *Dione* crew grabbed the raft and swung it around. Four dead faces turned slowly toward the cutter. The men of the *Dione* recoiled as sightless eyes accused each of them in turn. One of the officers had to break the spell, ordering the raft pushed away.

Using boat hooks, the *Dione*'s men began to pull in the floating bodies to look them over for any signs of life. It was gruesome, tedious work and no one was exempt, not even Radioman Swede Larson. He had helped pull in two bodies when a youth from the engine room appeared beside him, dragging in draughts of air. Swede was suddenly sure he heard a signal coming in over the radio. "Here," he said to the boy, "hold this for a while." He handed over his boat hook and beat a hasty retreat to the radio room. Outside, he could hear the

grunts of his fellows as they worked and the thumps of the
boat hooks against the side. He did not stay in the radio room
for long. He willed his legs to carry him back on deck. The
boy was still there with the boat hook. Larson took it back and
the boy lurched away to the preferable heat and stink and
claustrophobia of the engine room below.

Alger turned the *Dione* toward a position designated on
a message board dropped by an airplane. Several miles
downcurrent, a lifeboat with ten survivors was found. After
talking to the *Osprey* and the *Umpqua*, Alger found out that
they had picked up one survivor apiece. The *Umpqua* captain
said their man was the one who had been with the flag on the
bow. Garland Henderson had survived.

The *Dione* moved back closer to the stern of the *Naeco* and
found two more men alive, though badly burned. They were
brought aboard, alternately screaming and whimpering their
pleas for the pain to be stopped. On the mess deck, Ensign
Oliver again found himself faced with acting as the medical
officer. One *Naeco* crewman had compound fractures in both
legs, the shiny white bones protruding through the skin. Oliver assisted the pharmacist's mate in applying traction and
staunching the blood flow by tying off blood vessels and applying ice packs. The man was in hideous pain, his teeth gritted,
eyes rolled back into his head. Oliver gave him a Syrette of
morphine, but it seemed to have little effect. He called the
naval hospital at Norfolk and requested and received permission to give the man more than the recommended number of
Syrettes. Finally, the man quieted, his cries trailing down to
pitiful whimpers.

Alger and McCormick conferred when the sonar operator
called out a contact. Should they head toward shore with the
wounded or attack? McCormick favored attack and Alger
agreed. He signaled his intentions to the *Roper* and began to
maneuver. More contacts were made as the *Roper* followed,
and soon Commander Howe's sonar operators had made contacts of their own. For over four hours, the two ships tracked
down contacts. Once, the echo was good enough for the *Roper*
to drop depth charges but the results were negative. The *Dione*
found the derelict hull of an old torpedoed wreck, only its

seaweed-covered bottom showing, but there were to be no
other signs of U-boats. Finally, Alger was forced to break off
the search. The *Dione* turned toward shore and safety for the
*Naeco* survivors. The *Umpqua* and *Osprey* followed.

Korvettenkapitän Walter Flachsenberg of the *U-71* moved
off Cape Hatteras as a replacement for the departing *U-124*
and almost immediately sank the small freighter *Oakmar*.[12]
Flachsenberg was not unaware of the stirring success of Mohr
and hoped to duplicate it. All the U-boat commanders wanted
to curry Doenitz's favor. He was very much a father figure to
them and, to a man, they hoped to please him. Sunken tankers,
Flachsenberg knew, pleased Doenitz more than anything else,
so he hoped to find at least one for the admiral. Flachsenberg
was probably certain, however, that Mohr's success would
have its price. Surely, the Americans would never let another
tanker sail past the capes of North Carolina alone again after
the carnage visited on them by the *U-124*!
    All night long on 25 and 26 March, Flachsenberg waited
near the Diamond Shoals Lighted Buoy, but nothing was seen
except some small fishing boats. By 0730, he was about to dive
and sleep for the day when his lookout spotted some masts on
the southern horizon. The sun was up, but Flachsenberg
waited to see if the vessel was of interest. It was. A tanker!
Almost disbelieving his eyes, Flachsenberg saw it was entirely
alone. He ordered the *U-71* down and began to maneuver to
get the tanker between him and shore.
    The tanker coming at the *U-71* was the Socony-Vacuum
*Dixie Arrow*, fully loaded with 96,000 barrels of crude oil. She
carried a crew of thirty-three men, her master an experienced
sea captain named Anders M. Johanson. The *Dixie Arrow* was
known to be a good ship to work aboard. Johanson was a kind
and gentle man and also a first-rate shiphandler. He had seen
to it that his ship had the best cook available and that work
schedules were kept reasonable. The crew was, as a result, a
close-knit, hard-working group, considered by the company to
be one of its most efficient.
    Johanson was very much concerned about taking his ship
past Hatteras. He had remarked to his chief engineer that he

had been instructed to follow the 40-fathom curve, a very difficult task considering the many ships in the vicinity, all traveling blacked out and as rapidly as possible. He had also received information that the navy had placed a minefield off
Cape Hatteras. With this in mind, Johanson had stopped a
navy patrol boat off St. John's River, Florida, and asked for
details. The patrol boat had put him off, telling him "there are
a couple of other navy boats up ahead—ask them." Captain
Johanson had tried to contact other naval ships, but they had
all avoided him. Since he couldn't get any other information,
Johanson had reluctantly decided to follow his orders.

It was almost 0900 when the first of the *U-71*'s torpedoes
arrived. Able Seaman Oscar Chappel, who was at the helm,
spotted it and sang out a warning but it was too late. The
torpedo exploded amidships and the *Dixie Arrow* heeled over.
Seconds later, another torpedo struck. Flachsenberg was taking no chances. The *Dixie Arrow* burst into flames, a gigantic
fireball streaming skyward. Six men were on the bridge along
with Seaman Chappel. He could see that most of the crew had
collected on the bow. To keep the flames away from them,
Chappel ordered the other men off the bridge and began to
turn the *Dixie Arrow* into the wind. On the bow, knots of men,
formerly stranded by flames, were suddenly freed. Seaman
Chappel held the wheel firmly while the wall of flames raced
toward him. He just had time to lock the wheel before he was
enveloped in the inferno.

Given a respite by the self-sacrifice of Chappel, the men of
the *Dixie Arrow* began to abandon ship. Captain Johanson
emerged from his cabin. He was dressed in full uniform. Most
of the men had never seen him in full uniform before. He was
resplendent in his crisp coat, cap and buttons. Stiffly, he
turned toward the bridge. Before he had taken more than a
few steps, a third torpedo from the *U-71* struck just beneath
him. Captain Johanson disappeared in a blaze of destruction.

Seaman Alex Waszczseyn stood on the bow with his best
friend, Seaman Frederick Spiese. "Pretty soon we'll have to
swim for it," Spiese said, "and I can't swim a stroke."

"It's a damn fine time to learn, Spiese," Waszczseyn said,
and then the two of them jumped. When Waszczseyn came to

the surface, he looked all around but there was no sign of Spiese. He cried out but there was no answer. Waszczseyn began to swim, dodging the burning oil. It was all he could do.

William R. Wolfe, the first assistant engineer, had stayed below to shut down the engines. By the time he reached the deck, he could see nothing but flames. The bridge was completely on fire and the noise of the burning oil was like a locomotive passing by. Finally, he found six other men preparing to launch a raft. He went into the sea with them and climbed aboard. The raft had no paddles, however, and they found themselves being blown into a patch of burning oil. Wolfe and five others abandoned the raft but one man remained, saying he couldn't swim. Wolfe begged him to jump but he refused. In an instant, the raft and the man were engulfed in flames. The man did not cry out. He simply disappeared.

Seaman Paul C. Myers was with six others on the forecastle head, trying to launch a liferaft. As soon as it hit the sea, it was set afire. Desperately, they wrestled hatchboards over the side and saw them catch on fire as well. The *Dixie Arrow* was drifting, since the engines had been cut and the fire was no longer being blown back. Myers and the others had no choice but to jump. They splashed into a clear space and began to swim for their lives. An hour later, Myers looked back. He could see the *Dixie Arrow*, still burning furiously, but he could also see another vessel. It was the destroyer USS *Tarbell*. The *Tarbell* began to maneuver back and forth around the tanker. She did not seem to be slowing to pick up survivors. She seemed to be hunting.

The *U-71* had waited to observe the tanker sink. Suddenly, there was another ship on the sea, an American destroyer! Flachsenberg yelled at his chief to take the U-boat down and to head east toward deeper water and safety. Above, he could hear the swishing propellers of the destroyer and then the ping of a solid sonar hit. The *U-71* was in trouble. The *Tarbell* moved in on the scent and then swept overhead, dropping a load of depth charges. Ordinary Seaman Woodrow P. Nayer was swimming toward the *Tarbell* and was approximately two hundred yards away when he saw the depth charges dropped.

When the first one went off, it felt like somebody had kicked him in the stomach. The next ones knocked him unconscious.

The *U-71* shook from end to end, bracketed by the *Tarbell*'s depth charges. Flachsenberg began to zigzag his U-boat, turning violently this way and that. Above, the sounds of the destroyer came nearer and then faded. Flachsenberg ordered full power. The *U-71* ran for her life.

Lt. Commander S. D. Willingham of the *Tarbell* had no choice but to abandon his attack. His lookouts had called his attention to the merchantmen in the water. The *Tarbell* was no stranger to U-boats. She had been with the old *Reuben James* when that American destroyer had been sunk by U-boats in the North Atlantic before the war. Willingham had attacked Topp's *U-552* then with no success and, once more, he had to stop short. Reluctantly, after a single depth-charge run, he slowed the *Tarbell* to pick up survivors. He would find twenty-two of them, some on rafts but most hanging to pieces of wreckage. One of the men brought on board was Alex Waszczseyn. Among the huddled knot of weary survivors, he spotted someone who looked familiar. The man was covered with oil but Waszczseyn recognized him all the same. "Spiese!"

Frederick Spiese smiled tiredly. "I learned how to swim, Alex," he said.[13]

The *Dione* had been miles away when alerted to go to the rescue of the *Dixie Arrow*, but no one had bothered to tell Lieutenant Alger that the *Tarbell* had already been there. The cutter was too late to do anything but, once again, observe bodies and wreckage. Alger was frustrated and angry. He ordered the *Dione* down toward Hatteras.

The U-boats kept shuttling in. By late March most of them were choosing to come straight in on the killing grounds of Cape Hatteras.[14] Kapitänleutnant Johannes Oestermann of the *U-754* was demonstrative of the complete disdain the arriving U-boat captains had for American defenses. Oestermann did not even bother to wait for dark when he arrived. He sailed off Norfolk for a few hours, practically daring the United States Navy to come out and do battle, and then moved north where he chanced upon the oceangoing tug *Menominee* towing three barges loaded with coal and lumber.

Stunned at the sudden appearance of a U-boat, the captain of the *Menominee* could clearly hear Oestermann yell out commands as the German gun crew furiously cranked their 88-mm gun around toward the barges. Aboard one of the barges was H. E. Riggin, his son Orris, Deckman Juton Eston, and a puppy, Snowball. Riggin had a small boat, but before he and the others could get to it, an 88-mm shell struck the barge. Knocked off their feet and showered with water and pulverized coal, the barge crew again tried to get to the boat. Finally, it was launched. But after a few oar pulls, Orris remembered he had forgotten Snowball. Reluctantly, the elder Riggin turned the boat around. Snowball was waiting for them, anxiously running back and forth. Orris pleaded to the tiny puppy to jump. The *U-754* fired again.

The other bargemen watched as Riggin's barge suddenly exploded, turned over and sank. Oestermann moved his U-boat around their sterns, pumping in round after round until another of the barges was sunk and the third was down by its bow, taking on water fast. Then he went after the tug, which had cut the tow-line and was going at maximum rpm's toward shore. Easily catching up with it, Oestermann ran alongside the tug for a while, patiently waiting for his gun crew to get perfectly lined up. Leslie Haynie, the *Menominee*'s captain, ordered the engines stopped and the crew to abandon ship. Oestermann stopped the *U-754* as well and ordered two rounds fired into the wallowing ship. Both hit amidships, blowing the tug completely out of the water and setting her on fire. Captain Haynie and H. R. Bateman, the chief engineer, found themselves hanging on to a small raft. They would be the only survivors, rescued later on the same day by the freighter *Northern Sun.*

It was almost dark when the 38-foot coast guard picket boat #*4345* approached the barge that had not quite sunk. Clinging to it were six men. After they were taken aboard, the six bargemen were surprised to be greeted by Riggin, his son, and Eston, all of whom had survived. In fact, they had almost managed to row to shore when the coast guard had found

them. Despite the grimness of the occasion, all of the bargemen got a laugh when young Orris Riggin pulled open his
jacket to show them Snowball—warm, dry, and stifling a huge
yawn.[15]

The *Dione* plowed the sea off Hatteras, determined to either kill one of the U-boats or so harass them that they would
come after the cutter rather than the merchant vessels. Alger
had devised a set of meticulous tables that used the speed of
the ship, the sink rate of the depth charges, and the depth
indicated, to put the depth charges right where required. Pro-
foundly affected by the *Naeco*, he ordered every echo attacked,
every shadow traced. Lookouts had orders to report everything they saw on the sea, no matter how seemingly insignifi-
cant. Even a small oil slick could mean a U-boat resting on the
bottom. Dawn and dusk found Lieutenant Alger first on the
port wing of the bridge and then on the starboard wing as
the cutter zigzagged. He believed this was a favorite time for
the U-boat commanders and the best time to catch one of them
on the surface.

It was a crisp dawn, with Alger searching the horizon,
when one of the U-boats decided to rid itself of the pesky
cutter. Alger and a lookout spotted the torpedo coming directly at the *Dione*. Alger snapped out an order and the *Dione*
turned just in time. McCormick was on the bridge. Swinging
the cutter's bow in the direction the torpedo had come, he
moved in for the attack. A series of depth charges were laid
and the attack maintained until even McCormick had to agree
the U-boat had gotten away. But chunks of decking left behind
indicated a near miss. It was at least one U-boat that would
have to spend some time doing repairs before it could attack a
freighter or tanker again.

The *Dione* badly needed yard work, but Alger grimly kept
the cutter on patrol. Blackout conditions were the rule, the
crew packed into the Glory Hole. The Graveyard weather
pounded the cutter. Days passed with nothing seen except the
hulks of torpedoed ships and great oil slicks and empty lifeboats and, always, the drifting bodies. Sleep became precious.

Crew-members at General Quarters would often fall asleep standing up or hanging on to a stanchion or a ladder.

An especially good echo in late March caused Alger to drop a whole series of depth charges in shallow water off Cape Lookout. As the *Dione* herself seemed to explode, two men in the engine room finally had had enough. They burst up on deck and shinnied up the foremast as the *Dione* pitched in the wake of the depth charges. Neither Alger nor McCormick took note of them. They were too intent on tracking the echo.

A stain of diesel fuel on the water indicated a hit, and the cutter turned once more to attack. The water was very shallow and everyone on board knew what was going to happen when Alger ordered the *Dione* slowed for a more accurate drop. It was as if a burst of concussive needles passed through the cutter. Every man was pinned by them, his body quivering in response. Alger did not stop the attack. All day and all night, he chased the wildly maneuvering U-boat, with the two men of the "black gang" remaining high on the mast as the *Dione* pitched and shuddered beneath. Finally, just before dawn, the men on the mast ran out of adrenalin and climbed down to slink off to their bunks. Just as they fell asleep, the *Dione* went on the attack again. Lockers were flung to the floor, wall bunks broken loose, deck plates popped and spun high into the air, but the two completely broken men slept through it. Hours later, Alger finally ordered the *Dione* to stand down. The U-boat had gotten away.

The coast guardsmen began to put their ship back together. No real damage had been done, but portions of the ship were a mess. Men's belongings were strewn across the deck. The galley looked as if a small bomb had gone off inside. Pots and pans and crockery lay heaped in a mound of rubble. The engines had been thrown out of synch and the entire ship reverberated in sympathetic harmonics. The engineers groped their way in darkness searching out shattered insulators and broken mounting bolts and brackets.

Before order was completely regained, another echo was heard, this one a solid return. Alger ordered McCormick to go after it and the men raced to General Quarters once again. McCormick grimly maneuvered the cutter, changing speeds, turning this way and then that, depth charges calculated and dropped. The men of the *Dione* held on as their cutter was knocked hard on her bow. The sound of broken glass and clanging deck plates told them all their repairs had been undone. No matter. The *Dione* kept on, stalking the killers on what had become an incredible sea of death.

# 10

# The Q-Ships

Kapitänleutnant Reinhard Hardegen was on his way back. After the *U-123*'s spectacular raid on American shipping in January and February, Kaleun Hardegen had wanted another chance at American shipping. This had been granted, and Hardegen had sailed directly for Cape Hatteras. On 22 March, just before reaching the Gulf Stream, he caught the tanker *Muskogee* and sent two torpedoes into her side. Hardegen waited until the crew got away on three lifeboats and a large raft and then moved in closer to question them. He started to ask the sullen Americans the name of their ship when suddenly the *Muskogee* exploded, a fountain of burning oil thrown high into the sky. Hardegen ducked below, ordering the *U-123* full astern and then submerged. After a few minutes, he surfaced again and climbed to the bridge in a greasy cloud of smoke. When the wind thinned the smoke a bit, he was witness to a grisly sight. The lifeboats were covered with burning oil and the men in them were on fire.[1]

Hardegen ordered the *U-123* west, heading toward what he believed would be more easy prey in American waters. This time, however, more would be waiting for Kapitänleutnant Hardegen than easy prey. This time something else would be on the sea, something Hardegen would consider

diabolical, something designed to do nothing else but kill
U-boats. And Hardegen and his *U-123* were heading directly
toward it.

Among the many ideas Admiral Andrews and his staff had
discussed to repel the U-boats from American shores had been
the use of Q-ships. Q-ships were heavily armed ships designed
to look like innocent freighters. They were usually filled with
cork or similarly buoyant cargo so that a torpedo would do
nothing but blow a hole in the side. Then, when the U-boat
would come in closer to investigate, the freighter's camouflage
would be thrown aside and the guns run out to blast the
U-boat. That was the theory, in any case, and it had worked a
few times during World War I.

Admiral King, oddly enough, was the catalyst behind the
use of Q-ships. It was he who suggested to Admiral Andrews
in February it might be a good idea to begin outfitting such
ships and, in the military, a suggestion from a superior officer
is tantamount to an order. Andrews, of course, responded positively. Through the U.S. Maritime Commission, his staff was
able to acquire three ships, the *Wave*, a trawler, and the *Carolyn*
and *Evelyn*, both small freighters. The ships were outfitted in
Portsmouth, New Hampshire, with an assortment of 4-inch
guns, .50-caliber machine guns, depth-charge throwers, .30-cal-
iber machine guns, sawed-off shotguns, rifles, pistols, and hand
grenades. To confuse potential spies, the names of the three
ships were changed. The *Carolyn* became the *Atik*, the *Evelyn*
became the *Asterion*, and the *Wave* became the *Eagle*. Everything about the operation was top secret.

Admiral Andrews himself gave the commanders of the
three ships their orders. Lieutenant Commander L. F. Rogers
was given command of the *Eagle* while Lieutenant Commander G. W. Legwen got the *Asterion* and Lieutenant Commander Harry L. Hicks the *Atik*. Andrews braced them by
admitting that if they got into trouble, help would not be
likely. Every ship and plane he had, he told the officers, was
already committed. Rescue of a Q-ship would be low-priority.
Because of that, he went on to say, service aboard the Q-ships
would be strictly voluntary and the crews were to be told that.

The crews were told, but no one withdrew. For all the secrecy, every man aboard had known for some time the mission of the converted ships. In a sense, they had already volunteered by not putting in for a transfer. Accordingly, fully manned, the three ships sailed on 23 March. It became immediately obvious to all aboard the ships, however, that theirs was not to be an easy mission. The ships, despite the work done at Portsmouth, were very old and barely seaworthy. Moreover, none of the crew and few of the officers had been briefed on how a Q-ship was supposed to operate. The captains had read some literature on the operations of Q-ships in World War I and that was about it.[2]

On the same day the Q-ships sailed, the *U-123* was still purposefully sailing for American waters but was having some problems. Spotting a large tanker, Hardegen ordered a torpedo fired. The torpedo got stuck in its tube, however, and there it remained, the reverberations of its whining propellers shaking the entire U-boat. After it wound down, Hardegen ordered it ejected. It was, but an inattentive torpedoman in the stern also thought he heard an order to fire and independently launched another torpedo. Hardegen was disgusted. "It is bitter to accept," he wrote in his log, "that during a difficult attack when finally everything falls in place on the bridge, avoidable failure of old veterans can keep the boat from scoring an easy victory." He chased after the tanker, noting that "I almost lost her on the dark horizon because of her wild tacking. She is now running at 12 knots, tacking for her life." He also noted that there were guns on her deck, causing him to keep a respectable distance away. When he was finally able to line up, he fired a double salvo. A minute later, the entire tanker seemed to explode before his eyes. All he could see was a sea of flames, and he was certain the tanker had gone down, but then his radioman reported that messages were being sent. He called up his deck-gun crew and ordered them to finish the tanker off. For five and a half hours, Hardegen would circle the tanker (she was the British *Empire Steel*) until, at last, the 88 had holed her enough to sink her. "A tough customer," Hardegen would call the tanker, but "it is amazing that during the attack she was not able to fire even one shot with her cannon or machine guns . . . Poor lookout and poor training of the gun crews!"[3]

Hardegen kept moving west. A few days later, in American waters again at last, his lookouts spotted a small freighter moving slowly south. Her running lights were on. This was just like the American shipping he remembered! Hardegen readied for the attack.

But something stopped him.

He couldn't put his finger on it, but there was something not quite right about the little merchantman. He called up his navigating officer and a midshipman and asked them if they could determine anything suspicious about the ship. Neither could, so Hardegen decided to go ahead with the attack from the surface, firing a single torpedo. The torpedo sped straight and true from a distance of about 650 yards. The ship stopped and a fire broke out on board. Hardegen's radioman picked up her distress signals. "*Carolyn* torpedoed," was the signal. "Burning. Not bad." And then she gave her position. She began to list and one lifeboat was dropped into the water.

"Not bad?" sniffed Hardegen. "We'll see about that."[4]

The *U-123* moved around to the freighter's stern while the 88-mm gun crew got ready. Hardegen unconcernedly sat on the bridge rail and watched while the smoking freighter's second lifeboat was launched. He ordered his gun crew to wait until it got clear before firing. Suddenly, the *Carolyn (Atik)* began to move toward the U-boat. His suspicions renewed, Hardegen ordered half-speed and turned away. The *Carolyn (Atik)* turned with him. Hardegen ordered three-quarter speed and again turned. The *Carolyn (Atik)* turned once more and then, before a startled Hardegen, suddenly came to life. Canvas was pulled aside and trapdoors dropped, revealing the true intentions of the seemingly innocent freighter. Hardegen ordered full-speed but it was too late. The guns of the *Carolyn (Atik)* opened up and the midshipman beside Hardegen collapsed with a groan.

Hardegen screamed for the bridge to be cleared. He and the first lieutenant knelt beside the wounded midshipman. The boy's right leg was smashed by a .50 caliber round. The Q-ship, for it was obvious now what had been encountered, was still firing as fast as she could. Splinters from the *U-123*'s deck rained down on Hardegen. When he looked up, he saw a big black object sailing directly toward him and it occurred to him that the Q-ship was using its depth-charge throwers. The midshipman was howling in pain and the men were having trouble moving him, so all Hardegen could do was watch the depth charge loop in. It missed the conn by a few feet and sank beneath the U-boat, exploding 100 feet below. Railing at his men to get the midshipman down no matter what it took, Hardegen watched the *Atik (Carolyn)* disappear in the cloud of diesel smoke the *U-123* was producing. Hardegen gathered his wits. He had been tricked as if he were a rank amateur. But he wasn't going to run. He was going to rid the world of this nuisance!

Below, the deck was slick with blood as Hardegen descended to the attack periscope. The midshipman was stretched out in Hardegen's own bunk while the navigator made a tourniquet with his belt. The young officer was still conscious but made no sound. His eyes were large and vacant. Hardegen lifted a towel that had been placed over the boy's shattered leg and immediately saw it was hopeless. He ordered an injection of morphine and then took the *U-123* down to periscope depth. In cold anger, he observed the Q-ship. Apparently, the two lifeboats that had been launched had returned. She had sunk no deeper than before and her men were still at her guns, waiting for some sign of the U-boat. Hardegen patiently maneuvered until he had the *Atik's (Carolyn's)* engine room in his sights. It took twenty-four seconds for the torpedo to find its target. The *Atik (Carolyn)* was rocked by a big plume of smoke and fire and then began to sink, her stern arched high above the sea. Once again, the lifeboats were manned but this time in earnest. A few minutes later the *Atik (Carolyn)* sank, her depth charges going off as she went down.

Meanwhile, the *Atik's (Carolyn's)* sister, the *Asterion (Evelyn)*, was racing toward the site. She had picked up the *Atik's (Carolyn's)* signals, the first a calm "SSSS" followed by an "SOS" and then, in the clear, the same message the *U-123* had picked up. A little later, however, came another message, this one no trick. "Torpedo attack. Burning forward. Require assistance."

While the *Asterion (Evelyn)* raced to help, no one else in the navy was paying much attention. Just as Admiral Andrews had warned, there was little the navy could do. Moreover, the secrecy of the entire mission hampered any response. As far as the duty officers of the Eastern Sea Frontier knew, the *Carolyn (Atik)* was just another small freighter being sunk by a U-boat, an almost nightly occurrence. By the time word had filtered up to those officers who knew what was going on, it was too late. A bomber, a tug, and a destroyer were dispatched, but the weather had turned nasty and none of them could reach the position recorded. Only the *Asterion (Evelyn)* fought through the stormy sea to rescue her sister, but by the time she got there, there was no sign of either the *Atik (Carolyn)* or any of her crew. Almost plaintively, the *Asterion (Evelyn)* inquired of passing freighters if any of them had sighted survivors or wreckage, but nothing had been seen.

Late that night, the wounded midshipman in the *U-123* died with Hardegen at his side. Silently, the U-boat crewmen wrapped the young officer in a canvas hammock and then stretched him out on Hardegen's blood-soaked bunk. An all-night vigil was kept, and the next morning Hardegen ordered the *U-123* to surface. The storm had abated and the sky was bright and brilliantly golden as the *U-123* rose from the deep with a roar of air and foam. The U-boat stood starkly alone against the vast blue Atlantic. Hardegen climbed to the bridge followed by an honor guard with the canvas-wrapped body. Below, in silence, the rest of the crew stood at attention, looking up. Hardegen intoned the Lord's Prayer, his words carried away into the emptiness of the sea by a light wind. At his signal, the midshipman's body was slipped into the sea. As it sank in a shimmer of reflected sunlight, the honor guard stood at attention and saluted.[5]

The search for the *Atik (Carolyn)* continued with no success. Finally, on 9 April, a German radio broadcast reported that a Q-ship had been sunk by an unidentified U-boat off the American coast. "The Q-ship," the broadcast said, "was sunk by a torpedo after a battle fought partly on the surface with

artillery and partly beneath the water with bombs and torpedoes."[6] Admiral Andrews knew then what had happened, but
could not understand why there had been no survivors from
the *Atik (Carolyn)*. There was some talk that perhaps the
U-boat had machine-gunned the navy crew. The likely explanation was simpler, however. When the *Atik (Carolyn)* had
sunk, her depth charges had gone off. Hardegen and the *U-123*
had been shaken by the blasts even though they were some
distance away. Most likely, the men of the *Atik (Carolyn)* had
been killed by their own depth charges.

The Q-ships kept operating even after the death of the *Atik
(Carolyn)*. Admiral Andrews had no choice in the matter. Fortunately, however, never again in the war would one of them
meet up with a U-boat. Hardegen, for his part, kept going on
his second American patrol, but he had been shaken by the
encounter. Although he had easily disposed of the Q-ship, he
had sustained his first casualty. More than that, he sensed a
change in the "American Shooting Gallery." The United
States had been stupid at the beginning of the war, but Hardegen was also aware of its awesome potential. His lookouts
were spotting more and more aircraft, and there were destroyers and patrol craft to dodge where before there had only been
smooth seas and fat tankers and freighters.

The *U-123* would have to be more careful.

All the U-boats would.

# 11

# The *Hambleton* and *Emmons* Cruise

I t was midnight, 26 March, when the *Dione* could go no
farther. Out of depth charges and nearly out of fuel, Lieutenant Alger ordered the ship and her tired crew to stand
in to Portsmouth. There was a glow on the horizon behind
her, the glow of the torpedoed Panamanian freighter *Equipoise*.
Alger had received the report on the freighter, but there was
nothing he could do about it. Repairs were needed, and supplies. The destroyer *Greer* was in the area and was dispatched
instead. One torpedo from Lassen's *U-160* had struck the ship,
with the loss of forty crewmen. All the *Greer* found was a
single lifeboat and dozens of bodies.[1] There would have been
little the *Dione* could have done, in any case.

Alger knew his men desperately needed shore leave to get
away from the unceasing General Quarters and the frustrations of fruitless attacks, so he granted a liberal leave and pass
policy. As soon as the *Dione* had moored and the ship put in
order, men began to stream off her, a few bound for home and
family, others to hit the bars and bordellos of Norfolk.

The men of the *Dione* had a favorite bar, a Mom and Pop
operation that catered to the coast guardsmen. It was a
friendly place, a place where the *Dione* men could put their
feet up on the chairs and drink beer and forget, if only for a

little while, the things they had seen. Sometimes, however, they found themselves in the same bars as sailors from the regular navy, most of whom had seen nothing in the war except the Norfolk shipyards. It was tempting to the coast guardsmen to brag about their duty, but most did not. They knew it was going to be a long war and just about everybody in uniform was going to get into it, sooner or later. They also knew that the United States, while not losing, definitely was not winning, either. It was best to drink and listen to the Andrews sisters or Tony Martin on the juke box and tell stories to each other and passing waitresses and forget the war for just a little while.

One of the favorite tales was that of the USS *Tuscaraura*. It, like every sea story told by every sailor of every nation, always began the same.

"Now, listen you guys, this is no bull——!"

And then the story was told with elaboration allowed by everyone within earshot.

"The *Tuscaraura* was a river gunboat up the Yang-tzee and the Whang-poo."

"She had thirteen decks and a straw bottom."

"She had a rubber smokestack so she could go under low bridges."

"She had hinges in her hull so she could turn corners."

"She had sidewheels and when the river dried up they put treads on them and used her like a tank."

"A Marine was posted port and starboard to keep the water buffalo from eating her hull."

And the ending was the same the world over, too. "Now that's no lie. If you'll fill this glass again, Miss, I'd be pleased to tell you more!"

Lieutenants Alger and McCormick stayed aboard. There was too much work to be done to get the cutter ready for sea as soon as possible. Before McCormick could get much accomplished, however, a set of written orders arrived and were carried directly to him with copies to Alger. After he had read the orders, McCormick began to look around the *Dione*, now busy with supplies being stacked on her deck for storage later. It did not seem possible that he had been chosen but there it was. He read the orders again and then sought out Alger for advice. Although widely apart in temperament and background, the two men had nonetheless forged a deep respect for one another during their grueling days at sea. Self-assured, almost to the point of arrogance, McCormick had rarely, if ever, sought the advice or confidence of anyone. But this time, things were different. In fact, things were to never again be the same. McCormick was leaving the *Dione*. He was going to be given that which Alger had deprived him of and that which he deserved and needed: command.

Admiral Andrews and his Eastern Sea Frontier staff kept track of every ship under their command, so they knew when the *Dione* had gone in. It left a gap in the defenses, but there was nothing that could be done about it, although it was hoped that the destroyer *Greer* would be able to continue cruising nearby. Admiral Andrews still wanted destroyers like the *Greer* more than anything else. He believed that the destruction sustained by the merchant fleet in March had proved his warnings to be correct. Because of it, he hoped King would relent and give him enough destroyers to challenge the U-boats directly. His plan was to put dozens of the swift ships out into the sea-lanes, armed to the teeth and ready to swarm to the attack no matter where a U-boat might be spotted. As the March 1942 *Eastern Sea Frontier War Diary* noted, the destroyer "with its speed, maneuverability, superior sound gear, and ability to keep at sea in conditions that drive smaller craft into port, is the deadly and traditional enemy of the submarine." This reflected Admiral Andrews's thinking exactly. It was only a matter of numbers, he believed. If $x$ number of destroyers were on hand, $y$ number of U-boats would be sunk.

The only other alternative to the destroyers was the use of convoys. But Admiral Andrews wondered if convoys were suitable for the conditions he faced. In February he had expounded at some length in the *Eastern Sea Frontier War Diary* against the use of a convoy system to protect the merchant fleet. He had admitted that the convoy was "the classic procedure" for defending merchant shipping against submarine attack, "but the lessons of history cannot be read without some reservations." Coastal sea-lanes were different, it was argued, from overseas trade routes. Merchant ships along the coast could "seek the protection that daylight affords" and also "break their passage by lying over in sheltered harbors at night. In addition, vessels far at sea are deprived of the air coverage afforded by planes operating from shore bases." Andrews felt, also, because of the limited forces then at his disposal, that "the hazards to merchant vessels gathered together in large and insufficiently protected concentrations are increased, rather than diminished."

In his quest for destroyers, Admiral Andrews was being listened to, finally, if not by Admiral King, at least by the civilians responsible for the nation's economy. The sinkings of the freighters and tankers along the coast were causing serious economic dislocations. Something had to be done or it might come to a choice of continuing the war or letting the Northeast freeze. If the admiral thought destroyers were the answer, then maybe, these civilians thought, more should be given him. Pressure was brought to bear on Admiral King.[2]

Admiral King was not much impressed by anything any civilian had to say short of Roosevelt. It was his navy and he would run it as he pleased. In response to the complaints from the logistics managers in the Roosevelt administration, from the governor of North Carolina (whose residents were becoming distraught by the amount of destruction they were witnessing from their shores), and from Admiral Andrews, King finally managed a lukewarm dispatch on 8 March that at first glance might have appeared to be a positive response. A careful reader, however, would note that King's policy was exactly the same as it had been from the beginning.

"When such employment is practicable," the dispatch read, "and does not interfere with escort fleet vessels, tasks, and fleet operations, destroyers and other suitable escort ships making passage through Sea Frontier Zones incident to scheduled movements should be utilized to the fullest extent in the protection of merchant shipping."[3] In other words, the destroyers were only available when they didn't have anything else to do. When the commander of the Fifth Naval District (which included Cape Hatteras) urgently requested four destroyers to constantly patrol his area, Andrews used the request as an excuse to again ask Admiral King for more destroyers. King responded curtly, telling Andrews that "your knowledge of other demands for [destroyers] as imperative as your own is not given sufficient credit in your [dispatch]."[4] That was about as close as the official language used in naval dispatches could come to telling Andrews to shut up.

Admiral Andrews lapsed into silence. He had no choice if he wanted to keep his job.

As April began, just as Admiral King had promised, two destroyers with no other assignments were temporarily released to the Eastern Sea Frontier. They were the U.S. Navy destroyers *Hambleton*, commanded by Lieutenant Commander Forrest Close, and the *Emmons*, commanded by Lieutenant Commander T. C. Ragan. They were both very capable commanders and ships. In fact, the *Hambleton* and *Emmons* were to become famous in World War II, always in the thick of battle from the Murmansk convoy runs to the North African and Normandy invasions. But this was early 1942, and those victories were still well into the future. Admiral Andrews ordered the two destroyers to patrol from Wimble Shoals to Cape Lookout. Both commanders exuded confidence, certain that they would sweep the seas clear of any U-boats that dared to get in their way. Admiral Andrews also believed they would do well and wished them luck and success. He had no way of knowing, of course, but the patrol the two destroyers were about to accomplish would indeed be a very special one, one that would, in fact, cause a change in the direction of the entire battle against the U-boats.

But not because of their success.

## The First Day

On the first day of the patrol of the *Hambleton* and the *Emmons*, Kaleun Hardegen and his *U-123* moved back into position off Cape Hatteras. Hardegen was not in a good mood. He had spent several days after his battle with the Q-ship giving his crew some rest and also carefully going over his U-boat, inspecting her for damage. He was ready to get back to work. There were also seven other U-boats in the general area on 1 April. They were Lassen's *U-160*, Oestermann's *U-754*, Topp's *U-552*, Möhlmann's *U-571*, Flachsenberg's *U-71*, Linder's *U-202*, and Mützelburg's *U-203*. Working down the coast toward them was Greger's *U-85*. Hardegen and Lassen were the only ones with the larger Type IX boats. The rest were Type VIIs, indicating Doenitz's intention to get any U-boat across the Atlantic that he could.[5]

Despite Admiral Andrews's impressive efforts at gaining air and sea support during March, the U-boat assault beginning in April was the same old story. Just before midnight on 31 March, the *U-71* sank the British freighter *Eastmoor* 100 miles off Cape Hatteras.[6] An hour later, just over the horizon from Cape Lookout, the *U-754* burst to the surface and fired a single torpedo into the side of the Socony-Vacuum *Tiger*. A fireman in the engine room was killed, but the rest of the crew, including six navy gun crewmen, were able to escape in three lifeboats.[7]

On their first morning off North Carolina, the seas were calm and smooth for the *Hambleton* and *Emmons*, and it was hard to believe that a war was going on at all. Several freighters and tankers were seen, all moving peacefully and without escort. Neither destroyer was aware of the two sinkings just hours before. Later that morning, however, a frantic signal was received from the freighter *Delsud*. She could see a U-boat nearby, she said, maybe two. She needed help. The *Hambleton* and *Emmons* charged off at full speed to the rescue. But instead of being glad to see them, the *Delsud* opened fire as soon as the destroyers got near. Dodging the shells, the destroyers frantically radioed in the clear their identity. When the *Delsud* finally stopped its wild firing, the destroyers moved alongside to determine what had happened. The master of the freighter did not seem the least bit embarrassed by his attack. In these waters, he indicated, every ship had to look out for themselves. Anyway, he thought the two destroyers had looked an awful lot like submarines.[8]

While the *Hambleton* and *Emmons* were trying to sort things out with the *Delsud*, Kaleun Georg Lassen of the *U-160*, which had sunk the *City of New York* a few days earlier, came across the British freighter *Rio Blanco* 60 miles out from Cape Hatteras. A single torpedo was used to sink the ship, which was loaded with iron ore. There were only nine survivors out of a crew of forty. These were to drift in a lifeboat for two weeks before being found by a North Carolina fishing boat.[9]

To complete the opening salvo of April, the veteran commander Kapitänleutnant Hans-Heinz Linder of the *U-202* waited until dusk to sink the British freighter *Loch Don* near the wreck of the *Eastmoor*.[10] Thus, the first day of the patrol by the *Hambleton* and the *Emmons* ended. Four ships had been sunk in their area, but all that had happened to them was that they had been shot at by one of their own freighters. Unaware of the sinkings and still confident, they steamed south.

## The Second and Third Day

Hardegen, as unaware of the *Hambleton* and *Emmons* as they of him, got back into the fray on 2 April, an hour after midnight. As usual, he was after a tanker. This one was the 7,057-ton Socony-Vacuum *Liebre.* Hardegen was still enamored with using his deck gun and saving his torpedoes. The skipper of the *Liebre,* Captain Frank C. Girardeau, was on the bridge when more than twenty 88-mm shells in rapid succession came sailing in at him out of the darkness. Girardeau sent his tanker into a series of rapid zigzags and then turned to put his stern into the face of his attacker. Big fireballs ripped the deck of the *Liebre,* but since she was heading south in ballast, there were no secondary explosions. It appeared the tanker was going to get away, but then one of Hardegen's shells struck the engine room, cutting the main steam line to the starboard generator. With his ship plunged into darkness and engines failing, Girardeau had no choice but to order the tanker abandoned.

Two lifeboats were launched in an orderly manner and a head count immediately made. Of the thirty-four crewmen, two had been killed by the *U-123*'s shells, seven were missing and believed drowned, and four had serious wounds. Hardegen maneuvered his U-boat past the lifeboats and inspected the tanker. To the crewmen of the *Liebre,* the U-boat was like a lion sniffing its kill. Just then, the sun broke over the horizon, sending shafts of gold and red shimmering across the calm sea. Hardegen, fearful of aircraft, immediately left the bridge of the *U-123* and ordered her submerged. For an hour afterwards, the men of the *Liebre* drifted, waiting for their ship to sink. When it didn't, the boat containing Captain Girardeau returned and climbed aboard. The radioman went to his set and began sending signals, requesting help. Soon, the tug *Resolute*, guarded by the British trawler HMS *St. Zeno*, arrived. Hardegen had been cheated out of his kill as the *Liebre* was successfully towed into Morehead City.[11]

Meanwhile, the *Hambleton* and *Emmons* were beginning to be vaguely aware of the killing going on around them since they had picked up a spate of SSSSs and SOSs over the radio. Still staying close to one another, they came across two "suspicious craft" at about the same time the *Liebre* was being torpedoed.[12] For hours, the destroyers maneuvered around the ships, trying not to get too close and at the same time trying to determine why the "mysterious" ships were in such unfriendly waters and not following any set course. Perhaps they were the ships that had been rumored all along to be helping the U-boats. Finally, identification was made. One of the ships turned out to be a Hatteras fishing boat and the other a lost American freighter. At least, neither of them had fired at the two destroyers. That was an improvement. When word was received from the *Esso Augusta* that there was possibly a U-boat some 40 miles away, the *Emmons* raced in the direction given while the *Hambleton* hung back to keep patrolling off Lookout. The *Hambleton* spent a nervous night alone.[13]

Korvettenkapitän Topp of the *U-552*, completely oblivious of the two stalking destroyers, was at work that night. Just 10 miles off Chincoteague, Virginia, he came across the freighter *David H. Atwater*. The *Atwater*, with a full load of coal bound for Norfolk, was struck by an 88-mm shell in the darkness and then strafed by machine-gun fire. Topp had learned from Hardegen to try to save his torpedoes. Topp, however, used little discretion in his attack. With the ship sinking barely more than 600 yards away, he directed his machine gunners to continue their fire, hitting the American crew trying to man their lifeboats. The master of the freighter, Captain William Webster, was felled by the fire and his crew panicked, jumping into the sea before the boats were successfully launched. When the small coast guard patrol boat #218 arrived, only three survivors and three bodies were found out of a crew of twenty-six. The coast guard cutter *Legare*, which had heard the gunfire and immediately headed toward the scene, could detect no trace of the *U-552* and only found one lifeboat containing a body. The lifeboat was riddled by Topp's gunfire, enforcing the widespread belief that the U-boats often tried to murder the survivors of torpedoed ships.[14]

Continuing the destruction the next morning, the *U-754* torpedoed the *Otho*, a small American freighter loaded with manganese, tin, and palm oil, sailing in to Norfolk from Africa. Twenty-three crewmen, five navy men, and three passengers were lost; only fourteen survivors were picked up by the navy ship *Zircon* a few days later.[15]

As the sun rose on 3 April, the *Emmons* came back from her patrol out in the Gulf Stream. Despite all the death and destruction going on all around them, she had seen nothing and neither had the *Hambleton*. The two destroyers clustered together again and began to patrol around Wimble Shoals until a report of a U-boat near Diamond Shoals sent them flying south. It was night by the time they reached the reported location and almost immediately their sonar operators reported "firm contacts." Star shells were fired, which illuminated only a large American tanker dawdling along. There was no submarine. But for the next few hours, the two destroyers and stations all along the coast would receive frantic reports from merchant vessels that a U-boat had been observed shooting star shells into the sky.[16]

## The Fourth and Fifth Day

On 4 April, the commanders of the two destroyers were losing, if not their confidence, at least some of their enthusiasm. They had kept their crews at General Quarters for much of the patrol, and the men, as well as the officers, were wearing out. A report from the freighter *Chester Sun* on a submarine contact resulted in a few hours of futile search followed by a run down to Ocracoke to investigate a report by the freighter *Phoenix*. That night, with the two destroyers well south, Topp's *U-552* surfaced off Currituck just as the tanker *Byron D. Benson* came into view. The British trawler HMS *Norwich City* had been escorting the tanker until dusk but had dropped away, unable to keep up. The torpedo hit between two full tanks and the *Benson* exploded in a mighty gush of flame that spread across the deck, incinerating many men where they stood. The crew immediately abandoned their ship, many of them jumping into the water while the tanker, still under power, turned to starboard, leaving behind a swath of burning oil.

The *Dione* had returned to sea at midnight on 3 April fully provisioned and nearly rested. When the *Benson* exploded, the lookouts on the *Dione* saw it, and Alger changed course and headed in that direction. It was a dark night with no moon. As the *Dione* sped toward the boil of orange and red that marked the *Benson*, she saw that two other ships were also nearby. One of them was the *Norwich City*, having finally caught up with the tanker. The other was the destroyer *Hamilton* assigned to Admiral Andrews for two days to supplement the *Hambleton* and *Emmons*. Radio calls soon established that the *Hamilton* had picked up twenty-seven men while the *Norwich City* had found one. Ten men were reported missing. Alger moved his cutter between burning patches of oil, searching carefully. No other crewmen were found. The *Byron D. Benson* was to burn and drift for three days before sinking, its great smoke cloud covering hundreds of square miles and casting a pall along the entire North Carolina coast.[17]

While the *Dione* spent the day picking through the wreckage of the *Benson* and patrolling nearby in the hope the U-boat would come back, the *Hambleton* and *Emmons* decided to sail east to look around. That night the freighter *Bidwell* was torpedoed by the *U-160* within sight of them. The explosion blew up two oil tanks and sprayed burning oil across the decks, covering the second mate who ran, screaming, to the side and jumped overboard. The explosion also carried away all of the tanker's steering control and she began to carve huge

circles on the ocean. The master of the tanker took to a lifeboat along with several of his officers and began to row away.
The chief engineer, however, went below and began to direct
the men in the after section to connect the emergency steering
gear. Although many of the men complained, he ordered them
to keep working and not to abandon ship.

The *Hambleton* and *Emmons* rushed to help but were confronted with a burning tanker that was out of control. Every
time a heading was taken to search for the U-boat, the destroyers found themselves dodging the tanker as it turned. Under
these circumstances, not a single firm sonar contact was made.
After an hour or so of this, the steering gear was finally repaired and the *Bidwell* slowed and stopped. All the fires aboard
were put out. Several hundred yards away, the lifeboat containing the master turned and sheepishly made its way back to
the tanker.

After the master was aboard, the *Hambleton* and *Emmons*
offered their help. It was refused. The implication from the
thoroughly embarrassed and angry master was that he
thought the *Bidwell* was better off without the navy around.
About then, the *Hambleton* developed trouble with her port
turbine, so escort was impossible, anyway. Her crewmen were
working on it when, as luck would have it, the *Emmons* suddenly developed an excellent sound contact. The *Hambleton*
joined her as best she could, and together the destroyers
dropped several patterns of depth charges before realizing that
all they were doing was attacking the disturbed water produced by the *Emmons*'s first attack. After they regrouped, neither destroyer could gain any kind of contact at all.[18]

## The Sixth and Seventh Day

On the evening of 6 April, the British tanker *British Splendour*, carrying 10,000 tons of gasoline, tried to get past Cape
Hatteras by going full speed after dark as near the shoals as
she could get. It was Topp again in his *U-552* that was waiting,
pretending to be a blinking buoy. The *Splendour*'s master saw
the "buoy" and maneuvered his ship to run several hundred
yards away from it at a perfect right angle. Topp unleashed a

torpedo into the port side of the tanker. It struck the engine
room, killing twelve men and starting a fire that threatened to
spread to the gasoline bunkers. The tanker was quickly abandoned by the survivors, who watched it sink until it stabilized
bow up with its stern on the bottom. There it rested, burning.[19]

Satisfied, Topp sat right where he was until sunrise and
then started to move out to sea to deeper water to rest for the
day. Before he got far, the Norwegian tanker *Lancing* appeared, heading north. Topp turned around and sent a torpedo into the tanker's starboard side, killing one man, flooding
the engine room, and knocking out all the radio equipment.
The remaining crew abandoned ship successfully and were
later picked up by the American tanker *Pan Rhode Island* and
the British trawler HMS *Hertfordshire*.[20]

While the *Hambleton* and *Emmons* zigzagged back to the
north seeing and hearing nothing, Lieutenant Alger took the
*Dione* south toward Hatteras. The activity of the night before
was enough for him to try to stake out the area. He soon found
the hulk of the *British Splendour*, still burning. Alger sent the
*Dione* on a search pattern and was rewarded by a good echo.
He called General Quarters and watched his crew race to their
duty stations. After weeks of being in the middle of the battle,
the *Dione*'s crew were like a well-oiled machine. Alger took his
position on the bridge and ordered an attack. The Y-gun
roared, sending two depth-charge mallets soaring away while
the *Dione* began her turn. The Y-guns were quickly reloaded
and standing by, ready. Alger had a moment to contemplate
their efficiency. If there was a more professional crew in the
United States Coast Guard and Navy, he would have liked to
have seen them. They were the best. He looked over at Mc-
Cormick. He was going to hate losing McCormick, but there
was no time to worry about it. The *Dione* had finished her
turn. Alger received the soundmen's reports. The target was
running, heading for deep water.

If it was Topp and his *U-552* below, he was running with
the United States Coast Guard on his tail. An hour later, Alger stood down from General Quarters. The U-boat had gotten away, but the trap that had sunk two tankers was at least

temporarily closed down. Alger cut his engines and drifted, listening. If the U-boat came back, he'd spring his own trap. Meanwhile, the *Hambleton* and *Emmons* were cutting across the Gulf Stream. As far as they could see in every direction, the sea was completely empty. Dolphins, however, were seen. And also some flying fish.

## The Eighth Day

On 8 April, the two destroyers moved back south, near the *Dione*. Hardegen observed the increased naval activity around Hatteras and moved even farther south until he was off the Georgia coast. There, just after midnight, he saw the big American tanker *Oklahoma* coming at him. It was loaded with a cargo of 100,000 barrels of refined petroleum. Hardegen fired a torpedo into the tanker's engine room, which blew a hole big enough to also flood the crew compartment. Seventeen men were instantly drowned, but there was no fire and that gave Captain T. P. Davenport time to organize an orderly evacuation of the eighteen survivors. Before the lifeboats had gotten far, however, one of the men said that there was still a wounded man on board, so Davenport turned his lifeboat around. Hardegen had maneuvered in closer with his deckgun crew at the ready, but when he saw the lifeboat going back to the tanker, he waved his gunners off. Davenport, along with Second Engineer Henry Maah and Third Officer Malcolm McPhee, climbed aboard and waded through waist-deep water until they found seaman William Howell. Howell was bleeding profusely but was still alive. Picking him up, the three men carried him back to the lifeboat and pushed off again.

Hardegen waited until the lifeboat was clear and then ordered the tanker shelled. Twelve rounds were fired, but still the tanker did not catch fire.[21] Convinced it would sink anyway, Hardegen headed out to sea and then turned back in time to ambush the tanker *Esso Baton Rouge*. The *Baton Rouge* was loaded with 70,000 barrels of lubricating oil and 20,000 gallons of heating oil. She had already been torpedoed once in the war, off the Azores by the *U-202*. Hardegen, from the surface, sent a torpedo into her starboard side between the bunkers and the engine room. The bunkers exploded and tore out her side, flooding the crew's quarters. Captain James S. Roche had also been the tanker's master during the Azores torpedoing and calmly gathered his surviving crew into two lifeboats. One of the crewmen, however, refused to get aboard a lifeboat. He had been born in Germany and was the object of some suspicion by the crew even before the torpedoing. He yelled something at Captain Roche that the captain couldn't understand and then jumped into the sea. Roche looked for him but couldn't see him after that.

Hardegen brought the *U-123* in closer, motoring in between the two lifeboats. A searchlight swept over the boats and then toward the tanker. "Come over here. We'll save you," someone said from the *U-123*'s conning tower.

"Are those bastards talking to us?" Captain Roche wondered.

The *U-123* continued on. Perhaps Hardegen had heard the German crewman yelling for help. In any case, he didn't stop. Captain Roche and his crew continued to row away until they were joined by a lifeboat from the *Oklahoma*. Roche took his bearings and headed west. By late afternoon the same day, the lifeboats landed safely on the beach near Brunswick, Georgia.[22] Hardegen and his *U-123* headed for deep water to rest for the day. Both the *Oklahoma* and the *Esso Baton Rouge*, as it would turn out, would be salvaged and repaired and put back into the war effort within eight months.[23]

## The Ninth Day

On the final day of the patrol of the *Hambleton* and *Emmons*, the U-boats went on a spree that recalled the murderous days of March. Topp in the *U-552* struck first against the American tanker *Atlas* within sight of the Cape Lookout Lighthouse. Two torpedoes were fired at a range of 300 yards. The *Atlas* stopped, and all of the crew got off safely before the tanker sank. Topp did not stay around. He swept past the lifeboats and headed north. One of the lifeboats drifted into a patch of burning gasoline and two of the crewmen jumped off. They were burned to death.[24]

At about the same time, Hardegen, still off Georgia, swept in under the cover of darkness and torpedoed the American freighter *Esparta*. The torpedo blew the hatch covers off the holds of the banana-laden ship and released the ammonia used in the refrigeration system. The fumes were so overwhelming several men had to jump overboard to escape. Hardegen apparently got a whiff of the stuff as well and was last seen departing hastily westward. In an hour, the *Esparta* went under.[25]

Finishing the murderous night, Lassen and the *U-160* found the American freighter *Malchace* off Cape Lookout with a cargo of 3,628 tons of soda ash. The *U-160*'s torpedo broke the back of the small freighter and set fire to the cargo. Only one man was lost when he jumped overboard before the lifeboats could be launched. The Mexican tanker *Faja de Oro* picked up the remainder of the crew the next day.[26]

The *Hambleton* and the *Emmons* journeyed slowly back to Norfolk in the afternoon, but before they had securely docked, Mützelburg in the *U-203* bagged the British tanker *San Delfino* off Cape Lookout. Two full lifeboats pushed off from the blazing tanker, but only one would be there when rescue finally came. The other had been pushed by a strong current back into a huge cauldron of burning oil. All the men in the surviving lifeboat could do was watch agape while their mates screamed for help.[27] The British trawler *Norwich City* rushed to rescue the survivors and while she did so, Topp, a few miles farther south, blasted the American tanker *Tamaulipas* with a single torpedo. The *Norwich City* moved down to pick up those survivors as well, one of whom reported that the U-boat had come in so close, he "could have dropped baseballs on it."[28]

On the last day of the *Hambleton* and *Emmons* patrol, the U-boats had sunk five allied merchantmen. Both of the destroyers had managed to limp back to Norfolk, but had little to show for their efforts besides the strain placed on their captains and crew. Disturbed by their lack of success, Admiral Andrews studied the reports from the destroyers and then asked for a list of the other forces he had in the area at the same time. To his surprise, there had been eight destroyers, along with the *Dione*, the *Calypso*, and a number of other coast guard and navy vessels. Yet, since the beginning of April, the U-boats had sunk twenty-two allied merchantmen all in the same general area.

Andrews began to rethink his position as a result of the report. What if he had had twenty destroyers out there? Thirty? Would it have made any difference? Andrews had issued routing orders to the merchant vessels, ordered blackouts aboard the ships, and had all the warships and airplanes under his command actively patrolling. He had even managed to get the Roosevelt administration to agree to a blackout of lights along the Atlantic coast. But none of that had stopped the U-boats. The conclusion Andrews reached surprised him, but after he had reached it, he realized it was both inevitable and undeniable.

But how, after his months of badgering for one thing, was Andrews now to ask for another? And for something he himself had argued against? Nothing about Admiral Andrews ever suggested he was shy. It was only a matter of how best to go about it. The reports from the *Hambleton* and *Emmons* had convinced him of what to do. Why not try to convince Admiral King the same way? Andrews sent Admiral King a condensed version of the two destroyers' reports, accompanied by a letter from the commander of Destroyer Division 19, which included among its number the *Hambleton* and *Emmons*. Their lack of success had upset him and he knew that Admirals King and Andrews would be upset as well. In the time-honored tradition of the military, the division commander therefore sat down and wrote a letter that he hoped would cover him and stave off criticism of his command. It was a letter that pleased Admiral Andrews very much.

"It will be extremely rare," the commander had written, "for patrolling destroyers to make actual contact with a submarine in which an alert submarine commander attempts to avoid contact." Also, "At night, destroyers are easier to see than submarines." And, "While patrolling operations of this type are of some value in combatting enemy submarine activities, the submarine menace on our Atlantic Coast [the following is emphasized by the author] *can be defeated only through the operation of a coastal convoy system."*

Through one of Admiral King's own subordinates, a canny Admiral Andrews had fired the first salvo in his new campaign for the development of a convoy system for the American coast, the only thing, Andrews now believed, that could save America's merchant fleet from total destruction. Later, a staff officer would present Andrews with a study made of the navy's battle against the U-boats that had attacked American coastal shipping during World War I. Andrews found that the initial response along the American east coast had been exactly the same in that war as this one—single warships had been sent after the U-boats to no avail. Even President Woodrow Wilson had despaired over the tactic, saying it was like "hunting hornets all over the farm." Finally, convoys had been instituted on the Atlantic coast in 1918 and that had finally staved off the U-boats. It had taken some weeks of bitter experience but Admiral Adolphus Andrews had finally learned the same hard lesson.[29]

The *Hambleton* and *Emmons* were moored in Norfolk, the admirals were rethinking their positions, and changes were coming.

But still the *Dione* was at sea, patrolling alone.

Just before dawn on 10 April she came across the burning tanker *San Delfino* drifting off Cape Hatteras. It was an eerie sight in the dark. Flames were spewing and popping from jagged holes in the side of the wreck and all around it floated pieces of wreckage in a gigantic black pool of glistening oil. A lookout spotted a body in the orange glow of the flames and Alger ordered the *Dione* alongside. It was not the usual practice to pick up bodies, but Alger wasn't certain which tanker he had found and hoped for some identification papers to be on the dead man. The sailor was fished aboard by boat hooks and was discovered to be a young man, probably in his twenties. This was unusual. The merchantmen were usually older, the young men all in the military. A lifeboat was spotted and the *Dione*, moving carefully through the oil, edged over to it. It was empty except for some blankets and survival gear and some papers that identified it as being from a British tanker. The boat was stripped and then machine-gunned until it sank. The body was laid out on deck and covered with a tarp.

Alger ordered the *Dione* in to turn over the body and the papers to the proper authorities. Before he got very far, however, the sonar operator called back an excellent echo. He could also hear propeller beats, he said. Alger was on the bridge. McCormick was there, too. Go in or follow up the echo? It took Alger about one second to decide.

"General Quarters!"

There was the thunder of feet, many of them bare, on the deck of the *Dione*, the swoosh of tarps thrown aside from machine guns, the clank of depth-charge racks being unsafed, the clanging of the annunciator as the engine room was given the word.

The *Dione* attacked, turned, and attacked again. What seemed chaos was in fact planned and orderly. The ocean lit up and then a huge water spout burst to the surface sending tons of steam and water skyward. Before it settled, the *Dione* was already cutting through the shower, drenching the men on deck. There were shouts to ready more charges while below, as always, the black gang held on in the darkness as the shock wave swept through them. Alger was on the starboard wing. The Y-gun blasted out two charges that flew up and then dropped steeply. The men in the engine room heard the Y-gun, then the splashes. There was silence and then an ear-shattering roar. Someone yelled in fear and confusion and then there was silence again.

The *Dione* swept past the burning *San Delfino* and dropped some more explosives. A dense smoke covered everything and the sun, just creeping above the horizon, was like a distant, cold disk drifting across the pale and yellow sky. White plumes from the depth charges burst skyward. The wreck glistened from the spray and then groaned as it eased deeper into the cold water. Red flames spat and sputtered.

It was an image of hell.

But still the *Dione* hunted the U-boat.

# 12

# The Night of the *Roper*

**N**ot yet aware of the arguments coming his way concerning the use of convoys, Admiral King kept releasing single destroyers to Admiral Andrews as they became available. One of the destroyers Andrews would be allowed to use temporarily was the USS *Roper* (DD 147). She was to have a remarkable cruise in the service of the Eastern Sea Frontier. In many ways, in fact, her service would be the most excruciatingly painful of all the warships thrown singly into the combat against the U-boats. She would be strained to the limit of her endurance . . . until she would face a sudden, violent event on a dark, cold night that would, in fact, mark a turning point of sorts in the battle against the U-boats. It was to be a night of pain, a night of fear, and a night of death.

On 8 March 1942, the *Roper* began her first antisubmarine patrol in the Eastern Sea Frontier.[1] She had been ordered into the battle against the U-boats, her captain had been told, as a replacement for the *Jacob Jones*. The captain of the *Roper*, Lieutenant Commander Hamilton W. Howe, harbored no illusions about his assignment. For one thing, he had been in the same company and class at the Naval Academy as the *Jacob Jones*'s skipper, Hugh David Black. He knew that there was not a more competent officer in the destroyer service than "Dubie"

Black, yet the U-boats had easily sunk him and the shipping he had been trying to defend without a single loss of their own.

Howe also knew his own command and even though he was proud of his destroyer, she was old, having been launched in August of 1918. Referred to as a "four-piper" by the navy because of her four oil-fired boilers and stacks, the *Roper* was 314 feet long with a displacement of only 1,600 tons. Because of her cramped size, she was only lightly armed with five 3-inch guns, six 21-inch torpedoes, and four .50-caliber machine guns in addition to her two racks of depth charges and a K- and a Y-gun for propelling the charges on different patterns. She was, in fact, almost identical in age and appearance to her sister ship, the *Jacob Jones.*[2]

If the *Roper* had one strength, Howe knew it was her speed. She could officially make 28 knots, but on power trials had easily reached 30. The *Roper*, then, could outrun any known German U-boat. Still, the *Jacob Jones* had been capable of the same speed and it had not saved her. The *Roper* and the *Jacob Jones* had often patrolled together and even moored beside each other all up and down the coast. When they were together, it was remarkable how they seemed almost reflections of one another. The *Roper* had even been in the vicinity of the *Jacob Jones* the night she was sunk. There had been radio contact between the two as the *Roper* had passed through the "Jakie's" patrol area on her way to her new station. The fate of the *Jacob Jones*, Howe was chillingly aware, could also easily be that of her twin, the *Roper.*[3]

The *Roper* had one piece of equipment that the *Jacob Jones* could have used. It was a primitive radar of British design that Howe hoped would at least help him spot trouble before it reached him. The equipment was very heavy and part of it, the "bedspring" antenna, had to be installed high on the mast. Like all the 4-stackers, the *Roper* had a tendency to be topheavy, and the antenna made this worse. To compensate, 100 tons of lead had been placed beneath the boilers. Howe hoped it would be enough. The *Roper* had already come close to turning over during his command. On a convoy run in January 1942 to Londonderry, an awesome wave had struck the *Roper* in the North Atlantic, tilting her first 54 degrees to starboard

and then 47 degrees to port. A little more and they would have
gone over. It had been a close call.[4]

A 1926 graduate of the Naval Academy, Lieutenant Commander Howe had served in various ships in the peacetime
navy, including the battleship *Arizona* with a junior lieutenant
named Arleigh Burke. Promotions had been slow in this period for everyone in the navy, and it had taken Howe ten years
to reach lieutenant, but he had stayed on. He liked the navy
and, besides, he had received good assignments along the way,
including a tour with the Asiatic Fleet. He had served first
aboard the minesweeper *Bittern* and then in the gunboat *Tulsa*
out of Sin Ho, China, on the Hai River guarding the Standard
Oil Station there. His family was able to join him on this tour,
living in Tin Sin near Peking, so it was one of the more satisfying of his career. His next assignment had been very much a
plum—instructor in the Department of Electrical Engineering at the Naval Academy. After that, destroyers had seemed
his lot. First had been the *Bainbridge*, where he had served as
gunnery officer, and then the old *Reuben James*, where he had
been the executive officer.

Destroyers, cramped and uncomfortable, were not considered good duty, but Howe felt service with them would lead to
what every young naval officer desired more than anything in
the world: command. At last, in September 1941, orders came
down to him by dispatch. The destroyer USS *Roper* was his.
Since then, besides the Londonderry convoy, the *Roper* had
been on antisubmarine patrol or North Atlantic convoy activities, always in the company of other ships. It was made clear
that this would not be the case when Howe received his latest
orders. He was to take the *Roper* on patrol alone, working the
destroyer back and forth between the entrance to Chesapeake
Bay and Cape Lookout.

The *Roper* was flying her solid blue SOPA (Senior Officer
Present Afloat) pennant. Although Howe was the captain of
the *Roper*, Commander Stanley C. Norton, commander of Destroyer Division 54, of which the *Roper* was the flagship, was
also aboard. "Commodore" Norton had spent his formative
years in China. He was a brusque, no-nonsense commander
who had suddenly found himself in command of a destroyer

division that had been spread too thin for him to do much more than observe its activities. One of those destroyers had been the *Jacob Jones*. The others, the *Dickerson* and the *Herbert*, were on alternating antisubmarine patrol and North Atlantic convoy duty. It was only the *Roper* that Norton could influence but, in theory, his role even there was only that of advisor. It was a frustrating command experience. Howe was aware of the frustration and did his best to defer to Norton and to keep him informed of the *Roper*'s activities. Still, his presence was not a comfortable one.

The *Roper*'s first day in Torpedo Junction almost proved to be disastrous. Howe had been ordered to rendezvous just south of Wimble Shoals with the *Dione*. The *Roper*, uncertain of the area, entangled her starboard screw in the cable holding buoy #52 just as the *Dione* came up. The *Dione* did not hesitate. She immediately began to screen the destroyer just as if she were nothing more than a merchantman in trouble while the *Roper*'s embarrassed crew struggled to clear the heavy cable. When that proved impossible from the deck, the *Roper*'s engineer officer, Ensign Bill Mouquin, finally had to dive into the sea to pull it loose.

After Mouquin returned, dripping but successful, the *Roper* began to make way only to have her steering gear jam. Hand steering was hastily substituted, and the *Roper* doggedly kept going until the *Dione* led the way over an unidentified wreck. Lieutenant Commander Howe thought this might be an excellent location to test out the new "teardrop" 600-pound depth charges he had on board, charges double the standard size and streamlined like a bomb rather than the usual ash-can shape. They were aboard as an experiment, and Howe figured he had better determine if they could be successfully dropped.

The *Dione* moved a respectful distance away while the *Roper*, moving slowly, rolled the charges off her stern. One thing that would be learned immediately about the new weapons was that they fell faster than the old "ash cans." The *Roper* just barely managed to get out of the way before the sea erupted in a mighty roar of white foam, brown mud, and pieces of wreckage. The *Roper*, her seams opening and rivets popping out of her hull, shuddered in the tremendous shock

wave. Immediately, there were calls to the bridge from all over
the ship. The *Roper*, if not sinking, was at least leaking badly.
Howe had no choice but to abandon his patrol and turn the
*Roper* and head her back to the Portsmouth Navy Yard for
repairs. He reported as such to the *Dione*'s skipper. Lieutenant
Alger made no comment except acknowledgment. The men of
the coast guard silently watched the self-wounded United
States Navy destroyer depart, and then the *Dione* turned to
continue her lonely, dangerous patrol. As the *Roper* droned
north toward the safety of Portsmouth, there was a suppressed
feeling of humiliation aboard. Nothing, however, could be
done. The repairs would have to be made before the *Roper* was
seaworthy again.

On 20 March 1942, after almost two weeks of extensive
repairs, the *Roper* once again put to sea. When she reached her
station, she was entirely alone, the *Dione* off patrolling farther
south. On the way out of Norfolk, the *Roper* had encountered
the *Dickerson* hurrying into port. This was a surprise. The
*Dickerson* had also been ordered on antisubmarine patrol and
was not supposed to leave her station until relieved by the
*Roper*. The *Dickerson* did not answer any signals and she was
traveling much too fast for the channels. Although no one
bothered to let the *Roper* know at the time, it was later learned
that the *Dickerson* was coming in with her critically wounded
captain, Lieutenant Commander J. K. Reybold, another class-
mate of Howe's.

A gigantic oil slick was immediately encountered just
south of Wimble Island Shoals. There was an ugly smell in the
air, and the sea was heavy and black and sluggish from the
thick oily layer. Howe decided to seek its source. Fires were
spotted burning along the eastern horizon, sending stacks of
black smoke churning skyward. The *Roper* turned toward the
smoke and then away, her path a planned zigzag to keep from
giving any U-boats an easy shot. A body floated by, spread-
eagled, on its face, still in its life preserver. The lookout
sighted it, yelled down, but the *Roper* kept going, her prow
pushing aside splintered lumber and crates and more bodies
bobbing in her path. Now and again, the old ship shuddered
her length as Howe ordered her to speed up and then slow

down, her speed changes, it was hoped, doing as much to confuse any stalking U-boats as the zigzags. Another call from the
lookout was unnecessary. The radar operator had already
spotted the stern of a tanker ahead. Howe eased the *Roper* over
to it, looking for signs of life. There were none.

The tanker, the *W. E. Hutton*, was not burning, but it was
the source of the oil slick and it was an obvious navigational
hazard. Howe ordered the *Roper*'s 3-inch guns to sink the hulk
and they spat once and then twice, holing the stern. The .50
calibers opened up as well, adding more holes to the rusty,
barnacle-coated bottom. Still, the stern kept floating. The crew
of the *Roper* had lined the rail to watch the effort at sinking the
wreck and had seen for the first time dead American sailors. It
had been a sobering experience for them. The *Roper* circled
once and then Howe ordered the destroyer to move away
through the oil and the splintered lumber and the crates and
the bodies. The U-boat that had done this carnage might be
just out of sight, waiting for the *Roper* to make a mistake and
offer a nice side view of herself. Always mindful of the lesson
of the *Jacob Jones*, Howe meant to make no such mistake.

The *Roper* continued south. Late in the afternoon, another
dead man in a lifejacket drifted by. Howe kept zigzagging, his
soundmen pinging and listening. As night descended on the
destroyer, the crew on deck were presented with a remarkable
sight. Looking toward shore, they could see the bright glow of
many lights. War or no war, the Americans along the coast
were still freely burning street and advertising lights. Even
the rawest bluejacket understood how this was helping the
U-boats. All the Germans had to do was maneuver out far
enough to get their target between them and the lights. When
the freighter or tanker came along, blacked out or not, they
would be like sitting ducks.

A cry from the lookout on the mast sent a chill through the
crew on the bridge. Torpedo! It was too late to do anything
but pray. The gray streak the lookout had seen sped toward
the racing destroyer and then passed well under the stern.
Howe ordered General Quarters and asked for sound contacts.
There were none. Perhaps all that had been seen was a dolphin. He ordered a depth charge dropped anyway and then

put the *Roper* about. A few minutes later, the soundman yelled
back a contact. That was enough for Howe. He ordered a pattern of ten depth charges dropped and directed the *Roper* away
from the scene. He recognized that the advantage was entirely
to the U-boats, especially at night.

Daybreak found the *Roper* just off Cape Hatteras, heading
south. Howe had ordered Ensign Mouquin to oversee the operation of the radar. Mouquin had known next to nothing
about radar but had learned by trial and error. He still didn't
know everything about it, but at least he could turn the damn
thing on and more or less know what was happening on its
screen. Figuring out the way things worked was a specialty of
Mouquin's on board the *Roper*. And why not? Howe had put
him in charge of the *Roper*'s engines and boilers. If he could
learn about naval steam engines, he could certainly figure out
radar. Actually, it wasn't that hard. It just took practice. As its
sweep went back and forth, a disturbance in the field showed
up on the radar scope as a "blip." Mouquin kept the radar on
constantly, its purpose dedicated to picking up ship traffic or
perhaps even a periscope. Practice and more practice, that was
the idea.

Just as the sun was coming up over the horizon, Mouquin
noted a contact. Howe turned to investigate and found the
*Gulf Bird*, an American freighter, traveling past the capes all
alone. The *Roper* escorted the *Gulf Bird* for a couple of hours,
ensuring its safety at least for that time. When a sinking
freighter hove into view, the *Roper* left the *Gulf Bird* to investigate. The freighter was almost all the way down so no name
could be taken off her. (Author's note: this was probably the
freighter *Teresa*.) Howe dropped a depth charge after the
soundman said he had a contact, and then the radar operator
reported another "blip" and the *Roper* charged off to find the
tanker *Gargoyle*, also traveling alone. The *Roper* fell in with the
tanker for an hour and then broke off only to find the freighters *Tidewater* and *Cocique* loitering along, fat targets. Howe
considered escorting the two, but the other adversary in the
Graveyard of the Atlantic, the weather, was making its presence felt. By nightfall, a full-blown squall was in progress. It

lasted the night, and in the morning the *Roper* was riding a tumultuous sea.

Howe did not stop his zigzagging, despite the weather. All day, the *Roper* patrolled alone on an angry and miserably cold, gray sea. With the heavy new radar topside, some of the officers wondered about the old ship's stability. The Graveyard was known for huge waves that would appear from seemingly nowhere. The *Roper* attacked the waves, lowering her prow into them, then sitting back on her stern, finally wallowing from side to side. But she kept going. It was uncomfortable but safe. That night, under orders from Norfolk, the destroyer finally was able to get out of the weather by standing in to Morehead City where a load of sixty depth charges, trucked down from Norfolk, waited for them. As they were being loaded, there was a flash on the horizon and then an ominous rumble. It was a freighter, struck by a torpedo. Suddenly, the men of the U.S. Army's 28th Division, on beach patrol and guard duty, appeared and began to help the *Roper*'s tired crew load the depth charges. Side by side, army and navy men worked together and soon the *Roper* was ready to go.

Rather than wait for morning, Howe elected to proceed out of Beaufort Inlet and to sea. By midnight, the *Roper* was back on patrol. Almost immediately, a torpedo track was spotted and the klaxon for General Quarters was grunting its anxious "URK-URK-URK!" The men of the *Roper* were beginning to wonder if and when they might ever sleep again. Boatswain's Mate Harry Heyman, a muscular young volunteer from Pennsylvania, was making an attempt at keeping a journal during the *Roper*'s stint in the Graveyard. By the time the *Roper* had seen the grisly results of the *Naeco* sinking and turned once again toward Norfolk for repairs, it seemed to Heyman and all his fellow sailors that they had been caught up in something diabolical. "This torpedo junction," he wrote succinctly, "is hell." Had Lieutenant Commander Howe been able to enter Heyman's thought in the official log, he would have probably added only an "amen." Howe was tired and his ship and crew were, too. He no longer saw any way that he could succeed in his mission. The U-boats held too many cards. All the *Roper* had become was just another potential victim.[5]

On 21 March 1942, the *U-85*, commanded by Oberleutnant Eberhard Greger, left St. Nazaire bound for America. This was to be the *U-85*'s fourth war cruise.[6]

Greger, a respected member of the German Naval Academy class of 1935, was known as an aggressive commander, the type who did not mind taking a chance for success and, therefore, the type Doenitz liked. Typical of Greger's aggressive style was his action on the *U-85*'s first war cruise off Greenland. There, the *U-85* had joined a "wolfpack" of U-boats vectored in by Doenitz on a convoy. After a day of failure, the others had gone on in search of easier prey, but Greger had stayed. After dodging depth charges from a destroyer, Greger had finally managed a hit on a 7,000-ton steamer. A few minutes later, the *U-85*'s crew were grinning at each other as another hit was made and then another. Their grins soon faded, however. As Greger must have known they would, the protective screen of British destroyers began to move in. Diving, the *U-85* was shaken again and again by a heavy barrage of depth charges. Three times the tenacious Greger would try to surface to work the convoy over, and three times he would be forced back down to weather yet another depth-charge barrage. It was only after his U-boat began to suffer numerous leaks that Greger had reluctantly called off his attack and returned to St. Nazaire.[7] Doenitz had taken note of Greger's aggressive style. When *Paukenschlag* had begun, he and his *U-85* were sent to the "American Shooting Gallery."[8]

After getting outside the harbor entrance, Greger took the *U-85* down. British aircraft were everywhere and seemed to know exactly where and when the U-boats would attempt to break out of their French ports to the open sea. The interior of the U-boat was a jumble of men and equipment and food. Even the spare water closet was packed with food, and several of the water tanks had been converted to carry diesel fuel. The men laughingly nicknamed the *U-85*, like the other Type VIIs crossing the Atlantic, their "Great German Floating Warehouse." Her crew could hardly move up and down the narrow

corridor without ducking something extra, whether it be a
string of sausages or a rack of engine belts. All of it was necessary. Once the *U-85* left St. Nazaire, she was on her own for at
least a month.

Amidst all the confusion, Seaman Erich Degenkolb
worked diligently with his shipmates to get the *U-85* organized. Although he paid attention to his duties, he was also
paying attention to his stomach. On the *U-85*'s third war
cruise, a cruise in the North Atlantic that had taken the submarine close to New York City, the 25-year-old Degenkolb,
blonde and blue-eyed and otherwise healthy, had been terribly
seasick for almost a week. "Oh! Neptune!" he had wailed in
his diary. "Badly seasick" and "No end to it." He prayed that
the sickness would not return on this cruise. Fortunately, the
*U-85* encountered only good weather the first few days out.
Several times, Degenkolb and his mates were allowed to go up
on deck, away from the ubiquitous odors of diesel fuel, mold-
ing food, and body sweat below. There, they found, to their
delight, the sea "as smooth as a table" and were able to observe
"magnificent sunrises." By the time some heavy weather had
set in, Degenkolb had found, to his relief, that he had acquired
his sea legs. A week out and whales were sighted, the great
beasts sounding nearby before racing ahead of the U-boat. On
their way to America to destroy or be destroyed, the men of
the *U-85* were enjoying themselves immensely.

Greger, for his part, was ever the professional, keeping his
men busy by simulating aircraft attacks again and again. At
the alarm, all the crew not otherwise at a duty station would
race to the bow torpedo room, causing the bow to dip down a
little faster and saving a few seconds that might mean the
difference between life and death. This drill was important,
not only for the seconds saved but to keep the men sharp. A
constant watch was also kept, even in the mid-Atlantic, for
both potential victims and adversaries. Torpedo drills were
run. As soon as the *U-85* came on station, Greger meant for his
U-boat to be ready for anything.

On 4 April 1942, the *U-85* crossed into the Gulf Stream. It
was unseasonably warm, and many of the men immediately
peeled down to their underwear. Degenkolb, unused to the

heat as most of the Germans, complained in his diary that it
was "abominable." Still, the sunshine and clear skies were
welcome because it meant the sea would not be rolling and
there would be no seasickness. To celebrate their journey and
their entrance into American waters, the cook baked a big
cake that was enjoyed by all. Still, despite everything,
Degenkolb, like most of the men, was homesick. There were
very few professional sailors in the youthful U-boat crew.
Their thoughts kept wandering back to the cool, green pas-
tures of Germany and family and girlfriends. Wishing, however, did no good. This was war and the *U-85* had come to do
her part. Degenkolb would do his as well. They all would.[9]

On 28 March, the *Roper* was patched well enough to go
back on station. Her crew was now used to what was found,
more drifting wreckage and liferafts and bodies. Stopping to
pick up the bodies was never considered. The *Roper* had neither the time nor the facilities for that. If she had, she might
not have done much else since there were so many. The bad
part was when the bodies were seen floating on their backs.
The work of birds on their faces was a hard thing for most of
the men to stomach. Small, privately owned craft were also
observed operating miles off the coast. There was some discussion in the wardroom as to why they were there. Some of
them were fishing boats, that was understood, but the others
seemed to have no purpose. The origin of most of them was
the North Carolina coast and the skippers, when questioned,
invariably answered to a man that they were on the sea only to
rescue shipwrecked American and Allied seamen. Somebody
had to do it, they griped, since the navy and coast guard
seemed unable to stop the U-boats. While it was true that the
residents of the Graveyard's coast had a long history of rescu-
ing ships in distress, it was also known that their ancestors had
indulged in a darker, though legal, pursuit—the salvage of the
numerous wrecks and their drifting cargo along that murderous coast. It was also possible, so the wardroom gossip went,
that one or more of these small craft were servicing the
U-boats, bringing them food, fuel, and news, all for a price, of
course. It was all speculation but still a source of frustration to

the *Roper*'s officers and crew and especially to the radar operators, who constantly received back the blips of something
small—a U-boat or a small craft, there was no way of telling.

Three days of patrolling down toward Cape Lookout
passed. On the second day, the soundmen were constantly
making contact, and thirty-two depth charges were dropped.
It was nerve-wracking. The klaxon seemed never to stop. The
crew, eyes red-rimmed and short of temper, trudged sullenly
back and forth to their stations. Coffee began to be drunk in
prodigious quantities, some of the men drinking 30–40 cups
per day. On the third day out, a radio transmission from an
unknown source reported a U-boat on the surface off Cape
Lookout. Howe ordered the *Roper* in hot pursuit. Lieutenant
(j.g.) Winfield DeLong, the torpedo officer, ordered his crew to
check out the torpedoes, set on both sides of the destroyer, and
the depth charges on the stern. Win DeLong had had friends
aboard the *Jacob Jones* and the *Reuben James*, both U-boat victims. He was very much aware of how vulnerable the *Roper*
was. He also knew that if there was a U-boat operating brazenly on the surface ahead, it was likely that his torpedoes
would be called on to sink it. He ordered the torpedoes set on
a 90-degree curved firing course. This meant that even though
the torpedoes were launched from the side of the destroyer,
they would immediately turn and head for wherever the bow
was aimed. In a short time, DeLong was satisfied that both his
torpedoes and his depth charges were set and ready to go.
There was no U-boat found, however, only a large wooden
section of a deck and a cargo hatch of yet another sunken
freighter. Still, Howe kept the *Roper* in the vicinity, patrolling,
looking, and listening.

It was just after midnight when a lookout reported seeing
some white flashes in the dark. Another lookout reported that
the flashes were spelling out "SOS" in Morse code. Cautiously, Howe ordered the *Roper* toward the signal, half-sus-
pecting a U-boat trick. It was not. It was a lifeboat crammed
with 27 survivors from the torpedoed *City of New York*, a passenger ship out of Cape Town, South Africa, bound for New
York. One of the survivors, a crewman, reported that the ship

had sunk and that there were more lifeboats all around filled
with terrified and wounded civilians.

Howe had to make a very difficult decision. He had already
taken a chance, bringing the *Roper* to a full stop at night to
rescue the survivors in the lifeboat. There was certainly one
and probably more U-boats in the area and the *Roper* would be
an easy target if Howe tried to initiate a rescue operation that
would call for slow speeds and more stops. He considered the
fact that it was not, after all, the *Roper*'s mission to act as a
rescue vessel. No one could blame him if he called for assistance from the *Dione* or some other small coast guard vessels
while he took the *Roper* on to hunt for the U-boat that had
done the damage. Still, for all his usual caution, Howe never
had any doubts as to what he should and would do. He called
in his position and asked for help and then proceeded ahead to
the approximate location of the sinking.

Fortunately, there was a physician aboard, Dr. Winton H.
Johnson. Dr. "Johnny," as he was affectionately known to the
officers' wives of the *Roper*, was a calm presence aboard the old
destroyer. The *Roper*'s crew was glad he was there and so was
he. He enjoyed the duty and the life at sea, sensing it to be the
great adventure of his life. When the battered *City of New York*
survivors were brought to him, he was ready. By 0200, however, Dr. Johnson had lost his first patient, a badly burned
crewman. Since he had no clinic as such, he had set up a temporary hospital in the officers' wardroom. If more survivors
came aboard, he wasn't sure he was going to be able to handle
them, his small medicine chest already strained. Still he kept
at his work. It was that way all over the *Roper*. Men who had
been so tired they were having trouble standing only minutes
before were now alert and wide awake, anxiously peering into
the darkness. At last, the *Roper* was doing something besides
hunting and running from phantoms!

At 0240, a red flare was spotted and the *Roper* stopped beside a liferaft, several men clinging to it. Two more liferafts
appeared out of the gloom just as the soundman yelled back a
solid contact. It was a U-boat, the soundman was sure of it.
Nervelessly, Howe kept the *Roper* stopped until nine more
crewmen were picked up and only then ordered a single depth

charge dropped to cover the destroyer's slow movement forward. A few minutes later, there was another red flare and twelve more survivors were brought aboard. At 0430, another flare brought the *Roper* to a lifeboat crammed with twenty-two survivors, one of them a newborn baby!

The *Roper*'s crew rushed to the side to help. A human chain soon formed, the survivors hauled up to the deck by sailors hanging on netting draped over the side. One of the survivors was a small girl handed directly to Howe. The child was shivering, her little legs icy cold. She clung to Howe as tightly as she could while he carried her forward to a bunk in the officers' quarters. Gently, Howe laid the little girl down on the bunk and covered her with a blanket. He suddenly found himself thinking of his own daughter who was about the same age. Filled with sadness, anger, and frustration, he hurried back to the bridge. On deck, Dr. "Johnny" had taken an hours-old infant and wrapped it in a windbreaker and was watching incredulously as the baby's mother climbed up the cargo net under her own power. She was, as it turned out, Desanka Mohorovicic, the wife of an official in the Yugoslavian government-in-exile. After the Germans had taken over her country, her family had begun an odyssey to get away that had led to Jerusalem to Cairo and then to South Africa. When the Yugoslavian government had ordered her husband, Joseph, to New York, Mrs. Mohorovicic could not get a berth on the same ship. A month later, however, space on the *City of New York* had come open. Even though her baby was due in about a month, she decided to follow along with her two-year-old daughter Vesna. She had almost made it, being twenty-three days out with two days to go when the first of two torpedoes from the *U-160* had struck.

In minutes, Mrs. Mohorovicic had found herself in a crowded lifeboat giving birth. The ship's doctor, Dr. L. H. Conly, was called to help. Dr. Conly had deliberately followed Mrs. Mohorovicic to the lifeboat but had slipped and fallen when a huge wave had knocked him off balance. That had left him with two broken ribs. The other passengers rigged some canvas to cover them while the doctor shrugged off his own pain to aid Mrs. Mohorovicic. There was a massive Hatteras

storm on the sea. The lifeboat was being pitched about by 15-
and 20-foot waves that intermittently crashed down on the
small boat, flooding it with seawater. Dr. Conly caught the
baby, a boy, just as one particularly huge wave crashed aboard.
Miraculously, all it did was wash the baby off and start his first
breath. After Dr. Conly had cut the cord with a pair of small
scissors from the first-aid kit, Mrs. Mohorovicic took the baby,
swaddled it in a turban offered by a fellow passenger, and put
it in her blouse next to her skin and leaned happily back while
the other survivors stared at her, amazed at the pluck of this
tiny woman.

Soon, Mrs. Mohorovicic, Vesna (as it turned out, she was
the tiny girl Howe had carried to safety), and healthy baby son
were bedded down in the officers' quarters. Once her origin
was determined, Harry Heyman was called on to try to speak
to her since he had grown up among people who spoke Serbo-
Croatian. Unable to remember the word for husband, Heyman asked her, "Where is your daughter's father?" Grinning,
she explained and soon the word had spread throughout the
ship—the wife of a Yugoslavian government official, later ex-
aggerated to *the* ambassador to the U.S.A., had been rescued by
the *Roper*. The *Roper* was named after a nineteenth-century
naval hero, Jesse Sims Roper. When it was announced that
Mrs. Mohorovicic had decided to name her baby Jesse Roper
Mohorovicic, the crew, to a man, almost burst with pride. A
sum of $200 would be raised for the baby that night by the
bluejackets.

All night long and well into the morning, Howe and his
officers and crew continued to ignore their own peril to keep
searching. More lifeboats were found but no more survivors.
Despite the tragic circumstances, there was a light mood
aboard the *Roper*. Children raced up and down the narrow
corridors of the destroyer and young women—nurses from
South Africa and Holland—stopped to smile and talk with the
bedazzled crewmen. Late that night, the *Roper* proudly entered
Norfolk harbor with sixty-nine survivors from the *City of New
York*.[10] It was to be, perhaps, the proudest moment in the existence of the old warship.

The *Roper*'s crew were given exactly one day to savor their accomplishment, and then the *Roper* was sent out once more to take up the same patrol. Five days later, she returned, leaking again, her crew exhausted and frustrated and, in many ways, defeated. The *Roper* had seen more burning freighters and tankers, had passed through massive oil slicks, drifting wreckage and floating bodies, but had managed only a few sound contacts. Howe was intensely aware that since the *Roper* had first gone on patrol, thirty freighters and tankers had been sunk in his patrol area. The U-boats were as invulnerable as ever.

Howe allowed a liberal leave policy. He had kept his crew almost constantly at battle stations for five days, a policy that had not endeared him to any of his men. The euphoria over the successful rescue of the *City of New York* survivors had not lasted long. There was grumbling below deck, and some of the officers were unhappy as well. Nerves that had been taut were now raw. The *Roper* was not anywhere close to mutiny but she was unhappy. There was really little Howe could do about it. He had the ship and the crew to keep safe and his mission to accomplish. He was doing both the only way he could see to do it, right or wrong.[11]

The *U-85* was a Type VIIB German submarine.[12] Considered medium in size, she was only 218 feet long, 20 1/4 feet wide at her midpoint, and but 15 1/2 feet high measured from her keel to the top of the conning tower. Her inner dimensions, inside the pressure hull that housed her forty-five crewmen, two 1,400-horsepower diesel engines, two 275-horsepower electric motors, forty-four huge wet-cell batteries, twelve torpedoes, five torpedo tubes (four in the bow, one aft), the steering and control rooms, and all the intricate ducting and tubing of her buoyancy-control systems, were crammed into an even smaller space, a narrow steel cylinder only 150 feet long and 14 feet wide at its widest point. There were three main compartments aboard the *U-85*, connected by a corridor that started at the bow torpedo room, went through a circular hatch to narrow bunks for the crew and past a tiny curtained "cabin" for the captain, widened briefly for the busy and crowded control room, and then continued on back through the din of the engines to the after torpedo room.

The odor inside this "iron coffin," as the crewmen often referred to it, was sickening. Diesel fuel seemed to be everywhere. Even the food and water tasted of it. Uncanned food brought for long missions moldered and rotted before it could be eaten. There was very little water aboard, and bathing, even the washing of one's face, was discouraged. Moreover, there was only one toilet for the entire crew, the second one used for storage. Seasickness and dysentery were not uncommon aboard the U-boat, so the toilet stayed in constant use, its filthy odors adding to the pollution. Even that one toilet could not be used below the depth of 80 feet, so many crewmen were often forced to use coffee cans or buckets while submerged. The only way a crewman could escape the noise and stink and cramped conditions was to be called on watch atop the conning tower when the U-boat was surfaced. This was not only a welcome job but a necessary one. The *U-85*, as all German U-boats at that stage of the war, had no radar, only the eyes of her crew to spot the enemy.[13]

In very many ways, the Type VII boat was a limited weapon. It was not very fast; a maximum 17 knots was all it could do on the surface, 7 knots submerged. The Type VII's design depth was fairly shallow, not much deeper than 250 feet. Its submerged range was only about 80 miles at very slow, conservative speeds, and but 12 miles at top speed. That meant most of its operations had to be conducted from the surface, where it was extremely vulnerable to aircraft attack. Yet, 691 of them were to be built during World War II, possibly the largest series of a warship type ever built in history.[14]

Despite the Type VII's drawbacks, it was extremely resilient and seaworthy because of its size, construction, and low center of gravity. It could slash through the seas at top speed through the nastiest weather with only its tiny, streamlined conning tower offering any resistance to the wind. It had good range, 6,500 miles at 12 knots on the surface, and its engines were powerful and easy to maintain. There was not a thing superfluous about the Type VII. It was a killing machine designed for one purpose only—to sink ships. This it did. Type

VII captains and crews were renowned for wringing the last ounce of performance from their machines, some even taking them down to as much as 600 feet to escape depth-charge attacks and then rising to assault the astonished enemy.[15]

The men of the *U-85* were very much aware of the limitations but, like all Type VII crews, were proud of their craft. The *U-85* had survived three war cruises and had sunk four enemy vessels. She was a successful U-boat heading into the waters of the hapless Americans and their fat, wallowing merchant fleet. Both captain and crew were confident of the outcome.

On 7 April 1942, Greger made an announcement: the *U-85* was 300 nautical miles from land and, as he put it, "660 miles from Washington." [16] A day passed as the *U-85* maneuvered, the outside temperature dropping drastically until it was only a few degrees above freezing. On 9 April, the watch on the conn spotted a blinking light, and Greger, thinking it was a ship, crash-dived only to find he had been fooled by a lighted buoy. The next night, things went better. A lone freighter was spotted, its running lights on. Greger fired a fan of two torpedoes, both slamming into the ship. She was the small Swedish freighter, *Christina Knudson*, en route from New York to New Orleans. The *Knudson* sank with no survivors.[17] Erich Degenkolb, aware only that the *U-85* had successfully sunk a "steamer," proudly entered the sinking in his diary. On the back page, he also noted the birthday of his girlfriend, Lieselotte Lang—16 July. As a reminder and just to be sure he didn't forget or make a mistake, he had also carefully written down her shoe and glove sizes. As soon as the war cruise to America was over, he would do his shopping in St. Nazaire and then go on leave, perhaps in time for Lieselotte's birthday.

Greger kept moving the *U-85* around, trying to position the U-boat where he might catch the most traffic. Sticking to the tactical doctrine still recommended by Doenitz, he kept his U-boat asleep on the bottom during the day, ignoring the sounds of ship traffic passing overhead, and then rose to the surface at night to hunt for ships. On the early morning watch of 13 April, Degenkolb climbed to the bridge of the conning tower and the fresh, cold, and clear Atlantic air. There were no targets, only "American beacons and searchlights visible at night." With this terse phrase in his diary, Degenkolb had sensed the truth: as the *U-85* hunted for victims, so was she also being hunted and by an enemy that was hungry for success and revenge.

It was late afternoon on 13 April when the *Roper*, patched once more, wearily stood out of Norfolk for yet another patrol. There had been rumors among the crew that the *Roper* would go north, perhaps back to convoy duty, but that rumor, more of an unexpressed hope, was soon dashed as the destroyer turned south. During the *Roper*'s absence, six more tankers had been sunk in the Graveyard. By 2110, the *Roper* had cleared False Cape Buoy and was zigzagging. The night was clear with many stars visible, and there was virtually no wind. At 2238, there was a contact. Howe veered the *Roper* off but did not sound General Quarters. He wanted to give his men as much rest as possible. He ordered one depth charge dropped and then resumed the base course. After assuring himself that everything was in order, Howe looked around the bridge and then decided it was a good time to turn in. He was exhausted and Ensign Kenneth Tebo was the officer of the deck. Howe trusted Tebo. Everybody trusted Tebo. The first lieutenant, Tebo had graduated from the Naval Academy only fourteen months previously, but his service aboard the *Roper* had been outstanding from the beginning. His attention to detail and personal integrity were his greatest assets. Howe thought that Tebo had a great future in the navy if he was fortunate enough to survive the war. After he had seen his commander off the bridge, Tebo stared through the bridge window into the deep black of the night. Ahead lay a void with only an occasional wisp of phosphorescence spewing over the bow to mark forward progress. The old ship droned south, blacked out, knifing through a flat sea.

It was six minutes after midnight when Ensign Mouquin saw a peculiar blip on his radar screen. It seemed to him to be unusually dense, as if whatever was out there was just a solid chunk of iron. At the same time, the soundman, a seaman the officers and crew called "Professor" Black, heard the distant noise of rapidly turning propellers. Since the sonar/radar shack was just behind the bridge with the door open, all Mouquin had to do was to call out to Tebo. He had something unusual, he told the deck officer, possibly a small craft of some sort but different than anything he had ever seen. Whatever it was, it was no more than 2,700 yards ahead. Black seconded Mouquin's report. Something was definitely out there. Tebo acknowledged and ordered the captain informed. Quartermaster George Hamilton immediately called Howe and advised him of the situation.

Howe had been in a deep sleep. He heard the words but was slow to understand their meaning. "What is our course?" he asked and then, "What time is it?"

Quartermaster Hamilton answered Howe's questions and then told him Tebo wanted to investigate. At first, Howe was reluctant. Even in his groggy state, he was certain that the *Roper* was doing nothing but following either a coast guard vessel or another one of those crazy North Carolina power boats out on a salvage or fishing run. To follow it would mean going off the *Roper*'s planned zigzags and a delay in the patrol schedule. Hamilton reported, however, that Tebo thought the craft ahead might be a U-boat. "Very well," Howe finally rumbled, still doubting. "Permission granted." He wearily sat up and then put one foot followed by another on the floor. He was still in his uniform. He had made a habit of sleeping in it on the *Roper*. Groggily, he rose to make his way to the bridge.

Ensign Ken Tebo did not wait for his captain. He had the permission he wanted and wasted no time in using it. He turned the *Roper*'s bow after whatever it was that was out there. Tebo was not a man who ordinarily went on hunches. He was an engineer, thoughtful and analytical in demeanor. After all the disappointments, his analysis of the situation should have brought him to the same conclusion Howe had reached. There was no U-boat out there, certainly not one that was going to allow the *Roper* to catch it. Still, for this one time, Tebo was going on more than logic. It was in his gut and he could not explain it. It *was* a U-boat. He was certain of it!

When the *Roper* pulled within 2,100 yards of whatever was ahead, a wake could be seen. The sea was calm and very phos-

phorescent. Tebo, aware that German U-boats had stern torpedo tubes, ordered the *Roper* starboard of the wake and then
increased the speed of the destroyer to 20 knots. He knew the
*Roper* could not go much faster without losing her sonar capability. Still, the *Roper* was gradually overhauling the craft
ahead. The executive officer, W. W. "Bill" Vanous, appeared
on deck. He had sensed some slight change in the *Roper*'s routine while in his cabin. Perhaps it was the cessation of the
*Roper*'s usual, careful zigzagging or perhaps it was just the
intuition of an experienced officer. Whatever it was, Vanous
appeared on the bridge at a critical moment, took stock of the
situation, and advised Tebo to keep right on doing what he
was doing. Vanous thought the young ensign just might be
right. Whatever was out there was definitely acting suspi-
ciously. Commander Norton and Howe arrived soon after-
ward. Howe told Tebo to keep the conn. He still believed that
ahead was some sort of a coastal vessel, but he decided to allow
Tebo to continue the chase for the experience. He would allow
it, however, for only a few more minutes, and then he would
order it broken off so that the *Roper* could continue south on
schedule. Norton watched for a few moments and then impa-
tiently went outside and climbed up on the flying bridge for a
better look.

The wake ahead turned sharply to port and then to starboard. Whatever was out there had discovered the destroyer
on its tail and was trying to lose it. The soundman, Black,
yelled out that he had a good sonar contact. That meant the
craft ahead was not a low-draft vessel. To Tebo, that ruled out
at least the North Carolina salvagers and probably the coast
guard as well. He calmly kept the *Roper* on track while Vanous
went outside and up on the flying bridge with Norton to get a
better look. Standing behind Tebo, Lieutenant Commander
Howe weighed the evidence and tried to decide what to do.
He did not want to order General Quarters. The men were
exhausted. It was beginning to look as if Tebo might be right,
but it could still be another false alarm. What about the devas-
tation done to the *Dickerson* by the *Liberator*? He did not want
to have a reverse occurrence and accidentally fire on one of his
own ships. Interpreting sonar echoes was more of an art than

a science. It could still be an American vessel out there. It could be so many things . . . but a U-boat? How could it be a U-boat after all these weeks of failure? U-boats hid beneath the sea, striking out in secret and then disappearing without a trace. This thing, whatever it was, was out in the open. A U-boat? It just couldn't be! Howe's thoughts were interrupted by a shout from the lookout on the port side. *Torpedo!* It came from ahead and sizzled past the destroyer's bow before being swallowed in the dark. Howe dropped all of his doubts and immediately ordered General Quarters with orders given to prepare the machine guns, the 3-inch guns, the torpedoes, and the depth-charge batteries for action. Blearily, the men of the *Roper* slowly climbed out of their bunks and staggered up on deck to find the destroyer leaping ahead, her sharp bow slashing through the waves, sheets of phosphorescence flashing astern. What the devil was happening?

The chase continued for ten minutes. Tebo, still in charge of the bridge, constantly kept the *Roper* to one side of the wake. Vanous ordered the 24-inch searchlight on the flying bridge switched on and then climbed up the mainmast for a better view from the searchlight platform. The searchlight's powerful beam swept up the churning wake until—*there!*—turning sharply to starboard 300 yards ahead, a German U-boat could be seen on the surface, its conning tower and deck gun clearly illuminated. Vanous started calling down directions to Tebo. Howe's first thought was to get on the radio, to alert the navy to what was happening and perhaps get help. He knew there was a B-18 bomber patrolling the coast, codename: Apple. "Jesse to Apple," he called. "Jesse to Apple." Only static answered him.

Tebo ordered the *Roper* hard to starboard after the fleeing submarine. The U-boat, however, had a much sharper turning radius than the destroyer and was coming around quicker. Tebo was not certain if the U-boat was running or turning to fight, but he was going to catch it and that was that! Commander Norton ordered the searchlight turned off. He thought it made the *Roper* too much of a target. There may be one U-boat out there in the light but there might also be a second just waiting to spring a trap. Lieutenant DeLong, on his way to his torpedoes, appeared and advised Tebo to ram the U-boat. Tebo kept his course while Vanous yelled at the guns to fire. If he heard Norton's order to turn the searchlight off, he chose not to follow it, keeping the light on and playing it across the U-boat deck, which was now only 200 yards to starboard and coming around fast.

Suddenly, U-boat crewmen scrambled out of the conning tower and raced toward the 88-mm deck gun. The U-boat was turning to fight with a gun powerful enough to blow the *Roper* right out of the water. Still, no fire came from the *Roper* even though Commander Norton had climbed up on the flying bridge and was exhorting the men to fire their machine guns.

Chief Jack Wright at his duty station near the bridge could no longer stand it. Cursing, he shoved a gunner out of his seat and jacked back the handle on a .50-caliber, clearing it. Maybe nobody else on this tub knew what to do but, by God, he did! Instantly, the big gun spat and Chief Wright swiveled it around, sending a line of tracers and bullets slashing across the U-boat deck, cutting the gun crew down. He kept up his fire, the heavy slugs clearly banging into the side of the submarine, which kept turning. Tebo kept the *Roper* turning with it. Soon, the U-boat had come around 180 degrees, its starboard side toward the *Roper*. Amidst a hail of .50-caliber fire, one man and then another were observed climbing out of the conn and jumping into the sea. Was the U-boat giving up? Not yet. Men were still trying to man the 88-mm deck gun. Only Wright's bullets kept them at bay behind the conning tower. There was not, however, another .50-caliber gun on the *Roper* firing. Their crews sat or stood behind their silent weapons as if frozen in place.

The U-boat completed its turn, its port side facing the *Roper*, and then slowed and stopped, the sea streaming across its deck. Besides Chief Wright, only Harry Heyman, captain of 3-inch gun #5 and the sailor who had translated for Mrs. Mohorovicic, was ready to take advantage of the situation. By then, all the other 3-inchers were inoperative, their excited crews having pulled the triggers in advance of loading the shells, thus tripping the solenoids. The result was an apparent jam or dud round. Still steeped in peacetime-navy rules and regulations, the 3-inch gun crews, one by one, were stopping and incredibly pointing their barrels skyward for the required ten minutes before attempting to reload, while in front of them, just yards away, sat a German U-boat still capable of sinking them.

With Vanous calling down directions and Norton still imploring more of the guns to fire, Tebo ordered the *Roper* slowed to keep from losing the U-boat in the dark. This gave Harry Heyman and his crew their chance. The quartermaster called over the telephone lines to find out if any of the 3-inch guns were ready. When it was Heyman's turn, he alone called out "Ready, sir!" and then calmly ordered his men to load. There were six men on the gun crew, Heyman, a sight setter, a pointer, and three loaders. Of the loaders, the #3 loader was to take a shell from the magazine rack, #2 to pass it on, and #1 to throw it in as Heyman opened the breach. At Heyman's command, the #3 loader froze. Behind the #5 gun, on top of the galley, sat a number of the "snipes," Mouquin's "black gang" of machinists and boilermen. One of them, Machinist's Mate Frank Bukovich, saw the problem, raced over, grabbed a shell, and passed it on. Heyman slammed the breach closed and ordered the gun aimed. A moment later, Heyman yelled "Fire!" and the 3-inch gun spat an armor-piercing shell at the U-boat. The "snipes" cheered and clapped when a flash of light and shrapnel spinning away into the darkness indicated a hit on the conning tower. Heyman quickly loaded again, the #3 loader now back in action. As the men behind them continued to cheer, the #5 gun crew fired again and then again.

Lieutenant DeLong had, in the meantime, been having his problems. He had been ordered to fire his torpedoes, but his torpedo crewmen were still not all on station, the rest probably standing somewhere on deck, stunned at what was happening. Moreover, the U-boat was lying just off the *Roper*'s starboard side and DeLong's torpedoes were adjusted for curved fire. To hit the U-boat, the torpedoes would have to be reset. Crawling down under the torpedo tubes, DeLong laboriously began to hand rotate the aiming mechanism on a torpedo. Before he could complete the task, he heard Heyman's 3-inch gun ring out again and then there were shouts. He looked up just as the submarine began to sink, stern-first. Men were pouring out of it, going into the sea, yelling and waving at the men of the *Roper*. It was too late for the torpedoes. The *Roper* had sunk a U-boat!

Or had it? As the U-boat disappeared under the sea in a swirl of phosphorescence, Howe, silent until then, ordered Tebo to move the *Roper* away. He was not convinced that the U-boat had been sunk or scuttled. The British had advised their American counterparts that U-boat skippers would do anything to win, even abandoning part of their crew to make their attackers think they were sunk, only to move out of the killing zone and then turn back to put a torpedo into the attacking force. The *Roper* surged ahead and then turned as Black yelled out a strong sonar contact. Howe surmised it was either another U-boat or the same one, still maneuvering—there was no way to tell. It didn't matter. The best defense, the British had also said, was to attack. Howe ordered the *Roper* toward the contact.

The old destroyer plunged forward, her long guywire moaning and then howling in the wind like a mournful, crying banshee. Ahead, the crew of the U-boat, each in a lifejacket, were yelling in both German and English, their anguished voices drifting up to the stunned *Roper* crew. "*Bitte* (Please)! *Bitte!*," they were yelling. "*Kamerade.* Please! Help me! Save me!"

The *Roper* kept roaring ahead until she plowed into the struggling, yelling Germans. Lieutenant DeLong, still at his torpedoes, leaned over the side and looked at one youthful German as he swept by. "*Kamerade, bitte!*" the U-boat crewman pleaded, clawing at the side of the destroyer. In a frozen moment, American and German made contact, one looking helplessly down while the other opened his mouth in dreadful supplication. Then the moment was past, the *Roper* sweeping on. Dr. Johnson was also at the rail toward the bow. When he heard the yelling and saw the men in the water, he tried to release a large lifering but found the bolts painted over and frozen. He, like the other men on deck, could do nothing for the pleading Germans. Many of them didn't want to, in any case. These were the men responsible for all of the death and destruction they had been witness to for weeks. Let them drown!

If there had been confusion and hesitation on the bridge of the *Roper* at the start of the engagement, there was now nothing but calm and clarity of purpose. The soundman had placed the target. At just the proper interval, Tebo gave the order and eleven depth charges rolled off the stern of the *Roper*. They were set for 100 feet. The *Roper* kept going. The German crew, bobbing in the destroyer's furious wake, saw the charges drop into their midst and began to scream.

The exploding charges were felt on the *Roper*. WHUMP! The old ship trembled. There were leaks. WHUMP!-WHUMP!-WHUMP! Ten times, the ocean lit up in an expanding white circle of death that suddenly contracted and pushed up in a geyser of tremendous force. The *Roper* turned to make another run, but Black was no longer getting any solid sonar returns. The Germans in the water weren't yelling anymore, either. Howe ordered the *Roper* slowed. Her cable stopped moaning and soon the only sound that came from her was from her quietly throbbing engines. Somebody snapped the searchlight off and the *Roper* slid forward, a dark apparition on a slick sea, as an eerie silence crept across the black water. The officers on the bridge looked at one another for a moment, and then Commander Norton turned on his heel and made his way to his cabin to write his report. What had been done had been done. Some sense would have to be made of it. The first German U-boat had been sunk by an American surface vessel in World War II. Who had done what and when? The navy would demand to know.

For the rest of the long night, the *Roper* steamed back and forth in the vicinity of the sinking, always listening and looking. If there was another U-boat in the area, or if the one thought sunk was still somehow operating, Howe was not going to allow the *Roper* to be attacked by it. At 0120, the men were allowed to secure from General Quarters. Still not quite understanding what had happened, many of them remained on deck, quietly talking over the events. At 0201, three small vessels, presumably coast guard, came into view showing their masthead lights and playing searchlights around the horizon.

At 0607, with a crimson dawn spreading across the eastern
sky, a PBY seaplane contacted the *Roper* with a report of a
large oil slick and a mass of debris. It marked the slick with a
smoke bomb and then circled while Howe moved the *Roper*
over and dropped two obligatory depth charges. Another airplane appeared and then another and excitedly reported seeing men in the water. Howe directed the *Roper* to the area. He
ordered Dr. Johnson into the whaleboat with the admonition
to bring back everyone he found, dead or alive.

Dr. Johnson, with two crewmen, set forth into a nightmar-
ish scene. Dozens of German U-boat crewmen were floating in
the oily water, their arms and legs spread-eagled, stomachs
pushed in, eyes clots of blood, pink froth running from their
mouths. Dr. Johnson and the crewmen grimly began to pull
the bodies, most of them still in their escape lungs, aboard. He
expected to find some of the Germans alive at first, but then he
realized they were all going to be dead. Just as with the *Jacob
Jones*'s crewmen, the internal organs of the crew of the U-boat
had been ruptured when the *Roper*'s depth charges had gone
off beneath them. Before Dr. Johnson could finish picking up
the bodies, however, the soundman on duty on the *Roper* made
a sharp sonar contact. Howe still thought there might be another U-boat in the area. The British he had talked to had
insisted the Germans never patrolled alone. After ensuring
that Dr. Johnson was out of harm's way, he moved his ship
over the stationary contact. Large air bubbles rose steadily to
the surface. Four depth charges were dropped on the site and
then an orange buoy was put out to mark it. He was now
certain this was the wreck of the U-boat the *Roper* had sunk the
night before. To speed the recovery of the bodies, Howe ordered Tebo to man a second whaleboat and assist Dr. Johnson.
It was an ugly assignment for the young Annapolis graduate.
The warming day had caused the bodies to bloat and one of
them had been hit in the face with a .50-caliber round. Tebo
could only thank God it was the Germans who had lost the
battle and not the crew of the *Roper*. In all, the two boats
would return to the destroyer with twenty-nine bodies. His
diary tucked into a pocket, Erich Degenkolb was one of them.
That diary along with other papers floating in the debris

would confirm that the U-boat sunk was the *U-85*. Two bodies, riddled by Chief Wright's machine gun, were searched by
Tebo and then allowed to sink. Of the bodies recovered, two
were officers. The captain of the *U-85*, Eberhard Greger, was
not found.

Howe ordered the bodies stacked amidships on deck. *Roper*
crewmen began to gather around them. They wanted souve-
nirs. There was anger throughout the ship. At first, it had
been turned inward, men arguing with each other on what
could or should have been done the night before. Now, the
anger turned toward the bodies. Everybody thought they deserved something from the Germans, these *bastards* who had
caused all of the death they had witnessed. To defuse the situation, Howe ordered canvas spread over the bodies and sent a
crewman to stand guard. Seven airplanes orbited above the
*Roper* along with a blimp. A British trawler was also heaving
into the area, her crew experienced antisubmarine personnel.
Howe was more than ready to leave it all to them. He turned
his destroyer toward Norfolk and left at high speed. After the
*Roper* stood in at Lynnhaven Roads, a navy tug appeared and
her captain told Howe he had been sent for the Germans. The
bodies and their belongings were transferred and the tug
pulled away. As the men of the *Roper* watched in disbelief,
some of the crew of the tug descended on the corpses and
began to go through their pockets. No one said anything
aboard the *Roper*. They were all too exhausted at that point to
bother. They just watched.[18]

The *Roper* did not stay anchored long. Ten minutes after
the crew of the *U-85* were transferred, Howe ordered the destroyer back out to sea. On the same night the *U-85* was sunk,
another U-boat had sunk the tanker *Empire Thrush* off Hatteras.[19] The *Roper*'s war was still on. The war was not quite
over for the *U-85* and her crewmen, either. Naval Intelligence
received the bodies in Norfolk and took them immediately to a
small hangar at the Naval Air Station. There, they were
spread out on a canvas mat for search and analysis. It was
sourly noted by the officers in charge of the investigation that
many articles had probably already been taken from the bod-

ies prior to their delivery. After photographs were taken, each *U-85* crewman was stripped to his underclothing and a thorough search made for personal effects. Any found were then placed in individual envelopes keyed to a number assigned each body. Identification proved to be easy by either identification discs, name tapes on clothing, or other effects. Fingerprint cards were made and these, along with the envelopes containing the personal effects, the clothing, and four enlarged photographs (two side views and two front views) were wrapped in individual packages so that they could be easily identified. A naval medical doctor was called in and told to carefully examine each body to establish the cause of death. An individual report on each body was made up. Typical was Erich Degenkolb's:

Age: 25
Height: 72″
Weight: 170 lbs.
Hair: Blonde
Eyes: Blue
Beard: Yes
Tattoos: None
Condition: Good
Color: Face blue, ears purple, neck and chest spotted pink
Bruises: Forehead
Wounds: None
Life Preserver Apparatus: Rubberized air pocket type, yellow
Clothing: Cover-all top, trousers, no cap
Date of Death: 14 April 1942
Time of Death: 0050

After the analysis, a decision had to be quickly made on what to do with the bodies. At the Naval Air Station word had spread about the *U-85* crew, and the curious were already gathering. The commander of the station also wanted his hangar back. It was decided, therefore, to bury the bodies the same day and to do so, if not secretly, then as quietly as possible. Despite newspaper articles about it and the evidence that swept up on American shores every day, the war off the East Coast was still very much a military secret. To try to explain away the bodies of a U-boat crew to the public would have created an embarrassing flap. When it had to, Navy Intelligence could act quickly. When it was discovered that neither civilian morticians in the area nor the U.S. Naval Hospital in Portsmouth could immediately provide enough caskets, twenty-nine standard caskets and shipping boxes were found and quickly purchased from the Veterans Administration for a total cost of $1,193.55. Each body, still in its underclothing, was placed in an individual casket that was in turn sealed in a shipping box.

After it was dark, a convoy of trucks arrived, picked up the boxes, and transported them, several officers, a Catholic chaplain, a Protestant chaplain, and a firing party of twenty-four seamen to the National Cemetery in Hampton, Virginia. The convoy was met at the cemetery by a Provost Marshal major, eight army officers, twenty Military Police (to act as honorary pallbearers), and fifty-two prisoners, all from Fort Monroe, Virginia. The prisoners were there to dig and later fill in the graves. The caskets, still in their shipping boxes, were placed in the graves with burial services read by the Catholic chaplain followed by the Protestant chaplain. The sailors fired three volleys, Taps was sounded, the graves were filled, and everyone left.[20] To this day, all twenty-nine *U-85* crewmen are still buried in their numbered plots at the National Cemetery in Hampton.[21]

# 13

# The Bucket Brigades

There was little elation at 90 Church Street over the sinking of the *U-85* by the *Roper*. In fact, it was feared that the success might give credence to Admiral King's belief that a few destroyers on limited patrol were enough to stop the U-boats. But shortly after the sinking of the *U-85*, Admiral King issued a directive to the Atlantic Fleet headquarters ordering the permanent reassignment of three ships to Admiral Andrews at once and "others to bring destroyer strength . . . to a total of nine as soon as may be."[1] These three destroyers were immediately and almost, it seemed, eagerly reassigned. Why? The answer lay in the political pressure mounting on King to do something about the U-boats. The Petroleum Industry War Council Committee, a private group of big oilmen, had investigated the continuing sinkings of their tankers along the Atlantic coast and had determined that if the rate of attrition continued as it had in January, February, and March, there would not be enough oil available to continue the war effort past 1942.[2] These men had the ear of Roosevelt, the one man Admiral King listened to.

Even before Admiral King had reassigned the destroyers, the Eastern Sea Frontier was at least making progress toward becoming a reasonable adversary for the U-boats. On 1 April,

Admiral Andrews had a surface fleet of twenty-three large (90-foot and up) and forty-two small (75- and 83-foot) coast guard cutters, three 173-foot PCs, twelve old Eagle boats and converted yachts, and fourteen British armed trawlers. The trawlers, though hampered by their plodding speed, had already proved to be effective with their tough, aggressive crews. Moreover, eighty-four army and eighty-six navy planes located at nineteen bases from Bangor, Maine, to Jacksonville, Florida, were available for antisubmarine patrol.[3]

Although Admiral Andrews had come to the conclusion that a convoy system was the only way to successfully fight the U-boats, he had tried many other ideas. One that had come his way was that of using a fleet of auxiliary sailing yachts and motorboats as observers and pickets. The man behind it was Alfred Stanford of New York, commodore of the Cruising Club of America. Admiral King himself supported this idea, and eventually the famed "Hooligan Navy" was formed. This assorted collection of yachtsmen and Sunday sailors would serve with distinction and verve, if not effectiveness.[4]

In the same volunteer vein, Admiral Andrews made use of the civil air patrol (CAP) for reconnaissance, fire patrol, rescue work, and carrier and freighting service. At first, these light planes flown by private, volunteer pilots were only equipped with two-way radios, but later they would be armed with bombs. They were to become, in effect, an air force without "red tape," a group of men and women with boundless energy and enthusiasm who were willing to fly even in weather that kept the military grounded and, while doing so, pay for their own gas, equipment, and repairs. Their contribution to the U-boat war was to eventually be significant because the U-boat commanders were all deathly afraid of airplanes. The British, with their secret airborne radar, had managed to surprise many U-boats. As a result, it was a standing rule throughout the U-boat fleet to dive at the mere sight of an airplane. With the numbers of planes that CAP was able to put into the air daily, they almost surely disrupted many a U-boat commander's careful plans.[5]

On the technical front, as had already been shown with the *Roper*'s kill of the *U-85*, the application of radar in antisub-

marine warfare was obviously a good idea. The manufacture
of radar sets for naval use was becoming a high-priority item.
Another innovation waiting to come on line was high-fre-
quency direction-finders (HF/DF or "Huff-Duff"). These instruments took advantage of Doenitz's requirement that his
commanders radio headquarters at least once a day if possible.
As soon as a U-boat's aerial stuck up above the waves, the
Huff-Duffs, on both ships and land, would soon be taking
bearings on them all up and down the east coast. If there were
any ships and planes in the area, they would be immediately
vectored in on the unsuspecting submarine.[6]

Sonar and listening gear were also being improved and,
more importantly, the training of soundmen was getting better. A special school at Key West, Florida, had been developed
for officers and enlisted men alike to learn the techniques of
sonar in antisubmarine warfare. No longer did a man picked
to be soundman have to spend weeks and months learning on
the job and being trained and supervised by officers usually
more ignorant of the subject than he. A man coming out of
Key West could go aboard any ship and be ready to apply his
trade immediately.[7]

In April, Professor Philip M. Morse, a Massachusetts Institute of Technology physicist specializing in sound waves, accepted the directorship of a small group of physicists and stat-
isticians called the Anti-Submarine Warfare Operational
Research Group (ASWORG). Part of Captain Wilder D. Baker's Anti-Submarine Warfare Unit of the Atlantic Fleet, this
group of dedicated men were to begin applying scientific
methods to killing submarines. While the U-boat commanders
would continue to work the old way, using wile and cunning
and experience, the Americans were beginning to mobilize
their strengths, the strengths of organization and technology.[8]

All these things were coming. But Admiral Andrews still
had not managed to gain that which he believed he needed
most—the cooperation from the masters of the endangered
merchant vessels. Ever since the U-boats had arrived, these
men, wise in the ways of the sea and their vessels but hard-
headed, stubborn, and disrespectful when it came to the
United States Navy, had consistently ignored Andrews's sug-

gestions and orders. Each master seemed to have his own ideas on how to outsmart the U-boats. Some of them had steamed perilously close to shore and buoy markers, others far out to sea, off the regular trade routes. Some continued to display lights in darkness, most never bothered to zigzag, and radio security remained poor; names of ships and cargoes still, even after all the carnage of the first three months of 1942, were being radioed in the clear. All the technological and organizational innovations in the world would not help if this continued.

In early April, Admiral Andrews tried again to gain the merchantmen's cooperation. He issued a series of memoranda, encouraging the masters to pay attention to his suggestions and commands. In the memos, the merchantmen were praised for their courage and skill. They were vital to the war effort, it was said, and the navy recognized their importance. But it was also important that the masters pay attention to routing instructions, to zigzag both day and night, to keep their radios at 500 kilocycles for routing instructions, to traverse especially dangerous areas, such as Cape Hatteras, by day only, and to keep their ships darkened at night with lookouts alert. The U-boats were using every failure to comply with these instructions to sink ships and kill men.[9]

There were many elements in the navy that were not impressed with Admiral Andrews's memos and thought he was wasting his time. They contended that the only way to ever control the merchantmen, and particularly the tankers, was to have them all confiscated, manned, and operated by the navy.[10] Admiral Andrews thought that idea, though attractive, to be impractical. There was, however, one certain way to ensure the safety of the tankers. Admiral Andrews had thought about proposing it for some time if adequate forces were not otherwise provided to him. On 10 April, he wrote the secretary of the navy and advised him that "the sinking of ships, tankers especially, on this coast is a serious matter resulting, if continued, in dire consequences to our war effort." After requesting more fast ships to combat the U-boats, Admiral Andrews went on to say, "If such forces are not supplied in the near future, it is recommended that *consideration be given to the stoppage of tanker sailings* [italics author's own] until escort vessels become available."[11]

With this letter, the uniformed portion of the navy had admitted to its civilian supervisors that it could not, with the present forces available, control the U-boat menace just off American shores. Although Admiral King had supported Admiral Andrews's statements in the letter, it put him under even more pressure to do something, anything, to solve the U-boat problem. That was perhaps the reason he did not argue with Andrews when the Eastern Sea Frontier commander proposed a convoy system, even though Andrews himself had opposed such a system for months. King appointed an informal board with representatives from COMINICH, CINCLANT and the commanders of the Eastern, Caribbean, and Gulf Sea Frontiers to provide him with plans for convoys. This board was dominated by Admiral Andrews and Admiral Royal E. Ingersoll, commander in chief of the Atlantic Fleet. Admiral King took the recommendations from the board and wrote, "The principles enunciated and the general procedure suggested in this excellent report are concurred in." Admiral Andrews was given "all necessary authority to integrate this plan and to deal directly with agencies concerned."[12]

"Dolly" Andrews was pleased, even though he knew that his force was still too small to have a total convoy system. For one thing, the tankers and freighters were coming in from everywhere—the Caribbean, the Gulf of Mexico, even straight across the Atlantic. It was impossible for him to organize all of these ships into a single, unified convoy system. But Andrews was sure he could, with perseverance and ingenuity, make convoying work. He and his staff devised a temporary convoying system labeled the "Bucket Brigade," whereby ships would be moved from anchorage to anchorage by whatever local escort vessels were available. Andrews's staff had noticed that north of Hatteras good harbors were available approximately every 120 miles, which was about as far as a slow merchantman was likely to go in a day. There were not as many harbors available south of Hatteras, but where no harbors were available, net-protected anchorages would be established. There would be an estimated 120 to 130 ships requiring protection every day, but Andrews was certain he could manage if all of his ships stayed at sea as much as possible.[13]

While Andrews hurried to ready his "Bucket Brigade" system, the freighters and tankers continued to sail and the U-boats continued to attack them. Doenitz, anxious to sink as many ships in the American area as possible before countermeasures could be taken, radioed his commanders in early April that they had ". . . freedom of action according to fuel and state of defense. In order to make full use of the present favorable conditions for attack (new moon) they are ordered to start their return passage without fuel reserves. In emergency they can be supplied from tanker." The admiral was pushing his U-boats to the limit, stretching their endurance, gambling with the lives of the crews to sink tonnage before the Americans woke up and did something about it.[14]

He would receive no arguments from his "sea wolves." Five miles off Jacksonville, Florida, on the night of 10 April, the tanker *Gulfamerica* was silhouetted nicely against the city's lights for Hardegen and his *U-123*. In quick succession, Hardegen sent two torpedoes into the tanker's starboard side and then maneuvered in closer. The navy gun crew on the stern of the *Gulfamerica* started to man their 4-inch gun and then thought better of it when red tracers from the *U-123*'s machine gun spewed past them. For six days, the *Gulfamerica* would drift until finally sinking. Of her crew of forty-one civilians and seven navy gun crew, seventeen civilians and two navy men were lost.[15]

Kaleun Rolf Mützelburg of the *U-203* had taken Hardegen's place on the Cape Lookout station. Just before sunrise on 11 April, he torpedoed the tanker *Harry F. Sinclair, Jr.* The volatile cargo of gasoline and fuel oil immediately exploded, incinerating the captain, the radioman, and all the deck officers. Twenty-six crewmembers were picked up several hours later by the destroyer USS *Herbert* and the British trawler HMS *Hertsfordshire*. The *Sinclair* did not sink immediately, but the flames from her burning cargo kept the rescue ships away, so she was left to drift. Drift she did for four days until the *Senateur Duhamel*, another British trawler, managed to get a towing hawser on her. She was eventually towed to Baltimore, refitted, and returned to service as the *Annibal*.[16]

The destruction of the British freighter *Ulysses* provided an excellent example of the continuing disregard of Admiral Andrews's advice by the merchant masters. The *Ulysses*, her cargo primarily refugees from the war zone in the Far East, had proceeded directly up the coast toward Norfolk without informing either the Eastern Sea Frontier or the Port Director in New York of her intentions. Her master was certain that by providing a careful lookout, he could avoid any U-boats that might be lurking in the area. On the afternoon of 11 April, the *Ulysses* was approximately 40 miles southeast of Cape Lookout. The wind was moderate, the sea choppy, the visibility good. The lookouts saw nothing. Lassen of the *U-160* saw them quite well, however.

The first torpedo struck about 5 feet below the waterline. The master of the *Ulysses* immediately ordered a distress signal sent out, the first signal of any kind he had sent the authorities since entering the dangerous east coast waters. Ten lifeboats got away, all of the passengers and crew including a cat and three kittens safely aboard. Lassen would drill a total of four torpedoes into the ship before it finally sank.[17]

Surprised that the *Ulysses* was even in the area, the navy still responded fairly efficiently. Forty-five minutes after the first torpedo had struck, a navy Catalina flying boat and an army Flying Fortress were circling the scene of the attack. The destroyer USS *Manley*, en route from Norfolk to Charleston, S.C., was redirected to go to the rescue. She arrived several hours later and rescued, as her captain put it, "95 passengers, 128 white crew, and 67 Chinese crew." The two airplanes left as soon as the destroyer arrived, prompting the *Manley*'s captain to complain that he had been left as a perfect target for any nearby U-boat. Still, he persevered, and soon, passengers and crew, both "white and Chinese," were on their way safely to Charleston.[18]

The next morning, Mützelburg's *U-203* heavily damaged the Panamanian freighter *Stanvac Melbourne* off Cape Fear.[19] Hardegen and the *U-123*, still having a "happy time" off Georgia, torpedoed the sugar freighter *Leslie* on the night of 12

April. Four crewmembers were killed in the explosion, and one was blown overboard. The surviving twenty-seven pushed off in two lifeboats. Though a distress signal had been sent, no one came to investigate. Late the next morning, the *Leslie*'s lifeboats came ashore about a mile north of Cape Canaveral Lighthouse. The crewman knocked overboard was miraculously found by the tanker *Esso Bayonne* and put safely ashore in Key West.[20]

By mid-April, the U-boats had been attacking shipping off the American east coast for three months. It appeared that their successes would continue indefinitely, and Admiral Doenitz could not resist crowing about it. "Before the U-boat attack on America was begun," he wrote, "it was suspected that American anti-submarine activity would be weak and inexperienced; this conjecture has been fully confirmed . . . The crews [on anti-submarine vessels] are careless, inexperienced and little persevering in a hunt. In several cases, escort vessels—coast guard ships and destroyers—having established the presence of a U-boat, made off instead of attacking her . . . On the whole . . . the boats' successes are so great, that their operation near the coast is further justified and will continue."[21]

Despite Doenitz's trumpeting, Admiral Andrews was still on the job. Lieutenant Alger had been prepared to take the *Dione* to sea, but on the morning of 14 April was instead ordered to report to the commander, Fifth Naval District, in Norfolk for a briefing. The briefing turned out to be the plans Admiral Andrews had devised for his "Bucket Brigade" convoys. Alger and the others of the coastal patrol were told that, henceforth, they, in concert with navy destroyers, would be responsible for convoying all tankers and freighters around Cape Hatteras to Wimble Shoals. All merchantmen requiring to pass this dangerous stretch of sea had been ordered to put into safe harbors for the night and then, each morning, assemble in an assigned area for convoying.

Alger hurried back to the *Dione*, anxious to go to sea. Although he had his doubts, he hoped that the limited convoy system would work. Even while the meeting had been going on, Mützelburg had sunk the big freighter *Empire Thrush*

within sight of the Cape Hatteras Lighthouse. The freighter
sank in shallow water, her mast and funnel remaining above
water. There she would remain for many days, a stark reminder of the U-boats' mastery of the American coast.[22]

At twelve noon on 14 April, the *Dione* rendezvoused with
the *Dickerson* near the Diamond Shoals lighted bell buoy. Although McCormick was on the bridge with Alger, Lieutenant
(j.g.) Dick Bacchus now stood as the navigator and executive
officer. Bacchus had arrived on 11 April from the coast guard
cutter *Modoc*. A native of Norfolk, he had rejoiced at his orders
to the *Dione*, since it would allow him to be close to home. The
day of his arrival, he had headed over to the Norfolk Yacht and
Country Club to do "a little elbow bending." While there, he
had met another coast guard officer, introduced as "Jimmy
Alger." When asked where he was headed, Bacchus had replied, "The *Dione*. Know anything about her?" Alger had
laughed. "Hell, man. That's my ship! Welcome aboard!"
Bacchus couldn't remember what time he and Alger had left
the club that night, but by the time they did, they had become
good friends.
    Now, however, they were on the bridge of a fighting coast
guard cutter, and Alger was the commander and Bacchus his
exec. Friendship could not exist in that setting. Bacchus was
also very much aware of the critical eye being constantly cast
on him by the man he had replaced, Lieutenant McCormick.
McCormick had decided to stay on board as long as he could
so as to help Bacchus learn his duties.
    Alger watched the *Dickerson* plow ahead, going faster than
the *Dione* could keep up. The destroyer seemed enormously
confident, flashing her lights at the two merchant vessels that
had shown up for the convoy and swerving around them almost like a sheep dog barking at the heels of his flock. When
the coast guard cutter *Cayuboga* arrived, Alger was somewhat
amused. The escorts outnumbered the escorted. The *Dickerson*,
however, persisted and soon had the small convoy lumbering
north. Zigzagging was the doctrine for a fast convoy or for
small ones with a narrow front, but, because of the short distances involved, the Bucket Brigades would generally follow a

straight course. The *Dione* was ordered to take up a position on the port bow of the leading merchantman. Six hours later, both cutters were released by the navy destroyer, and the two freighters left to go their own way up the coast. Alger turned the *Dione* south. He would patrol during the night, working his way toward the next convoy rendezvous point. He thought about the enthusiasm of the *Dickerson* that day and wondered if it would last. "It would not surprise me," he said half-seriously to McCormick and Bacchus, "if one day we arrive at the rendezvous point and find ourselves all alone."

The *Dione* went back to patrolling for the night around Lookout Shoals. The next morning, Alger got back to the Cape Lookout lighted bell buoy in time to meet the *Dickerson* again and two British trawlers. This time there were three merchantmen in the convoy, two American tankers and a freighter. The two tankers were modern and fast, so by noon they and the *Dickerson* had disappeared over the horizon leaving the *Dione* and the trawlers and the freighter behind. Alger decided to be aggressive as a convoy escort even though the doctrine called for him to keep his ship close alongside. He ordered the *Dione* to range out and drop depth charges on suspected echoes. He felt he had a far better chance of keeping the U-boat off balance through this tactic. As McCormick had done when first taking the *Dione* on patrol, Alger was now devising new tactics to fit the situation. By late afternoon, the *Dione* dropped off the freighter and once more went on patrol.

The morning of the 16th again found the *Dickerson* patiently waiting at the Cape Lookout rendezvous for the *Dione* and any merchantmen that wanted to be convoyed. This time she even had the destroyer *Noa* with her. There were five ships in the convoy, three tankers and two freighters and, once again, the ships were safely escorted around Hatteras and released. The "Bucket Brigades," as advertised, were working.

That night, the *Dione*'s sonar operator got an excellent echo, so Alger stayed up through all the watches, ordering a number of depth-charge runs. McCormick and Bacchus stayed up with him. The results were negative. At sunrise, the *Dione* was back at the rendezvous. The *Dickerson* wasn't there but the *Roper* was, still on its arduous patrol after the fateful *U-85*

sinking. Two tankers and two freighters were escorted with
no problems, although an echo caused the *Dione* to veer off and
depth-charge the contact. Wreckage from the Norwegian
whaling factory ship *Lancing,* sunk by Topp's *U-552* on 7
April, came floating to the surface.

The *Dione* and her crew had now fallen into a routine.
Meet the navy in the morning and convoy all day and then
patrol alone all night. Since the Bucket Brigades had begun,
not a single ship had been torpedoed near Cape Hatteras or
Lookout. One hundred miles out, however, Hirsacker in the
*U-572* had bagged the small freighter *Desert Light* on 16 April.
Hirsacker had attacked in broad daylight, launching two torpedoes. One man aboard the Panamanian-registered ship was
drowned in the fireroom, but the rest of the thirty crewmembers were able to get off in a single lifeboat.[23]

On the morning of 19 April, the *Dione* showed up at the
Cape Lookout Shoals lighted whistle buoy to rendezvous with
the convoy as usual. She had spent part of the night just off
Wimble Shoals working an excellent echo but had reluctantly
broken off the contact as dawn neared. Waiting for her was an
impressive variety of merchantmen, the *M. F. Elliot,* the *Pan
New York,* the *Pan Virginia,* the *Nortind,* the *Axtell J. Byles,* the
*Hampton Lodge,* the *E. W. Sinclair,* and the *Hopetarn.* It was the
biggest Bucket Brigade convoy yet. But just as Alger had
feared would eventually happen, the navy wasn't there. Radio
transmissions soon established that the destroyers had been
called elsewhere. Soon, however, a British trawler and then
another came chugging into the area followed by an 88-foot
coast guard vessel.

At least the *Dione* wasn't completely alone. She was, however, the senior vessel, and Alger had no choice but to form up
the group and head north as best he could. Some of his officers
were disgruntled with the navy and voiced that in no uncertain terms. Alger, however, said nothing. It was a case of too
many jobs and too few ships. But there were some tempting
targets in the convoy, especially the big tankers *Axtell J. Byles*
and *E. W. Sinclair.* Alger ordered the *Dione* into the lead of the
convoy and began to screen ahead. The British trawlers and
the small CG boat could do little except strain to keep up.

When Cape Hatteras loomed into view, tension crackled aboard every ship in the convoy. The convoy was vulnerable, anyone could see that. Without a fast destroyer to sweep out to the horizon and back, the slow escorts could do little beyond providing themselves as targets. Still, bit by bit, the convoy moved north without incident. By 1800 hours, the convoy was nearing the drop-off point, and Alger was beginning to think they had made it. He had used the *Dione* as if she were a destroyer, aggressively screening and even flying back to pick up stragglers several times, blinking angrily at them to keep up. The *Dione* had put in a tough day and was looking forward to dropping off the sometimes maddeningly independent merchantmen. But still they were proud of what they and their ship had accomplished.

One of the *Dione*'s crewmen, however, was feeling something other than pride. Seaman First Class John J. Fleming had gone to his bunk after his watch was over, but instead of dropping off to sleep as usual, he found himself having one of the strangest experiences of his life. It was as if a presence had entered the cabin, climbed up on his bunk, and sat on his chest. Gasping for breath, Fleming was consumed with unreasonable fear and close to panic. Although he hadn't touched it since he had been aboard the *Dione*, he reached into his sea chest, grabbed his rosary, and started praying. Gradually, the weight lifted, but when his time came to go back on duty, Fleming was still haunted by the spectre of some unknown menace. Just as he got to his station on the flying bridge, he looked out to sea. Coming directly at him and the *Dione* was a torpedo.

Before Fleming could say a word, an airplane, coming out of the sun, suddenly dived over the convoy. It was a navy plane and it was anxiously rocking its wings. "Oh no," Alger thought. "What does he see that I don't?"

That question was quickly answered. Radioman Swede Larson had just emerged from the mess deck and was talking to Chief Electrician's Mate Pugh about some electrical problems when a younger seaman grasped his shirt and tugged, saying "Look, look!" and pointing right down the airplane's track. Swede's conversation with Pugh ended as he saw a tor-

pedo heading straight for the *Dione*. He looked up at the bridge
and saw that Lieutenant Alger had also seen the torpedo.
Above him on the flying bridge stood John Fleming, trans-
fixed, as if he were seeing an angel of death.

Swede ran forward to his General Quarters station just as
Alger gave the order for full right rudder and full speed ahead.
The *Dione* heeled over, gaining speed while her crew hung on.
Swede saw the torpedo pass the *Dione*'s starboard quarter,
missing by about 20 yards. He turned to follow its track and
saw it was heading directly for the tanker beside them. Aboard
that tanker, the *Axtell J. Byles*, lookouts also followed the airplane's course and then looked down at the water. Speeding
toward them were the torpedo that had missed the *Dione* plus
one other from Kapitänleutnant Heinrich Zimmermann's
*U-136*. Captain John D. Baldwin yelled "hard aport!" and gave
the alarm but it was too late. Although he dodged the torpedo
meant for the *Dione*, the second torpedo struck on the starboard side, tearing a gaping hole in the hull above and below
the waterline and collapsing the bridge and midship house.

Alger thought he had spotted a periscope and turned toward it. He soon had the *Dione* pouring over the spot, dropping eight depth charges on two runs. When navy bombers
began to dive-bomb, he returned to the torpedoed tanker. The
*Axtell J. Byles*, loaded to the brim with 87,000 barrels of crude
oil, was leaking from her wound, but luckily the oil had not
ignited.[24]

Alger spoke to Captain Baldwin, who advised that he
could still proceed. Alger maneuvered the convoy back together and began to move them northward, while behind
more airplanes joined the attack on Zimmermann. The *U-136*,
however, had retreated as soon as its torpedoes had been
launched and was snaking for deep water.

There was chagrin and anger aboard the *Dione*. This time,
a U-boat had attacked a vessel directly under their care, and
that had made it a personal, direct affront. The shepherds had
watched the wolf maul their flock. The death and destruction
that had covered their ocean now filled their hearts.

# 14

# The Tankers Are Stopped

On the afternoon of 17 April 1942, Kapitänleutnant Adalbert Schnee of the *U-201* attacked the neutral Argentine motor tanker *Victoria*.[1] This attack would initiate a diplomatic brawl that would eventually involve the Roosevelt administration, the Argentinian government, and even the German Nazi government.

Of all the South American countries, Argentina had tried from the very first to maintain a strict stance of neutrality in the war. This gave her the right, her government believed, to get rich by trading with both sides. So it was that one of her tankers, the *Victoria*, was plowing into a typically strong northwest wind off Cape Hatteras when Schnee fired two torpedoes into her side. Schnee, one of Doenitz's favorites, was a very successful commander, having already sunk fifteen tankers and freighters since he had become a U-boat commander in 1940.[2] His crew doted on him, proudly painting a snowman on the conning tower in honor of his name (Schnee translates to Snow in German). When Schnee won the Knight's Cross, his men painted a cross on the snowman as well.[3]

In 1945, Schnee would receive the ultimate honor from Doenitz, command of the *U-2511*, one of only two Type XXI U-boats to ever go to sea. The Type XXI was the most advanced submarine built during World War II. It was twice as large as the old Type VII and able to stay underwater longer and dive deeper than any submarine up to that time.[4] But on the afternoon of 17 April 1942, Kaleun Schnee was just another young Type VII U-boat skipper who had made the long arduous journey across the Atlantic to get some of the easy kills off the United States. And along came the *Victoria*, big spotlights playing on bright Argentinian flags painted on her sides. Schnee either didn't notice the flags or didn't care. A tanker was a tanker.

Since the *Victoria* had left Argentina, she had heard many distress signals from Allied tankers and freighters being attacked by German raiders. The *Victoria*'s captain, however, was a firm believer in his country's neutrality and felt going to the aid of an Allied ship, no matter what the situation, might be construed to be a violation of this stance. His duty was to deliver his load of linseed oil to New York, pick up another cargo, and carry it back home and that was all. Everything changed, however, when the first of Schnee's torpedoes plowed into the port side of his ship.

The captain rang the alarm and ordered his radioman to send out a distress signal. Within minutes there was an acknowledgment from the United States Navy. The captain then ordered identification flags to be sent up in prominent display to stop another attack. Then, along with the rest of his crew, he hastily departed in two lifeboats.

Forty miles away at that moment, the old minesweeper USS *Owl* was sailing southeast from New York to Bermuda with an oil barge in tow. When she heard the *Victoria*'s distress signal, the minesweeper changed course and went as fast as she could to the rescue. Five hours later, the *Victoria* was found, completely deserted. There was a strong light illuminating the Argentine flag and other lights that showed the still bravely flapping identification pennants, but that was all. As the sun rose the next morning, two large holes could be seen in the *Victoria*'s port side, but little damage could be seen beneath the waterline. The captain of the *Owl* decided that the *Victoria* was still seaworthy and salvageable. He called the Naval Operating Base at Bermuda to inform them of this, let his crew have breakfast, released the oil barge, and began towing the tanker.

When Admiral Andrews was fully informed of the *Owl's* plight, he radioed that he was sending the USS *Sagamore* to assist. In the meantime, the *Owl* had come across a lifeboat that contained none other than the chief officer and twenty other members of the crew of the *Victoria*. The *Owl* picked them up, and soon the *Victoria* was operating under her own power, the *Owl* escorting.

Before they had gone far, the destroyer *Nicholson* appeared. Aboard her was the *Victoria's* captain and the remaining crew-members. Although this set of survivors seemed reluctant to leave the safety of the destroyer, they were finally convinced and the small convoy continued westward, a full crew manning the *Victoria*. On the morning of 20 April, the *Sagamore* appeared and relieved the *Owl* and soon the tanker was safely in port. The United States, by any yardstick, had done Argentina a very large favor.

But the Argentines didn't quite see things that way. Although the *Victoria's* owners coughed up a gift of $20,000 for the Navy Relief Society to show their appreciation, the Argentinian Foreign Office questioned that their ship had been attacked by a German submarine at all. Maybe what had really happened was that the *Victoria* had struck two American mines. The United States Navy gruffly replied that it was not in the habit of placing minefields in primary sea-lanes, but for six weeks afterwards the Argentines hid behind this flimsy possibility. Finally, the Argentinian Minister of Marine issued a two-hundred-page report on the incident squarely placing the blame on the Germans. Subsequently, the Nazi government apologized, the Argentines accepted, and it was hoped by the two nations that it would all be forgotten.

As it turned out, the United States War Shipping Administration would have the last word. Busy as always trying to gain any possible vessel for convoying across the Atlantic, the federal agency happened upon the *Victoria* in July 1942 and "requisitioned" her. Argentina was paid a fair price, the *Victoria* renamed, and soon she was part of the American merchant marine. She would never again fly the Argentine flag. It had

been one of the stranger ship transfers of the war. As it was,
all concerned were glad to dispense with it.[5]

In mid-April, the U-boats discovered by chance that there
was another Torpedo Junction besides the one just off the
North Carolina coast. For weeks, freighters and tankers had
been sweeping far out to sea off Cape Hatteras, nearly 300
miles out, and had been escaping most of the carnage and also,
not incidentally, the navy's limited convoy system.[6]

At this new spot on the night of 19 April, Hirsacker in the
*U-572* sank the large British freighter *Empire Dryden* and then,
an hour later and a bit to the south, Oberleutnant Ludwig
Forster launched a torpedo into the port side of the American
freighter *Steelmaker*. A big hole was ripped in the ship's side
and the cargo, tons of war materiel destined for Iran, began to
spill out. The master, Leonard Dukes, ordered his ship abandoned. All engines were stopped and two lifeboats launched.
Forster watched, playing his searchlight over the ship and the
lifeboats, and then moved in for a closer inspection. He found
the lifeboat containing Dukes and questioned him carefully
about the name of the ship he had sunk, the cargo, destination,
and tonnage. Dukes answered truthfully, knowing he was at
the U-boat commander's mercy. Forster leaned forward on the
conning tower fairing and listened, and then said that he was
sorry he had had to sink Dukes's ship. "But this is war," Forster explained unnecessarily. "You will be rescued, however.
Do not worry. I shall send your position by radio. Thank you
for the name of your ship."[7]

Forster disappeared below with several German lookouts
left on the conn. Some further conversation was attempted,
but none of the youthful lookouts seemed to know much English. After about fifteen minutes, the lookouts disappeared
and the *U-654* began to move away. Soon it had disappeared
into the darkness, leaving the two lifeboats alone. Dukes ordered sea anchors put out to keep them in the area in case
Forster had radioed in their position as promised. But by the
next afternoon, rescue had not come, so the lifeboats put up
sails and set a course to the west-northwest. Try as they might,
the two lifeboats could not stay together and by nightfall had

lost sight of each other. Two days later, one boat with eighteen crewmembers and five navy gunners was found by the navy destroyer *Rowan*. The other lifeboat, the one containing Dukes, was not so fortunate. It would take ten days before it was found by the British freighter *Pacific Explorer* about 50 miles off Frying Pan Shoals Lightship. Two men had died of exposure in it, but the rest, twenty-seven men, were taken safely in to Morehead City.[8]

Meanwhile, the new Torpedo Junction was becoming a killing ground. Like cattle before a slaughterhouse, dozens of merchantmen were plodding toward it, unaware that the Germans were onto their new route. An hour after the *Steelmaker* had gone down, the British tanker *Harpagon* was torpedoed by the *U-109*. Only eight men would survive, all picked up from a raft by the Argentine ship *Rio Diamante* over a month later. They would be landed at Buenos Aires, half a world away.[9]

Eighteen hours after the *Harpagon* was sunk, Forster destroyed the small Swedish freighter *Agra*.[10] Kapitänleutnant Horst Uphoff in the *U-84* sent down the Panamanian tanker *Chenango* shortly afterwards, killing all but two of the crew.[11] Schnee, also alert to the new area and in his first attack since the *Victoria*, torpedoed the small Norwegian steamer *Bris* on the night of 20 April. Two lifeboats got away, but some of the men died when they dived overboard and were sucked into the propeller. Thirteen men in one of the lifeboats would survive after a harrowing journey all the way to the South Carolina coast.[12]

At noon on the 21st, the American freighter *Pipestone County*, en route from Trinidad to New York with 4,970 tons of bauxite, had managed to get 100 miles north of this new killing ground but unluckily droned right into the sights of the *U-576* just as that U-boat was coming in from its transatlantic journey. Kapitänleutnant Hans-Dieter Heinicke immediately shot a torpedo at the freighter. The crew of the *Pipestone County*, with remarkable calm, managed to launch four well-supplied lifeboats without sustaining any casualties, even though their ship sank within 20 minutes of being torpedoed. The crew in one of the lifeboats would be rescued by the *Dione*'s sister ship *Calypso*. Two of the other lifeboats were

picked up by the British freighter *Tropic Star* and taken into
Boston. The fourth lifeboat would make a landing at Cape
May, New Jersey. Remarkably, not one crewmember had been
lost in the ordeal.[13]

Schnee stayed at the new killing grounds as long as he
could. He had no idea of the uproar he had caused by sinking
the *Victoria* and only wanted to sink as many ships as he could
with the torpedoes remaining. On the night of 21 April in
bright moonlight, his lookouts spotted the American passen-
ger/motor transport *San Jacinto* out of New York en route to
San Juan, Puerto Rico, with 79 crewmembers, 104 passengers,
and a general cargo. Schnee sent a single torpedo into the side
of the ship and then directed his searchlight over it to see the
results. He saw that he had hit a passenger ship and ordered a
cease-fire until the ship had been abandoned. Aboard the *San
Jacinto*, the elderly master, Captain Robert W. Hart of Ruther-
ford, New Jersey, ordered his ship stopped and the lifeboats
manned. Although his officers implored him to do so, he refused to leave the bridge, although he did agree to wear a life
vest.

One of the passengers was eighteen-year-old Lawrence W.
Earle, son of a former Pennsylvania governor, traveling with
Harry O. King, also eighteen. The boys were on a holiday,
going to visit Lawrence's brother in the Bahamas. So ignorant
had they and their parents been of the carnage going on offshore, they had thought little of the U-boat menace when making their plans. Together with the rest of the passengers and
crew, they headed for the lifeboats and rafts. Soon, all but
Captain Hart and his first officer were off the *San Jacinto*,
which was rapidly settling. The officer pleaded with Captain
Hart but the old man just sadly shook his head. It was his
duty, he believed, to go down with his ship. The last time
anyone would see Captain Hart, he would still be on his
bridge with a resigned but calm expression on his face.

Schnee had watched until he believed that all had gotten
off the *San Jacinto*. Then he unlimbered his 88-mm deck gun
and proceeded to circle the ship, shelling it repeatedly. In an
hour, the *San Jacinto* slipped forever beneath the waves.
Schnee submerged shortly afterwards.

All night long, the lifeboats and rafts drifted on the cold, dark sea. Miss Louise Harshbarger, 26, of Fort Wayne, Indiana, was in one of the lifeboats. What she believed to be her great adventure in life, a secretary's job at the Naval Air Station in San Juan, had ended in a crowded lifeboat in the Graveyard of the Atlantic. Many of the people had been injured, including three children who had bad cuts. Using a flashlight she found, she used salt water and then iodine from a small medicine kit to clean the wounds as best she could. In another lifeboat, young Lawrence Earle and Harry King were sitting in stunned silence as the war finally came home. Across from them, a five-year-old boy whimpered in the arms of his grandmother. He had both of his legs broken, the bones sticking through his skin. Blood flowed in a gush at every heartbeat. There was nothing anyone could do but pray. Within an hour, the boy died. When the sun finally rose the next morning, the woman still cradled her grandchild. Some crewmembers gently took the boy away from her and, after a short service, slid him overboard. When they turned back to console the grandmother, they found that she had also died. Shortly afterwards, she was also gently placed in the sea.

In the early afternoon, the destroyer *Rowan* arrived for rescue. Louise Harshbarger watched as survivors in two of the lifeboats were picked up, but then the destroyer seemed to lose interest in the rest of them and picked up steam. Two depth charges were dropped by the *Rowan* and then the ship turned and attacked again. This attack brought up oil and debris, and the survivors in the remaining lifeboats and rafts let out a cheer. They believed the *Rowan* had gotten a piece of the U-boat that had attacked them. Actually, all the *Rowan* had done was bring up a part of the *San Jacinto*. Schnee, by then, had sunk the British freighter *Derryheen* just a few miles away and then headed east for home. All of the remaining survivors of the *San Jacinto* were eventually taken aboard the *Rowan*. Five crewmembers, including Captain Hart, and nine passengers had died.[14] There is no record as to whether Louise Harshbarger was able to continue seeking her adventure in Puerto Rico or whether the two boys, Lawrence Earle and

Harry King, ever had their vacation with Lawrence's brother in the Bahamas.

Lieutenant (j.g.) Nelson McCormick saluted the standard one last time and departed his beloved *Dione*. He was on his way to Key West per his orders to assume his new command. In some ways, it was a traumatic moment for the young officer. He felt no sense of satisfaction or accomplishment as he left, despite the hearty send-off his brother officers and the crew had given him. It seemed to McCormick that he had worked and fought for nearly five months in vain. For all of his aggressiveness both as commander and then as executive officer of one of the finest fighting ships afloat, he had seen nothing but the death and destruction of that which he had been charged to protect. In fact, his last day aboard had seen the *Axtell J. Byles* torpedoed, a ship that had been directly under the *Dione*'s protection. To McCormick, that had been humiliating. He took one last, long look at the *Dione* and then turned away. Hunching his shoulders against the chill wind off the bay at Little Creek, he carried his meager belongings toward the bus stop.

Lieutenant Alger watched McCormick go. He understood the man's unhappiness and dissatisfaction but could do nothing about it. The *Dione* was only in port for a short time, and there was always so much to do. In fact, Alger was anxious to get under way. A contact that had been made near Wimble Shoals the day before had been bothering him. There was no wreck nearby, to his knowledge, but something had definitely been down there, and he was fairly certain he had hit it with a depth charge. He wanted to go back again and sniff around. Maybe, just maybe, there was a damaged U-boat there. He had heard of it happening before. A U-boat could be so wounded that it could not surface until the crew, working feverishly around the clock, could make repairs. If this was the case, Alger wanted to get back, to stop that effort as soon as possible.

When Alger looked again, McCormick had disappeared behind a row of warehouses on the busy navy base. Alger doubted he would ever see him again. This war, he understood at that moment, was going to do that regularly, take a friend and send him away just when you were at last beginning to know and understand him.

Nothing he could do.

Back to work.

There was also little Lieutenant Alger and the *Dione* could do about the new round of killing going on several hundred miles away. Their responsibility still lay closer in. Besides, Alger was determined to find out what he had hit off Wimble Shoals. On 22 April, he went back and put a buoy on the spot and then began to cover the area with depth charges. The navy destroyers *Swanson* and *Nicholson*, attracted by his activity, moved in to nose around and soon their sonar operators were also excitedly reporting a good contact. The *Swanson* moved in and dropped a big 600-pound depth charge but, disappointingly, nothing came up. Alger then dragged an anchor over the spot until something was hooked. He then ordered the *Dione* backed, trying to tear something away below, but the line broke and the anchor was lost. Before any more could be done, Swede reported a communication from the *Dickerson*. She was leading a convoy along with the *Roper* and needed assistance. Reluctantly, Alger headed out to them, rendezvousing at midnight. The very next morning, however, he had the *Dione* back at his buoy at Wimble Shoals. All day long, he maneuvered or drifted in the area, listening, looking for something that might help him. Once more, the navy called and Alger departed, heading out to meet a night-running Bucket Brigade. But as soon as he had done his chores there, he was right back at Wimble Shoals. This time he dropped three depth charges, but still nothing came up.

For several days, Alger repeated the pattern. The Bucket Brigades were running at night since the *Axtell J. Byles* had been hit, so after he had assisted with them, he took the *Dione* back to the Wimble Shoals Buoy. On 25 April, he began an exercise in demolitions. Perhaps he could tear the wreck below apart and finally discover what he had hit. Working in a dense smoke coming from a swamp fire ashore, he asked for volunteers to go aboard a raft and lower two depth charges

tied together. Seaman John Fleming, recovered from the
strange premonition of the torpedo meant for the *Dione*, was
one of the volunteers. The resulting blast, electrically fired,
shook the *Dione* but that was all. All day long, Alger continued
to drop depth charges. The officers and crew of the *Dione* were
now convinced that they had a U-boat below. A freighter or
tanker would have come apart with all the explosives the *Dione*
had expended. The feeling was that if it wasn't a U-boat, by
God, it sure was a damn good imitation.

For the rest of April, the *Dione* would continue her frustrating investigation of the Wimble Shoals object when not
escorting Bucket Brigades. Finally, on 29 April, she was ordered to report back to Little Creek. There, some badly
needed repairs were to be undertaken plus a refitting of new
armament. The men of the *Dione* were not ready to stand
down. They were still trying to even the score, somehow.
They were also trying to prove that maybe they had already
done so, with the thing below their buoy at Wimble Shoals.
But headquarters was adamant. It was past time for the *Dione*
to rest and that went for her crew, too.

The U-boats were not resting. For the remaining days of
the month, they continued to exploit their new Torpedo Junction. This was bad enough but, on 29 April, the *U-402*, under
Korvettenkapitän Siegfried von Forstner, slipped back into
the familiar waters just off Cape Lookout to catch the Russian
tanker *Ashkhabad* trying to sneak by at night. The *Ashkhabad*
had not waited for a Bucket Brigade to form. Von Forstner
put a single torpedo into her and she began to sink immediately, her stern striking the shallow sea bottom and leaving
her bow afloat. Before their ship sank completely, the Russians
tried to use their deck gun, but were wide of the mark and had
to make for the lifeboats. They were soon picked up by the
British trawler *Lady Elsa*.[15]

Von Forstner continued on, attacking the United States
Navy armed yacht *Cythera* off Cape Fear. The *Cythera* sank
after two *U-402* torpedoes struck her, her depth charges going
off beneath her struggling crew. There would only be two
survivors out of a crew of seventy-one. Both were picked up

by von Forstner and carried back to France. In a letter to his wife, von Forstner would later recall the incident: "We should really have kept them locked up and all that, but a U-boat is not spacious as you know and they were nice chaps and friendly—they joined us in our meals, and we brought them home in our own way, and nobody was the worse for it. At our arrival, they were met by an escort and taken away in the usual manner thought fit for prisoners of war, much to the consternation of my crew, whom they had invited to come and see them back home in the States after the war."[16]

Von Forstner could, of course, afford to be generous to Americans. His destruction of the *Ashkhabad* had helped to end the month of April on an ignominious note for Admiral Andrews and his staff. New tactics and new equipment had been installed with some success throughout the month, but still the Germans ruled the east coast. In the 30 April 1942 *BdU War Diary*, Admiral Doenitz wrote: "Attacking conditions in the American area continue to be very good. Anti-S/M activity has increased, but its fighting power, its concentration, its determination to attack and destroy are small." He could not resist further chiding the Americans. "Those who fight are not sailors, but people who are being paid for their presence in the area endangered by U-boats. C.O.'s are all of the same opinion, namely that the American area will remain a highly favorable area for attacks for some months to come and that a high percentage of successes can be scored with very few losses."

Admiral Andrews was probably not aware of Admiral Doenitz's contempt for his men, but he was aware that he could not continue to accept the losses being inflicted by the Germans. Something truly drastic had to be done or the war effort was going to end in a huge oil slick spread from New York to Key West. He again went to Admiral King and reported that he had done all he could do under the present policies to control the U-boat assault, especially on the tankers. It was obvious that the tankers were the major targets and it was the tanker masters who had proven to be the most independent and obstinate. King was in a mood to listen and, with the Roosevelt administration's agreement, it was done quickly.

The message went out: "Commercial oil tankers for Gulf and
Caribbean and U.S. Atlantic ports shall be held in port pending further orders." All U.S. tankers were vested in Admiral
Andrews's hands "with the necessary authority to direct their
sailings as required by the existing situation."[17]

Admiral Andrews was now the czar of all American
tanker traffic, but all he could do was to order them to stay
safely in port while he devised more safeguards. He knew he
had to hurry. The east coast, and the war in Europe, would be
living off rapidly dwindling oil reserves until he could get the
tankers moving again. After all these months, after all that had
been tried, the situation was still desperate.

# 15

# Proud Day, Bitter Day

---

**O**n the morning of 4 April 1942, Kapitänleutnant Hellmut Rathke signaled his crew to cast off all lines. Obediently, they sprang to their stations and the *U-352* edged into St. Nazaire harbor. No band disturbed the misty quiet of the French port city. There had been a time when no U-boat crew could leave on a cruise without a German oompah band to send them on their way. But those days were gone forever. The less attention given their departures the better. All too many in the U-boat force were dead, victims of British aircraft and destroyers that always seemed to know when a U-boat took to sea. Rathke was glad to get away from the city. The entire German occupation force in St. Nazaire was edgy. Only a week before, a British commando raid had thrown the port into confusion, and much of the city's carefree charm had disappeared.

As the *U-352* cleared the small St. Nazaire lock, Rathke's thoughts focused on his submarine. He had, according to Admiral Doenitz's orders, followed his *Unterseeboot 352*, a Type VIIC, from the moment her keel was laid. On the first war cruise, Rathke had taken his boat to sea for five weeks, nearing Iceland at one point. Twice he had attacked, once sending a spread of four torpedoes at a British destroyer. But he had not managed to hit anything. Or maybe his torpedoes had been duds or had been sabotaged in some way. Whatever the truth, he did not trust the fourteen "fish" his U-boat carried.

An observer on shore would have noticed that there was a blotch of black paint on the conning tower of the *U-352.* Rathke had ordered it to cover the Flensburg coat of arms that had once been displayed there. The German coastal city where his wife and small daughter lived had adopted his U-boat. He could not help but wonder when and if he would see them again. All the other U-boat skippers Rathke had known were aggressively self-confident. Even the ideology of the National Socialist party and all of its propaganda, much of which the thirty-two-year-old Rathke believed, could not help take away his worries. He had orders to proceed to America, take up a position off the North Carolina coast, and disrupt as much shipping as possible. He knew how enormously success-ful other U-boats had been in American coastal waters and that it was imperative that he also succeed for both the glory of the Fatherland and for his career as well. But would he be up to it? He had never felt so much pressure.

After reaching the open sea safely, Rathke kept the *U-352* on the surface and ordered *"langsame Fahrt,"* slow speed, for the trip across the Atlantic. He would try to conserve as much fuel as possible on the crossing. Rathke believed he would need every drop of it once the *U-352* went into action against the Americans.[1]

On the other side of the Atlantic from the *U-352,* the USCG Cutter *Icarus* was continuing her constant, though fruitless, antisubmarine patrols of the coastal waters from New York to Atlantic City. Though frustrated like the rest of the *Icarus*'s crew by their lack of success against the U-boats, Gunner's Mate 2d Class John Bruce, twenty-four, liked serv-ing aboard the *Icarus* and believed his ship would eventually do well. Toward that end, he kept the guns on board clean and well oiled. The *Icarus* was the twin of the *Dione* and the *Ca-lypso.* Abaft amidships, she was armed with depth-charge racks, a World War I-vintage Y-gun, and two .50-caliber Browning water-cooled machine guns. Forward, mounted on the bow, were two more .50-caliber guns and a 3-inch deck gun. On the flying bridge were two .30-caliber Lewis machine guns, and locked up in the armory were two .45 pistols, two Thompson submachine guns, a number of .30-caliber Springfields, and several hand grenades. The gun crews had not had any target practice for over a year. Even though the war had ended all ammunition restrictions, the ship's commander, Lieutenant Maurice D. Jester, had still not allowed it.

Lieutenant Jester was something of an enigma to the young crew under his command. A native of Chincoteague, Virginia, Jester had entered the coast guard as a surfman in 1917 and worked his way up the ranks until he was commissioned in 1941. By the time he took command of the *Icarus*, he was fifty-two years old. The crew respected his knowledge of the sea but thought him tough as nails and somewhat aloof. His only contact with them seemed to be when they served him coffee or when he meted out punishment for minor infractions.

In late April, the *Icarus* received new orders. She was to proceed to Key West, Florida, to become part of the southern end of escorts for Admiral Andrews's Bucket Brigades. These orders were not received happily by all the crewmen. For several years, the *Icarus*'s home station had been the town of Stapleton on Staten Island, and many of her crew had established themselves in the local community. But all leaves and passes were canceled, and early on 8 May the *Icarus* pulled away from her berth. Key West seemed a long way away.[2]

The *U-352* crossed into what Rathke considered American waters several hundred miles off the coast of New Jersey on the morning of 2 May. Rathke had made the four-week crossing as productive as he could. The average crewman on board his U-boat was twenty-two years old and ten of them were only nineteen. Few among them were professional seamen, and Rathke knew they could use all the training he could give them. He had simulated attacks both on the surface and underwater, periodically ordering crash dives, timing how long it took to submerge until he was satisfied with the results. He had also held evacuation drills. At the order, his men would

pull on their lifejackets and escape lungs and line up to practice escape. Only one man could pass through the control
room and conning tower hatches at a time, so speed and order
was critical. The other hatches on the deck, the galley hatch
and torpedo-loading hatches, could not be used in the drill.
They might be underwater.

To soften the training, Rathke had also allowed short sun-
bathing periods for three or four men at a time while they
were in mid-ocean and out of aircraft range. As the U-boat
neared the United States, Rathke even permitted the radiomen
to tune in American jazz programs, although he personally
considered the music decadent. By the time the *U-352* started
to work her way toward Cape Hatteras, Rathke was satisfied
with the training, spirit, and morale of his crew. He decided to
stay on the surface and look for targets as he moved south. If
what he had been told was true, they should be fat and easy.
Before he got far, however, several patrol planes harassed him
into crash-diving. None of the reports he had read from the
other U-boat skippers had mentioned there being so many airplanes around. Did the Americans know he was there? Was he
in a trap? His worries mounted.

On 5 May, Rathke brought the *U-352* into the area of the
new Torpedo Junction, approximately 300 miles off Cape Hatteras. He had been briefed on this new, lucrative area and
hoped for some good luck. Per Doenitz's standing recommen-
dation, he stayed submerged for most of the day and then
came to the surface at darkness. There, he patiently waited
under a bright moon. At 2100, he was rewarded by the sight
of a medium-sized cargo freighter droning north at a speed of
only about 8 knots. The freighter, according to an analysis of
the records, was the Swedish *Freden*. She was not zigzagging,
so all Rathke had to do was wait until the freighter crossed his
bow. This he did and at 2130 launched his first torpedo.

The *Freden* had two lookouts on watch. The one on the
starboard side saw the torpedo and sang out a warning. It was
too late for the *Freden*'s master to turn his ship, but it didn't
matter as Rathke's torpedo missed by the length of the ship,
passing in front of the bow. After more than five minutes had

passed and the *Freden* had continued on unscathed, Rathke knew he would have to try again.

Aboard the *Freden*, an atmosphere of near panic prevailed. All of her officers and crew were topside, ready to abandon ship at the first opportunity. At 2200, Rathke was ready. He carefully lined up and fired. The *Freden*'s crew on her starboard side cried out when they saw the torpedo coming their way. In a moment, her crew on the port side also cried out at Rathke's torpedo, but this time it was heading away from them. The torpedo had been perfectly lined up but had been set too deep, passing well underneath the *Freden*.

As far as the *Freden*'s crew was concerned, it was definitely time to get off. The master stopped the *Freden* and a boat was lowered. As its crew started to pull away, the master had a change of heart. After all, his ship was in perfect condition. Wouldn't they all be safer aboard her? Shore was a very long way away and he had heard of lifeboats drifting for weeks before being found. He hailed the lifeboat and ordered everyone back. It apparently never occurred to him to send out a radio call for help. The *Freden*'s boilers were fired up and the ship headed north again.

Rathke was chasing the *Freden*, but when the freighter stopped to let the crew get off and then back on again, he apparently passed it without seeing it. After a short search, he decided to continue on a northerly heading. After a few hours, his lookouts spotted the *Freden* again, this time coming up behind the U-boat. Rathke turned the *U-352* toward the freighter and sent another bow torpedo on its way. This time, the depth had been corrected and Rathke had moved in even closer. What could possibly go wrong?

The *Freden*'s crew were still topside, anxiously watching. Once more, it was the crew on the starboard side who saw Rathke's torpedo coming at them. And, once more, it was her crew on the port side who saw it emerge from the other side and keep going. There was now some discussion as to the intelligence of the U-boat skipper that was attacking them. There was no doubt that he had gotten their range, but he was definitely having trouble gauging their draft.

At 2230, Rathke took his last chance at the *Freden*. The

*Freden*'s crew watched the torpedo coming. It had obviously
been set at its shallowest setting, occasionally even jumping
out of the water like a dolphin. This time it was the port-side
crew that got to watch the torpedo coming at them. And this
time, the starboard-side crew got to watch it jump on by, just
missing the bow by a few feet. That was enough for the
Swedes. They were perhaps being attacked by the most inept
U-boat commander in the Atlantic Ocean, but he had at last
gotten just about everything right. The next torpedo was
probably going to get them. In fact, the U-boat had come in so
close, the *Freden*'s crew could see the German commander and
his lookouts on the conning tower. The *Freden*'s master ordered his ship swung away with her stern toward the U-boat.
That would give the Germans less of a target while he abandoned ship. Rathke watched the freighter turn and disconso-
lately assumed it was running away. All he could do was order
the *U-352* submerged. He was so depressed he apparently forgot about the 88-mm gun on his deck. He just took his U-boat
down to wait for a better day.

While the *U-352* moved away, the *Freden* had come to a
complete stop, her crew getting aboard two lifeboats. All
night long they would drift. The Swedes fully expected to
have to endure a nightmare on the sea but at dawn they could
see the *Freden* had drifted along with them and was only a few
hundred yards away. The rest of the ocean was empty. Regain-
ing their confidence as the sun rose, they reboarded the *Freden*
at 0830 and continued uneventfully on to New York. Their
adventures would be referred to as "incredible" by the navy
intelligence officer who would later interview them.[3]

At about the same time the Swedes were reboarding their
ship and just a few miles away, Rathke brought the *U-352* to
the surface. He and his lookouts clambered to the conning
tower bridge and began to scan around them. Almost immediately, one of the lookouts cried out. Rathke whirled and looked
where the man was pointing. Four miles away at 600 feet, a
twin-engined plane was barreling in on a direct course for the
*U-352*. Rathke pushed the watch in ahead of him and then
jumped through the hatch to the deck seven feet below, landing painfully on a knee that he had badly wrenched in a skiing

accident some years earlier. As Rathke writhed in pain, the
U-352 began its crash dive.

Seconds that seemed as long as minutes ticked by. Finally,
the U-boat was submerged. Rathke stumbled to his feet, but he
was having to grit his teeth against the awful pain. Because of
everything else that had happened to him, he was certain that
he was going to be bombed, but when no explosion came after
an hour, he surfaced and looked around. The sea and sky were
empty.

Over the next few days, Rathke kept moving closer to
shore, attacking three more freighters with still no hits. On 7
May, an airplane coming out of the sun almost caught him
again. His boat was barely submerged when the bombs struck,
doing no damage but leaving Rathke completely pessimistic
about the entire mission. But he could not fail. What would
the other U-boat commanders think? And what about Admiral
Doenitz? Something had to be done to change his luck.

Rathke decided to move to the 20-meter line off Cape
Lookout where Hardegen had experienced such success in the
early days of the American campaign. He knew nothing of
Admiral Andrews's recently instituted Bucket Brigades. All
that he knew was there had to be shipping there. How else
could Hardegen have had all of his success? Rathke sat on the
surface for two nights without seeing a single ship.

Late on the afternoon of 9 May, he decided to break the
rule of only attacking at night and came to the surface. Immediately, he was rewarded by the sight of a mast rising above
the horizon. He ordered a crash dive and maneuvered toward
the ship. Maybe, finally, his luck had changed. He ordered the
attack periscope up but wasted no time on identification. He
meant to sink the ship, no matter what it was. He ordered two
of the bow torpedo tubes flooded and fired in quick succession.
The U-352 shuddered and then began to rise with the sudden
buoyancy caused by the departure of the torpedoes. The executive officer, Leutnant Josef Ernst, adjusted the submarine's
trim, but the adjustment was too severe and Rathke lost sight
of his target as the periscope dipped under the sea. Suddenly,
the U-boat shook from the shock of a distant explosion. Rathke
ordered the U-352 back up to periscope depth so he could ob-

serve the target. He believed it to be a small freighter. It was, however, the U.S. Coast Guard Cutter *Icarus*.[4]

On 9 May, the crew of the *Icarus* were feeling very much alone. Once they had left their home district, they felt as if they were intruders wherever they sailed. When Ensign Charles Pool, the communications officer, sent a message to the commandant of the Sixth Naval District advising him of the *Icarus*'s entry into the area, the response had been a cold, noncommittal *Received*. This had not been the first snub of the day, either. Earlier, off the Virginia coast, a convoy of three freighters and an escorting destroyer going north had sailed into view. Curious, the officer of the bridge had swung the *Icarus* closer to see if anyone recognized the ships. Instantly, the destroyer had charged the cutter, swerved in front of it, and angrily blinked a warning to keep well away. The *Icarus* plowed doggedly along, running across the next convoy just south of Wimble Shoals. This time the *Icarus* had learned her lesson and kept her distance.

Gunner's Mate John Bruce had spent the day doing a number of small sailor's chores. He had also checked his guns and was as satisfied as he could be with their readiness. He wanted to test them just once, but no order for target practice had come. He couldn't understand that. He knew the *Icarus* had entered the biggest U-boat killing ground along the coast. Wouldn't it be wise to test the weapons just once? He thought about mentioning that to one of the officers but decided against it. It was apparent they were having their own problems.

The day was warm and overcast, the sea almost flat, and many of the men had spent some time on deck speculating on their duty in Key West and on how to win the war. When the air cooled late in the afternoon, most, including Bruce, drifted off to their quarters. Soon, the *Icarus* was quiet except for the constant muffled roar of her two Winton diesel engines.

At 1615, Lieutenant Edward D. Howard, the executive officer, had the bridge. Lieutenant Jester had retired to his quarters. Howard kept the course steady at a speed of 14 knots. Below in the soundroom, soundman William L. Rabich listened intently into his earphones. Through the normal clutter, he suddenly thought he heard something unusual. He called crewman Santiago Quinones to listen in. Quinones immediately called Howard and told him that he believed there was a submarine nearby, probably no more than 100 yards away.

Howard considered calling General Quarters but decided to summon Jester to the bridge instead. He ordered Quinones to keep listening. Another soundman, Arthur Laskowski, joined Rabich and Quinones. They were more certain than ever that they were hearing submarine sounds. They could not understand why the *Icarus* was not taking at least evasive action. The contact began to fade. Quinones now placed the object at 2,000 yards off the port bow. At 1625, the contact suddenly improved. Still, the *Icarus* plowed straight ahead. Lieutenant Howard wanted to be absolutely sure of his target. He did not want to waste any depth charges. He knew there would be hell to pay from Jester if he did.

At 1629, almost ten minutes after Rabich had made his first contact, Jester was still not on the bridge.

Quinones was now convinced that the contact was a submarine and that it was maneuvering parallel to the *Icarus*, probably trying to get ahead to make an attack. Just as he picked up the phone to call the bridge, a tremendous explosion rocked the ship. Quinones reeled against the shock. What he had feared had already occurred.

Below, John Bruce was relaxing in his bunk when the *Icarus* suddenly shook as if she had run aground. Deck plates were jarred and lights flickered. Bruce was out of his bed and running to the deck even before General Quarters was called. Once there, he saw a huge swirl of mud and water 200 yards off the port quarter.

Lieutenant Howard kept the bridge calm while he analyzed the situation. He suspected that a torpedo had missed the *Icarus* and had struck the sea bed and exploded. Perhaps the torpedo's depth mechanism had been set too deep. If so, that had been very lucky for both Howard and the *Icarus* since he had taken no evasive action while waiting for Jester to show up. From what Quinones had told him, Howard placed the U-boat still off the port beam and reported this to Jester as the commanding officer puffed onto the bridge. Jester was decisive. He immediately ordered the *Icarus* hard aport and called down to warn Warrant Machinist Henry Cookson to stand by with his mechanics in the engine room. He knew they were about to be shaken up badly by the explosions of depth charges in the shallow water.[5]

When the *U-352*'s periscope rose above the water's surface, Kapitänleutnant Hellmut Rathke expected to see a burning freighter. Instead, almost disbelieving his eyes, he saw a boiling brown sea and a fast, armed subchaser maneuvering in front of him. Certain that his periscope had been seen, he blurted out an order to dive. What could he do? The water was shallow, limiting his maneuverability. He had to think! What would the other U-boat skippers do in such a situation? Rathke's initial response was to move behind the subchaser to try to hide in its wake, but then he remembered the muddy turmoil he had seen in his periscope. His torpedo must have caused this. What better place to hide? It was a clever move worthy of Hardegen himself!

The *U-352* moved toward the muddy swirl and then sank to the bottom where her nose pushed gently into the soft mud churned up by the torpedo. Rathke ordered complete silence. He planned to wait for one pass from the subchaser and then either to surface to periscope depth for a torpedo attack or, remembering it this time, coming all the way to the surface to attack with his deck gun. He was suddenly feeling very confident. The ship above was a small cutter, not a destroyer. He was in a Type VIIC German U-boat, probably the deadliest ship that had ever sailed. Rathke believed he could destroy his adversary.

It was now 1630. Only two minutes had elapsed since Rathke's torpedo had missed, and the *Icarus* was ready for attack with all hands at battle stations. Lieutenant Jester set his ship on the course Lieutenant Howard recommended and saw that his bow was aimed directly toward the muddy stain left by the torpedo. That seemed to him to be a good place to start his attack. At 180 yards from the mud, the soundmen lost contact. Jester calculated what he thought to be a proper interval and ordered a diamond pattern of five depth charges laid. First, the crew dropped one charge from the rack, followed by two from the Y-gun, then one from the rack, and later, another from the rack. The depth charges splashed into the muddy water. Their explosive mechanisms were set for 100 feet. Jester ordered the *Icarus* into another sharp turn.

The crew of the *U-352* heard the *Icarus* and cringed as the cutter roared directly overhead. Rathke listened intently, trying to gauge his attacker's course so he could surface and finish it off quickly. Outside, the first depth charge from the *Icarus* dropped toward the submarine's deck gun. Two other charges drifted down next to the conning tower. Another plummeted directly for the U-boat's engine room, while the last charge fell about 50 feet behind her stern.

The *Icarus* trembled under the impact of her own explosives. Fuses blew and deck plates heaved. The black gang in the engine room held on to anything they could grab and then raced to the diesels to check for damage.

On board the *U-352*, every gauge in the control room and in the tower suddenly shattered. Sharp glass flew through the air. Leutnant Ernst was flung headfirst into a control panel, his body flopping lifelessly to the deck. Lights flickered throughout the U-boat and then died. Rathke gradually forced himself out of a red haze. He dragged himself up by hanging on to the attack periscope, now bent and ruined. The tower floor was slick with blood. The emergency lights burned dimly while Rathke examined Ernst. His skull was crushed. Rathke felt his stomach begin to heave so he turned away. After a moment, he gained control of himself and called for a damage report from the engine room. Could he still maneuver? The reply was negative. Both electric motors had been knocked off their mounts, although one machine was operating intermittently.

Rathke reviewed his situation. His second-in-command was dead, he had lost most of his instruments, and he could not maneuver underwater. The only chance he had was to play dead. Perhaps the American ship did not know it had hit him. Perhaps if he stayed right where he was, the *U-352* might yet survive. What Rathke did not know, what he could not tell without his instruments, was that his U-boat was on the move. The depth charges had blown away the *U-352*'s deck gun plus a good portion of the sheet metal surrounding the tower, altering her buoyancy. The *U-352* was drifting, her bow up, her stern occasionally dragging on the smooth white sand, toward the west.

Aboard the *Icarus*, the three soundmen knew by the sounds they were getting from the U-boat that it was still moving but not very fast. They relayed the information to the bridge. Jester began to turn the *Icarus* around, heading toward the contact. He made several passes trying to line up exactly. At 1645, he ordered a second attack, with the depth charges to be thrown out at his command.

The *U-352* was a dead boat. Every man sat or stood absolutely still. The only sound to be heard was their breathing and a constant dripping from one of the torpedo tubes. When the dripping became a spurt, one of the torpedomen called out. Rathke sent a runner back to stop the talking. Obermaschinist Grandke came forward from the engine room and requested permission to work on the one electric motor not completely destroyed. Rathke and Grandke had never gotten along. Grandke was older and had served on several successful U-boats before being assigned to the *U-352*. It seemed to Rathke that Grandke was constantly questioning his orders. Rathke turned Grandke down, angrily putting his finger to his lips. He could still hear the American ship patrolling above, but no depth charges had fallen for fifteen minutes. The *U-352* might still escape as long as they could remain undetected. The *Icarus*'s engine noises faded and then grew ominously strong.

The *Icarus* had been searching, making question marks on the sea, but now she was lined up for her second attack. Jester gave the command and a "V" pattern, one charge from the rack and two from the Y-gun, splashed into the water. The rack charge fell toward the submarine's bow, while the Y-gun explosives fell to one side.

The charges slammed the *U-352*. She keeled over on her port side and then settled to the bottom, one of her buoyancy tanks ruptured. Rathke called for a damage report. The pres-

sure hull had held, one of his officers reported back, but he was
not sure it could withstand another such attack. The *Icarus*,
already on her way back for another round, quickly provided
the answer. This time a single depth charge was dropped on
the spot where bubbles were rising from the split buoyancy
tank. At 1708, the *Icarus* dropped another charge on the bubbles. This one missed but came close enough to force a decision on Rathke. He ordered his men into their escape lungs.
With no other option, Rathke ordered all remaining tanks
blown and his gun crews to stand by. The *U-352* was coming
up![6]

The *Icarus* was coming around for yet another pass. The
gun crews on the cutter had been at their battle stations for
thirty-nine minutes with a spectacular view but little to do.
Once, during the attack, a patrol plane had flown in from the
southwest over the port bow, waggled its wings, and exchanged recognition signals. The men at their guns had
waved, but the plane did not stop or seem to realize a battle
was going on. The gun crews had settled back, not expecting
to go into action. Submarines either got sunk or slipped away
and that was that.

On the bridge, Lieutenant Howard spotted signs of the
*U-352* first. A thousand yards to starboard, a huge bubble
burst up from the sea, leaving a wake of spreading white foam.
Howard thought he could see a dark shape underneath and
called it to Jester's attention just as the U-boat's bow broke the
surface. It was 1709. The bow, at a 45-degree angle, pushed
farther out of the water until the conning tower became visible. The *U-352* immediately settled with all of the deck awash
except for about eight feet of the bow. No order came to the
gunners, but the men on the starboard side and the flying
bridge opened fire. Jester sent word to the gunners to keep
firing. He believed that if the Germans reached their deck
gun, the *Icarus* could be blasted out of the water with one shot.
No one on board the cutter realized the U-boat's deck gun had
been blown off during the first attack.[7]

Rathke threw open the conning tower hatch and saw a
horrifying sight. The tower bridge was a jumble of twisted

steel and grotesquely bent equipment. Moreover, his U-boat was barely afloat, the sea only four inches below the rim of the hatch. He threw his secret codes out and gave the order to abandon ship. The quartermaster ran from the control room to the stern yelling, "All men out!" But as the men of the *U-352* lined up, Obermaschinist Grandke stormed through them until he reached Rathke. "You crazy dogs!" he roared, "we can still run for it on our diesels!" Rathke raged back at him to be silent and then motioned for the crew to begin evacuation.

As the first few men clambered through the hatch, they were struck by the *Icarus*'s machine guns and fell, screaming. Grandke began to yell at the men to stop, that they would only die if they continued. Rathke ignored him and kept his men going. He believed his attackers would soon stop firing after they saw he was surrendering.

At that moment, however, the *Icarus* was lining up to put her 3-inch gun into action. Jester meant to have this U-boat. Charles E. Mueller was manning the 3-inch gun. He had not had much in the way of practice, but he was still an excellent shot. The first shell hit in front of the *U-352*'s tower and ricocheted into and off it. The second shell landed behind the tower. The third hit it dead center.

Maschinistmaat Gerhard Reussel was climbing out of the *U-352* tower hatch just as the shell struck. He was thrown high in the air, blood spurting from a severed leg. Rathke ordered the last of his men out, but his engineering officer, Oberleutnant Heinz Tretz, refused, disappearing back into the boat to ensure scuttling was complete. Rathke screamed back at him to get out, but there was no answer. He started after him, but suddenly the *U-352* lurched and started to slide downward. Amidst a hail of 3-inch shells and machine-gun fire, Rathke climbed out of the conning tower hatch and jumped.[8]

There was chaos aboard the *Icarus*. The 3-inch gun was punching out shells as fast as it could be loaded, and every gun that could bear on the target was blazing. One gunner on a .50-caliber became so anxious he bent the restraining frame with brute force and shot up his own bulkhead. John Bruce was in the middle of all this frenzy, jumping from gun to gun, clearing jams and solving problems. When one of the .30-caliber machine guns on the flying bridge jammed, they called for him. By the time he was able to make his way there, the gunner had field-stripped the gun completely and parts were strewn all over the deck. Bruce cursed the man and then began gathering up parts. At least he had a good view from the flying bridge. He could see tracers soaring out at the U-boat, hitting the tower and hull and richocheting off into space. He was impressed at the continued orderliness of the submarine's evacuation in the face of such intense fire. He also thought them to be very dark complexioned. Maybe they were Japanese!

The men of the *U-352* swam away from their boat. Rathke looked for Reussel and found him in a sea of blood. Pulling off his belt, he tried to tie a tourniquet around the stump of the young man's leg but there was little left to keep the belt from slipping off. Rathke looked up and saw his U-boat sink. He called to his men to have courage but still the firing continued from the *Icarus*. Rathke screamed at the Americans to stop, and his men picked up the cry for mercy. "*Bitte,*" they begged. "*Kamerade, Mein Gott . . . Bitte!*" Rathke was certain he heard the Americans reply through a megaphone, "Damned Germans. Go to Hell!"

John Bruce saw the U-boat go down. From his station aft he saw the gunners still firing. "For God's sake!" he yelled. "Don't shoot them in the water!"

The gunners on the stern stopped but the forward gunners kept shooting. One of the aft crewmen, as if coming out of a trance, turned toward Bruce. "You must not be mad at anybody, John," he growled.

Bruce was disgusted. "That could have just as easily been us in the water," he snapped and then began to pick up the empty cartridge casings scattered on the deck.

Three minutes had passed since the *U-352* had gone down before Jester sent a runner from the bridge to each gun ordering a cease-fire. The time was 1717. The soundmen were still getting contacts from the U-boat, so Jester ordered one last attack. Running over the bubbles, one depth charge was dropped. No more sounds came from below. Jester, concerned that other U-boats might be in the area, ordered the *Icarus* on a course away from the scene.

Rathke watched incredulously as the *Icarus* began to steam away. After machine-gunning them in the water, did the Americans now intend to let them drown? Actually, Jester was unsure of his authority to do anything other than sink submarines. Now that the attack was over, he had reverted to his usual caution. Before he would do anything, he would ask permission and that included the rescue of German U-boat survivors.

Ensign Pool began a series of frustrating radio calls. First, he called Norfolk with the message, "Have sunk submarine. 30–40 men in the water. Shall *Icarus* pick up any of the men?" There was no reply. Next, he tried Charleston with the same message. The message was received, but again there was no answer. Pool waited ten minutes and sent, "Have you any message for us?" A minute later a coded message came back. Decoded, it read "No."

Eight minutes later, at 1740, Pool tried the commandant of the Sixth Naval District with the message, "Shall *Icarus* pick up prisoners?" No answer. He desperately tried again. The *Icarus* was drawing farther and farther away from the U-boat crew. "32 German submarine men in the water," he radioed. "Shall we pick them up?" Finally, at 1749, a message came back. "Pick up survivors. Bring to Charleston." Pool snatched the message and rushed it to the bridge. Jester immediately ordered the *Icarus* around.

Rathke saw the *Icarus* returning. It occurred to him that the small warship might be returning to finish the job of massacring his crew. He called to his men to stay together and help support the wounded. It was all he could do besides pray. He had held Reussel in his arms the entire time he was in the water. The crewman was very weak but still alive. Rathke spoke to the men around him. "Remember your duty," he counseled. "Do not tell the enemy anything."

The *Icarus* came closer and then stopped. Using his limited English, Rathke asked that his wounded be taken aboard first. This was done. John Bruce helped position a 55-gallon drum

Admiral Karl Doenitz, commander of the German U-boat
fleet. After the surprise attack on Pearl Harbor and the entry
of the United States into the war, he quickly improvised a plan
for an attack across the Atlantic. He called it *Paukenschlag*
("drumroll"). (U.S. Naval Institute)

The crew of the *U-123* celebrates a successful attack while Kapitänleutnant Hardegen watches through binoculars. Hardegen would use the *U-123*'s 88-mm deck gun shown in the foreground for the first time on the tanker *Malay*. Although some of his officers were skeptical of using the gun to attack shipping, Hardegen showed that it could be done effectively. (Bibliothek feur Zeitgeschichte)

Kapitänleutnant Hardegen receives a welcoming bouquet after
returning from *Paukenschlag*. On the crossing back to France,
Admiral Doenitz had radioed the news that Hardegen had been
awarded the Knight's Cross. Hardegen's report to Doenitz was
enthusiastic. Any U-boat that could get across the Atlantic was
certain to be successful. (Bibliothek feur Zeitgeschichte)

When the U-boats arrived off Cape Hatteras in January 1942,
there was only one large antisubmarine ship there to oppose
them—the United States Coast Guard Cutter *Dione*. (U.S.
Naval Institute)

Lieutenant James (Jimmy) Alger, commander, United States Coast Guard Cutter *Dione*. (Courtesy Admiral James Alger, USCG (Ret.))

"Swede" Larson on duty in the radio room of the *Dione*. Here he would listen to the dying ships of "Torpedo Junction" as they desperately begged for help over the international calling and distress frequency. "SSSS" meant that a U-boat had been spotted. Almost without fail, that signal was followed by "SOS": the U-boat had attacked. (Collection of Major Harold Larson, USMC (Ret.))

In the middle of a typical "Graveyard of the Atlantic" gale, the men of the *Dione* race once more to their duty stations. While they readied the depth charges, Lieutenant Alger maneuvered the cutter, stalking the killers on what had become an incredible sea of death. (Dick Bacchus collection)

Burning and sinking, the *Dixie Arrow* was the victim of the
*U-71*. Many of her crew were saved by the sacrifice of Able
Seaman Oscar Chappel, who turned the tanker into the wind
to keep the flames from them. In doing so, a wall of fire
enveloped the bridge. (U.S. Naval Institute)

On the night of 4 April 1942, Topp's *U-552* attacked the
tanker *Byron D. Benson* off Currituck, North Carolina. The
*Benson* was to burn and drift for three days before sinking, its
great smoke cloud covering hundreds of square miles and
casting a pall along the entire North Carolina coast. (National
Archives)

The crew of the *U-352* is marched off with Kapitänleutnant Rathke in the lead. The entire crew would remain as POWs for the rest of the war. (National Archives)

Kapitänleutnant Hellmut Rathke (*second from left*) and Leutnant Oskar Bernard (*third from left*) are interrogated by intelligence officers shortly after leaving the *Icarus*. (National Archives)

Constant watch was necessary aboard the *Dione*. Here, Lieutenant (j.g.) Dick Bacchus takes his turn while waiting for a Bucket Brigade convoy to form. (Dick Bacchus collection)

beside the gangway on which the prisoners deposited their belongings as they came aboard. Only a few coins and pocket knives turned up. Rathke was the last man out of the water. Bruce and crewman John Freda reached down to help him, but he shrugged their hands away and climbed aboard on his own power. His small dark eyes burned with righteous anger. Limping, he pushed his way through the Americans to where Reussel lay. There he knelt and took the boy's hand. "It was all for the Fatherland," he said. Reussel looked back vacantly. He would die four hours later.[9]

As the *Icarus* droned toward Charleston, a surprising thing began to happen. The Germans were placed in one of the wardrooms and a guard assigned to watch. Rathke told his men to say nothing to the Americans, but the American coast guardsmen began to slip down to see their prisoners and the two crews began to talk to each other. Soon the Americans who could speak some German and the Germans who could speak some English were swapping jokes and war stories. It was even discovered that some of the Germans had relatives in the United States. And before long, trays of sandwiches from the galley and boxes of cigarettes from the ship's stores were finding their way to the Germans' compartment. After that, the mood among the Germans, except for Rathke, became buoyant. The young submariners realized that they had escaped and were on their way to the richest country in the world for internment. For them, the war was over. And they were alive!

During all this, Pharmacist's Mate Kahn was doing all he could for the injured. But his tiny medicine chest could offer little help to Reussel or to the several other severely wounded men, one of whom had lost an arm. By the time the *Icarus* tied up at Charleston on 10 May, the crew of the cutter were feeling positively brotherly toward their German captives and expressed hope to them that they would be treated well. Through their new second-in-command, Leutnant Oscar Bernard, they relayed their thanks back for the crew's many kindnesses. Rathke, however, refused to join in the gesture. He was bitterly angry at the men of the *Icarus* and especially Lieutenant Jester because his crew had been machine-gunned in the water. This was something he believed no U-boat commander would ever allow. He meant to report Jester to the first person of authority he came across.

As Rathke came up from below into the bright South Carolina sunshine, he was completely back in control of himself. He had decided that he would be the kind of prisoner the National Socialist Party would want him to be. He would be proud, arrogant, and unyielding in principle until the day the war was won and he was released, not in shame from the loss of his U-boat, but in glory. Marines with fixed bayonets and scores of American and British intelligence officers were waiting at the foot of the gangplank. Rathke lined his crew up and marched them, heads up, down the plank. John Bruce winced as the Germans, most of them barefooted, were forced to stand on the brutally hot concrete and railroad tracks next to the dock. Rathke kept them standing at complete attention. Not one complaint came from their ranks. After about thirty minutes, some silent signal was apparently given and the Marines clustered about the Germans and marched them away. No one on the *Icarus* would ever hear of them again.[10]

On the same day that the *Icarus* sank the *U-352*, the *Dione* was ending her days in dry dock in Norfolk. She was now even more formidable. Two 20-mm guns had been added and her 3-inch gun had been replaced with a more powerful dual-purpose gun. The old Y-gun had been removed and new depth-charge racks added along with four modern K-guns. Her wooden mast had also been replaced by a steel one with a radar platform. Although no radar was yet available, it was promised to be installed soon. During the time in dry dock, Lieutenant Alger had sent his gunners to Dan Neck for training. They had returned very enthusiastic over their new weapons.

As it happened, Alger was in the Fifth Naval District Headquarters building, clearing the *Dione* for her return to sea, when the news about the *Icarus*'s sinking of the *U-352* came in. At first, it wasn't clear where the sinking had occurred, but after a few more dispatches, it was ascertained that the *U-352* had gone down only about 20 miles south of Cape

Lookout. This was exactly where the *Dione* would have been patrolling had she not been in dry dock. Alger knew Maurice Jester and his exec, Lieutenant Howard. They were good men, he allowed to the navy officers at Headquarters, and deserved the kill. If he was disappointed that it was the *Icarus* and not the *Dione* that had bagged the U-boat, Alger would not show it.

The *Icarus*, the twin of the *Dione*, had just happened to be passing through the *Dione*'s patrol area, an area where the *Dione* had seen for so long so much blood and death. The *Icarus* had just happened to run across the *U-352* right off Lookout where the *Dione* had spent night after night, day after day, of constant patrol, of dodging torpedoes, of depth-charge attack after attack. The *Icarus* had just happened to run across the *U-352* and had sunk her.

Those were the facts. Maurice Jester would receive the Navy Cross for his actions. Jim Alger and the *Dione* still had a war to fight.

So be it.

# 16

# The Bravest
# Little Ships

In mid-February 1942, a strange flotilla sailed from Britain, heading west. Twenty-four British antisubmarine trawlers, experienced in fighting U-boats in Britain's coastal waters and the Norwegian fjords, had been ordered to make their way across the Atlantic to assist the Americans. In many ways, it was a rescue mission. After weeks of urging Admiral King to institute a convoy system and being rebuffed, the admirals of the Royal Navy had hit upon the idea of sending the trawlers. Prime Minister Winston Churchill had quickly agreed with the plan and had alerted President Roosevelt that the ships would soon be on their way. It was clear to Churchill and his admirals, if not to Admiral King, that something had to be done and quickly. The great success of the U-boats along the American Atlantic coast wasn't just hurting the Americans. Without the supplies daily plunging to the bottom of the Graveyard of the Atlantic and elsewhere in American waters, Britain could not last long.[1]

For the trawlers the trip across the Atlantic proved to be a rough one. There were vast storms on the Atlantic during the winter of 1942, and one of them descended onto the little ships when they were only about halfway across. One of the trawlers, the *Northern Princess*, was caught by a huge wave and swamped, going down quickly. Her sisters nosed around her grave briefly, finding no survivors, and then continued on. There was no time for rescue operations. Each trawler carried 180 to 200 tons of coal, enough for only eighteen days' steaming. When they arrived in Nova Scotia, the trawlers would only have a few tons left.[2]

Because of the lack of proper fuel and repair, it would not be until 31 March that the trawlers finally sailed into American harbors. The line officers of the U.S. Navy had been eagerly anticipating their arrival. The Royal Navy, the experts in antisubmarine warfare, had promised to help their sister service get through a bad time. When the Americans got a look at the little ships, however, there was only disappointment. Manned, for the most part, by British ex-merchantmen, the trawlers were tiny vessels, barely 170 feet long, and obviously very slow, capable of a mere 12 knots at best. Any U-boat could easily outrun them. Moreover, the trawlers were all in bad need of overhaul and none of them had, as the *Eastern Sea Frontier War Diary* would put it, "so much as a wrench aboard" to accomplish it. It also became apparent that the little British ships would need a high grade of coal to operate efficiently, a grade of coal difficult for the navy to acquire. It was a reluctant United States Navy, then, that took the trawlers into dry dock for repair. The British, in turn, were all too aware of the keen American disappointment and were put off somewhat by their reception. When they received their ships back from the Brooklyn Navy Yard, they were shocked. The fine white teak decks of their trawlers had been coated with a thick layer of blue-gray paint as had everything else. Many, many hours would be spent by the British in removing it.[3]

In April, fourteen of the trawlers were patched up well enough to be placed on duty in the Eastern Sea Frontier. Once on station, they quickly proved their worth. Despite their size, they were formidably armed. A 4-inch quick-fire deck gun was aboard along with .30-caliber Lewis machine guns. There was also an assortment of depth-charge racks and launchers on their sterns that could allow them to drop a pattern of ten charges at a time. Moreover, they had the latest model sonar equipment (which they called ASDIC). The crews of the trawlers, consisting of four officers and thirty-three enlisted men, were nearly as formidable as their weapons. These men, after two years of fighting the Germans, were eager to confront the U-boats on a new battleground. Nothing seemed to bother them, not even the tumultuous winter weather of the American Atlantic coast. They were willing to steam anywhere, anytime they were needed. Immediately, their names began to be mentioned over and over in the Eastern Sea Frontier dispatches as being either already there or on the way to the rescue of torpedoed freighters and tankers. It didn't take long before their reputation spread and the U.S. Navy and Coast Guard, at least at their working levels, began to breathe a collective sigh of relief any time the tough little ships were in the area.

Two of the trawlers, however, would be destroyed by the very merchant fleet and navy they had been sent to assist. On 11 April, HMS *St. Cathan* collided with the freighter *Hebe* off Cape Lookout, with both ships sinking. All of the merchantmen would get off safely, but only nine British crewmen would survive.[4]

A month later, HMS *Senateur Duhamel* would have an unfortunate rendezvous with the destroyer USS *Semmes*, an old four-stacker commanded by Lieutenant Commander W. L. Pryor, Jr., and part of the *Roper*'s Destroyer Division 54. On 5 May, the *Semmes* was on patrol off Cape Lookout. She had spent the day there, zigzagging and on the alert for U-boats. At 0320 in the morning, Pryor was notified that the radar set was not working. A half hour later, it was repaired, and almost immediately an object was seen on her scope. The bearing of the object was fixed and determined to be no more than 2 miles away. Aware of the *Roper*'s experience with the *U-85*, Pryor ordered the *Semmes* to turn toward the object. Lookouts were ordered onto the wings of the destroyer, and when the *Semmes* was approximately one mile away, the object was seen to be some sort of ship. What kind of ship could not be determined as it turned a very bright spotlight onto the *Semmes* and left it there. Pryor shaded his eyes with his hand and tried to peer through the light to no avail. He ordered the signal "WHAT SHIP?" sent by blinker light. There was no response. Pryor had heard of U-boats using their searchlights on ships while they lined up for an attack. He kept the *Semmes* going straight toward the light, at ramming speed. Behind him, the radar operator excitedly called out the distance from the object. Suddenly he fell silent. The lookouts on the wings started yelling and Pryor rushed outside just in time to see a ship crossing the *Semmes*'s starboard bow.

It was too late for Lieutenant Commander Pryor to do anything except to watch the inexorable progress of the *Semmes* toward the unknown ship. Signalman Alvin C. Daly, however, dropped his blinker gun and hit the general alarm without waiting for orders just seconds before the *Semmes* struck the ship amidships. With a mighty roar of rending steel and splintering wood, the *Semmes* rode up and then smashed down on top of the little ship.

Pryor picked himself up as did the rest of the men on the bridge and looked down. The *Semmes* was still locked to the ship, which had fallen silent and dark. Pryor took a megaphone and yelled down. "What ship are you?" Some hoarse voices answered. It was one of the British trawlers, HMS *Senateur Duhamel*. Pryor ordered the *Roper* called, to tell Commander Norton what had happened, and then tried to back off of the *Duhamel*. After several attempts, she slid free, the sound of more rending metal evidence that great damage had been done to the trawler.

The *Roper* soon came into view, standing clear to assist as required. The harried *Duhamel* skipper used a flashing light to ask the *Semmes* to also stay in the area while he sorted things out. A shout from the water below revealed that one of the British seamen, one J. Wood, had been knocked into the sea by the collision. He was taken aboard the *Semmes*. Pryor ordered a boat lowered to pick up any other British who might be in the water. The *Roper* did the same. By 0514, the *Roper*'s lookouts reported that the *Duhamel* was no longer in sight and apparently had sunk. At sunrise, the trawler's masts could be seen, the ship sitting on the bottom. Remarkably, all of the *Senateur Duhamel*'s crew would be rescued. The *Semmes* was also lucky; there were no casualties except for some severe bruises. Although a tragedy had been somehow avoided, there was one less ship to help the Americans.[5]

Destined to become perhaps the most famous and tragic of the trawlers was HMS *Bedfordshire*. The officers and crew of the *Dione* knew her. She had been the trawler helping the *Dione* the day the *Harry S. Sinclair, Jr.*, had been torpedoed.[6] Lieutenant Alger and several of his officers visited the *Bedfordshire* after that incident to thank the British for their assistance. Alger would later recall the officers and crew of the trawlers to be "very gallant gentlemen who went out of their way to bear a hand when it was most needed. They were the bravest little ships you could imagine."[7]

It was in late April that the chain of events leading to tragedy began. The *Bedfordshire* was in Norfolk for supplies when two North Carolinians met two of her officers in a restaurant. The North Carolinians were Wahab Howard of Ocracoke and Shanklyn Austin of Hatteras. One of the British officers was Sub-Lieutenant Thomas Cunningham, a thin young man with a dark black beard and a delightfully British sense of humor. During the meal, Cunningham regaled the Americans with several anecdotes of life in the Royal Navy. When Howard told him he was from Ocracoke, North Carolina, Cunningham wanted to know where that was. When told, the two officers told Howard and Austin that they were heading in that direction, to nearby Morehead City. When the dinner was over, Howard expressed hope that he would get to see them again. Cunningham said that he hoped so, too, and held out his hand. As Howard said goodbye, he noticed the young officer's unusual yellow-gold watch with a black leather band and his yellow-gold ring with initials set in black onyx. As it would turn out, he would have reason to remember these things.[8]

In late April, the *Bedfordshire* was indeed working out of Morehead City, often in company with the *Dione* and the *Calypso*, and also with her sister trawler, the *Senateur Dubamel*. While the trawler was in port one day, Aycock Brown, a civilian special investigator for the Office of Naval Intelligence, had reason to make an official call. Bodies from the British ship *San Delfino*, sunk by the *U-203*, had washed ashore along the Outer Banks and needed to be buried. Brown met Lieutenant R. B. Davis, the *Bedfordshire*'s skipper, and also Sub-Lieutenant Cunningham and made his request. Might the trawler assist in properly burying these men? Needed were some British flags and also perhaps a British burial party. Cunningham regretted that patrol duties would keep him from supplying any men for a burial party, but he might be able to supply the flags. He disappeared below, returning soon afterwards with a stack of neatly folded Union Jacks. Brown thanked the British officer and started to leave but was stopped by an offer of a portion of Royal Navy rum. Brown agreed to this idea and before the afternoon was over, he had become friends with the slight young officer. During their conversation, Cunningham related the happy news that he and his wife were soon expecting their first child. By coincidence, Lieutenant Davis and his wife were also expecting. When the babies came, Cunningham said, the *Bedfordshire* would be holding a party that he was certain Morehead City would never forget. Would Brown be interested in attending? Aycock Brown said that he would, indeed, and hoped to see Cunningham before that as well. Cunningham said that he hoped so, too, but that the *Bedfordshire* had almost finished her reprovisioning and would shortly take to sea. It would be possibly weeks before the *Bedfordshire* would return to port. When Brown left the British ship, however, he had the strange feeling that he would see Cunningham very soon. But a few days later, he went by the trawler's berth and saw that she had left on her patrol. He silently wished her all the luck and went about his duties.[9]

Also on patrol off Morehead City was another ship, the German U-boat *U-558*. A very successful U-boat, the Type VIIC *U-558* had been credited with sinking ten ships in previous patrols. It had also already encountered the United States Navy. Even before the Americans had entered the war, the destroyer USS *Kearny*, while trying to screen a convoy in the North Atlantic, had been severely damaged by a *U-558* torpedo attack.[10] The *U-558*'s skipper, Kapitänleutnant Günther Krech, was only twenty-eight years old but was an aggressive, colorful officer who had trained under one of Germany's best U-boat aces, Kapitänleutnant Joachim Schepke of the *U-100*.

Part of the *U-558*'s fame lay with Krech's seagoing aquarium. In a tank in the control room were a variety of tropical fish, each named for the leaders of the countries at war with Germany. Krech's favorite fish was Churchill, a small, mean-tempered pirate fish. When Churchill died after three patrols, he was placed in an alcohol-filled glass tube and hung, with proper ceremony, from a lamp in the wardroom where the crew could touch him for luck. On 12 April, Krech took the *U-558* out of Brest and headed for America. Along the way, he rendezvoused with one of the new "milch-cows," huge new U-boats built to carry oil, diesel fuel, torpedoes, and other supplies to keep the fighting U-boats at sea as long as possible. Admiral Andrews and his staff had heard rumors concerning these new U-boats, but were not certain of their existence. But exist they did and after refueling, Krech continued, arriving on 5 May off Cape Lookout.[11]

For a week, Krech maneuvered around Lookout. Hardegen and all the other U-boat skippers had said this was a lucrative area, but no targets came into view except, briefly, one of the Bucket Brigades. Krech went after it, but it was a fast-moving convoy and after a 50-mile chase reluctantly had to give up. He was now southeast of Cape Lookout, near Frying Pan Shoals. He spent two days there, slowly circling, without seeing anything. At 1400 on 11 May, however, he heard the sound of propellers. Coming to periscope depth, he saw two small vessels coming toward him. Every crewmember of the *U-558* involuntarily shuddered when they suddenly heard the *ping* of British ASDIC. Whatever the vessels were, they weren't merchantmen. They were obviously U-boat hunters of some sort.

Krech took the *U-558* down and waited. Four hours later, he heard depth-charge detonations in the distance and then more propeller sounds. Fearful the vessels might be closing in on him, he waited for an hour before coming to periscope depth to look around. The sun was just setting, and silhouetted against the horizon were the two patrol vessels, still in a search pattern. It was only a matter of time, Krech realized, before these two persistent vessels would find him. He made a decision. He would wait forty-five minutes and then come to the surface and make a run for it using his diesels. This he did, heading south at the *U-558*'s maximum speed of 18 knots.

Lookouts on the conning tower called Krech's attention to a flashing white light behind them. The light was switched off, but Krech ordered the lookouts to continue their watch. It was apparent something was following them. After running for two hours, the lookouts called out to Krech again. They had spotted a ship coming up on their stern. Krech followed their pointing fingers with his binoculars. *There!* Whatever it was wasn't gaining on them but it was definitely following. It was also small and all alone. Krech found it hard to believe such a ship would dare chase him. Perhaps, however, he was being chased into a trap. In that case, there was only one thing to do. Kapitänleutnant Günther Krech was never one for running. Sinking ships, any kind of ships, that was his specialty. Krech turned the *U-558* around. He was going to take the small warship on, one on one.

The *U-558* slid under the waves while Krech turned his white cap around and swung his leg over the seat behind the attack periscope in the control room. He grasped the handles on the periscope and swiveled it around. As his U-boat got closer, he recognized his quarry. It was one of the British antisubmarine trawlers. That explained its aggressiveness. When the trawler was 1,000 meters away, Krech ordered two torpedoes fired and then took his U-boat down to await the sound of their explosions. After several minutes, however, it was evident that the torpedoes had missed. Cautiously, Krech took the *U-558* back up and looked around. The trawler was still there and now barely 600 meters away and turning in Krech's direction. Had he been seen? He didn't wait to find out. He made a quick calculation, lining the *U-558*'s bow directly toward the trawler. *"Los!"* Krech snapped and a third torpedo was on its way.

This time, Krech didn't take his U-boat down. He didn't dare. He had to see what happened to the trawler. If this torpedo missed, the British were going to be right on top of him. A man was behind Krech, quietly counting, an infinity seeming to pass between each second. At count number 36, there was a huge explosion. The trawler had turned at the last mo-

ment and the torpedo had caught it squarely amidships. The
trawler, which was the *Bedfordshire*, was thrown up on her
bow, her stern jerking upward. Krech blinked and in that instant, the *Bedfordshire* was gone, leaving nothing but a spreading wake over the rippling sea. The soundman below reported
scraping sounds, the noise of a dying ship going to its grave.
Remembering the other patrol vessel that had been with the
trawler, Krech took the *U-558* down and headed south. The
last signal the *Bedfordshire* had sent out had been a routine
message at 1512 EWT, 11 May 1942. As far as the United
States Navy knew, the *Bedfordshire* was still on her patrol between buoys 4 and 14 south of Cape Lookout. She had no set
time to call in. HMS *Bedfordshire* was dead and no one knew
but Günther Krech and the men of the *U-558*.[12]

Three days passed. It was spring along the North Carolina
capes, a beautiful but capricious time of gusty winds and sudden storms. On the morning of 14 May, however, the sky was
clear and blue. Only a slight breeze occasionally rippled the
fields of sea oats growing wild among the sand dunes of the
Outer Banks. A single coast guard truck traveling slowly
down the beach was the only thing disturbing the peaceful
morning. Inside the truck were two young coast guardsmen,
one of them Arnold Tolson, a native of the nearby Buxton. At
about 0700, Tolson thought he saw something in the surf. It
appeared to be a man waving. Tolson knew it couldn't be a
swimmer. There was no one who lived anywhere nearby and,
anyway, the sea was too cold at that time of year. No, anyone
in the sea off the Outer Banks that morning was either crazy
. . . or dead. Tolson stopped the truck and jumped out. At the
surf, he took off his shoes and waded out until he reached the
body. It was fully clothed in what appeared to be a black uniform. Tolson and the other coast guardsman loaded the body
in the back of their truck and took off toward the Ocracoke
Coast Guard Station. Before they got there, however, a local
fisherman stopped them and told them he had also seen a body
in the surf, near the inlet. Tolson turned his truck around and
drove back toward the point, searching the waves carefully.
Before too long, he saw it. Tolson again waded out and re-
trieved the body, loaded it in the back of the truck, and headed

once more for the station. The chief of the station, Homer Gray, took the two bodies and placed them in a room at the back of the station and then called navy headquarters in Morehead City to report what had happened.[13]

In Morehead City, it was Aycock Brown who was ordered to respond. He procured an amphibian aircraft from Cherry Point and flew to Ocracoke where Gray met him and led him to the back room of the station. When the tarpaulin covering the two bodies was thrown back, Brown started at the sight of one of them, a young man with a beard. "I know that man," he gasped. "He's from the *Bedfordshire*!"[14]

It was Sub-Lieutenant Thomas Cunningham. Papers in the man's pocket confirmed it. Sunglasses and a bankbook from a Morehead City bank were in his Royal Navy sweater and a Morehead City newspaper was in his hip pocket. There were no wounds on the body at all.

As required by regulations, Brown gently removed Cunningham's sweater and his shoes for identification and placed them along with the papers and personal effects into a small box. Included were the ring and watch that Wahab Howard had noticed in the Norfolk restaurant. The next day, when word of the event spread through Ocracoke, Howard would learn that his friend had died. Papers and a name on his shirt identified the other body as Stanley Craig, ordinary telegraphist, Royal Navy. A local doctor, Charles L. Swindell, was called in to determine the cause of death. Since there were no external wounds, Dr. Swindell concluded that the men had probably been killed by either concussion or drowning or both. After Dr. Swindell left, Brown turned to the next step: burial. Regulations, as well as Outer Banks custom, required burial as soon as possible. There were no morticians on the Outer Banks, and Dr. Swindell had estimated that the men had been dead for several days. Some sort of arrangements would have to be made immediately.

Aycock Brown and Chief Homer Gray had initiative. Gray remembered that two large wooden boxes had recently been found near Ocracoke. These boxes, in shape and size similar to coffins, were called by the locals "battery" or "sink" boxes. Duck hunters would lie on their backs in them while floating beside their decoys and then, as the ducks approached, rise up and fire away. To assure propriety, the Ocracoke postmaster, considered by all to be the local authority on all things legal or otherwise, gave his considered opinion that the boxes were abandoned property and could be confiscated for any use by the coast guard.

The funeral was solemn and dignified, as befitted two heroes who had come from a foreign land to protect American lives and property. Plots were donated by the Williams family beside their own in the little Ocracoke cemetery. A United States Coast Guard honor guard acted as pallbearers, and the caskets were draped in two of the Union Jacks that Cunningham had given Brown. Amasa Fulcher, a lay preacher for the Methodist (and only) Church in Ocracoke, conducted the service and even sang an appropriate hymn. It was, in many ways, a typical Outer Banks funeral given by a people who had known all their lives the hardships rendered by the sea.*

After the funeral, Brown finally got around to calling his headquarters to report what he had found. He was greeted with consternation. The men could not be from the *Bedfordshire*, he was told sharply. There had been no distress call from that ship. She was still on patrol. When pressed by Brown, the officer at headquarters went to check his file. When he returned, he was more sympathetic. The last time anyone had heard from the *Bedfordshire* had been on 11 May. Perhaps she had indeed run into trouble. Or, maybe, the officer brightened, the two men had simply fallen overboard and drowned! Brown could only shake his head at that idea. It was not feasible that two trained British seamen were going to fall overboard and be left by their mates to drown.[15] It would not be until 16 May that the navy would finally admit that the *Bedfordshire* was missing in action and probably lost.[16]

A week later, Arnold Tolson, on board the USCG patrol boat *63-067*, would again have an encounter with the crew of the British trawler. On patrol 5 miles northeast of Ocracoke

---

* Cared for by coast guardsmen from the Ocracoke Station, the graves are still there. British warships still occasionally send memorial parties to visit them.

Inlet, the little 63-footer hove to beside two floating bodies, and Tolson helped pull them aboard. They were in bad condition, but Tolson recognized them by their dark blue turtleneck sweaters. They were men from the *Bedfordshire*. Aycock Brown was again called in to make identification. These bodies, however, proved to be too deteriorated to positively identify. Also no battery boxes were available, but the men at the coast guard station knew of a local resident who had, some years earlier, purchased a supply of lumber to build a new outhouse. The man was approached. Since he had never gotten around to using the lumber as intended, would he be willing to donate some of it to build caskets for two of our valiant allies? The man quickly agreed, and several local carpenters volunteered to do the work. Another Outer Banks funeral was held, and the two men were laid to rest beside Cunningham and Craig. Two more bodies would be found from the *Bedfordshire*. One, identified as Seaman Alfred Dryden, would be found in late May and interred at the Oak Grove Baptist Cemetery at Creeds, Virginia. He would be buried with full military honors, with a contingent of officers and men from the other British trawlers in attendance. The last body, only tentatively identified as a *Bedfordshire* crewman, was buried near the coast guard station at Cape Hatteras. All the other *Bedfordshire* crewmen remained missing forever.[17]

Other trawlers would yet die in the battle and all of them would be battered and wounded, but still they would fight the U-boats. They were slow and ungainly and easily sunk, but in many ways, they would have the Royal Navy's finest moment ever in American waters. Each day, they went out to meet an enemy that was bigger, faster, more heavily armed, and able to remain hidden until it was ready to strike. Even though they would receive more casualties than they would inflict, they kept coming, fighting America's battle. They were, indeed, "the bravest little ships."

# 17

# Torpedo Junction
# Moves South

At the end of April 1942, Admiral Andrews was still holding all American tankers in port, except for an occasional Bucket Brigade, until a full convoy system could be devised. Tankers of other countries and all freighters were, however, still sailing and often alone. Reports received by Admiral Doenitz indicated that much of this unprotected traffic was occurring off the Florida Atlantic coast, so he decided to expand his operations there.[1] In effect, Torpedo Junction was moving south. As May 1942 opened, the *U-109* torpedoed the British tanker *La Paz* just off Miami. The *U-109*'s skipper, Kapitänleutnant Heinrich Bleichrodt, waited until he saw the tanker settle to the bottom and then turned and brazenly ran north on his diesels within full view of startled citizens driving along the Florida coastal highway.[2] When he got 10 miles southeast of Cape Canaveral, he blasted the tiny Nicaraguan banana boat *Worden* out of the water with his deck gun.[3] People on the beach saw the U-boat clearly, and soon the navy and coast guard offices were besieged with reports. It seemed as if the entire Florida Atlantic coast had been attacked by a fleet of U-boats, when in fact it was only Bleichrodt enjoying himself immensely. In any case, the navy did little in response. Convoy duty was the first priority and there just weren't enough ships left for much antisubmarine activity.

It did not seem to be a good time to be aboard a banana boat. On 3 May, the *U-506*, commanded by Kapitänleutnant Erich Würdemann, was heading determinedly south off Fort Lauderdale when lookouts on the conn spotted the *Sama*. Würdemann sent a single torpedo at the small Nicaraguan freighter, blowing it in two. Remarkably, all of the fourteen members of the crew were able to get off in lifeboats, although a few of them were injured when they fell on canted decks slippery with crushed bananas.[4]

Close behind Würdemann was Korvettenkapitän Reinhard Suhren of the *U-564*. Suhren decided to patrol between the navigational lights of Cape Canaveral and Jupiter Inlet and was rewarded with the kill of the freighter *Ocean Venus*, her surviving crew rowing ashore at Cape Canaveral.[5] Bleichrodt was still in the area, and two hours after the *Ocean Venus* was sunk, the *U-109* attacked the Dutch freighter *Laertes* and sank her and her cargo of lend-lease material destined for India (three airplanes, seventeen medium tanks, and twenty trucks). Although the radio operator on the *Laertes* called for help, no one answered. While lifeboats were being lowered, Bleichrodt sent another torpedo streaming in. Eighteen men were blown to bits.[6]

The next day, Suhren was maneuvering just off Boca Raton in broad daylight and in full view of sunbathers on the beach when the British tanker *Eclipse* came sailing up the 10-fathom line, paralleling the coast. The *Eclipse*'s second officer saw the *U-564*'s torpedo coming in and ordered a "hard-a-starboard," but it was too late. The torpedo struck one of the after bunkers and blew up, the shock wave rolling over the frightened people on shore like thunder.[7] Suhren continued his assault by blasting the American freighter *Delisle* and her cargo of camouflage paint. Just as with the *Eclipse*, however, the ship was abandoned but later towed in for repairs.[8] In any case, the word quickly went out to other U-boats. The Florida Torpedo Junction was open.

* * *

One of the U-boat commanders eager to share in the spoils of a patrol to America was the remarkable Kapitänleutnant Peter Cremer of the *U-333*. Bright and aggressive, Cremer was one of Doenitz's favorites and was widely believed to be headed toward higher command. Although his family had expected him to be a lawyer, Cremer, at the age of eighteen, instead applied to the German Navy for a commission. By the time he was twenty-nine, Peter Cremer was a U-boat commander and destined to become one of the best.[9]

On 30 March 1942, Cremer took his *U-333* out of one of the massive concrete bunkers at La Pallice and headed west. With lookouts on the tower anxiously studying the gray, dangerous skies, he carefully worked his way to the open sea and then took his U-boat down. Assigned to her in July 1941, Cremer had been the *U-333*'s only commander and had worried over every detail of her construction from bulkheads to blankets. Emblazoned on her side were "three little fishes," taken from the American hit tune of the same name and also meant to represent the 3 "3s" of the *unterseeboot*.[10]

By March 1942, the *U-333* had already been on several war cruises and had been credited with sinking three ships for a total of 14,000 tons.[11] But Cremer and his crew had thirsted for greater tonnage and glory, of which both, in 1942, were supposed to be abundant only in the waters of the New World. Brazenly, Cremer had asked Admiral Doenitz for an assignment there and, after receiving it, had further compounded his forwardness by asking for liberty in Paris first. Amused, Doenitz had granted the leave and burst out laughing when Cremer had then asked for a loan.[12]

On board the *U-333*, Cremer could not help but smile as he thought of that moment and the next days in Paris. His loan had not lasted long. In fact, he had run out of francs while sitting in a fancy restaurant with three long-limbed Parisian beauties. To cover the debt, he had written a note that Admiral Doenitz would pay, figuring that he would be at sea when his commander received the bill.[13]

And that's exactly what had happened. When Doenitz received the note demanding payment from the restaurant, the *U-333* was two-thirds of the way across the Atlantic and preparing to rendezvous with the *U-459*, a "milch cow" commanded by Fregattenkapitän Graf Georg von Wilamowitz-Moellendorf. Von Wilamowitz-Moellendorf was to Cremer "an old gentleman from the Kaiser's time" but still very much a competent submarine skipper.[14] After refueling from the tanker U-boat, Cremer kept heading west. Cremer, unlike Rathke in the *U-352*, which was coming across the Atlantic at nearly the same time, was supremely confident in the abilities of himself and his crew, not to mention his own personal *fingerspitzenzeful*. Several days later, however, something happened that could only be ascribed to bad luck. The *U-333* was motoring on the surface in a dense fog when, out of the gloom, a big tanker suddenly materialized dead ahead. When the tanker was 200 yards away, Cremer fired two torpedoes. As they sped away, the sudden lightening of the U-boat caused it to rise to the surface and then wallow before sinking back down. Cremer, distracted by the destabilization, turned back to his periscope only when he heard two heavy thumps. He jammed his eyes against the eyepiece and then snapped his head back, yelling, "Hard to starboard, Chief!"

The *U-333* sluggishly turned while every eye in the control room searched Cremer's face for an answer. Then they heard it. Hideous groans and massive spews of bubbles surrounded the U-boat. Was the tanker sinking on top of them? A huge impact knocked the German crew to the deck as the tanker slammed down on the *U-333*'s bow. Locked in a deathly embrace, it seemed to Cremer that U-boat and tanker were beginning the long journey to the bottom, some 5,000 feet below. *"Blow all tanks! Blow everything!"*

The *U-333*, its bow forced almost straight down, tore her way across the tanker's bottom, and then popped to the surface. Cremer threw open the conning-tower hatch. The tanker was still there. It had rammed the *U-333* and had not been sinking as he had thought. The tanker, the *British Prestige*, seemed to be undamaged. The *U-333*, on the other hand, was in poor shape. Her bow was twisted and mangled, her bridge completely flattened with the attack periscope snapped off. A quick inspection also revealed the direction-finder destroyed along with the surface torpedo-aiming sight. A report also came back that the caps on two of the bow torpedo tubes were jammed. "What a ----ing mess!" his engineer had summed up.[15]

Cremer, suddenly beset with many problems to solve, could do nothing but let the *British Prestige* continue on her journey. As it would later be learned, the tanker had not gotten away unscathed. Although Cremer's torpedoes had been duds, his U-boat's bow and bridge had managed to slice neatly through the entire length of the outer hull of the tanker. Luckily, the inner hull had remained intact. The cargo of the *British Prestige* had been volatile airplane fuel. If the *U-333* had penetrated the inner hull, one spark would have set it all off, destroying both tanker and U-boat. At least Cremer had managed that little bit of luck, unrecognized though it was at the time.[16]

The *U-333* limped on, the crew completely absorbed in repairing the damage as much as possible. Most of the conning tower fairing, crushed like paper, was stripped off, the direction-finder made watertight with cement and wooden pegs, and the mangled conduit in the conning tower straightened and welded. To substitute for the direction-finder, Cremer mounted his binoculars on a rail. If he had to, he intended to simply aim his entire U-boat. To underscore his perseverance, Cremer entered the following entry into his log: "Intention—ahead into the Straits of Florida. Surfaced by day, in no circumstances return home without steamer."[17]

The *U-333*, only barely operational by any definition, was nevertheless still going in to fight the Americans. To outsiders, it might have seemed a desperate plan. To Cremer and his crew, it was glorious. Paris now seemed a very, very long time ago.

On 4 May 1942, the *U-333* arrived to take her station in the Straits of Florida, the narrow gap between the Florida Atlantic coast and the Bahamas. After carefully inspecting the area with his remaining periscope, Cremer brought the *U-333* up onto an unbelievably placid sea. It was evening and the men of the *U-333* could not help but rub their eyes in wonder. Behind them was a blacked-out Europe. Here, the buoys were still blinking and the Jupiter Lighthouse was sweeping its bright beam of light far out to sea. The *U-333* was cruising parallel to the coastal road and there could be seen the headlights of many cars traveling back and forth. Intrigued, Cremer took his U-boat in so close he could read the neon signs on the garish hotels lining the beach. To the south, a great glow announced Miami. It was incredible. After nearly five months of war, there was still no blackout off Florida. All Cremer had to do was to back out to sea and wait until something came between him and those lights. Whatever it was, he vowed, would die.[18]

On 5 May, his vow was fulfilled. The big 8,327-ton Socony-Vacuum Oil tanker *Java Arrow*, plowing unconcernedly south in ballast, motored right into his makeshift binocular sights. The *Java Arrow* had straggled from her Bucket Brigade convoy and was not zigzagging. Two torpedoes struck her in her port side, sending her captain and crew to the lifeboats.[19]

A few hours later, a small freighter, the 2,000-ton *Amazone*, appeared, and Cremer pumped two more torpedoes into her. The *Amazone*'s stern broke off, and then both sections caught fire after her crew had escaped.[20]

Grimly satisfied, Cremer listened while the navy and coast guard called back and forth in the clear to each other and other merchantmen. There seemed to be no radio discipline whatsoever. Cremer easily avoided several coastal picket boats and then submerged. Soon, the sounds of another ship passing nearby reached him, and he came to the surface to identify it. It was the 6,986-ton tanker *Halsey*, traveling north all alone (and in violation of Admiral Andrews's orders) with 80,000 barrels of naptha and fuel oil. Cremer sent two torpedoes slamming into her, destroying two lifeboats and ripping open the entire port side. Two hours later, in an atmosphere of almost pure naptha, her nearly asphyxiated crew of thirty-two pulled away in the remaining two lifeboats. The *U-333* nosed in closer and sent in another torpedo to finish the tanker off. It missed, but shortly afterwards the *Halsey* exploded anyway with huge pieces of her hull thrown hundreds of feet into the air. As the *Halsey* rained down around him, Cremer hurriedly ordered the *U-333* submerged.[21]

Despite the crippled condition of their U-boat, Cremer and his crew had managed to do enormous damage to the

Americans. But within a few hours of sinking the *Halsey*, an American subchaser found the *U-333* and immediately began to attack. As the sound of propellers filled the ears of the crew of the *U-333*, they knew they were in trouble.

Cremer had the *U-333* down to 60 feet when the first depth charge from the coast guard patrol vessel *PC 451* came tumbling down. The explosion snapped the *U-333*'s bow upward, sending her crew howling to the deck while food and equipment rained down on them. A shouted report informed Cremer that the hydroplanes of his U-boat were frozen. Cremer ordered all ballast tanks flooded to keep the *U-333* from breaking the surface. The U-boat dropped like a stone, its stern crunching into the sandy bottom first. While the crew hung on, the *U-333* turned on the fulcrum of her stern and then slammed down on the sand. Before they could recover, propeller noises followed by splashes overhead told the crew more hell was on its way. The *U-333* was shaken and then knocked over on her side by the depth charges. There were more pings of American sonar. Another depth-charge run was coming.

Cremer wasn't sure if his U-boat was going to be able to take the punishment. Diving tanks and oil bunkers were already leaking and certainly telling the Americans his location. The emergency lighting system was barely operational, the lights providing only a pale, yellow glow. More reports came back. The depth gauge and rudder indicator were *kaput*, the engine-room telegraph broken, the diesel air-supply mast and exhaust-system valves leaking. The sea was determinedly gaining access to the *U-333* from a dozen and more different places. There was only one thing to do. *Run.*[22]

An attempt to rise from the bottom failed. The stern was too heavy. More depth charges came down. Cremer ordered the electric engines full ahead. He trundled through the sand, going east, toward deeper water. Seven hours later, he was still wallowing through what had turned to mud, his attackers swarming overhead. Exhausted, he wondered how much longer his crew and his boat could take it. Suddenly, word came back from his soundman. The attackers were withdrawing. What had happened, in fact, was that the cutter *Vigilant*

and the two other coast guard patrol boats that had been attacking Cremer had been ordered to return to Fort Pierce to
accompany a convoy. It had been luck, pure luck, but Cremer
and the *U-333* had survived. He surfaced just as the destroyer
*Dallas* arrived to continue the attack. Cremer took the *U-333*
down again. The *Dallas*, however, could never quite get a fix
on the *U-333* and, after a series of short attacks, wandered
away.[23]

Cremer again took his U-boat up. He had to in order to get
the seawater out of his boat and to improve the foul air he and
his men were breathing. The *U-333* rose into a dark, clear
night, and Cremer threw open the conning-tower hatch and
clambered outside. Below, his men clustered beneath the single hatch, taking in great draughts of fresh, cool air. One of his
lookouts clutched Cremer's arm. The *Dallas* was nearby, only
2,000 yards away. It was still maneuvering and as Cremer
watched, a pattern of depth charges was dropped. Cremer
turned the *U-333* away from the destroyer and slipped away,
bound for the open sea. He kept maneuvering in the deeper
water while his crew struggled with the repairs.[24]

As luck would have it, also on the sea the next morning
was the 38-foot week-end cabin cruiser, *Jay-Tee*. The *Jay-Tee*
was a member of the civilian volunteer "Hooligan Navy" and,
though completely unarmed, was on antisubmarine patrol.
Her crew consisted entirely of a Fort Lauderdale fishing boat
skipper, Willard Lewis, and "Uncle Bill," an ancient Fort Lauderdale character who had never given anyone his last name.
Lewis and Uncle Bill had been asked to look for a torpedoed
ship, but what they found instead was the *U-333* on the surface, her crew frantically at work on the frozen hydroplanes.
Lewis swung the wheel over and fired up the converted Buick
automobile engine in the tiny boat and headed for the submarine. He wasn't certain what he was going to do when he got
there, but maybe he could at least scare the thing away. Luckily, before he got to it, the U-boat dived. Lewis headed for the
spot of spreading oil that marked its last location. But by
the time the *Jay-Tee* got there, there was no other sign of the
raider. After a few minutes, Uncle Bill spotted it again some
1,000 yards away, and once more Lewis turned the cabin

cruiser after the "Gray Wolf." Cremer, testing his hydroplanes
and not even aware of the tiny boat, took the *U-333* down
before the *Jay-Tee* got near him.

"Dammit, we've lost her!" Lewis griped after fifteen minutes had gone by with no sign of the U-boat. "The boys back
at base will never believe we saw a sub."

Uncle Bill gravely nodded agreement. The old man was
not a talkative soul. But he let out a whoop of astonishment
when the *Jay-Tee* shuddered once, lurched, and then began to
rise. Cremer, still completely unaware of the *Jay-Tee*, had surfaced his U-boat directly beneath the cabin cruiser. While
Lewis and Uncle Bill staggered on deck like drunken sailors,
the *Jay-Tee* went up, up, up, all the while rattling around on
the U-boat's deck. Cremer and his crew, below, looked up
with knitted brows. What the hell was that? He ordered the
*U-333* back down and the *Jay-Tee* slid off. Lewis crawled to the
gun'l and looked over. He could see the phosphorescent out-
line of the big submarine drawing away. Could they follow it?
Uncle Bill wasn't interested. His advice was to get the hell out
of the area before the damn thing came back. Lewis agreed.
The *Jay-Tee* ran for it, her bottom scored with blue and black
paint and planks ripped and torn from her side. With that as
evidence, Lewis had little trouble convincing the other members of the Hooligan Navy that he had, indeed, seen a U-boat.[25]

Cremer, perhaps puzzled but otherwise unaware of his encounter with the *Jay-Tee*, decided to keep heading west. Before
long, the freighter *Clan Skene* came into view and he drilled
two torpedoes into her, waiting around just long enough to see
the ship sink.[26] Cremer had a feeling his luck was about to run
out if he stayed any longer. The *U-333*, almost mortally
wounded, sailed for France. She would never again return to
American waters, but for Cremer and crew, it had been a
grand and glorious adventure.[27]

The assault continued along the Florida coast for the remainder of the month. Suhren, moving a little south, caught
the freighter *Ohioan* at high noon lolling along close to shore
between Boca Raton and Pompano Beach. The *U-564*'s torpedo struck the freighter, loaded with manganese ore, wool,
and licorice root, on her starboard side. The ship went down

so quickly that there was no chance of anyone getting into the lifeboats. Luckily, however, some liferafts broke free and twenty-two survivors were able to climb onto them. Fifteen of their crewmates drowned.[28]

That night, Suhren continued his success by sinking the Panamanian tanker *Lubrafol* close in to Pompano Beach. The thunder of his torpedoes rattled the windows of the sleepy little community and sent many citizens streaming to the beach, where they were confronted with the sight of the blazing tanker.[29]

Suhren moved south to see what he could find nearer Miami. Five days later, he spotted the Mexican tanker *Potrero Del Llano* coming at him neither zigzagging nor observing any blackout precautions whatsoever. In fact, the vessel was brilliantly lighted with four spotlights illuminating the Mexican flag that had been painted on a canvas frame and mounted amidships. The captain of the *Potrero Del Llano* firmly believed that his vessel's nationality would keep him from being torpedoed. Suhren had no time to wonder what the spotlights were for. He laid a torpedo into the side of the tanker at five minutes to midnight. One of the *Potrero Del Llano*'s bunkers blew, completely demolishing the bridge. The chief engineer, left in charge, ordered the engines stopped, but that was the last coherent thing accomplished. Crewmembers fashioned all manner of rafts out of planks and anything else that would float and jumped overboard. As the tanker groaned and sank, the *U-564* was observed slowly circling her kill. Later that night, two coast guard patrol boats came into the area and picked up the twenty-two crewmembers still alive. Thirteen had been killed either by the explosion or by drowning.[30]

Luck still was bad for anyone on a banana boat anywhere near Florida. The small American trader *Nicarao*, carrying a cargo of 21,700 banana stems, 1,400 bags of coconuts, and some charcoal was hit by a torpedo from Kapitänleutnant Gerhard Bigalk's *U-751* on the night of 15 May. No one aboard the ship saw the U-boat, but her captain saw the torpedo's track. There was no time for manuever, however, and the torpedo struck about 5 feet below the waterline. That broke the ship's back, and she went down quickly in a rough sea. There would be thirty-one survivors out of a crew of thirty-nine. These would be picked up by the tanker *Esso Augusta* the next day.[31]

Bigalk kept going. In fact, most of the U-boats were on the move again. Admiral Doenitz was diverting his U-boats once more. The target this time: the Gulf of Mexico.[32]

# 18

# Into the Gulf

To the U-boats, the Gulf of Mexico was a vast new sea to exploit. There were dozens of ways to slip into it, and the primary trade routes were well known. All a U-boat commander had to do was to position himself near one of those routes and wait. In May, the first U-boat into the Gulf was Korvettenkapitän Harro Schacht and his *U-507*.[1]

Schacht gained his first kill by sinking the small freighter *Norlindo* on 4 May 80 miles northwest of the Dry Tortugas. Since there was no time to launch the lifeboats, the *Norlindo*'s crew was forced to jump overboard. Eight hours later, just before nightfall, the Honduran banana boat *San Blas* happened upon the tired, cold, and shocked men and pulled them aboard.[2]

Schacht had not waited to see the fate of the crew. Doenitz had ordered him to patrol deep into the Gulf and that was his intention. When he was approximately 100 miles southwest of Naples, he made a vicious attack on the *Munger T. Ball*, laden with a full cargo of gasoline. After sending two torpedoes into the American tanker, he rose to the surface and ordered the machine guns unlimbered. While the crew of the tanker milled around on deck, Schacht fired indiscriminately in an attempt to set the gasoline in the bunkers on fire. Instead, he

set the gasoline on the water ablaze, incinerating the crewmen
who had jumped overboard to get away from the machine-gun
fire. Although Schacht apparently was not deliberately aiming
his guns at them, others of the crew were hit and killed on
deck. Fifteen minutes after the first torpedo had struck the
tanker, she sank. There were only four survivors left by then.
As these men struggled in the water, Schacht ran nearby and
then kept going. Miraculously, that night, the four survivors
were spotted by the freighter *Katy*, rescued, and taken to Key
West.[3]

Three hours after sinking the *Munger T. Ball*, the *U-507*
and the coldly efficient Schacht struck again. The victim this
time was another tanker, the *Joseph M. Cudaby*. The *Cudaby*'s
master, Walter E. Reed, had seen the *Munger T. Ball* burst into
flames about 9 miles south of his location and had turned his
ship toward Tampa in an attempt to run for it. Schacht, however, had spotted the *Cudaby* and was in hot pursuit. When he
caught her, he sent a single torpedo into her starboard side.
Instantly, the ship exploded and was enveloped in flames from
amidships to the after end. The next morning, a navy PBY
plane, ordered to search for survivors based on the distress
signals received, found Reed and eight men in a lifeboat. One
other survivor was picked up the same morning. Of the crew
of thirty-seven, twenty-seven were lost.[4]

Schacht was far from through with his killing spree. By
noon on 6 May, he had managed to take the *U-507* all the way
to the mouth of the Mississippi and on the shipping lane leading into the port of Mobile, Alabama. There, the *Alcoa Puritan*,
loaded with 10,000 tons of bauxite, steamed into his sights.
Aboard the freighter were also eight survivors from the Esso
tanker *T. C. McCobb*, sunk about 600 miles east of Georgetown,
British Guiana, by the Italian submarine *Pietro Calvi*. Lookouts on the stern spotted the *U-507*'s torpedo and alerted the
master, Y. A. Krantz. Krantz called down to his chief engineer
and told him to "hook her up!" The *Alcoa Puritan* churned
ahead, dodging the torpedo. Schacht began to chase the
freighter, with his deck gun firing. After about 25 minutes of
wild shelling, one of the rounds hit the fantail, causing the
ship to swing out of control. Krantz saw that he had no

chance, so he ordered the ship stopped and abandoned.
Schacht seemed to take no notice. He kept shelling. One lifeboat was blown up just before the men crawled into it and
another was riddled with shrapnel. This boat was launched
anyway, even though constant bailing was required to keep it
afloat. The rest of the crew jumped overboard and clung to a
raft. Schacht barely let the lifeboat get out of the way before
he sent another torpedo streaming into the side of the burning
tanker. The tanker shuddered and settled, burning furiously
but still afloat.[5]

Schacht, apparently suddenly aware of the crew, maneuvered the U-507 alongside the lifeboat and spoke to Krantz.
"You can thank Mr. Roosevelt for this," he lectured and then
expressed hope the lifeboat would make it to shore safely. He
then disappeared below and the U-507 submerged. That afternoon, the survivors were picked up by the U.S. Coast Guard
Cutter Boutwell after being spotted by a patrol bomber.[6] The
bomber did not spot the U-507, however, and Schacht was able
to continue his destructive plunge into the Gulf with the complete destruction of the Honduran banana boat Ontario and the
tiny Norwegian freighter Torny.[7]

Another future ace followed Schacht into the Gulf. This
was Kapitänleutnant Erich Würdemann of the U-506. Actually, Würdemann could have beaten Schacht into the Gulf but
had been slowed by the temptation of the banana boat Sama off
the east coast of Florida.[8] After he sank the Sama, Würdemann
headed south and then west, linking up with Schacht in
the Gulf and making a combined attack against the Socony-
Vacuum tanker Aurora at 0230 on 10 May.

Würdemann struck first, his torpedo slamming into the
Aurora's starboard side just abaft of the bridge, blowing a hole
in the hull. The master, William H. Sheldon, kept calm, corrected the list to starboard by shifting ballast, and prepared to
keep sailing. Würdemann, however, sent two more torpedoes
into the starboard side and then surfaced and began blasting
away with his deck gun. Captain Sheldon ordered his ship
abandoned. Although Würdemann ceased fire while Sheldon
and his crew readied their lifeboats and liferafts, Schacht surfaced and ordered his deck-gun crew to shell the Aurora at will.

The first shell from Schacht severely wounded two of the
tanker crewmen. The remainder of the crew managed to get
off safely. The next morning, the survivors were picked up by
the patrol crafts, USS *Onyx* and *PY 157*. Remarkably, the *Aurora* never sank and was eventually towed to Algiers, Louisiana, and repaired. She returned to service with the War Shipping Administration as the *Jamestown*.[9]

Würdemann and Schacht continued to operate in close
proximity, but after two days of not seeing any targets,
Schacht decided to move right into the mouth of the Mississippi. He radioed BdU of this fact and added: "Mississippi
lights as in peacetime. Frequent mist off Mississippi. Dirty
water gives good cover at periscope depth, but bad listening
conditions. Off Southwest Pass boat difficult to handle because
of unaccountable drifts and very variable density of water. No
traffic at night. Patrol by 2 PC-boats. At dawn large number of
inward and outward bound tankers and steamers of considerable tonnage. Single steamers the whole day long. Air patrol
along main shipping routes."[10]

Schacht was quickly rewarded for his audacity by catching
the tanker *Virginia*, laden with 180,000 barrels of gasoline, after she had stopped to pick up a pilot for the journey upriver
to Baton Rouge. Schacht was so contemptuous of the American defenders, in fact, that he had placed his U-boat so that it
was between his target and shore. He sent three torpedoes into
the big tanker, causing a huge explosion. The *Virginia* began to
burn furiously while her crew, many of them on fire, threw
themselves overboard in a desperate attempt to escape. Of a
crew of forty, only fourteen would survive.[11]

By the next day, Schacht and Würdemann had set up a
gauntlet for American ships trying to enter or leave the Mississippi River ports. Operating 30 miles outside the mouth of
the river, Würdemann caught the ones coming out that
Schacht had missed closer in and vice versa. At 1450 on 13
May, Würdemann finally sank a tanker, the Gulf Oil Company *Gulfpenn*. The *Gulfpenn* was en route, alone and unarmed,
from Port Arthur, Texas, to Philadelphia loaded with fuel oil.
Würdemann sent a torpedo into her engine room, which killed
all of the engine crew and demolished the engines. Captain

Arthur S. Hodges, the tanker's master, was given no time for thoughtful orders. The ship went down within five minutes of being struck. Of the crew of thirty-eight, twenty-six would make it to the lifeboats where they would drift for three hours until the Honduran vessel *Telde* happened by and picked them up.[12]

Würdemann took his *U-506* down to rest beside the remains of the *Gulfpenn* until dark. Then he came to the surface, moved a little south and surprised the tanker *David McKelvey* sailing alone from Corpus Christi, Texas, bound for Bayonne, New Jersey, with a load of crude oil. Würdemann's torpedo caused an explosion that immediately engulfed the entire ship in flames. The burned-out hulk of the *David McKelvey* would drift for days, finally beaching herself on the Louisiana coast.[13]

Ship traffic avoided the entrance to the Mississippi for two days after these attacks so, even though he was out of torpedoes, Schacht traveled south in an attempt to catch anything that might be trying to slip by. His tactic worked on the overcast, rainy afternoon of 15 May when his lookouts spied the Honduran freighter *Amapala*. Lookouts on board the *Amapala* also spotted the *U-507* and an attempt was made to get away. When Schacht saw what the freighter was trying to do, he hurriedly ordered the 88-mm gun fired. The first round missed by a wide margin, but the next one was nearer. The *U-507*'s radio operator called up a warning to Schacht. The freighter was signaling for help over and over. Schacht ordered all his guns to concentrate their fire on the radio room. This was done with devastating effect. On board the *Amapala*, the master threw over the confidential codes in a cardboard box weighted with concrete and ordered his vessel abandoned. Three lifeboats were used, carrying away the entire crew of fifty-seven. One of the lifeboats was accosted by Schacht who ordered a line attached to the boat. The *Amapala*'s second officer identified himself and was told by Schacht that he was to take members of the submarine crew to the freighter in the lifeboat and help them place explosives aboard to sink the vessel. The Honduran officer was confused as to what he was supposed to do and clambered aboard the U-boat to talk to Schacht. Schacht, however, was disgusted with the man and

disappeared below, leaving his subordinates to continue to try
to make the necessary arrangements.

As was done so often during the course of the U-boats'
assault of shipping in American waters, the *U-507* was thought
to be Italian by the *Amapala*'s crew although it was obvious
that the submarine was crewed by Germans. Just as the
*Amapala*'s second officer got back into the lifeboat, finally understanding what was expected of him, an order was shouted
from the conning tower and the tow line cut. All the Germans
disappeared inside the U-boat and it began to move away. The
reason for that was quickly obvious. A navy dive-bomber suddenly appeared, two canisters of depth charges under its
wings. Schacht crash-dived the *U-507* and was submerged before the airplane could completely line up. It dropped the
depth charges anyway, and the resulting explosions convinced
the *Amapala*'s crew that the U-boat had been blown up. Soon,
the freighter *Gonzales* came into view and rescued the crew.
The *Amapala* would be taken in tow the next day by the coast
guard cutter *Boutwell* but would sink before it could be
brought to a port.[14]

Schacht had gotten through the airplane attack unscathed
but decided it was futile to stay in the Gulf without torpedoes.
Consequently, he signaled BdU that he was about to make the
long journey back to France.[15] Würdemann and the *U-506*
were still in good shape, however, with an ample supply of
torpedoes. On the morning of 16 May, while waiting on the
surface near Southwest Pass, Louisiana, his lookouts spotted
the tanker *William C. McTarnahan*. Würdemann sent a torpedo
into her starboard side and then another into the engine room.
All the men in the engine room and the after quarters were
killed instantly. The *U-506* surfaced and began to shell the
tanker. Amidst the blasting shells and the thunder of the burning ship, the remaining American crew abandoned ship.
Würdemann kept shelling the tanker but could not get it to
sink. It would be later towed to Mobile for repairs and returned to service as the *St. James*. The survivors would be
picked up by several fishing boats.[16]

Several hours later, still in the same shipping lane, the
*U-506*'s lookouts spotted the big Sun Oil Company tanker *Sun*.

The *Sun* was a gutsy, tough ship. She had already been attacked once by a U-boat, von Rosenstiel's *U-502*, on 23 February 1942 just north of Aruba. That attack had ripped the side and bottom completely out of the center of the vessel but, after temporary repairs, Captain Cornelius Van Gemert still managed to get his ship back to an American shipyard for repairs. With her new master, Captain John P. Bakke, she was, when the *U-506* spotted her, en route from the shipyard in ballast to Beaumont, Texas, for a load of fuel oil. Würdemann drilled a torpedo into the tanker's port bow. It exploded, opening up a huge hole that slowed but did not stop the ship. Bakke ordered the *Sun* into a zigzag pattern at full speed, leaving the *U-506* wallowing in her wake.[17]

Nonplussed, Würdemann stayed right where he was and was rewarded by catching the tanker *Gulf Oil* with a full load of petroleum products. Würdemann hit her amidships with a torpedo, and the tanker began to list. Würdemann put another torpedo into her starboard side at the engine room. The ship went down rapidly after that, stern first. There would only be nineteen survivors left hanging on to two liferafts. They would drift for a day and a half until picked up by the Esso tanker *Benjamin Brewster*.[18]

On 19 May, almost as a guest U-boat, the *U-103* and its famous commander, Kapitänleutnant Werner Winter, ventured out of its assigned Caribbean area into the southern reaches of the Gulf of Mexico and torpedoed the freighter *Ogontz*. The *Ogontz*, loaded with nitrates and manned by a crew of thirty-seven plus four navy guards, immediately began to sink. The ship was ordered abandoned by Captain Adolph M. Wennerlund, and two lifeboats and two rafts were launched. Remaining behind were two of the navy guards, Hayden George and Woodrow Wilson Harrison, still at their guns and hoping to get a shot at the U-boat if it surfaced. Surface it did, Winter taking his U-boat up to talk to the survivors. As he surfaced, several tragic but remarkable things happened at once. Harrison got a single shot off at the U-boat just as the *Ogontz* began to roll over. Winter and his lookouts ducked as the shell sang by, splashing harmlessly behind them. The *Ogontz* continued to roll, her mast arcing over and crash-

ing down right on top of one of the lifeboats, killing nineteen men, including Captain Wennerlund. The *Ogontz* then
promptly sank, taking Harrison and George with her.

George, whose foot was tangled in a rope, managed to get
free and claw his way to the surface. The *U-103* picked him
and another crewman up and took them to the remaining lifeboat. Winter came out on deck and checked the two men over,
personally treating a gash on one of them with alcohol. Winter, who was wearing shorts and had a deep tan, spoke to the
*Ogontz* crew in what was described as perfect English with an
Oxford accent. "Are you American boys?" he asked. "Sorry
we had to do this but this is war." He then saw that the two
men were put safely aboard the lifeboat, ordered cigarettes
and some food provided, waved, and took the *U-103* down. A
day later, the *Ogontz*'s survivors would be picked up by the
tanker *Esso Dover*. Winter moved south, back into the Caribbean, leaving the Gulf to Würdemann and the others coming
in to relieve him.[19]

That was fine with Würdemann. He didn't need Winter to
horn in on his solo performance. On the morning of 19 May,
he mercilessly attacked the small United Fruit Company
freighter *Heredia* with three torpedoes, blowing the decks of
the ship completely off and tearing the lifeboats to bits. Only
two rafts would get away with twenty-three survivors out of a
complement of forty-eight crew, six navy guards, and seven
passengers. All but three of the survivors would be picked up
by shrimp trawlers the next morning. The others would be
picked up by seaplane.[20]

The next morning, a little to the south of the attack against
the *Heredia*, Würdemann used the remainder of his torpedoes
against the Cities Service Oil Company tanker *Halo* as it sailed
toward New Orleans with a load of crude oil. The results
were to be horrendous. The *U-506*'s first torpedo struck the
starboard side of the tanker just under the bridge, killing Captain Ulrick Fred Moller. Moments later, a second torpedo arrived, just forward of the engine room. This one tore the ship
apart and she sank by the bow within three minutes. Twenty-
three men were still alive. By nightfall, sixteen men had died
from burns or wounds or drowning or shock or the sharks that

kept sweeping in and out. The seven remaining were alive only because they had managed to construct two crude rafts from boards tied together with strips of canvas from their life preservers. Five days later, the Mexican freighter *Oaxaca* sighted the oil and debris and came over to investigate. There, the Mexicans found three men, one of them dead. The body was buried at sea and the two survivors taken aboard. One of these men would die before the *Oaxaca* reached its destination of Tampico, Mexico. The other raft was found on 27 May by the British tanker *Orina*. Only two men, badly burned and dehydrated, were saved.[21]

By the time the last of the survivors of the *Halo* was rescued, Würdemann and the men of the *U-506* were on their way back across the Atlantic to accept the accolades of Admiral Doenitz and the rest of their U-boat brethren. Two other U-boats, however, had moved in behind them to keep up the pressure in the Gulf of Mexico. They were the *U-106*, commanded by Kapitänleutnant Herman Rasch, and the *U-753*, commanded by Korvettenkapitän Alfred Manhardt von Mannstein. Rasch at first had meant to stay off Cape Hatteras but was ordered into the Gulf to take advantage of that situation.[22] Doenitz had tasted the sweet blood of the Gulf and wanted more. Always more. Until no more ships would dare sail off America.

# 19
# The First Convoys

By mid-May, Admiral Andrews was well along on his planning for a complete coastal convoy system. He also was able to report to Admiral King several effective attacks on the U-boats, signaling that the American antisubmarine forces were becoming more experienced and confident. The sinking of the *U-352* by the *Icarus* was cited along with a report about an attack made by the USS *Broome* while on patrol off Cape Fear on 2 May. When her sonar operators had picked up a good echo, the crew of the destroyer had immediately gone to General Quarters and made a depth-charge attack. Oil and air bubbles had come to the surface and then the sonar operators had excitedly reported that they could also hear propeller noises. The U-boat below had then gone into some wild maneuvers in an attempt to get away. The *Broome* remained dogged, however, and the U-boat—probably the *U-106* commanded by Rasch—tried to surface only to be beaten back down by machine-gun fire from the destroyer. For another three hours, the *Broome* continued her attack. Pieces of the U-boat's deck began to come up after sixty depth charges were dropped. In the end, the wily Rasch got away to move on down into the Gulf of Mexico, but the important thing was that the *Broome* had found a U-boat and then attacked it with skill and discipline.[1]

Another attack Andrews reported was a combined operation. A coast guard airplane had taken off from Elizabeth City, North Carolina, on 15 May on a normal patrol. About 30 miles out, the pilot of the plane had spotted a U-boat. As was often the case, the German U-boat was mistaken for an Italian submarine (reportedly of the "Enrico-Tazzoli type"), but the pilot didn't care where the sub came from. He meant to kill it. Twelve men were spotted on the deck of the U-boat just as the airplane began its bombing run. The U-boat, at the same moment, began to dive. Ten of the submariners were able to get down the conning tower hatch but two men were left, one crouched alongside the conning tower while the other crawled toward the stern on his hands and knees.

The plane barreled in, dropping two depth charges 150 feet ahead of the conning tower. The U-boat went under the sea in a spew of white foam, leaving the two men on her deck struggling in her wash, and then sank while the two depth charges exploded. The pilot of the plane continued to circle the spot. He could no longer see the two men that had been on the U-boat deck, but he did see pieces of wood rising to the surface and then an oil slick. More planes arrived and then an airship took up station followed closely by the destroyer *Ellis*. The *Ellis* dropped more depth charges and large quantities of oil were observed bubbling to the surface.[2]

Excited by the reports he received, the commanding officer of the Elizabeth City Air Base flew out to observe the action. Upon arrival, he saw air bubbles and oil rising to the surface after each attack. He was certain that his men had managed to sink a U-boat. The next day he flew out to the same location to confirm the kill. Once there, he spotted pillows, life belts, canned food, a canvas folding chair, numerous papers, small cartons, and, then, as his eyes strained against the glare of the bright sun against the water, the body of a uniformed man in a life belt. This would be the confirmation needed!

A Bucket Brigade was in the area so he flew over to it and blinked a signal to the escorts to pick up the body. This was done. But, to the consternation of all, the body was not that of a German but a Brazilian, a sailor from the ship *Buarque* sunk on 16 February. In fact, the *Ellis* had not attacked a U-boat at all but only an old wreck.³ Still, the coast guard plane had made a nearly successful attack on an actual U-boat and most probably killed the two U-boat crewmen stranded on deck.

Even one of the converted yachts Admiral Andrews had pressed into service almost bagged a U-boat. The *Alabaster* was a German-built 148-footer, a beautiful pleasure craft whose sleek lines had been changed only by the addition of a 3-inch gun, four .50-caliber machine guns, and, bolted on the stern, a single depth-charge rack. She also had some old World War I listening gear aboard and was manned by an all-navy crew. The *Alabaster* had been assigned the duty of escorting Bucket Brigades from the Chesapeake Bay to points north, and that was what she was doing on a beautiful May morning when one of her lookouts, struck dumb by the sight, suddenly began to point frantically back toward land at what was very definitely a periscope. After months of practice on the many wrecks that lined the coast there, the *Alabaster*'s crew knew exactly what to do. The *Alabaster*'s skipper turned his ship in the direction of the periscope and ordered up flank speed, some 18 knots, more than enough to overhaul a submerged U-boat.

Noting the shallow water he was in, the *Alabaster*'s skipper ordered the depth charges set at 50 feet and then dropped a charge. Nothing happened. Either the depth charge had been a dud or the trigger depth of the charge was set too deep. The next depth charge was set shallower and again the *Alabaster* made her run, dropping the depth charge almost exactly where it had dropped the first. The aim, as it would become quickly evident, was excellent. Down dropped the depth charge right on top of the first one. When both of them went off at once, the resulting explosion practically blew the yacht right out of the water. The deck grills in the engine room were propelled into the air, flipped over like iron flap jacks as they went up, and came down with a deafening clang. On deck, the crew for the 3-inch deck gun were standing by, ready for action when one of the ammunition passers suddenly found himself cradling the compass repeater, which had jumped completely out of its stand. When the *Alabaster* came down, it landed in an oil slick. After a quick check revealed no leaks or significant damage, a bucket was put down to bring up an oil sample. There was so much oil the *Alabaster* was confident it had sunk a U-boat. As it would turn out, the U-boat had gotten away, but all that oil gave the *Alabaster* good reason to think it had caused some significant damage. In any case, the convoy was spared by the *Alabaster*'s quick reaction.[4]

The changes that had occurred, especially the curtailing of tanker sailings, were apparent to Admiral Doenitz as well. For the first time since *Paukenschlag*, his *BdU War Log* expressed some unhappiness with the American campaign. "Attacking conditions on the North coast of America from Cape Fear to New York have been extremely unfavorable since 20 April," it was written on 17 May 1942. "[U-]Boats which are lying immediately under the coast and off the main ports report no traffic. It appears as if the traffic has temporarily ceased or has been so re-organized that so far the [U-]boats have not been able to pick it up."

Despite the apparent increased effectiveness of Admiral Andrews's forces and Admiral Doenitz's concerns, the U-boats were still finding targets. On 14 May, the Greek freighter *Stavros* (although of Greek registry, it had been chartered by the Swiss government and as such flew a Swiss flag, which theoretically made it neutral) was hit at high noon 70 miles southeast of New York City by a single torpedo from Kaleun Gerd Kelbling's *U-593*. A day later, the *Stavros*, with a large hole in her starboard bow, proudly reentered New York harbor. A calm, disciplined crew had saved the day.[5]

On 17 May, Kaleun Viktor Vogel of the *U-588* sank the tiny Norwegian freighter *Skottland* 200 miles out from Nantucket (the survivors were brought in by a lobster boat) and then found no targets at all for four days. On 21 May, however, he caught the *Plow City* while the American freighter had stopped to pick up eighteen survivors from the British freighter *Peisander*, sunk by the *U-653* four days earlier. With plenty of torpedoes aboard, Vogel sent three slamming into the *Plow City*. Although the attack had been vicious for such a small target, only one man was lost when he was knocked off

the bridge by the impact of the second torpedo. Vogel brought
the *U-588* in among the lifeboats to look over the survivors. He
pointed at one of the crew and his men reached down and took
the man by the arms and dragged him aboard the U-boat. Vogel met the man in the control room. Wide-eyed, the American crewman saw what he believed to be a mixed crew of
German and Italian "big, husky youth." Vogel put him at ease
by his quiet questions, delivered in excellent English. When a
report came below that gunfire could be heard to the east,
Vogel snapped an order and the crewman was taken by the
arms and dragged again, this time back to the lifeboat. Vogel
took his U-boat down after that and was last seen heading
seaward.[6]

Vogel would not find another target until two days later
when he destroyed the British freighter *Margot*, loaded with
6,000 tons of planes, tanks, and explosives. Vogel, preferring
to attack during the day, struck the *Margot* with a single torpedo and then surfaced about a mile off and fired his machine
gun at her. There were no hits, but the *Margot*'s skipper received Vogel's message clearly and ordered his ship abandoned. Vogel waited until all the lifeboats were clear and then
pumped twenty rounds of 88-mm shells into the freighter. Vogel again went among the lifeboats and inquired of the second
officer the name of the ship, destination, cargo, and port of
departure. While one of the U-boat officers filmed the event
with a motion picture camera, Vogel called below for some
rum. A bottle was brought up and given to the second officer.
Vogel then asked which lifeboat had the captain. After being
told, Vogel moved over and also gave the captain a bottle of
rum. The captain took the gift and thanked the U-boat commander and then asked Vogel to tow him to shore. "Sorry,
have no time," Vogel answered crisply and then took the
*U-588* around the *Margot* to fire more rounds into her. After
several hits at the waterline, the ship sank and Vogel took his
U-boat down and away. It would be four days before the crew
of the *Margot*, still in fairly good condition, would be picked
up by the Swedish freighter *Sagoland.*[7]

Kelbling and the *U-593* were also still off the Atlantic coast
but had spent much of the time after sinking the *Stavros* being

pursued by coast guard vessels and forced to dive by pesky aircraft. It was apparent to Kelbling that something had changed to the detriment of the U-boats along the east coast of the "American Shooting Gallery." The Americans were finally improving. Nevertheless, Kelbling persisted until he was rewarded by the sight of a Bucket Brigade convoy rounding a cape two and a half miles east of Barnegat Light, New Jersey. It was a bright early afternoon, but Kelbling decided to go ahead and risk detection because of the lack of targets at night. He stayed submerged and moved to line up.

At 1458, a torpedo exploded on the starboard side of the *Persephone*, a big tanker fully loaded with 80,000 barrels of crude oil. The oil did not explode, but some of it did begin to burn and quickly the entire ship was covered with thick, oily smoke. The tanker's master, Helge Quistgaard, gave orders to abandon ship. Since the water was only 8 fathoms deep at that point, the stern of the *Persephone* almost immediately struck bottom and stuck there. The survivors in the lifeboats calmly waited until a coast guard patrol boat came to pick them up.

The *U-593*, meanwhile, was forced to run for her life. The convoy escorts, supported by aircraft, pummelled the U-boat again and again, only losing her when Kelbling managed to find a trough of deep water to hide in. After that, he had no choice but to head back to France for repairs and resupply. The *Persephone*, although destroyed, would still remain useful to the war effort. Her forward part would be towed into New York harbor and 21,000 barrels of oil taken off by barges. Even later, her midships house would be removed intact and fitted to another tanker, the *Livingston Roe*.⁸

The U-boats, then, were still managing success off the eastern seaboard but at a much decreased rate and at much greater risk. There was no doubt that Admiral Andrews's forces had made progress. Andrews, increasingly relaxed and confident after months of pessimism and tension, only had one more knot to add to the noose he hoped would hang the U-boats once and for all: the full convoy system. Facilities had been developed for anchorage, inspection, and assembly of the convoys all along the coast. New personnel had been acquired and indoctrinated. Schedules had been devised to permit maxi-

mum efficiency. In a very short time, in fact, many separate
elements had been organized into an integrated, efficient, and
smoothly working machine dedicated to the support of the
convoys.

On 11 May, Andrews sent a dispatch to his command out-
lining his expectations for the system. Very little had been left
to chance, including air support. A circle with a radius of 20
miles was to be patrolled around the ships of the convoy, and
searches were to be made along the track of the convoy 25
miles in either direction. Southbound convoys leaving Hampton Roads would be covered on the first day by planes from
Langley Field, Norfolk, and Elizabeth City. On the second
day, aircraft from Cherry Point, North Carolina, would cover
them at daybreak, and then the convoy would be picked up by
aircraft from Wilmington and Charleston. On the third day of
a convoy, the planes from Charleston would stay with it all the
way to Jacksonville and land there. On the fourth day, planes
from Banana River would pick up the convoy and, on the fifth
day, planes from Miami would take over. By this plan, strong
and constant air coverage was believed to be assured.

Surface forces had also been carefully organized. Seven
surface craft were designated per convoy—two destroyers, one
corvette, two coast guard patrol craft, and two British trawlers. A group of these vessels were always to be kept in reserve
in case of overhaul or repair of any of the primary vessels. On
4 May, Admiral Andrews released a timetable to be followed
by the convoys. Every three days, one convoy of forty-five
vessels was to set out from Hampton Roads and head south for
Key West. Similarly, one northbound convoy of forty-five vessels was to leave Key West every three days. The schedule was
so staggered that incoming convoys would arrive a day before
the departure of the outgoing vessels and thus give the escorts
time to regroup and refuel.

Finally, and in recognition of one of the most vexing problems that had plagued the admiral since the beginning of the
battle, he demanded and received from the major shipping
companies a list of the more experienced and reliable merchant masters. From this list, he would choose his convoy

"commodores," captains he hoped he could rely on to keep the other civilians in line.

Despite all of the planning, there would be no way to determine what else needed to be done unless test convoys were made. Accordingly, on May 14th, a small convoy, numbered KS-500, left Hampton Roads bound for Key West. The next day, a northbound convoy, KN-100, left from Key West. There were many difficulties almost immediately encountered. For one thing, the merchant masters seemed to be almost completely ignorant of their own merchant signals, so much so that the navy commanders in charge of the convoys had to send frequent visual messages calling attention to principal paragraphs in the signal book. The merchantmen, in response, often did nothing or, worse, something different than ordered. The navy persevered, however, and the small convoys made it both ways without losses. Encouraged but still worried, Andrews decided to try another convoy, this one full-sized. He numbered it the KS-502.[9]

On 13 May 1942, the *Dione* finally completed her refit and returned to her war against the U-boats. But this time, things were different. Not only had Lieutenant Alger been told by headquarters that big changes were coming, he also had a problem he never expected aboard a small coast guard cutter at war—uninvited guests. As he ordered the *Dione* backed out of her berth in Norfolk, he took another look at the two civilians who had showed up on the dock that morning, clutching their freshly mimeographed orders. It was the famous writer Charles Rawlings, and his photographer, Jack Manning, both on assignment from the *Saturday Evening Post*. Rawlings announced to Alger as soon as he had climbed aboard that he had come to cover the "Battle of the Atlantic." He had asked for a small ship, he said, "humble but salty," and everyone at Admiral Andrews's headquarters had immediately thought of the *Dione*. She was always in the thick of things and that's where he wanted to be. In fact, Rawlings was told, the *Dione* had dropped more depth charges than any other ship in the Eastern Sea Frontier. She was also just about to get out of dry dock with a lot of new armament and everything else all fixed and painted. Admiral Andrews's staff had felt she was the best choice. That was how Alger found himself acting as host to a man as diverse from his own personality and lifestyle as perhaps could be possible. Moreover, Rawlings and his photographer were simply supercargo and that meant a special problem for Alger. In the military, every man has a function. He is a part of a larger scheme, and he must perform when called upon to do so. Rawlings and Manning, however, were just *there*, without any real thing to do. Alger could only look down from the bridge, study the two men, both of whom had immediately stripped to the waist to work on their tans, and then sigh and get on with his job. He had been ordered to show the two everything he was doing. Alger was an officer who believed orders were given for a reason, and he would follow them as best he could for as long as he could. Maybe, he hoped to himself, they would work out. Anything was possible.[10]

If Alger was a bit worried over his "supercargo," the crew of the *Dione* was reveling in their presence. The *Dione*'s bosun's mate was a good example. Almost as soon as the writer was on board, the man Rawlings would later call "Frenchy" in his story swaggered over to set Rawlings straight. Rawlings took one look at the "short, tough leather-voiced bos'n" and asked the one question that so far Alger had refused to answer. Had the *Dione* ever sunk a U-boat?

"Frenchy" was in his glory. "Now, you say it this way," he told Rawlings. "There's a fight on. We're in there just as close as we can get."[11] Cocking his eye so he could read Rawlings's notes as the reporter hurriedly jotted them down, he continued in a low, confidential tone. "There's a couple of greasy buoys out there got our number on 'em," he said. "Maybe it's sub oil. Maybe we struck some oil wells. You heard about Wimble Willy?"[12]

Rawlings confessed that he hadn't. His notebook poised, he breathlessly waited. "Listen, bud," the bosun said grandly, "we fish down Periscope Lane. Torpedo Junction, Hatteras way, that's where we live. You ask"—this with an advisory wink—"about Wimble Willy, bud."[13]

In fact, even without Rawlings wanting to see it, Lieutenant Alger had in mind a return to the "thing" off Wimble

Shoals that the men were calling Wimble Willy. He still hoped, and halfway believed, that the *Dione* had indeed sunk a U-boat there. Perhaps while the cutter had been in dry dock something had broken loose and floated up, something that would tell Alger what he had attacked. As soon as the *Dione* had reached the open sea, she was ordered to help convoy the tanker *Bessemer* and the Russian freighter *Sveti Duji.* Immediately after releasing them, Alger took the *Dione* down to Wimble Shoals. All hands were called to General Quarters when a contact was made. Several depth charges were dropped, including two from the new Y-gun. Soon, a spread of oil came from below and Alger knew he had found the thing that had frustrated him since April. But Alger would not say what Rawlings wanted to hear. Was the wreck below a dead U-boat? Alger didn't know. The next day, Rawlings tried again. "And I can't call Willy sunk?" he pleaded.

"No," he wrote that Alger had replied. "All you can say is that, in *Diana*'s [*Dione*'s] opinion, there is an object under her buoy that she has reason to believe is a successfully attacked submarine."[14]

That was enough for Rawlings. "My very unofficial stomach, where good hunches grow," he would write, "said that there were dead Germans down there—completely and gratifyingly, if you will, dead."[15]

But Wimble Willy, whatever it was, was past history and no longer really that important to Alger and the men of the *Dione.* Since their return to the Graveyard for patrol, they had taken note of more and more American warships, including an uncommonly large number of destroyers. Something was very definitely afoot, something big, and Alger guessed his *Dione* was going to be part of it.

At 0600 on 16 May, three freighters, the *Bluefields, Schickshinny,* and the *C. O. Stillman* sailed inconspicuously out of New York harbor and turned south, heading for Hampton Roads. As the clear spring morning brightened, the three ships continued their journey, while overhead, navy, coast guard, and civilian air patrol aircraft moved in and began to circle, keeping constant vigil. Seaward, coast guard YPs and

83-footers plus a few civilian boats of the Hooligan Navy searched back and forth, their sound gear activated, their depth-charge racks ready. At the mouth of Delaware Bay, the ships left the sea and entered the bay's quiet waters. After sailing its entire length, they entered the canal leading from the Delaware to the Chesapeake Bay. By then, it was nightfall. It would take another day for the ships to complete the first stage of their long journey. When they arrived at Hampton Roads, they found other merchant ships already in the anchorage. They were the *M. F. Elliot, Delaware Sun, Livingston Roe, New Jersey, Sir James, Clark Ross, Vagrant, Mogy,* and the *Nueva Granada*. On 18 May, the navy destroyer USS *McCormick* also sailed from New York. Heading down the coast on the most direct route to Norfolk, she ran at a speed of 20 knots and by evening of the same day, arrived at her berth at the Section Base to refuel. Early the next morning, she moved to Hampton Roads. Soon, other warships joined her. The navy destroyer *Ellis* arrived first and then two British trawlers, HMS *Cape Warwick* and HMS *Coventry City*. Three coast guard vessels joined them as well, the *PC 68* (the ex-*Dixie V*, a 47-foot former pleasure craft), the *PC 462* (a picket boat), and, after a week of escorting Bucket Brigades and patrol, the cutter *Dione*. This was the full complement for the KS-502 convoy to Key West.[16]

Admiral Andrews and his staff in New York City could do nothing now but wait and hope. All their plans so painstakingly put together over the weeks were only so many pieces of paper after all. Now the gauntlet would actually have to be run. Intelligence reports had placed U-boats operating at increments from Cape Hatteras to Key West. KS-502—ten freighters and tankers escorted by two old World War I destroyers, two converted trawlers, two coast guard craft meant for harbor patrol, and one designed to stop Prohibition smuggling—would have to sail past these proven killers. If a single ship were to be torpedoed, Admiral Andrews's convoy system might be considered a failure.

Charles Rawlings, still aboard the *Dione*, was having a fine time. In fact, he had talked the navy and his editor into letting him stay aboard for the entire convoy to Key West. At 0450 on

20 May, Alger gave the signal to unmoor the *Dione*. A report from below worried him. The port engine was acting up. But KS-502 could not wait. The *Dione* would just have to proceed on the starboard engine while repairs were made on the other one. He alerted the commander of the convoy, Lieutenant Commander J. M. Kennaday, of his problem and was told to proceed. Kennaday was thankful to have the seasoned *Dione* along on the convoy. He had been given an extremely pessimistic report on U-boat activities along his planned route. He had been promised that vessels of the various naval districts he would pass through would be engaged in antisubmarine operations, but that had never stopped the U-boats before. No, Kennaday realized, KS-502 would have to rely on itself, staying together and alert with no stragglers, if it was to survive.

Before the day was over, Kennaday was feeling better. Cape Hatteras had been successfully negotiated with no problem. The *Dione* had been assigned the starboard quarter of the convoy and there she zigzagged, occasionally ranging farther out to listen. The convoy was not supposed to go any faster than its slowest ship, but that proved to be the Brazilian ship *Mogy*, which was unable to keep up even at the slow speed of 10 knots. The *Mogy* fell back and Alger responded by circling her, furiously blinking his light for her to rejoin. The Nicaraguan ship *Bluefields* added to the escorts' problems when her deck cargo of kapok, burlap, and scrap paper caught on fire. Kennaday sent the *Ellis* flying over to her. There, he found the merchant crew trying to fight a raging fire with only one inadequate hose. Kennaday ordered the master of the *Bluefields* to turn his burning ship to keep the wind on her beam in an attempt to retard the flames and then deftly maneuvered his destroyer close alongside in order to bring to bear his own fire hoses. This quick action saved the freighter, but the rest of the convoy had moved on, leaving the *Bluefields* and the *Ellis* in a very vulnerable position. Kennaday had no choice but to call back one of the trawlers, the HMS *Coventry City*, and detach it from KS-502 in order to escort the damaged *Bluefields* into Beaufort for repairs. The *Ellis* then turned and raced after the convoy, first catching the still-plodding *Mogy* and then the main body by early evening as they passed Southport, North Carolina.

The speed of the convoy was now down to 7 knots, an easy shot for a U-boat, especially with night approaching. The *Dione*, still urging the *Mogy* along, continued in her planned zigzags as the stars began to spread out over the deep navy-blue sky. The lights of first one freighter and then a tanker blinked prettily on, almost daring any U-boats in the area to put them out. Shortly, the strained voice of one of the *Ellis*'s officers crackled over the radio, ordering the running lights to be shut off. The lights, after an interval, were grudgingly extinguished, but Alger saw that there were still several portholes left open on one of the tankers, the bright lights inside streaming out to sea like beacons. He moved past the *Mogy* until he had the *Dione* right up alongside the offending tanker.

Swede Larson, getting a little air for the first time of the day, had never seen his skipper so angry. Alger had his megaphone out, practically yelling directly into the portholes, ordering the crewmen inside, in a very polite, civil, but determined manner, to close their portholes and draw the curtains at once. Startled faces appeared one by one at the portholes and then abruptly disappeared as the curtains were drawn. When this happened again later that night, and while Lieutenant Alger was asleep, the *Dione* once again slid up alongside the tanker. The officer at the helm this time quietly ordered several of the men to man the machine guns on the flying bridge and then, using profanity in a manner only available to those who have had a great deal of practice at it, advised the tanker crew of not only what was going to happen to them if they did not turn out their lights, but, among many other interesting things, their birthright, the probable moral behavior of their mothers, and that human aperture most descriptive of them. The last thing the tanker crewmen heard as they quickly shut their portholes was the sound of coast guard machine guns being jacked back, ready to put the lights out permanently. No more lights were observed that night.

By the morning of 22 May, KS-502 was off South Carolina and Alger was delivered good news. The *Dione*'s port engine

was running again. It was just in time. *PC 462* reported a
sound contact. Alger was contacted by the *Ellis* and ordered to
investigate. The contact was a good one, and the *Dione*, putting
on an excellent demonstration for the navy destroyers of how
to conduct a depth-charge attack, wheeled about and laid several patterns that totaled eighteen depth charges. After circling the area and listening until confident that whatever had
been down there had left, Alger hustled the *Dione* back to the
convoy. That night, the *Ellis* spotted something dark and fore-
boding coming toward the convoy and again dispatched the
*Dione* to investigate. Going to General Quarters, Alger swept
his cutter down on the dark shape and then closed with it,
ready to board what could very likely be a crippled U-boat on
the surface. Disappointingly, the thing proved to be a drifting
pilothouse, undoubtedly a remnant of a torpedoed ship. Further investigation revealed a radio direction finder still attached and then, as it turned and bobbed eerily, the name
*Ohioan*. It was wreckage from the steamship sunk by the *U-564*
on 8 May off Boca Raton.

The next morning, it was the *Ellis* that made the sound
contact and she initiated her own attack. Her first charges
brought up oil and a big eruption of bubbles, so she turned
and delivered another attack at the same spot with more oil
coming to the surface. The *Dione*, moving with the stern of the
convoy, soon entered the slick. The coast guardsmen sniffed
the air. The odor was all too familiar to them. High-grade
bunker oil. Whatever was below, it wasn't a U-boat. It was
most likely a U-boat victim. The *Ellis* raced back to the convoy, Kennaday unhappily aware that while his ship had been
attacking an old wreck, his convoy had been made vulnerable
by his absence. An important lesson was dawning on him and
all the escorting American ships. The most important thing
for an escort to maintain was convoy integrity. As tempting as
it was to investigate good sound contacts, most of them were
better left alone. Only when there was a definite U-boat sighting or contact should the escorts even consider leaving the
screen and then only long enough to relieve the immediate
danger of attack. Other ships and planes could then be called

in to sustain the tracking and attack of a submarine if necessary.

By 23 May, the convoy, still moving too slowly to suit any
of the escorts, finally reached Florida waters. That night, the
straggling got worse. Not only the old *Mogy* but all the merchant vessels began to spread apart. The *McCormick* and the
*Ellis*, at the van of the convoy, turned and blinked their lights
furiously at the wallowing merchantmen, ordering them to
keep their station. That night, Kennaday would grimly enter
the following notation in his log: ". . . the merchant ship custom is different from the Navy's in regard to complying with
signalled orders—the captains receive them, but frequently do
nothing about it." He had learned one of the basic facts that
had frustrated the harried defenders of the American coast
since the U-boats had arrived.

The sea was turning bluer and the air warmer. The carefully planned air cover for the convoy had gradually diminished as it had moved south and, as the dangerous Florida
Straits were approached, it disappeared entirely. Kennaday
kept the convoy going. Off Pompano Beach, where the
U-boats had been active only a few days before, the *C. O. Stillman* broke down and dropped far behind the convoy. The *Dione* was ordered to stand by her. After some anxious hours,
one engine was fixed and the *Stillman* proceeded. The convoy,
slowed to allow the *Dione* and the *Stillman* to catch up, finally
plodded past Alligator Reef and relative safety late on 25 May.
Shortly afterwards, the convoy was disbanded, each ship going her own way.[17]

The *Dione* was ordered to proceed on to Key West to pick
up another convoy going back to Hampton Roads. This she
did, and on the next afternoon she entered the crystal-clear
waters surrounding the tiny cay and made her way through
the channel past the rainbow-hued but dangerous reefs. For
the men of the *Dione*, used to the gray, angry seas and the
wind-swept dunes of the wintertime capes of North Carolina,
the sight of Key West was dazzling. The white-washed walls
and glittering tile roofs of the beach homes were like small
castles, sitting on beaches of sugar. It was as beautiful as it was
anticlimactic after the tense convoy down. But it also gave

Lieutenant Alger, his officers, and his men time to reflect on what they had helped accomplish. Despite all their trouble, the convoy had made it all the way without a single U-boat attack. Every ounce of the cargo that had been entrusted to them had made it. By that yardstick, the full convoy system had proven to be a success.

Charles Rawlings would reluctantly leave the *Dione* only after the cutter had successfully taken another convoy north to Hampton Roads. He had had his adventure, however, and had also, during all the excitement, been able to grasp what had been important about it. As he and Lieutenant Alger leaned on the rail of the wing deck, the convoy ahead presented an inspiring sight. "Here's a picture for you, Charles," Rawlings reported Alger saying, "a picture of victory . . . the future of coast-wise transportation in this war."

Rawlings had questioned the statement, not being totally aware of the awful destruction the U-boats had already inflicted on the Allied merchant fleet. But what about the *"Rudeltaktic,"* he had asked—the wolf pack? Would it not defeat the convoy system?

Alger had answered by handing Rawlings his binoculars and pointing at the screen of escorts. "We're masters of that," he had said. "No one can lick us at convoy."

"You're right," Rawlings had responded after a moment of study. "It's magnificent."[18]

Had Admiral Andrews been privy to the conversation of the writer and the junior officer, he would have happily agreed. After receiving the report concerning KS-502 and the convoy that followed it, the old admiral must have been filled with both relief and hope. After all these months, his American ships were finally doing what he believed they could do best.

Magnificent, indeed.

# 20

# The Tactics Change

There was a positively ebullient mood in the Eastern Sea Frontier as June 1942 began. In May, the full convoy system had been tested with excellent results. Not only that but there had been a 20 percent increase in ships and planes in the command available for patrol.[1] Admiral Andrews looked around and was certain he had nearly the right mix to defeat the U-boats at last. After all, it was not necessary for him to sink the Germans but only to keep them off balance— diving from planes, running from ships, harassed away from the convoys—it didn't matter as long as they weren't sinking ships. Moreover, it seemed clear that the Nazis had recognized the changing balance of forces and tactics by diverting more and more of their U-boats in the Western Hemisphere to the Caribbean and the South Atlantic.[2] There would still be sinkings in the Eastern Sea Frontier and in the Gulf, of that there was no doubt, but these could be kept to an acceptable level. The United States Navy was not yet declaring victory over the U-boats, but it was certain of one thing: the Germans would have to come up with something very different from their previous tactics to overcome the strength of the convoy and the increased patrol forces.

* * *

The man who would have to come up with that "something different" was Admiral Karl Doenitz. Ordered by Hitler to move from the French coast after a British commando raid on St. Nazaire, Doenitz had reluctantly taken his staff and set up new headquarters in a Paris suburb. Fearful that moving away from the coast would lessen his control over his "sea wolves," Doenitz wrote in the *BdU War Diary*—"This is a regrettable step back where administration is concerned, since the direct contact with the front, that is, the personal touch between commanding officer and his operational boats and crews, will not be possible to anything like the same extent from Paris."[3]

The move was only a symptom of the unfair treatment Doenitz felt he was getting from the government. It seemed incredible to him that during the weeks of his greatest success, Berlin had gone on making impossible demands of him and his submarines. During long walks with his chief of staff, Doenitz occasionally let his anger and bitterness spill over. "Hitler understands absolutely nothing about the sea," he said once. "He's said so himself. And the Naval high command is afraid to risk losing its beautiful ships. So, they use our U-boats for just about anything, no matter where or what. It's insanity, I tell you!"[4]

Despite Doenitz's angry words, he would, in the end, adhere exactly to orders. This was illustrated perfectly in the spring of 1942 when the admiral was ordered to send more submarines into the Mediterranean. Doenitz considered the Mediterranean to be a U-boat trap, blanketed by British anti-submarine forces. But Hitler's staff was desperate to save Rommel's army in Africa, and if it meant sacrificing a few submarines to do that, to them the loss was well worth the gain.[5]

"These fine gentlemen," Doenitz complained when he received the orders, "think only of victory on land. They've forgotten the essential principle of the art of war: Be as strong as possible at the critical spot. No one in Berlin thinks of the Battle of the Atlantic. I doubt that the higher-ups even know that there is such a thing. But there is where the war will be won or lost!"[6]

Doenitz was correct on all points. Still, he did not hesitate to send some of his best U-boat crews to their certain deaths in the Mediterranean simply because Hitler had deemed it to be so. Complying with those orders also left him only ten fighting U-boats in the Atlantic (the remainder being either in for repairs or en route to or from missions) at a very critical moment in the American campaign.[7]

Besides all of his other duties and concerns, Admiral Doenitz demanded daily reports from each *Unterseeboot* commander on sinkings, weather, supplies, fuel, and technical problems. After thoroughly digesting each report, he would then personally transmit operational orders, counsel on tactics, give technical advice, and, often, personal messages such as birthday greetings. "Uncle Karl," then, was never far from the hearts and minds of the U-boat skippers and their crews. Whether given orders to penetrate the Mediterranean or sit for days in an arctic blizzard waiting for a phantom Russian convoy, they did not blame Doenitz. To most of the German submariners—officers and men—their admiral could do no wrong. It was the Nazi government that was blamed. To keep their loyalty and trust so that he could send men uncomplainingly to their doom for that government meant that Doenitz had to stay in contact with his men. And that meant night and day in his headquarters.[8]

His workload increased even more in February 1942 when three submarines, the *U-82*, the *U-537*, and the *U-252* all disappeared without a trace. What could have happened to them? His staff were divided as to the cause. Some said sabotage, others thought Q-ships had gotten them. But Doenitz was afraid that the British had come up with something different, some kind of new technical advance. In March, a flood of reports came to him, telling of a series of bizarre events. Out of nowhere, his U-boats reported, enemy destroyers and airplanes were on top of them. Even on the darkest nights, a U-boat might be caught in the glare of a searchlight suddenly switched on by a destroyer or depth-charge-laden airplane.

Doenitz had immediately questioned Berlin. "Is it possible," he wrote, "for an aircraft to detect the presence of a submarine before it actually comes within sight of the vessel?"

Berlin had consulted German scientists and their reply was negative. It was impossible, they said, to find an object as small as a submarine on the surface of the vast sea without radar, and radar was just too big and heavy to be placed aboard aircraft. Doenitz accepted the scientists' appraisal but still wanted to know what was causing his U-boats to be sunk. He began to hound German intelligence operatives to ferret out the secret. Eventually, they would discover the truth. The British were, indeed, putting radar on their aircraft. But Doenitz did not wait until he knew this. He kept sending his U-boats out.[9]

By May, it was clear to Doenitz that Operation *Paukenschlag* was running out of steam. First, the *U-85* had been sunk and, barely a month later, the *U-352*. Although it was not clear at the time the manner in which the two submarines had gone down, Doenitz was certain it meant that the Americans were catching on to the hard lessons the British had already learned. When he received reports that his U-boats along the Atlantic coast were sitting for long stretches of time without seeing anything, he guessed that some sort of a convoy system had been set up. Soon, reports confirmed his guess. He responded in May by moving his heaviest concentration of U-boats away from the American eastern seaboard down to the Caribbean and Gulf.[10]

Despite the shift, Doenitz knew that the most lucrative area for his U-boats would always be the east coast, that "critical spot." To recapture the initiative there, he formulated a plan for an operation that would not only sink ships but defeat the new American convoy system as well. For such a mission, he knew, a special man was needed, a U-boat commander with a portion each of skill, competence, luck, and audacity, with the emphasis on the latter two qualities. His choice: Horst Degen of the *U-701*.

Admiral Doenitz tended to have favorites among his U-boat commanders, and there was little doubt that Horst Degen was included in this select group. The admiral had seen to it that Degen had been trained by one of the best of the U-boat skippers, Korvettenkapitän Erich Topp. Topp had taken De-

gen along on an early cruise in April of 1941 and had shown
the *Kommandantenschuler* (commander-pupil) by way of example that to succeed as a U-boat commander required daring
and recklessness combined with persistent attack and virtually
no evasive action.[11]

On his first war cruise in January 1942, Degen had only
sunk the small freighter *Baron Erskine* off the northwest coast
of England. But on his next cruise in March, he moved just
south of Iceland and recklessly engaged the armed British
trawlers *Notts Country* and *Stella Capella*. The trawlers were of
the same design as the ones later sent to the United States and
were armed to the teeth. Using three torpedoes, Degen sank
them both, earning him Doenitz's nickname, the "gallant Degen."[12]

When he was summoned to Doenitz's headquarters in
early May 1942, Degen was considered a seasoned commander.
He was also only 29 years old. When he entered Doenitz's
office, he found his commander busy as always. "The Eagle,"
one of several affectionate nicknames given Doenitz by his
U-boat men, had his head down over a desk laden with documents and was intently shuffling through them. Degen patiently waited until the admiral's narrow face looked up to
stare penetratingly into the eyes of the young commander.
"It's America, Degen," Doenitz said, and then told him that he
would be taking a group of highly trained saboteurs with him.
He was to drop them off in a designated spot on 13 June and
afterwards accomplish another special mission.

Degen was glad to hear about going to America, but his
U-boat was in the Brest shipyard. She would not be ready in
time to reach the American Atlantic coast by 13 June. Doenitz
frowned, absorbing the news. He threw his pen down and
rubbed his eyes. It was just as well, he told Degen. He didn't
have much faith in saboteurs, but the other mission was of
utmost importance. He would assign another submarine for
the saboteurs. But it was still America. He then explained the
mission in detail, adding that he didn't want Degen back until
he had accomplished it and used every one of his torpedoes.[13]

America! Degen was excited by the opportunity because
he had heard of the "happy time" going on there. He sought

out none other than Reinhard Hardegen for advice. Hardegen tempered Degen's enthusiasm a little by telling him of the convoy tactics recently adopted by the Americans and of nets and minefields being placed in the harbors. Worse, the Americans were increasing their aircraft surveillance. Eventually, Hardegen felt, one of them was going to catch a U-boat on the surface and know what to do about it. But it was still a potentially lucrative place for a U-boat commander, the veteran assured him, especially for the audacious. That was all Degen needed to hear. Despite the complexity of the mission Doenitz had given him, the "gallant Degen" was sure he had all the audacity he would need to succeed.[14]

On 1 June, the *U-404*, commanded by Korvettenkapitän Otto von Bülow, found the American freighter *West Notus* 300 miles off Cape Hatteras steaming in from Trinidad to New York with a load of 7,400 tons of flaxseed. The battle that ensued was indicative of a new attitude among the Americans. Von Bülow attacked with his deck gun, devastating the wheelhouse, knocking over the forward and aft masts, and smashing the poop quarters, foc'sle, and the crew's quarters. The steering controls were also shot away. Captain Gerner of the *West Notus*, however, did not meekly abandon his ship. Instead, he ordered his own gun crews to stand at their stations. As von Bülow confidently moved in closer for the kill, they opened up, strafing the U-boat. A brief duel erupted, but the mobile *U-404* and her experienced 88-mm deck gunners were able to knock out the freighter's guns. Only then did Captain Gerner give the order to abandon ship. Just before Gerner stepped into a lifeboat, a round killed him and three other crewmembers.

Von Bülow ceased fire and then sent several of his crew to the freighter with a scuttling charge. When a wounded American was found still on board, von Bülow went to render first aid and then helped lower the man to one of the lifeboats. He then ordered Perrier mineral water and coffee to be distributed to all of the men in the lifeboats. After the demolition charge was set, von Bülow appeared on the deck of the U-boat and gave the senior American officer, W. C. Edwards, a scrap

of paper. On it was written—"Cape Hatteras," "320 mile,"
and "275 degrees." It was the course the lifeboats would need
to reach shore and safety. While the survivors of the *West Notus*
headed west, the Germans remained to detonate their charges
and send the freighter crashing to the bottom. Two days later,
one of the lifeboats with eighteen survivors was picked up by
the Greek freighter *Constantinos H.* The next day after that, the
rest of the crew was rescued by the Swiss *Saentis.*[15]

Von Bülow was one of several U-boat commanders who,
in June, had decided to wait well off the coast to prey on the
stray, solitary ships still to be found going to and from Atlantic ports. This tactic would provide only sporadic results. On 2
June, Korvettenkapitän Ernst-August Rehwinkel in his *U-578*
managed to ambush the Norwegian motorship *Berganger* coming in from Brazil loaded with coffee. He torpedoed her once
and surfaced but was surprised by six near-misses from the
*Berganger*'s 4-inch gun. Rehwinkel crash-dived and then waited
for the crew to abandon ship before slamming two more torpedoes into the freighter's side. One of the lifeboats wasn't
clear, however, and the explosions capsized it. Unhurt but
dazed, the crewmen were pulled into the other lifeboats. The
*U-578* surfaced nearby and Rehwinkel and some of his crew
came out on deck. None of them were wearing any uniforms,
just a collection of civilian clothes. The one military exception
was Rehwinkel's white captain's cap. Tanned, bearded, and
handsome, Rehwinkel looked to the Norwegians like an actor
from a Hollywood movie. Softly, he asked if any of the crewmen could speak German. When no reply came, he tried English, asking them the name of their ship, nationality, tonnage,
port of departure, port of destination, and whether an SOS
had been sent. All the questions were answered truthfully except about the SOS signals. One had been sent, but that was
denied. Shortly afterwards, the *U-578* disappeared, leaving the
Norwegians to their fate. The United States Navy destroyer
*Madison* would pick up some of them two days later and the
rest would be rescued by the freighter *Bavaderos* and a fishing
boat, the *Mary J. Landry.*[16]

Indicative of the scarcity of targets, Kaleun Heinz-Otto
Schultz's *U-432*, 250 miles out from Boston, had to settle for

two small American fishing trawlers, the *Aeolus* and the *Ben & Josephine*. The two trawlers had been fishing about 4 miles apart when Schultz spotted them on 3 June. He went after the *Ben & Josephine* first just as the sun rose over a calm sea. Schultz ordered his deck-gun crew into action and began to pummel the tiny ship with 88-mm shells and machine-gun fire. After the *Ben & Josephine*'s skipper, Captain Giuseppe Clarrutaro, ordered his crew of eight to abandon ship, Schultz moved in for the kill. As soon as the trawler had sunk, the *U-432* went after the *Aeolus*. The *Aeolus*'s skipper, Captain John O. Johnson, ordered his crew of eight men into a dory and then began to look for his best friend, a white Spitz named Spooks. With shells crashing down around him, Johnson looked everywhere but finally had to give up. Spooks had been so frightened he had apparently crawled up under something to hide. Tears were streaming down Captain Johnson's leathery cheeks as he pushed away in the dory with his crew. The *Aeolus* went down quickly afterwards, taking Spooks with her. Savvy seamen, the two fishing crews turned their dories toward the coast and, 36 hours later, landed safely.[17]

Schultz's victory, however, was somewhat Pyrrhic. Since the war had begun, the New England fishermen had maintained a nearly neutral stance, resisting any efforts to get them involved in reporting U-boat activities they observed. They believed it was none of their business and would only get them torpedoed for their trouble. After they heard what had happened to the *Aeolus* and the *Ben & Josephine*, however, they became much more receptive to the idea of calling in U-boat sightings. As the fishermen were, in effect, a picket of small boats off New England, their calls would thereafter result in many harassing attacks against the U-boats by aircraft patrols.[18]

On 19 May, Horst Degen received his U-boat back from the Brest shipyard and sailed down the French coast to another U-boat base at Lorient. There, he topped off his diesel fuel tanks and began a high-speed night run across the Bay of Biscay. In the bay, the *U-701* was extremely vulnerable to British land-based bombers, and it was imperative that the area be

crossed as quickly as possible, preferably under the cover of
darkness. Finally, the broad Atlantic was reached and Degen
turned the snout of the *U-701* toward the south and west for
the two-week trek to the American coast. As other U-boat
commanders before him, he would use that time for constant
training, especially for crash-diving. He gave his men 30 seconds and no more from the time his alarm went off until the
U-boat was completely submerged. Again and again, he had
his executive officer put the crew through the drills, the results never quite good enough to suit him. His executive officer was, in Degen's opinion, slow-moving and slow-witted. A
good commander required a good second-in-command; that
was one of the rules of thumb in any navy. But, somehow,
Degen had been saddled with an incompetent. Well, so be it.
Degen would work the man into shape. His mission was too
important to be held back by anyone.

Other than his executive officer, Degen felt he had a good
crew. Their spirits were high and they seemed to like and
respond to their officers. To keep them happy, Degen regularly allowed them to come up on the bridge to have some sun
and fresh air. He also allowed records to be played in the
wireless room over loudspeakers throughout the ship and, as
soon as the *U-701* came within range, to listen to news and
musical programs on U.S. radio stations.

When the *U-701* was one day out from the American
shore, Degen called his officers into the control room and
spread before them a nautical chart. He had been ordered to
conduct a different and dangerous form of U-boat warfare, he
told them—the laying of a minefield. Other U-boats would be
conducting similar operations up and down the coast, but the
*U-701* had been picked for the most difficult operation of them
all: the mining of the entrance to the Chesapeake Bay. Admiral Doenitz had given the orders personally, Degen said, and it
was a mission considered of utmost importance.[19]

The officers studied the chart depicting the approaches to
the Chesapeake. The executive officer and the other officers—
engineer Karl-Heinrich Bahr, navigator Günter Kunert, and
junior watch officers Bazies and Lange—all crowded around,
trying to discern from the fathom numbers and coordinates on

the chart some scheme to accomplish the mission. There was only a little more than 10 miles, tip to tip, between Cape Henry and Cape Charles. Through there passed not only freighter and tanker traffic but also most of the American Atlantic fleet. There were nets there as well and also an American minefield, the location of which was not certain. Moreover, at its deepest, the entrance was only 36 feet deep and there were dozens of shoals that were probably not even marked on the chart. It did not seem possible. They would have to operate in a narrow strait in shallow water very near the biggest United States Navy base on the Atlantic coast. Surely the Americans would be onto them from the first.

Degen made a proposal. The *U-701* would go in at night, not submerged, but on the surface. The Americans would not be expecting that. It would be audacious, but it might just work. The mines would take 60 hours to activate. Plenty of time to get away. After some discussion, all the officers agreed.[20]

On the night of 12 June, the *U-701* crept toward the Virginia coastline. Very soon, the sweeping lights of the Cape Charles and Cape Henry lighthouses could be clearly seen. It was, Degen would later remark, "a breathtaking moment."[21]

It was true. For all of the navy's insistence that the coast be blacked out, it had exempted itself, keeping bright the lights marking the entrance to the Chesapeake and the large navy and coast guard installations located just beyond. Degen carefully guided the U-boat toward the entrance. As he came closer, he turned to port toward the beach in order to avoid a large sandbank. Tensely, lookouts peered into the darkness. Along the beach, first one dim light and then another came into view. It was the town of Virginia Beach. Houses could be seen. Moving lights told of automobiles. As Degen steered ever closer to shore, people could be seen walking, holding hands, some of them lying on blankets on the beach. The young Germans' eyes widened. A couple on one of the blankets were embracing.[22]

The *U-701* turned sharply to starboard several hundred yards from the beach and began to run parallel to it. Degen was almost to the mouth of the Chesapeake.

"Kaleun!" It was one of the lookouts.

Degen peered forward. Just ahead, a patrol ship, one of the British trawlers from the look of her, was running without lights and cutting across the *U-701*'s bow at a sharp angle. If the trawler could be seen, so could the U-boat. Sweat trickled down Degen's face. He was completely helpless. The water was much too shallow to dive and his maneuverability was severely limited because of the shoals. If the trawler saw them, the *U-701* was doomed. Degen could do nothing but continue on. Maybe in the darkness, he would be mistaken for another patrol craft. Maybe . . .

Time seemed to slow to a crawl as the trawler continued on toward its intersection with the *U-701*'s path. Finally, it droned by and continued without any hint of recognition. Degen breathed out in relief. Now to lay the mines! As the Cape Henry Lighthouse passed by on the port side, Degen gave the order and the first mine was expelled from one of the bow torpedo tubes. There were three of them in each of the *U-701*'s five tubes. Every 60 seconds, a mine was launched to sink to the mud below. Just as the eighth mine was expelled, one of the lookouts spotted the trawler returning along the same east-west track. This time Degen took no chances. He ordered the noisy diesels shut down and the quiet electric motors turned on. As the trawler approached, Degen turned the *U-701* away, passing well clear of the patrol craft. He then turned again and went back to sowing his mines. Finally, when all of the torpedo-shaped weapons were gone, Degen ordered the diesels fired up.

Mission accomplished.

Degen turned the *U-701* and aimed it toward the open sea at full speed.[23]

# 21

# The Saboteurs

O ne of the stranger events in the battle would occur on 13 June when a U-boat brought agent-saboteurs (the ones Doenitz had originally scheduled for Degen to carry) to land on United States soil. It was just after midnight when the Type VIIC *U-202*, commanded by Kapitänleutnant Hans-Heinz Linder, slipped in close to the beach at Amagansett, Long Island. As lookouts on the conning tower scanned the beach, four civilians paddled toward shore in a collapsible boat. Linder watched until they had landed and then ordered a signal sent to Doenitz that all had gone well.[1]

All did seem to be going well for the agents even though they had unwittingly landed very near the East Amagansett Coast Guard Life-Saving Station and the headquarters of the 113th Mobile Infantry Unit. In fact, they had managed to land on the only beach within 100 miles that the coast guard patrolled 24 hours a day. That was why the Germans were surprised by a coast guardsman as soon as they struggled out of the surf. John C. Cullen, seaman second class and 21 years old, thought maybe he could help. "What's the trouble?" he asked pleasantly.

The men looked up but no one answered. Then one of

them started to walk toward Cullen. "Who are you?" Cullen asked him, pulling a flashlight from his hip pocket.

The man stopped. Perhaps he thought Cullen had reached for a gun. "Wait a minute," he blurted. "Are you coast guard?"

"Yes," Cullen answered. "Who are you?"

"A couple of fishermen from Southampton who have run aground."

Cullen relaxed. "Come up to the station and wait for daybreak."

The wind began to blow harder just then and a dense fog swirled in. The man who had walked toward him seemed to be thinking. "Wait a minute," he said finally. "You don't know what's going on. How old are you? Have you a father and mother? I wouldn't want to kill you."

While Cullen was absorbing this strange mixture of threat and concern, a fourth man in a bathing suit walked out of the fog. He was dragging a bag. Cullen heard him say something in German. "What's in the bag?" Cullen asked.

"Clams."

Clams? Cullen knew he was in trouble. There were no clams around for miles. He decided the safest thing for him to do was to play as dumb as possible. He stood mute while the first man who had spoken continued to study him. "Listen," the man said in a friendly voice, "why don't you forget the whole thing? Here is some money. One hundred dollars."

"I don't want it."

"Then take three hundred," the man said, his voice betraying some exasperation. He took more bills from his wallet and held them out.

Cullen thought he had better humor the man. "O.K.," he said.

The man handed him the money and then stepped in closer to the coast guardsman. "Now look me in the eyes," he said.

Cullen was afraid he was going to be hypnotized. He had seen it in the spy movies. "Would you recognize me if you saw me again?" the man asked once and then again. "Would you recognize me?"

To Cullen's relief, he hadn't been hypnotized, but he was

scared. How the hell could he not help but recognize the man if he kept insisting that Cullen look at him? Nevertheless, Cullen finally answered "No" and the man seemed satisfied.[2]

Cullen turned around and began to walk slowly back to the Coast Guard Station. When he was well into the fog, he began to run. Once at the station, he blurted out his story to Boatswain's Mate Jenette, who promptly telephoned his superiors, Warrant Officer Oden and Chief Boatswain's Mate Warren Barnes, who lived nearby. Fifteen minutes later, Jenette had gathered three other coast guardsmen at the station, given them and Cullen .30-caliber rifles, and returned to the beach. The fog was so dense that Cullen could not locate where he had seen the men. Since the men with him didn't know whether Cullen had hallucinated the whole thing or had stumbled on the advance party of an invasion force, the search was called off in five minutes. Being out on a dark beach in a dense fog when strange things were happening just didn't seem wise.

When the men got back to the station, Chief Barnes was there and took charge. Barnes took the men back down to the beach. He ordered his men to lie behind the sand dunes to resist the landings of any further Germans, but the fog was so thick that some of the men said they weren't sure that would do any good, so Barnes took them all back to the station. Once there, Cullen insisted on turning in his bribe money. Barnes counted the money and made Cullen a receipt. It was for $260. Cullen had been shortchanged forty dollars.[3]

Barnes called Coast Guard Headquarters in New York City and reported what had happened. The intelligence duty officer, a Lieutenant Nirshel, then phoned the Third Naval District Intelligence Office and relayed what he knew to the assistant duty officer, Ensign Fitzgerald. Fitzgerald then telephoned the assistant duty officer at the Eastern Sea Frontier, and that officer picked up the phone and called Coast Guard Headquarters in New York, completing a neat circle of calls. The Eastern Sea Frontier officer wanted to know if the army should be called in. He was informed by Headquarters that there were at least 100 coast guardsmen at the scene plus numerous coast guard craft searching the area. In fact, there were a total of only eight men at the station and no ships at all.[4]

At 0200, an army lieutenant arrived at the station with twenty armed men. The lieutenant explained that he had come because of a panicky call from the radioman at the Amagansett Naval Radio Station who had heard diesel motors and a diesel horn out to sea and guessed that the Germans were landing. Fearing for his family's life, the radioman had shooed them out of the station and into town. There, he had called the coast guard station. The man who answered said that he had been ordered not to discuss anything about German landings. The radioman wondered if, in fact, he was talking to a German agent so he hung up and called the 113th Mobile Infantry. The duty sergeant there told him that he was sorry but neither he nor any other infantryman could leave the premises without an order from the commander of the unit.

*Well, couldn't that order be given?* the radioman wondered.

He supposed so, the sergeant allowed . . . if the captain thought the reason good enough.

*Then . . . ?*

Reluctantly, the sergeant agreed to call his lieutenant who, in turn, called the captain. Permission was granted for the lieutenant and his men to head down to the beach.[5]

Meanwhile, in Eastern Sea Frontier Headquarters, the assistant duty officer had tried to reach the Federal Bureau of Investigation but found the FBI's wires busy. It later was learned that the army had notified the FBI, and agents were being called in.[6]

At first light, the fog began to lift a little and the coast guardsmen who had been barricaded in the Amagansett Station all night came out and made a search of the beach. The first thing found was a pack of German cigarettes half-buried in the sand. Then a furrow was seen in the sand as if some heavy object had been dragged over it. The furrow was followed until they reached a spot where it looked as if someone had dug a hole and filled it back up. A pair of wet swimming trunks was found nearby. The coast guardsmen began digging and soon uncovered four wooden cases. When these cases were torn open, more cases were found within, these made of tin.

Another disturbed area was found and an assortment of German clothing, including two dungaree outfits, a reversible civilian overcoat, a pair of overshoes and an overseas cap with a swastika were dug up.[7]

By 0600, the coast guard began to send some patrol craft out to look around at sea. Perhaps the U-boat was still nearby. Because of the fog, no planes could fly. By 1030, the first naval intelligence officer arrived in Amagansett accompanied by three undercover men. These men immediately took jobs in the area, one as a waiter in a restaurant and boardinghouse operated by a German suspect, another as a gas-station attendant, and the last as a helper on a wholesale fish truck.[8]

The naval intelligence zone officer from Riverhead, Long Island, arrived at 1035 and went to the coast guard station but was told by the officer there that he had been instructed to talk to no one, regardless of rank. After several phone calls, the zone officer was identified and the story told. At 1100, the commandant of the Third Naval District held a joint conference with the district intelligence officer, intelligence officers of the army, navy, and coast guard, and agents of the FBI. The FBI subsequently took over jurisdiction of the case. Later that night, four additional naval intelligence agents were sent into the area and moved into the coast guard lookout tower to watch out for enemy submarines. Two hours later, FBI agents arrived, ordered the navy agents out of the tower, and manned it themselves. They also began to walk the beach with newly armed coast guardsmen and even dug and manned foxholes near the spots where the Germans had buried their goods. Miffed, the naval intelligence agents set up their operations at the Amagansett Radio Station. From there, they could watch for German spies and keep tabs on the FBI as well. The FBI was well aware of their operation, however, and subsequently made every attempt to keep anything about the case a big secret from naval intelligence. Naval intelligence would later register a strong protest against the FBI over their behavior. The FBI, in its turn, would make a counter-complaint that vital evidence had been withheld from them, a vest found on the beach. Naval intelligence, as it was later to be learned, was innocent of this charge. The culprits had been coast guard officers who had gotten the vest from one of the search parties and had decided to conduct a private investigative effort of their own. The results of this would be that they would eventually accuse an innocent American citizen of being in on the sabotage scheme.[9]

Surprisingly, considering the initial turmoil, the first of the German saboteurs that landed on the Amagansett beach was arrested barely a week after his landing. The FBI made certain the newspapers gave them all the credit for cracking the case, although it would later be learned that they had done so only because one of the spies, Georg Johann Dasch, had turned himself in. Dasch was a German national who had been a resident in the United States for many years. He was even married to an American citizen. After he and the others had their scare with Cullen on the beach, he became nervous about his mission. After thinking about it, he decided to turn state's evidence. He first called the FBI on a Sunday evening, but it was the following Wednesday before he finally convinced someone there to talk to him. After that, all the FBI had to do was to go to the addresses Dasch gave them and pick up the other Germans.[10]

There was to be a second landing. The *U-584* placed four more saboteurs near Ponte Vedra, Florida, on 17 June, and this one went unobserved. The agents were even able to hide their explosives and get away, two of them to New York, two to Chicago. But Dasch's testimony would allow the FBI to catch them, too.[11] When it was all over, no damage had been done by any of the German saboteurs, and, eventually, all of them would be tried and convicted. Two of them, including Dasch, would receive prison terms. The rest would be executed.[12]

# 22

# Hopes Unfulfilled

On 11 June, the *Dione* sailed from Key West and headed north with her latest convoy. It had been an interesting time for the cutter's crew since the success of convoy KS-502 in May. After that convoy, Lieutenant Alger had come down with a case of the measles in Norfolk and had been taken ashore, leaving the cutter under the command of her young executive officer, Lieutenant (j.g.) Bacchus. Bacchus had handled the responsibility admirably, taking the *Dione* south with another convoy and then immediately turning around and taking yet another back to Key West. When she reached Key West, Alger was there waiting for her, having hopped trains and planes all the way down the coast. With very little rest for its escorts, a large convoy of tankers and freighters was formed and began to head north with the *Dione*, her sister cutter *Calypso*, the navy destroyers *Bainbridge* and *Decatur*, and the British trawlers *Lady Elsa* and *Kingston Ceylonite* escorting. Their destination: the Chesapeake Bay.[1]

On the same day as the *Dione*'s new convoy sailed, the Esso tanker *F. W. Abrams* was well ahead, just passing Cape Hatteras. She was on a dangerous voyage alone, violating Admiral Andrews's order that no American tanker could sail up the east coast unless in a convoy. On 10 June, as the *Abrams* neared

Hatteras, a coast guard patrol boat came across her and, recognizing the danger the tanker was in, ordered her to an anchorage. Her captain, Anthony J. Coumelis, reluctantly complied.

Coumelis waited until the next morning and followed the patrol boat back out to sea in an impromptu convoy. The sky was overcast and the visibility poor. When it started to rain and the seas began to rise, the tiny coast guard boat started to lose way. The *Abrams*, without a backward look, continued on. Less than an hour later, a tremendous explosion occurred on the tanker's starboard bow. Coumelis ordered a general alarm and opened the control valves to the fire-smothering system. After investigating the damage, it was determined that the *Abrams* could stay afloat, and Coumelis headed for shore. Less than thirty minutes later, another violent explosion occurred, again on the starboard side. Her decks now awash, the *Abrams* began to buckle. Coumelis had no choice. He ordered his tanker abandoned, but before that could be accomplished, an explosion, this one more violent than the previous two, occurred between the bow and the bridge on the port side. Hurriedly, Coumelis and his crew took to the lifeboats.

Several hours later, the crew of the *Abrams* landed safely near the Ocracoke Naval Station and reported that their ship had been torpedoed three times. Coumelis asked that he be taken back to the ship so that he could determine if she could be salvaged. The navy obliged and the Esso skipper was taken out. The *Abrams* was found, but she was almost submerged and had been battered further by heavy seas. There was no hope of salvage. During the trek out to the tanker, however, several of the navy men spotted some very ominous objects low in the water. Closer inspection revealed them to be mines. They were, in fact, part of the U.S. Navy's very own Cape Hatteras minefield. Traveling alone as she had, the *F. W. Abrams* had managed to blunder right into a "friendly" minefield, saving the U-boats the trouble of sinking her. Coumelis would later state that he had no information as to the American coastal defenses, minefields, or anything else because he was "under British charter." If Admiral Andrews needed any reminder of the continuing independent character of the commercial masters, Coumelis had provided it.[2]

Nevertheless, the tankers and freighters in the *Dione*'s convoy were behaving themselves fairly well. Discipline on not showing lights had been good at night, and the masters of the vessels had been as cooperative as they could about straggling. In fact, Alger considered it to be the best convoy yet. By late afternoon on 15 June, the convoy was nearing its end. At the *Bainbridge*'s signal, the *Dione* and the *Calypso* began to maneuver the herd of ships into single file preparatory to standing in to Chesapeake Bay. One by one, the tankers and freighters glided toward sanctuary. The lead vessel, the *Empire Sapphire*, contained the convoy's commodore. Pilot vessels led the big tanker past the red whistle buoy that marked the entrance to the Chesapeake. It was known to stand at one corner of the minefield placed to protect Hampton Roads, so care had to be taken in passing it. The convoy was proceeding slowly. Lieutenant Alger was on the bridge with Bacchus when one of the tankers, the fifth in line, suddenly shook as if it had hit something and then a huge plume of water and smoke erupted from its side. It was the American tanker *Robert C. Tuttle*.

"Oh no!" someone on the *Dione*'s bridge cried. It may have been everyone. Not again! After all these months, after everything that had been done for this convoy and all the rest, how could it be happening still?

On shore, thousands of vacationers stood up as one on the sandy beach opposite the Chesapeake entrance. Something was happening to those ships out there! Women screamed and men ran to the water's edge.

Alger was on the radio as the *Dione* ran toward the stricken tanker. The captain of the *Tuttle*, Martin Johansen, climbed back to his feet after the shock of the explosion and received reports. He heard that the *Dione* was coming, but he could feel the tanker going down under him. Whatever had hit him had opened up a huge hole. All the forward compartments were flooding. He ordered the *Tuttle* abandoned.

In Virginia Beach, word of the disaster spread rapidly. Soon, thousands more spectators crowded onto the beach. All that could be seen was a tanker, down by her bow, with other

big tankers still moving placidly past and smaller patrol
craft milling about. Suddenly, several small fighter-bombers
whooshed overhead and began to circle the convoy. One of
them dived, loosing a bomb. It exploded and the crowd nervously cheered. Before their cheer had died, however, it was
drowned out by a bigger explosion. It was the tanker *Esso Augusta*.

Lieutenant Alger was calling for sound contacts and his
soundmen were doing their best to comply. It was so shallow
where they were that the sonar was just bouncing back and
the sea was full of noise, the whop-whop of the tankers' and
freighters' propellers, the explosions, the bombs from the
planes . . . it was impossible. Alger took note of where the
*Tuttle* had been hit and did some mental calculations. If she
had been hit by a torpedo, the U-boat couldn't be far away.
Sweeping around the convoy, he took the *Dione* out to sea,
homing in on the track he guessed the torpedoes might have
taken. When he reached deeper water, he unloaded seven
depth charges.

The *Esso Augusta*'s skipper, Captain Eric R. Blomquist, had
meanwhile been checking over his ship. The torpedo, or whatever had hit him, had blown off the tanker's rudder and put
several holes in the hull under the tail shaft. Blomquist called
for a tow and HMS *Lady Elsa* came over to help. The tanker
was too heavy, however, and after the towline parted three
times from the little trawler, the work was abandoned. Blomquist then called in to shore, asking for assistance from there.

Out to sea with the *Dione* was the destroyer *Bainbridge*. Her
skipper had done the same as Alger and was attempting to at
least frighten the suspected U-boat away. When the *Bainbridge*'s soundman called out a "mushy" contact, the destroyer
dropped eight charges. The explosions went off one by one—
the men counted—*ONE! TWO! THREE! FOUR! FIVE! SIX!
SEVEN! EIGHT! NINE!* Nine? Eight depth charges had resulted in nine explosions, and one of them had been larger
than the rest by far and had shaken the destroyer from end to
end. The *Bainbridge*'s skipper knew immediately what had
happened. His depth charges had set off a mine. There was no

U-boat, at least not now. He and all of his convoy were in the middle of a German minefield!

Alger was alerted and ordered to stand by the *Augusta* to protect her from further harm. The *Calypso* was ordered to go south as fast as she could. There was another part of the convoy coming in, the *Delisle* in tow by the tug *Warbler* escorted by the trawler *Kingston Ceylonite*. They needed to be warned of the danger ahead.

As dark approached, the remainder of the convoy crept slowly past the *U-701*'s minefield and safely made it into Chesapeake. Several tugs relieved the *Dione* of the *Augusta* and began to tow the tanker to safety while Alger took his cutter into Little Creek. Everything seemed to be over. The *Calypso* had missed the *Kingston Ceylonite*, however, and shortly afterwards the British trawler led the way into the Chesapeake Bay. People still watching seaward in the darkness were witness to a sudden flash and a huge, rolling explosion. Aboard the *Delisle* and *Warbler*, seamen rushed to the rails as the shock wave blew past them. In the darkness, there were noises, the splashes of pieces of metal and wood and the remnants of British crewmen falling into the sea. For many minutes, the sky rained the remains of the *Kingston Ceylonite*. One of Degen's mines had done its job, blasting the trawler and its entire crew to pieces.[3]

At about the same time that the crew of the *Kingston Ceylonite* were paying for their service to the United States with their lives, the commander of the Inshore Patrol of the Fifth Naval District was planning the sweeping operations to begin at daylight the next day. Sweepers from the Navy Mine Warfare School at Yorktown and the Service Squadron of the Atlantic Fleet were given orders to report as soon as possible to the Section Base at Little Creek. That evening, a conference was held at the Section Base to decide how to conduct the sweeping operations. Plans were laid to conduct a thorough search of the channel. The channel was divided into three sections labeled "A," "B," and "C."

At daylight the next morning, minesweepers left Little Creek and began to work Area A, which lay south and west of one of the marked buoys. Working in pairs, the ships swept back and forth with magnetic gear. Five mines were found

and exploded. About the middle of the day, more minesweepers, these from the fleet, arrived and began their work. Then
sweepers arrived from the Navy Mine Warfare School. They
were instructed to sweep in Area B. Nothing was found and
the channel was declared clear.[4]

On the morning of 17 June, the regular south-bound convoy proceeded out of Hampton Roads, heading for Key West.
One of the ships, the *Santore*, a freighter loaded with coal, was
maneuvering into her convoy position in the area the minesweepers had designated Area B. Suddenly, she was ripped by
a terrific explosion. The ship immediately rolled over on her
side and began to sink rapidly. Captain Eric Nyborg was
thrown down to the deck, both of his legs broken. His mates
grabbed him and, with the surviving crewmen, jumped into
the sea.[5]

Aboard a coast guard 83-footer nearby was the newspaper
reporter J. Norman Lodge. It was one of the 83-footers that
had been especially designed for antisubmarine patrol duties.
Every inch of the little ship was packed with the implements
needed to carry out that requirement. Machine guns were
mounted around the deck with two depth-charge racks on her
stern. Below was a "sound room," actually not much more
than a broom closet, packed full of sonar and listening gear.
The 83-footers were known for their ride on rough seas, "like
a jeep on square wheels."[6] Bathing and shaving were unknown. The dozen crewmen manning them were a tough,
proud bunch. Lodge had been put aboard by a navy public-
relations officer who had promised him only an indoctrination
cruise that he would "probably find boring." Instead, he was
suddenly on a bounding ship turning to and fro and throwing
depth charges overboard at what appeared to be a real enemy.

"With a sound reminiscent of a distant thunder, the depth
charges exploded," Lodge would later write. "A geyser fully
fifty feet high appeared off the stern and our 83-footer left the
water momentarily. Again and again . . . the frail craft
jumped into the air."

"Suddenly the Bo'sun, who was navigating the subchaser,
shouted to the Ensign, Mr. John Dhue . . . 'Number ten just
got it.' "

"Number ten was the collier, 10th ship in line . . . The next few minutes were the most dramatic of my life . . ."[7]

What Lodge had witnessed was the *Santore* hitting one of Degen's mines. Several misunderstandings during the sweeping operations had left Area B still bobbing with explosives. The results of a later investigation of the minesweeping exercise would leave both Admiral King and Admiral Andrews furious and would result in orders from King to the commandant of the Fifth Naval District to completely overhaul his organization. This was the equivalent in military terms of a direct reprimand.[8]

But it was too late for reprimands to help the *Santore* or the *Kingston Ceylonite* or the *Tuttle* or the *Augusta*. Two ships sunk and two badly damaged. The mines of the *U-701* had done their job well.

Compared to the hopeful manner in which June had begun, things seemed to be falling apart for Admiral Andrews and his Eastern Sea Frontier by the middle of the month. This was underscored by the experiences of a convoy off Cape Cod the night of 15 June.

It was not a night when any trouble was expected from the U-boats. The weather was atrocious, a high wind blowing over a roaring, spewing sea. The convoy, six merchant vessels being escorted by five warships, struggled through heavy seas under a dark and moonless sky. The *Cathcart*, *Port Nicholson*, and *Pan York* led the way, followed by the *Malcrest*, *Norlago*, and the *Cherokee*. Ahead of them, two of the escort vessels plunged through the huge waves while an escort on either side attempted to protect the flanks. Behind came one more escort, her sonar sweeping right and left and ahead and behind. She was there to pick up any U-boats that might try to catch up with the convoy and also to alert the convoy commodore to any stragglers. Although the convoy was being carefully managed, the men on the escorts believed that if there were any U-boats around, the weather would force them to remain deeply submerged.

The weather, however, was not enough to deter the *U-87*. The *U-87*'s commander, Kapitänleutnant Joachim Berger, was

aware of the gale above, but when his soundman alerted him
to what sounded like a convoy, he decided to put up with it
and get himself some tonnage sunk. When the convoy got
close enough, he lined up on one of the lead ships and sent two
torpedoes from his bow tubes after it. It was the *Port Nicholson,*
a British ship. She took the first torpedo on her starboard side
and began to break up. Someone aboard her began to send up
rocket flares.

Twiggs Brown, the captain of the *Cherokee,* a passenger
ship containing 112 merchant crew, 41 army enlisted men, 4
Russian naval officers, 1 army air forces pilot, and 11 navy
guards, had immediately put his ship into a hard turn to starboard to get out of the light of the *Port Nicholson*'s flares.

"We shouldn't even be here!" Brown complained to the
bridge watch. "They should have let us go on!"

Brown was referring to the fact that he had brought his
ship across the Atlantic in a fast convoy but had then been
detached from it with no explanation and forced to stand in to
Halifax. Two days after that, he had been ordered to join a
slow 8-knot convoy for the remainder of the trip to New York.
This had made no sense at all to Brown since the *Cherokee* was
capable of 17 knots. It had been all that Brown could do, in
fact, to keep his ship going slow enough to stay with the convoy. Brown slammed his fist against his palm. "Damn!" he
railed. "Damn!" He strained his body forward, tipping up on
his toes. *Move, damn you, move!* Finally, he was going to use his
speed. He had to. The miserable convoy he had been ordered
to join had suddenly become a trap.

But no amount of speed could save Brown and his *Cherokee.*
Berger had the ship in his sights. He sent two more of his bow
torpedoes whining through the turbulent, roaring sea. The
first of them struck the *Cherokee* on the port side, devastating
the charthouse and the bridge. Captain Brown, bloodied and
dazed, lifted himself out of the wreckage and saw his men
standing around, looking at him. He angrily waved his arms at
them. "Save yourselves!" he growled. The crewmen scrambled
to follow Brown's orders, but the second torpedo slammed in,
blowing a huge hole in the forecastle. The *Cherokee* rolled over
and sank, taking with her dozens of screaming men.

All night long, in the terrible, blowing, frigid sea, the survivors of the *Cherokee* and *Port Nicholson* hung on to rafts and wreckage and each other. The next morning, the convoy had managed to circle back to the site of the torpedo attack. The sight that awaited them was sickening. Dozens of bodies floated in the water and there were sharks all about, snapping at them, jerking them to and fro. The survivors screamed pitifully for help. Remarkably, only five men of the *Port Nicholson* had lost their lives. But the *Cherokee* had lost sixty-five of her crew members (Captain Brown was one of the survivors) plus twenty of the army enlisted men and one of her navy guards. It had been one of the worst disasters ever in the history of the American Atlantic seaboard.[9]

On 24 June, Admiral Andrews received more bad news. Other U-boats had apparently layed more minefields. The tug *John R. Williams* had been the unlucky ship destined to first discover this. After going to the assistance of the *Port Darwin*, aground on Fenwick Island Shoal, the tug had been on her way back to Cape May. Although channels in the area in which she sailed had been swept of mines, her master either through ignorance or inattention strayed from the prescribed course and bumped right into a mine sown by Kaleun Paul-Karl Loeser's *U-373* almost two weeks before. Out of a crew of eighteen men, only four of them would survive. The *John R. Williams* sank almost immediately.[10]

In the halls and offices of the Eastern Sea Frontier Headquarters in New York as well as in the War Department, there was consternation. In Washington, a Senate naval affairs subcommittee had begun a preliminary investigation of the navy's antisubmarine campaign. Chaired by Senator Ellender of Louisiana, the committee indicated that it was not satisfied that everything possible had been done to halt the U-boat sinkings and that the entire matter was going to get a public hearing.[11]

In a matter of a few days, it seemed as if Admiral Doenitz had turned everything around and, in the process, ruined not a few United States Navy careers. On 19 June, General Marshall sent a strong letter of criticism to Admiral King. "The losses by submarines off our Atlantic seaboard and in the Caribbean now threaten our entire war effort," it said. Admiral

King shot back an angry reply, citing the shortage of ships he had to use against the U-boats. He had been forced, he wrote, "to improvise rapidly and on a large scale." Then, in a remarkable about-face, King went on to say, "I might say in this connection that [the convoy system] is not just *one* way of handling the submarine menace. It is the *only* way that gives any promise of success. The so-called patrol and hunting operations have time and again proved futile."[12]

After weeks of denying the usefulness of convoys, especially when the British had suggested using them, King had not only accepted the idea in his letter to Marshall but had even made the idea his own. Nevertheless, hardly a day went by that Admiral King's staff didn't hit Admiral Andrews with angry questions. Why were the convoys not working? And how was it that German mines seemed to be strewn everywhere and American minesweepers didn't seem to know enough to clear them? And what was the Eastern Sea Frontier going to do about it?[13]

Admiral Andrews remained calm in the storm of criticism. He had been in the navy for a long, long time, had seen changes and challenges come and go, and had been criticized only to triumph before. His hopes for the month had gone largely unfulfilled, but he believed that hard work and perseverance and the application of good tactics eventually paid off. It was that way in the navy, and it was that way in the world, too. Let them talk, let them investigate, let them criticize. He knew better than the young hotshots on King's staff and certainly better than some old windbag in the Senate. Doenitz had had his day. Andrews figured it was his turn now.

It was just a matter of time.

# 23

# The *YP 389* and the *U-701*

---

**W**hile Lieutenant Alger took the *Dione* back to sea for what looked to be a very long time, another American ship was already on patrol in the area, just outside the Cape Hatteras minefield. She was the U.S. Navy's *YP 389*, a Boston trawler pressed into service at the beginning of the war. She had been on duty off Cape Hatteras since early June, going up and down the Hatteras minefield perimeter, warning shipping not to stray into it. It was perhaps the only duty the *YP 389* was suited for in those dangerous waters. Even though the navy had bolted on her deck a 3-inch gun, two .30-caliber machine guns, and four depth charges on some stern racks, she was completely inadequate as a warship. She was slow, even by trawler standards, and she lacked any kind of underwater detection gear. In order for her to attack a U-boat, her crew would actually have to see one, a doubtful occurrence, and then catch it, an even more doubtful one. She also had no ventilating system or fresh-water showers for her twenty-two enlisted men and three officers, and her galley stove usually did not work. Still, for Admiral Andrews and his staff on the Eastern Sea Frontier, she represented a hull that could be sent to sea, one that could accomplish at least something, perhaps disrupt a U-boat's schedule or aim, or warn others of peril, or even offer herself as a target instead of a merchantman.[1]

Lieutenant R. J. Phillips, the *YP 389*'s commander, had tried to make his ship at least seaworthy. Since arriving in the Hatteras area, he had gotten his engines overhauled at Morehead City and tried to get the 3-inch gun fixed when it was found inoperable. The part needed for the gun was not available, however, so he was forced to go back to sea without it in working condition.[2] Since the *F. W. Abrams* had been sunk by the American minefield off Hatteras, the navy had been trying to decide whether to remove it or warn other ships of it in some manner. The U-boats were obviously aware of the minefield, having studiously avoided it, so its value was questionable. The *YP 389* was needed to patrol the minefield and warn shipping to stand clear until some decision was made.[3]

Since the *YP 389* had no degaussing equipment, Phillips had to be careful around the mines. He had very little room to maneuver. In order to accomplish his mission, he could not enter the minefield nor go very far away from it. His patrol area was locked in from the minefield's north and south buoys. It was thankless, drudging, frustrating duty.

Unknown to Lieutenant Phillips, there was another frustrated naval commander nearby. After the enormous success of his mine-laying mission, Kapitänleutnant Degen was looking to cause even more destruction and damage, this time with his torpedoes. Operating off Hatteras, Degen had expected the same success as Hardegen and the others before him. But after a week, very few targets had been seen and all of them had been well screened by escorts. Degen could neither understand nor accept it. Night after night, the *U-701* had risen to confront a dark and empty sea. The Hatteras Lighthouse, its flashing beacon once a lure for unsuspecting merchant ships sailing toward a U-boat trap, now seemed to mock Degen with its constant warning signals. There had been a big change in water temperature between January and June as well. The Gulf Stream was now a giant current of summer-heated water sweeping over the U-boat as it lay on a bed of white sand during the day. Temperature in the *U-701* would rise at times to over 90 degrees Fahrenheit, leaving Degen and his crew exhausted and nauseous. After days of this, the crew's morale had deteriorated, and they began to look forward to the nightly surfacings, not to sink enemy ships but simply to flush out the interior of the hot, cramped U-boat. Despite his attempts to control it, Degen's temper was also affected by the heat and was beginning to flare at the least pretext. Usually, he took it out on his executive officer. The man was just too slow-witted and Degen intended to replace him the moment the *U-701* arrived back in Brest.[4]

After a targetless week, Degen decided to temporarily change his tactics. He kept the *U-701* on the surface after sunrise and almost immediately spotted a convoy of ships heading south. It was close in-shore and moving too rapidly for Degen to catch, so he moved closer to the shoreline, figuring to catch the next one. After positioning himself, he waited. And waited. Finally, the next day, another convoy was spotted, this one going north but it was too far out for Degen to catch. "God Damn it!" he exploded at his exec. "I can't get a shot at them!"[5]

About then, one of Degen's lookouts spotted a tiny ship coming in over the horizon. Degen took the *U-701* down and looked the ship over. He thought at first it was some kind of fishing trawler, but then he noticed the 3-inch gun on its bow and the depth-charge racks on its stern. A naval patrol vessel, then. Degen considered going after it but then decided to leave it alone. There was no sense alerting the entire coast to his presence. Besides, the little ship might have more of a bite than she appeared to have. He continued his abortive attempts to position his U-boat to catch a convoy. Each time he moved, however, it seemed he would encounter the little patrol boat. It was almost as if the trawler were following him about. Was it part of a trap designed to sink the *U-701*?

Degen took the *U-701* down and spent the day of 18 June drifting underwater and thinking things over. Once more, the temperature gradually climbed inside the U-boat until it was almost unbearable. Overhead, Degen heard propellers. Probably the patrol boat. All of the U-boat commander's frustrations seemed to suddenly focus on the little ship. It was like a fly that kept buzzing in his ear. Degen ached to be rid of it by whatever means it took. As the day wore on and the propeller sounds were heard again and again, Degen kept getting angrier at the patrol boat. After dark had descended on the sea above, Degen took his *U-701* up. The first thing he saw when he stepped out on the conning tower bridge was the little ship. Degen decided he must be rid of it. He called up his gun crew.[6]

Nothing was suspected aboard the *YP 389*. Not once during the days since Degen had spotted the trawler had anyone aboard her had the slightest suspicion that there was a U-boat around. There was still no sound gear aboard the ship and, anyway, the *YP 389*'s job was to warn ships away from the minefield, not to look for U-boats. At the moment Degen spotted the trawler that night, she was about 5 miles west of Diamond Shoals on a northeasterly course. The sky was dark and moonless, the sea smooth. A lookout had been stationed on both wings of the bridge plus one on the flying bridge and one on the stern. While the *U-701* stalked her, the *YP 389* finished her run to the northern buoy of the minefield and then turned around and headed back on a southwesterly course. Degen waited, his own lookouts carefully watching. Finally, the slow little ship that had plagued him came back into view. Degen ordered the *U-701* forward.

At 0245 on 19 June, Lieutenant Phillips was on duty on the bridge. His executive officer, Ensign Ray P. Baker, Jr., and the engineering officer, Ensign R. M. McKellar, were both asleep in their bunks below. A cry from the starboard bridge watch caught Phillips's attention. He looked in that direction and was stunned to see a German U-boat suddenly appear out of the gloom. Instantaneously, his hand hit the alarm and then the U-boat opened fire.

Degen decided to use his 20-mm machine guns first. He didn't want to waste much ammunition on the little ship. He gave the order and the gun opened up behind him. Hot shells went flying across the U-boat deck as a stream of heavy slugs and red tracers slammed into the trawler.

Phillips was ducking and trying to help Signalman McPherson, the acting quartermaster, steer the *YP 389* at the same time. At Phillips's order, McPherson wrenched the wheel around, turning to port, trying to put his stern toward the U-boat. Phillips opened the *YP 389*'s engines wide. That gave him barely 7 knots. The *U-701* could go 18.

Degen ordered his 88-mm gun crew to open up at will. Their first round was wide of the mark, but the second caught the *YP 389*'s crew as they came up from below. One man was killed in the blast, another seriously injured. Still, the navy men kept coming. Machine-gun fire mixed with 88-mm shells began to tear away big chunks of the trawler's deck. But her crew ducked and weaved until they were at their battle stations. On the bridge, Lieutenant Phillips called the coast guard at Ocracoke and told them what was happening. The coast guard replied and told them to hold on. Help was coming. Phillips then put out a call to all ships and planes in the area, not for help, but to warn them of the presence of the *U-701*. Degen was informed of the *YP 389*'s call. "Damn!" he griped. "Sink that son of a bitch. *Now!*"

Phillips ordered his men to get the .30-caliber machine guns operating. Fireman 3/C Crabb manned the gun on the signal bridge, Fireman 1/C Wilson the gun on the boat deck. Soon, the old guns were barking, but the racket of incoming 20-mm and 88-mm rounds was so great they could scarcely be heard even by the gunners themselves. On deck, Ensign McKellar and others gathered the wounded into more protected areas and tried to administer what first aid they could. Miraculously, considering the pummelling the *YP 389* was taking, the wounds were mostly splinter wounds, ugly but not life threatening if treated in time.

Phillips began to head toward shore after swinging the *YP 389* around the buoy of the minefield. He knew it was their only chance. Maybe the German commander would be reluctant to head into shallow water after them. But the U-boat kept following. It was almost as if the commander of the U-boat had a vendetta against them. But what possibly could it be?

On the *U-701*, Degen knew he had matters under control but was frustrated by the misses of the deck gun. He chided the chief gunner, who replied that the low silhouette of the trawler made it difficult to hit. Degen moved in closer. A few of the .30-caliber rounds from the trawler whizzed past his head, but he ignored them in his single-minded dedication to ridding himself of the small warship. It was between him and success and had to die.

Phillips, seeing that the U-boat was going to continue to chase, decided on another desperate gamble. Perhaps if he dropped the depth charges, it might somehow scare the Germans away. And maybe if he set them shallow enough and dropped them in front of the U-boat, they might even cause some damage. Fireman 3/C Cole, in charge of the depth charges, prepared to drop them. McKellar dodged through the flying splinters to help. He sprawled out on deck beside Cole just as the stern seemed to disintegrate. A line of 20-mm rounds ripped past, and then an 88-mm round fell just behind. Cole, already wounded, snarled in agony as a piece of shrapnel caught him in the back. Still, with blood flowing from numerous wounds, the young man worked on his depth charges and then, finally, pulled the lever to send them trundling off. Although Degen slowed momentarily when the charges went off, the explosions were wide of their mark. Still, somehow, the Americans were fighting back. This he had not expected. He decided to use incendiary rounds. If he couldn't sink the pesky ship, maybe he could at least burn it down to the waterline. The first incendiary was on target, hitting the stern and killing Cole, who had been trying to somehow load another depth charge. Wilson dropped his machine gun and raced to help but fell in a heap after being struck by a 20-mm round.

Desperately, Phillips kept maneuvering, trying to keep the U-boat from getting a clear shot. But it seemed as if the Germans had managed to get their range. Phillips yelled up to the flying bridge and ordered Crabb to cease fire. He suspected the Germans were keying on the gun's tracers. Crabb finished out his drum of ammunition and was about to move when an incendiary round hit the wheelhouse, killing him and setting the bridge on fire. Shielding his face from the flames, Phillips ordered everyone still alive off the bridge. Another round looped in and then another. One of them set off the $CO_2$-fire-extinguishing system in the engine room, forcing the engine crew to abandon it. And the next hit one of the fuel tanks, and

an orange fireball puffed up from below, setting more of the
trawler ablaze. Phillips glanced at his watch. It was unbelievable. The *YP 389* had been pounded for over an hour by the
U-boat but was still afloat. But it was clear the end was near. It
was time to save the men.

The liferafts had been shot away and the lifeboats were too
exposed to gunfire to be launched, so Ensigns Baker and Mc-
Kellar went from man to man to make sure they had their
lifejackets on. Wounded men were helped to the side. At Phillips's signal, all the men jumped overboard. Phillips stayed at
the wheel until he saw the last man go and, then, leaving the
throttle wide open, clambered down through the shambles
that was left of his ship. After jumping, he looked up in time
to see the *U-701*, still in pursuit of the burning *YP 389*, plow
by. Soon, both ships were out of sight. Phillips called out to
his men and was happy to hear shouts in return.

Phillips swam toward the voices and found Baker, McKellar, and the surviving members of his crew. For the rest of the
night, he would keep them close, often swimming out to bring
in the weak and wounded, and constantly calling out words of
encouragement. The *U-701* was not seen again. At dawn, two
boats from the Ocracoke coast guard station found the small
band of American sailors and took them aboard. One of the
men had died during the night and five other men were missing. Ensign Baker was seriously wounded by splinter and
shrapnel wounds as were several of the men. On the way to
the hospital in the ambulance, Baker would insist on giving a
statement. Lieutenant Phillips was a true hero, he would say,
but the *YP 389* had been simply unsuited to the task given it.
She was a ship the navy had sent out against the U-boats without sound equipment to hear them, without a workable big
gun to fight them, and without speed or maneuverability to
even avoid them when attacked. The navy could do nothing
but read his report and agree.

Out on the sea, Degen knew nothing of this. He had followed the *YP 389* until finally one of his rounds had blown up
her engine room. Then, as he circled the drifting hulk, a few
final rounds had put the ship down to the bottom of the sea.

For the first time in days, Degen felt as if he was finally going to be able to accomplish his mission. A very real irritant had been eliminated. He made no attempt to look for survivors. He submerged and headed back toward deeper waters.[7]

# 24

# More Lessons Learned

Apprised of the merciless destruction of the *YP 389*, Lieutenant Alger and the *Dione* turned from their patrol off Cape Lookout and headed north to Hatteras to look for the killer sub. The *Dione* had orders to go to Lookout Bight in four days to join a northbound convoy (the Bucket Brigades still operating when necessary), so she would have to hurry if she was to have any chance of tracking the U-boat down. Nearly 350 miles were covered in 24 hours, the sonar constantly working. Alger was pleased with his soundmen. Their training and the weeks of experience since had made a big difference. No longer were they fooled much by schools of fish or rock outcroppings. Old wrecks were still picked up and misinterpreted, but Alger himself had become experienced enough to look at what came bubbling up after a depth charge or two to make a good, educated guess as to what he was attacking.

The sea itself was ideal for the hunt. The wind blew only lightly at night and hardly at all during the day, leaving the ocean flat calm. But the Graveyard of the Atlantic had its price for the calm. The men who had to work topside found themselves under a hot, unmerciful sun that seemed to be just inches away from the skin. On every quarter and on the mast,

Alger posted lookouts with orders to call out at the slightest suspicion of a periscope. For hours on end, the lookouts scanned the horizon, strips of tape on their backs often used to form untanned words or a girlfriend's initials.

At high noon on 20 June, the sonar gained a positive contact and Alger called General Quarters. Within two minutes, the crew were at their stations and a course set for a depth-charge pattern. Five depth charges were dropped and Alger waited to see what would come up. When nothing happened, he dropped another and then fired the Y-gun. The results were still negative. Whatever was below was constructed well but it was also immobile. Alger did not believe that a U-boat would accept such pummeling without moving, so after two hours of searching around, he left the probable wreck and kept going north. Along the way, he received new orders. He was to patrol along the Cape Hatteras minefield, temporarily replacing the *YP 389*. As soon as the *Dione* arrived, a strong underwater echo was picked up. The soundmen relayed the word to the bridge that the contact was moving. Alger tried to stay with it, but it twisted and turned and was lost. A U-boat. It had to be! Alger was certain he was on the trail of the killer sub. He decided to ask for support. In the previous months, the best he could have hoped for was perhaps a small YP to come grudgingly out of some faraway harbor. Now, however, four ships were immediately dispatched from nearby Morehead City. They were the 125-foot ("buck and a quarter class") subchasers *Jackson, Legare,* and *Rush* plus the *PC 524*. They came with orders to divide up the area off the minefield and make a careful search. That night, the *Dione* picked up some fast propeller beats in her area and then a slight echo. Alger sent the cutter after the sounds but they soon faded. The lieutenant now had little doubt. There was definitely a U-boat or U-boats nearby, and the *Dione* and the other ships were keeping it or them at least off-balance and running. All night long, Alger kept the *Dione* searching. Four hours after midnight, the U-boat was picked up again and Alger sent a depth charge down after it. The results were negative, but Alger was certain he had at least ruined a night of hunting for the Germans. But he wanted more than that. They all did. They wanted the killer of the *YP 389*.

Alger began to run back and forth along the buoy lines of the minefield. That was what the *YP 389* had done. Perhaps he could entice the killer U-boat to show itself in an attack. Just a single sighting was all he needed, Alger believed. His ship and crew were so well drilled, he was certain any U-boat they could find, they could sink.[1]

While the *Dione* searched for the *U-701*, Kapitänleutnant Hans-Heinz Linder of the *U-202* was heading south for Hatteras, while von Bülow's *U-404* was heading north after unsuccessfully looking for targets along the Georgia coast. Linder stopped off New Jersey long enough to stalk the *Rio Tercero*, an Argentine cargo-passenger ship. At sunrise on 22 June, one of Linder's torpedoes hit the *Rio Tercero*'s boiler room at the water level. The resulting explosion set off a secondary explosion of one of the boilers and a huge section of the ship's starboard side was blown away. Five men were killed. The Argentine captain calmly ordered an SOS sent with the ship's call letters, position, and the word "torpedoed" in the clear. The captain then placed his log under his arm and walked to the lifeboat assigned to him. He was angry and wished he could tell off the stupid U-boat commander. When were the Germans going to get it through their thick heads that Argentina was neutral? The identity of his ship could not be mistaken. There had been thirteen Argentine flags clearly painted on the ship—five on each side of the hull, one on a wooden sign on the poop deck, one on a big hatch cover, and one atop the bridge. Besides that, the name of the ship, clearly specified as Argentine in the Lloyd's ship manifest known to be carried by every U-boat commander, was painted nine times—three times on each side of the hull, once on the stern, and once on each side of the bow.

After glumly watching his ship sink before him, the Argentine captain was startled to see the *U-202*, a Type VIIC, slide in beside his lifeboat. The name "INSBRUCH" was painted on the front portion of the conning tower and a porcupine on its side. A German on the conning tower called to the Argentines, demanding that whoever was in command

come aboard. The Argentine captain identified himself and
clambered aboard the slick deck of the U-boat. He was escorted below and found himself confronting Linder himself.
The U-boat commander was obviously a very confident man,
about thirty-eight years old, blond hair, blue eyes, six feet tall,
well built and wearing khaki pants, suspenders, and a gray
sweater. Linder asked the Argentine captain if he had sent a
radio message, and the Argentine replied that he had not. Linder knew this to be a lie, and the Argentine suspected that
Linder knew it, but the conversation continued. Linder asked
for the ship's papers, but the captain told him they had gone
down with the ship. Linder then took the log. The Argentine
could not restrain himself further. He reminded Linder that
he and his ship were Argentine and thus neutral and that the
U-boat had no right to sink her. Linder coldly replied that the
captain should paint his ship more clearly so that it could be
seen. At a whisper, the U-boat commander sent his quartermaster back to his quarters and when he returned he had three
bottles of cognac and some shoes for the captain's naked feet.
"Perhaps this will help," Linder said. The *Rio Tercero*'s captain
took the gifts but asked for his log back. Linder refused. The
Argentine fumed and then demanded to look at Linder's list of
ships. He wanted to show that his ship was clearly marked as
being neutral.

A call from the conning tower snapped Linder's head up.
An airplane had been spotted. Linder nodded toward the Argentine and the captain was picked up and literally tossed out
of the U-boat hatch. As the airplane barreled in on the submarine, the captain scrambled down the conning tower and dived
into the lifeboat. The airplane dropped a bomb on the *U-202*'s
spreading wake, almost sinking the Argentine lifeboat but
leaving Linder and his men untouched. A little later, a blimp
arrived and dropped more bombs. It was a fiery pyrotechnic
display but to no avail. The unhappy Argentines were rescued
by the *PC 503* later that same afternoon and Linder, unscathed, continued south, still bound for Hatteras.[2]

Unaware that three U-boats were soon to be operating in
the *Dione*'s area, Lieutenant Alger was winding up his patrol
and preparing to join the convoy. On the morning of 23 June,

however, the *Norwich City*, a British trawler, joined him in stalking the *U-701* along the buoy line of the Hatteras minefield. Suspicious echoes were heard but no positive identifications made and both ships entered Morehead City the next morning for replenishment of fuel and depth charges. They then stood out of Beaufort Inlet and made their way to Lookout Bight. There, the ships *F. H. Bedford, Jr., Spokane, Manuela, Alcoa Voyager, Fred W. Weller, Hindanger, Thomas Sumnter, Governor John Lind, Nordal,* and the *Gypsum King* were waiting for them. By noon, Alger had them formed up and headed north, the *Dione,* the *Norwich City*, the CG #408 (an 80-foot patrol boat), and the CG #252 (a 75-foot "six-bitter"), escorting. No navy destroyers had shown up, so the four small warships knew that only luck would get them past Lookout and Hatteras, especially with the killer of the *YP 389* on the loose.

It wasn't Degen who spotted the convoy, however, but von Bülow and his *U-404*, fresh from sinking the Yugoslavian freighter *Ljubica Matkovic.*[3] As the sun set over the golden sands of the Outer Banks, Lieutenant Alger doubled the watch and alerted his sonar operators to be especially suspicious of any contacts. They replied almost immediately with a good one and Alger called the *Norwich City* to stay with the convoy while he attacked. Von Bülow, however, saw him coming and sped away, the *Dione*'s depth charges dropping well astern. He turned the *U-404* toward the convoy and ordered the periscope raised. He could hardly miss and it appeared he would be given little opposition. He had already left the American cutter behind, the British trawler was too slow to be an immediate threat, and the other two small escorts were laughable. Von Bülow swiveled around in his periscope chair, sighted on a large freighter and unleashed a single torpedo. It was the *Nordal,* a Panamanian ship loaded with general cargo. Helplessly, the men on the escorts watched as an explosion erupted from the freighter's starboard side followed by a large spout of water that went as high as the mast top. Dark smoke and licking flames poured out of the hole in the ship's side while the crew abandoned ship. The *Norwich City* moved over to pick them up.[4]

Alger sent the *Dione* flying back to the convoy, but there
was little he could do. One of von Bülow's torpedoes sped past
the cutter and into the side of the *Manuela*, an American
freighter loaded with 101,000 bags of refined sugar. Two men
were killed. The ship was abandoned. Twenty-three of the
crew escaped, including the captain, Conrad G. Nilson, in the
port lifeboat. Seventeen others jumped overboard and swam to
rafts. With Alger directing the rescue, the CG #408 towed the
lifeboat to the *Norwich City*, while the CG #483 stopped and
picked up the men on the rafts. Alger began to sweep around
the convoy, ordering all ships to stay together but to proceed.
The *Manuela* was left behind in a sinking condition, listing to
starboard.

Von Bülow began to maneuver again but caught sight of
the *Dione* coming after him. A *ping* against his side told the
cutter approximately where he was. There were a hundred
fathoms beneath him, however, and he took advantage of it,
dropping deep and turning away. Above, the *Dione* swept past,
the various thermocline layers fooling her sonar. After searching for thirty minutes, Alger took his cutter back to the convoy. He looked it over. It was plodding along at 8 knots, and
the *Dione* and the three other escorts were much too thin to
protect them from a U-boat willing to get in close. He called
shore and requested air support. Soon, there were planes overhead and a blimp. Such quick coverage had never happened
before. The planes swept in, their pilots eagerly dropping low
and covering huge swaths of ocean in a matter of seconds. For
as long as they had fuel, they buzzed around, almost daring a
U-boat to show even so much as a hint of itself. With the
airplanes securing his flanks, Alger was able to relax. When
they had to leave, he had to change his tactics. At an echo, he
would drop a depth charge as a warning, sweep in its direction, and then race back to the convoy, never leaving it for
long. The escorts varied their speeds, moving past or sliding
down the convoy, trying to stay between the freighters and
the U-boats. The idea was to keep the U-boats off-balance,
make them work to get in maneuvering position.

After the convoy got around Hatteras, it began to straggle,
and the *Dione* and the other escorts fitfully worked to keep it

together. When the planes returned, all could relax again. But
when they left, it was back to the exhausting duty. Finally,
with the crews of the four escorts completely worn out, Chesapeake Bay was ahead and safety. Lessons on convoying had
been learned again, lessons that would be used by others when
faced with a similar situation. Despite his exhaustion, Alger
was not disheartened. He had seen the air power available to
convoys and had been impressed by it. One of those hotshot
pilots was going to catch himself a U-boat. Alger was confident of that.[5]

But neither von Bülow, Linder, nor Degen would have
understood Alger's confidence at that moment. They had all
easily sunk ships and were busily setting up yet another
gauntlet around Capes Hatteras and Lookout, just as in the
bad old days of January, February, and March. It appeared to
the commanders of the U-202, the U-404, and the U-701 that
not much had changed since that "happy time" after all. But
one of their number was about to discover the truth.

# 25

# Harry Kane
# and the *U-701*

Horst Degen was certain his destiny was to repeat Hardegen's early successes in America and renew the "Second Happy Time." The jinx that had been his since he had mined the Chesapeake Bay seemed to have been broken by the destruction of the *YP 389* and his successful eluding of the *Dione*. After the *Dione* had left to escort the Bucket Brigade, Degen was free to attack as he wished around Hatteras. On the night of 25 June, he caught the *Tamesis*, a Norwegian freighter, sailing in sight of the dunes along Cape Hatteras. Degen attacked from the surface, sending a single torpedo into the starboard side of the freighter. According to a report from the crew, the *Tamesis* "bounced" high into the air when the torpedo struck and then fell back, wallowing on a spreading circle of white foam. Degen observed the hit, judged that it was sufficient to sink the ship, and submerged to look for another target. The *Tamesis*'s captain also thought his ship was sinking and ordered her abandoned. Four lifeboats were launched, one of which rowed ashore while the other three stayed near the ship.

At sunrise the following morning, the men aboard the three lifeboats saw that their ship had stabilized and decided to reboard her. After a cursory inspection of the torpedo hole, the captain thought his ship was still sinking. His engineer reported the engines were operational, however, so the captain decided to head for shallower water. Two hours later, the *Tamesis* ground ashore on a Hatteras beach near the fourth lifeboat. Since there was no evidence of the American military on the deserted beach, the captain feared the U-boat might sneak in and board him. Accordingly, he ceremoniously burned all of his codes and secret papers. A coast guard "six-bitter" soon found the Norwegians, however, and within the week, tugs had towed the *Tamesis* to port for repairs. A month later, she was in New York with all her cargo intact except some palm oil that had been contaminated with sea water.[1]

Unaware that the *Tamesis* had not been sunk, Degen kept the *U-701* submerged off Hatteras all day on 26 June, the heat inside the U-boat climbing steadily until it became difficult to breathe. The chemical air-freshening system stopped working during the day and, shortly afterwards, most of the *U-701* crew became sick. The one operational toilet became quickly clogged, and the men had no choice but to throw up where they stood or lay. The situation, Degen had to admit, was serious, perhaps serious enough to abort his mission. But Doenitz's admonition still rang in Degen's ears. He could not come back until he had fired his last torpedo.[2]

Degen, sick himself, still waited until dark to surface. The crew stood expectantly beneath all the hatches, anxiously waiting for Degen's signal to open them. After checking all around with the sky periscope, Degen nodded and the men leaped on the hatch wheels and twisted them open. As the hatches swung wide, the men strained their face upward, gulping in the fresh night air. Degen allowed them only a moment of pleasure before he barked at the first watch, ordering them to their duty. Those lucky enough to be on lookout duty gladly pulled themselves up the ladder to the conning tower bridge and clicked on their safety harnesses. Degen joined them. The night was dark and clear with only a slight breeze. The young Kaleun leaned against the tower fairing and waited for a target to present itself. He would wait all night with the watches changing behind him. Occasionally, he would turn to make certain his lookouts were alert. But it made no difference. All night the *U-701* sat alone on the black, placid sea.

The next day was as the previous one—hot, sticky, and, for the crew of the *U-701*, sickening. By mid-morning, Degen knew he had to surface to cool off or the men were going to be too ill to carry out their duties. He was actually as happy as anyone in his crew when he gave the order to surface. Some of the crew had already become so weak they were having trouble working, and most of them had become unnaturally depressed and only wanted to leave this awful place known as the Graveyard of the Atlantic and go home. But as the *U-701* rose, her soundman announced the distant beat of propellers—many of them. Convoy! Degen forgot the heat and the sickness and asked for a course. It was time to fight again. That, he was sure, would revitalize the men as nothing else could.[3]

The soundman aboard the *U-701* had, in fact, heard a small slow-moving convoy escorted by two U.S. Navy destroyers and the auxiliary yacht *St. Augustine*. Degen looked the convoy over. In the center was a fat tanker, the *British Freedom*. That was the one he would have. He began to maneuver his U-boat closer. When a destroyer turned in his direction, he dived deep, waited until it had passed, and then came up. A quick view through the periscope showed the side of the *British Freedom*, and Degen wasted no time in launching a torpedo at it. After the "fish" was away, both destroyers came at the *U-701* so Degen ordered the periscope lowered and took his U-boat down. Gently, the *U-701* leveled off just above the sea bottom while the destroyers thrummed overhead. Degen waited until their propeller sounds diminished and then came back up to periscope depth. The tanker had been hit and was sinking.[4]

Before Degen could line up to attack again, the *St. Augustine* brazenly moved into his line of fire and then turned toward him. Degen took the *U-701* down as the yacht dropped five depth charges nearby. For over an hour, the destroyers and the *St. Augustine* droned overhead, but no more depth charges were dropped.[5]

When he was certain his attackers were gone, Degen took the *U-701* to periscope depth and looked around. The convoy

was gone, including the *British Freedom*. He slumped back in
his swivel seat. If only he had had enough time to hit the
tanker with a second torpedo! Now, it appeared she had gotten
away, and he could not possibly catch up with the convoy.
There was only one thing to do. Submerge and wait for another target while sweltering in the awful heat.

The next day, Degen again was forced to the surface by
the heat and by his desire to try to spot more targets. At near
high noon, a smudge was seen on the horizon. Whatever was
coming their way looked big. Was it a tanker?

The ship coming toward the *U-701* was indeed a big ship
and also a tanker. It was, in fact, one of the biggest tankers in
the world, the *Wm. Rockefeller*. Moreover, she was loaded, carrying 140,389 barrels of fuel oil from Aruba to New York.
Degen fired a torpedo at her as she crossed in front of him and
watched happily as it struck her on the port side. The coast
guard picked up the *Rockefeller*'s transmissions and dispatched
an 83-footer to the rescue. Within a few hours of the torpedo
attack, all fifty of the tanker's crew were picked up. There was
nothing that could be done for the tanker, however. She
drifted for twelve hours, burning furiously, and then sank.[6]

Degen tracked the tanker until he was certain it was lost
and then triumphantly sent BdU a message announcing his
success. It was the moment he had longed for. Not only would
"Uncle Karl" be pleased, the young U-boat commander expected to be mentioned in a German High Command commu-
nique. Perhaps even the *Fuhrer* himself would see it. It was,
indeed, a "happy time" for Horst Degen![7]

While Degen and the crew of the *U-701* congratulated
themselves, a lone United States Army Lockheed Hudson
A-29 bomber rose from Cherry Point, North Carolina. Pilot-
ing the aircraft was a twenty-four-year-old lieutenant, Harry
Kane. Also aboard was a navigator, bombardier, a radioman,
and a flight engineer. All five young men were completely,
utterly bored. Since the war had begun, they had been assigned submarine patrol duty, first out of California over the
Pacific looking for Japanese subs, and now off North Carolina.
Their duty, along with most of the 396th Medium Bombard-

ment Squadron, was to patrol all day until there was only enough fuel to make it back to base, fly back, land, refuel, and fly out again. Day after day after day, all Kane and his crew-members saw was the vast expanse of the sea, unrelieved by any landmark besides whitecaps and the occasional debris of some unfortunate ship that had been torpedoed. Of course, occasionally a friendly ship was spotted and buzzed just to change the routine and to stay alert, but even those were few and far between.[8]

Lieutenant Kane did not know it, but his duty off North Carolina was the direct result of Admiral Andrews's successful in-fighting with Kane's army air forces superiors. At the very beginning of the U-boat campaign, the navy had requested that General H. A. "Hap" Arnold, chief of the army air forces, provide them two hundred B-24 bombers and nine hundred B-25s and B-26s for naval patrol duties. General Arnold did not take the request seriously enough to even reply to it. But, by March, at Admiral Andrews's request, Admiral King got involved and wrote General Arnold several personal letters, pointing out that it was imperative that U-boat patrols be increased from the air and the best way to accomplish that was with army bombers under navy control. General Arnold politely disagreed point by point. Admiral King then went over Arnold's head to General Marshall. Marshall was sensitive to the navy's needs at that moment as Prime Minister Churchill was sending some very unhappy messages to President Roosevelt concerning the U-boat successes. On 26 March, Marshall made his decision. Admiral Andrews would be given control of all airplanes of the army air forces that could fly antisubmarine search-and-destroy missions along the east coast. The commanding general of the 1st Bomber Command was to send as many assets as possible to fight the U-boats. Thus, Lieutenant Kane, his A-29, and the 396th Medium Bombardment Squadron flew across the country from California to Cherry Point, North Carolina, to help out the navy.[9]

Six sorties were flown every day—three to the south and three to the north, all along the North Carolina coast and over the primary shipping lanes. The first patrol began one hour before sunrise and the last an hour after sunset. It was routine and Lieutenant Kane and his crew quickly fell into the swing of it. Briefings were mercifully short as naval intelligence rarely had much to offer. The commander of the 396th believed that such intelligence was worthless, in any case. In order for his bombers to attack the U-boats, his pilots would have to see one with the naked eye. To know where they were the day before didn't help find them the day after. Success could come only from constant criss-crossing of the area and luck—plenty of luck. After a U-boat had been spotted, Kane had been told he would have only five minutes to drop his bombs. That was how long it took for a U-boat to submerge. On 7 July, Kane drew a mid-morning patrol flight and took off once more. The day was moderately cloudy and hot. A typical, boring day of flying was expected over the Graveyard of the Atlantic.[10]

Also spending a typically boring day in the Graveyard, actually on the bottom of it, was Horst Degen and the *U-701*. Nine days had passed since their triumphant sinking of the *Wm. Rockefeller*. During that nine days, not one target had been seen except a fast convoy well guarded by a number of destroyers and coast guard cutters. Degen had wisely stayed away from it, but it had left him frustrated and troubled. Perhaps the *Rockefeller* had been somewhat of a fluke. Perhaps there would be no more juicy targets. Perhaps, perhaps . . . Degen did not like variables. To him, control was everything.

Something else he could not control was the *U-701*'s air-freshening system, which was still *kaput*. To keep his crew healthy, he had taken to coming to the surface every few hours to flush out the interior. It put him in some danger, Degen realized, but he was confident that his lookouts could spot enemy airplanes or ships in time to submerge and get away. Although he still had several torpedoes left, his food and water were running low, and Degen knew that no matter what happened he would have to leave American waters in a few days and head back to France. It was imperative, then, that a target be found and soon.[11]

At noon, Lieutenant Kane was munching on his box lunch and scanning the ocean. Nothing had been seen all morning. Behind him was Lieutenant L. A. Murray, the navigator, and

the flight engineer, Corporal P. L. Broussard. Up in the Plexi-
glas nose of the twin-engine Lockheed Hudson sat Corporal
G. E. Bellamy, the bombardier. Kane had taken the A-29 out
past Cape Lookout and then headed south toward Charleston,
South Carolina. Although the standard operating procedure
was to fly low, sometimes as low as 50 feet, over the waves,
Kane had decided to keep his plane up at 1,000 feet so that he
could have a better view. At around 1230, Charleston was
reached and Kane turned around and headed back north, staying parallel to the shoreline.[12]

While the A-29 was completing its turn, Degen made his
decision to come to the surface once again. Although his crewmen had mostly stopped vomiting in the heat, they had become lethargic and Degen wanted them fresh for the hunt that
night. As soon as the U-701 came to the surface, Degen ordered the diesels fired up and took his U-boat at top speed
toward Cape Hatteras, 35 miles to the west. He ordered all the
hatches open and fresh air poured into the submarine. Degen
looked around at his crew. They were all grinning and going
about their duties. Good! He had done the right thing.[13]

Lieutenant Kane decided to drop down to 500 feet after he
left Charleston, but as Cape Hatteras neared, he spotted a line
of broken clouds at about 1,000 feet. Suddenly, he was struck
with an inspiration. Perhaps the reason he had never spotted a
U-boat was because they always saw him first. If so, maybe the
clouds could be used to advantage. Kane added power and
began to rise, soon plowing into the clouds. He called to the
crew to keep close watch as the plane broke in and out of the
clouds. It would be an interesting game, if nothing else, and
help dispel some of the boredom. At twelve minutes after two,
Kane thought he saw a distant object about 10 miles off his left
wing tip. Then the vision vanished as the A-29 buried itself
inside a cloud, only to reappear when the A-29 broke into the
clear. Kane called the crew to the flight deck. Could they see
it? They did. Kane turned left and started flying toward the
object. He stayed in the clouds and then throttled back to idle.
He would make as little noise as possible in slipping up on the
object. He couldn't believe it was a U-boat, but it was still an
interesting exercise—good practice, if nothing else.[14]

Horst Degen was on the conning tower, scanning the horizon with his binoculars. Nothing could be seen. But he was nervous. He had been on the surface much too long. When word came from the engine room that it was completely ventilated, he instantly decided to submerge. "Let's go down again," he commanded. "Take her down!"[15]

The *U-701* began to submerge while the lookouts unsnapped their harnesses and began to descend through the tower hatch. About 2 miles distant, Harry Kane's A-29 was coming fast. Kane anxiously peered forward into the bright white nothing in front. Suddenly—*there!*—it *was* a U-boat! Kane jammed the twin throttles to full power and shouted at the crew to prepare for a bombing run. He dropped the A-29 to 50 feet. The airspeed was 225 knots. Like a great metal hawk, Lieutenant Harry Kane and the crew of the A-29 raced toward the *U-701*.[16]

As Degen turned to climb down off the conning tower, he had no inkling of what was coming toward him. He paused to let his exec, who had also been on watch, go before him. The young officer stiffened and then cried, "Airplane, 200 degrees, coming in from port—aft!"

Degen pushed the man in front of him and then stole a glance over his shoulder before jumping into the hatch opening. He slammed the hatch down himself, all the while screaming the alarm. As the men of the *U-701* stampeded down the narrow corridor to the bow to increase the speed of the dive, Degen calmly hung his binoculars on a protruding stanchion and turned to his exec. "You saw it too late," he said.

"Yes," the officer meekly replied.[17]

Harry Kane barreled in on the swirling blue and white foam left by the *U-701*. He had his thumb on the red override button on the control wheels that would release the bombs. As the A-29 roared over the U-boat, Kane jammed the red button. Three 350-pound depth charges dropped away. One of them fell 25 feet short of the turbulence, the second in its center, the third another 80 feet beyond. The depth charges sank quickly, the second and third actually hitting the *U-701* and rolling off either side. They were set to go off at a depth of 50 feet. As the A-29 began to climb away, the depth charges exploded.[18]

Inside the *U-701*, the world suddenly went insane. The crew were shaken as if they were rag dolls, their ears ringing from the massive shock wave that passed through them and their U-boat. Then the water began to pour in from below, not slowly but in a rush. All power gone, the *U-701* dropped away, spiraling down, down until she punched bow-first into a sandy bottom, and then rolled over toward her starboard side.

The control room was filled with the moans and groans of the crew as they desperately attempted to equalize their ears and sinuses. Degen looked around. Somehow, at least half of his crew had been flushed back into the control room. Within seconds of hitting the bottom, however, the water had filled up to within one foot of the top of the room. Degen knew his U-boat was finished. Whatever he did next would determine the fate of his crew.

"We must abandon!" he shouted to everyone. His voice sounded unnaturally high-pitched. The remaining air had been compressed by the water to at least 8 atmospheres. All sound was different under that pressure. And to breathe air at that depth for long would be deadly. He had paid attention to the physiology classes in submarine school. Nitrogen narcosis, oxygen poisoning, decompression sickness, and air embolisms were all possibilities. He unscrewed the hatch. As he did, the pressure inside popped it open and he with it. Behind him, most of his crew were also shot out of the hatch, spiraling up in a towering, silvery column of air.[19]

Harry Kane banked to the right to see if he had made a hit. He looked over his shoulder in time to see Degen and then others bobbing to the surface in a spew of air. A big blue slick of oil or diesel fuel covered the sea where the Germans were swimming and continued to billow up from below. A fuel tank must have been ruptured. Kane completed his turn and came roaring back, a bare 300 feet over the survivors. "Throw out the lifejackets!" he yelled back to his crew.[20]

Degen heard the plane and ducked as it blasted overhead. He expected to be machine-gunned or have more depth charges dropped on top of him. Instead, five lifejackets and a liferaft came sailing down to plop nearby. Out of sight of him at that moment, eighteen of his men, the remainder of his crew, had managed to wrestle open the bow torpedo hatch and they, too, came blasting up to the surface. The current quickly separated the two groups, however, and they would never see one another again.[21]

Degen ordered all of the lifejackets available, including at least one from the airplane, made into a raft. The inflatable raft from the airplane had quickly drifted away on the current as did the other lifejackets. But Degen was certain that help would be on its way within a few hours, in any case. Kane thought so, too. He flew over the Germans again and then headed west. He had called in and given the location of the sinking (as best as he could determine it) to a coast guard station and reported the survivors. That was all he could do. He was low on fuel and had to head back to Cherry Point. Degen watched him go and then, in an attempt to keep the morale of his crew up, cheerfully remarked that all of them were going to get to spend some time in the United States of America.[22]

All day long, Degen and his men drifted. Then evening came. And night. The horizon and the skies had stayed empty. Still, Degen remained hopeful of rescue. He thought he was still in about the same position as where the *U-701* had gone down. In fact, however, he was in the Gulf Stream and heading northeast at a 3-knot clip. Rescue had been very near at the beginning, as it would later turn out, by both a coast guard patrol vessel and a Panamanian freighter. When requested by the coast guard to look for the Germans, the captain of the freighter had refused. Help a German U-boat crew after what they had done to the merchant ships? The captain was not interested. As for the patrol craft, Kane dropped a smoke bomb nearby and informed him by signal lamp and radio of the sinking of the submarine and the plight of the survivors. Kane had even led the vessel back to the site, but by then the current had already swept Degen and the others out of sight. The coast guard vessel was the 83-foot USCG #472, the same craft that had picked up survivors from the *Santore*. She searched for a while but found nothing and soon left for shore.[23]

Degen and his crew were on their own. The first of them, the coxswain, would die within three hours of sunset. He had just slipped under and not come back up. Throughout the night, other exhausted crewmen had done the same. Degen, dressed only in a pair of black shorts and shaking with cold, passed into delirium shortly before the first light of dawn. Several of his men kept him afloat. On the next morning, a small coast guard ship passed close by. The Germans cried for help, but the ship kept going. Six more men slipped under throughout the day. Planes flew constantly overhead, but none dropped down to look at the pitiful little struggling band. Just before sunset of the second day, 8 July, the handful of survivors, still keeping Degen supported, came across one of their comrades who had held on to two life preservers. Shortly after that, a lemon and then a coconut drifted by. One of the men splashed out to them and brought them back. The coconut was opened with great difficulty by using a valve on one of the life preservers to chop at it. Each survivor was then given a swallow of coconut milk and a little piece of lemon to suck and a small piece of coconut meat.

Degen, too delirious to eat or drink by himself, had his lemon and coconut forced down his throat. He would later remember dreaming that he was sitting on the shore washing oil from his body when a German-speaking man approached him and told him that he had been mentioned in the German High Command communiques of either June 29th or 30th.

That night, three more of the survivors of the *U-701* drowned. One of them, just before he went under for the last time, turned to Degen, who had come around a little after receiving the lemon and coconut, and told him "I die now. Please remember me to my comrades." Degen could only nod his head numbly.[24]

On the morning of 9 July, the United States Navy blimp *King-8* left its mooring point in Morehead City and headed out over the sea. It had been looking for the crew of the *U-701* for two days. Its commander, Ensign G. S. Middleton, had searched a quadrant designated number 1 the day before and had decided to shift over to number 2, which was northeast of number 1. It seemed to Middleton that the Gulf Stream might have swept anything from the sunken submarine in that direction. Two hours later, Middleton and his crew spotted a lone

man in the water. It was a *U-701* survivor. The German still
had enough strength to wave at the blimp. The *K-8* marked his
position and moved on, spotting two more survivors shortly
afterwards. Middleton called his headquarters and reported
what he had found. Then another survivor, this one apparently too weak to wave, was found. Middleton then turned
and dropped a liferaft to the first survivor who had been spotted, since he seemed stronger than the other three. It was
hoped he would go to the aid of the others. This he did and
shortly afterwards, the *K-8* moved over the raft and dropped
down blankets, a first-aid kit, a knife, and a jug of water. Leaving the raft momentarily, Middleton searched farther out.
Three dead men were found, along with a great number of
sharks, empty lifejackets, an oil slick, seaweed, and debris.
When returning to the liferaft, three more survivors were
spotted, these about a half-mile away.[25]

Meanwhile, the coast guard had dispatched an amphibious
aircraft piloted by Lieutenant Commander Richard L. Burke.
By early afternoon, Burke arrived in the vicinity of the *K-8*
and requested instructions from Middleton. Middleton complied by dropping flares near the survivors and Burke set his
airplane down. Seven survivors were picked up.[26] They were
all that was left of the forty-three crewmembers of the *U-701.*[27]

On 11 July, Lieutenant Harry Kane and his crew were
ordered by their squadron commander to board an airplane
bound for Norfolk Naval Air Station. They were not told the
reason. Waiting for them was a high-ranking delegation of
navy officers who escorted them to a hospital building guarded
by some dour civilians cradling submachine guns. Kane realized they were FBI agents. Kane and his crew went inside the
hospital, where more navy officers awaited them. Kane was
beckoned inside a large ward. There, a young man sat alone in
a chair. He was wearing shoes and a hospital robe over some
pajamas. His face was badly disfigured by sunburn and apparent exposure. A group of officers and civilians saw Kane and
came over to him. One of the civilians was introduced as Secretary of the Navy Frank Knox, who proceeded to shake
Kane's hand heartily and congratulate him.

While Kane was shaking the hands of the others and re-

ceiving their compliments, one of the officers went over to the
man in the chair and quietly said something to him. The man
turned quizzically toward Kane and then stood up. He was
obviously in pain and had some difficulty in standing straight.
Still, he managed to click his heels and salute. "Congratulations," he said through cracked, raw lips. "Good attack."

It was Kapitänleutnant Horst Degen.[28]

# 26
# Victory

Lieutenant Alger was forced to take the *Dione* into Norfolk at the end of June. There were repairs needed on the starboard engine that could not be accomplished at sea. Many of the men were allowed liberty, including radioman Swede Larson. Swede and the rest of the men headed in a rush to the garish strip of bars and joints and then stopped short. In the months before, there had been crowds of sailors and coast guardsmen and marines, but nothing such as that which confronted them now. It was a sea of heads, bobbing down the narrow street, hundreds, thousands of men on liberty, most of them in fresh, new uniforms. The crewmen of the *Dione* were jostled and pushed. When they poked into their old haunt, the *Dione* men found there was no room for them. Gone was the cheerful old couple who managed the place, replaced by a "slicker" with a thin moustache behind the bar and young, painted, hard women on the stools in front who knew how to get the "boys" to drink more. Every man in uniform was a hero even if he had not seen any more of the war than a basic training camp. The crew of the *Dione* found themselves ignored. Here they had once toasted "Cowboy" McCormick and drunk to forget the *Naeco* and excitedly discussed "Wimble Willy." But no one wanted to hear of that now. The war

wasn't close by. It was "out there," across the Atlantic and
Pacific where the Japanese and Germans had to be quivering
in fear and trepidation at what was being primed and aimed at
them.

Quietly, the crew of the *Dione* left Norfolk. It was no
longer theirs. And after they had thought about it, they
wanted more than the city could offer them in any case. It
seemed to be a good time to go home. Swede, too far from his
home to make it there and back, headed south with good
friend Walter Bond. Bond, as most of the *Dione* crewmen still
were, was a local boy, having been raised in the quiet North
Carolina fishing village of Hertford on Albemarle Sound. A
signalman and quartermaster, he was known as one of the
finest sailors on the bridge of the *Dione*.

Swede found Bond's home to be that of a working fisherman. Fish were even drying in the garage. But it was quiet and
peaceful, something Swede had not even realized he had
craved. He, along with most *Dione* men, had lost a great deal of
weight during the days of patrol and convoy. To successfully
live aboard the ship required constant muscle tension, pushing
this way against the sea, riding with it, and back and forth,
burning hundreds of calories without knowing it. When
Swede looked at himself in a mirror, he was shocked at the
gaunt face that stared back at him. The rings under his eyes
showed that sleep was something else he had missed as well
. . . and clean sheets . . . and showers. While in Hertford,
Swede would find himself taking several showers a day (fresh
water!), sleeping late in the morning, eating everything placed
before him, and going with Bond down to the local drug store
for ice cream and pie. It was as if the war no longer existed, as
if time had clicked back to a much happier time. When Swede
and Bond visited Bond's father's fishing boat, they would look
out to sea, and it was as if it were a different place from where
they had come. How could there have possibly been all that
death and destruction just a few miles away?

The days passed all too swiftly. In the morning, the sun
would creep over the placid sound and silently steal across the
sky. There was only the sound of the birds and perhaps the
doctor's old jalopy putt-putting down the street to disturb

the two exhausted *Dione* crewmen. And at night, there was only the sound of the crickets and the gentlest of sea breezes rustling the big oaks in the front yard. Swede would forever remember it as a respite, unrecognized but desperately needed.

While the *Dione* was being repaired and her men rested, Admiral Andrews and his officers were excitedly evaluating evidence of a startling change in the battle against the U-boats. It could be arguably said that both the sinking of the *U-85* and the *U-352* had been mere flukes. But the *U-701* had been sunk by a well-trained pilot and crew who knew exactly what to do after a U-boat was found. Admiral Andrews felt quite rightly that his command could take credit for that. They had, after all, fought all the bureaucratic battles that had brought Harry Kane and his squadron to the Atlantic seaboard. They had also placed the bombers at Cherry Point and determined their patrol route. Now, with the destruction of the *U-701*, Andrews and his staff sensed that more victories were about to follow.[1]

They were right. At the beginning of July 1942, the Eastern Sea Frontier estimated that there were more U-boats off the coast than had been there at any time since the war began.[2] Nevertheless, only six allied merchantmen would be torpedoed off the east coast during the entire month. Two of those would come on 15 July, about 20 miles east of Ocracoke Inlet, North Carolina, and would be made by the *U-576*, commanded by the experienced Kapitänleutnant Hans-Dieter Heinicke.[3]

It was Heinicke's second visit to American shores, the first in April 1942, when his *U-576* had easily sunk three ships and sailed back to France, completely unscathed.[4] This time, however, the *U-576* was greeted with a sea devoid of ships, a sure sign of some sort of convoy system in effect. Worse, the skies seemed to be swarming with patrol aircraft. But Heinicke had promised Doenitz more sinkings, so he aggressively began to search for targets, even during the day.[5]

On July 14, two navy OS2U-3 aircraft caught him on the surface. At a lookout's cry and stabbed finger toward the sky, Heinicke yelled out the alarm and began to make a crash dive.

The lead plane, piloted by Ensign William R. Jemison, dived down. Jemison's depth charges straddled the *U-576*'s conning tower, dropped beneath the U-boat and blew it back to the surface. As Jemison climbed, the second plane, piloted by Ensign George L. Schein, came barreling in. But before Schein could drop his depth charges, the *U-576* began to sink out of control. Schein dropped two depth charges anyway, the detonations further shaking the U-boat. As the planes circled, the *U-576* sank, eddies and swirls of oil and rust forming a huge stain on the sea.

For over an hour, the planes circled the stain, the phosphorescent shape of the *U-576*, apparently standing on its tail, clearly visible in the shallow water. Certain that they had sunk the U-boat, the two planes called in their report. Soon, an army bomber came out to help and stayed behind when Jemison and Schein had to return to base for fuel. The army pilot confirmed the navy pilots' report. There was a U-boat down and it was badly leaking oil. It was probably sunk.[6]

As it would later become clear, the *U-576* had somehow survived the near-perfect air attack. The Type VIIs were tough ships and Heinicke a tenacious, intelligent leader. That night, he reported the damage to BdU. One of his main ballast tanks had been shredded to such an extent repair was impossible. The next day, he reported that he could still move but the ballast tank was now completely flooded.[7]

From the amount of oil reported by the navy pilots, there is little doubt that Heinicke also had lost a good amount of his fuel, probably out of a ruptured saddle tank. If so, he likely knew that he did not have enough fuel to return to France. In that case, there was only one solution. The trip back had to be started immediately with a milch cow rendezvous along the way. But on 15 July, Heinicke spotted a convoy coming his way. He couldn't resist it. He had been sent to America to sink ships, and that was what he was going to do. Even though they were still trying to repair their submarine, the buoyancy control and steering systems barely functioning, Heinicke and his men strained to maneuver their U-boat into attack position. It was as audacious an attack as any German submarine ever attempted. With the forces ranged against the *U-576*, it was also suicide.

The *Chilore*, a small freighter carrying some dry cargo and ballast, would take the first of Heinicke's torpedoes on that day. The *U-576* had already been chased away once from the convoy by the USCG Cutter *Triton*, but Heinicke had managed to elude the cutter and work his way back. The *Chilore* was rocked by the explosion on her port side, but she did not immediately sink. The commodore of the convoy, who was aboard the Esso tanker *Mowinkel*, was a seasoned merchant skipper and former U.S. Navy captain. He saw the *Chilore* hit and started to take action, but then the *Mowinkel* was also hit, the torpedo blasting into her stern. While the convoy reacted in some confusion, the *Bluefields* also received a *U-576* torpedo, this one hitting her directly amidships. The *Bluefields* sank quickly, a clean kill by the *U-576*, but the *Chilore* and the *Mowinkel* were still salvageable.

The commodore ordered the *Mowinkel* and the *Chilore*, escorted by the destroyer *Spry*, to set sail due west to beach themselves in the shallow waters off Cape Hatteras. This was done, but no one aboard had considered the Hatteras minefield, the very one that had already claimed the *Abrams*. Several hours later, the *Chilore*, the *Mowinkel*, and the *Spry* all plowed into the minefield. The *Spry* would manage to elude the mines but not so the merchantmen. Both struck contact mines. Their ships severely damaged, the merchant crewmen got into their lifeboats and rowed to shore. The next day, two tugs came out in an attempt to get the two ships out of the minefield. One of the tugs would itself be sunk by a mine, but somehow both ships would eventually be brought out. The *Chilore* was found to be too damaged to tow and would be left to sink, but the *Mowinkel* would proceed safely and would, after repair, return to the merchant fleet.[8]

The *U-576*, then, had managed to sink two ships, even while severely damaged, an act worthy of Hardegen, Mohr, and Cremer. But this time Heinicke and the crew of the *U-576* would make no triumphant report to Doenitz. This time they did not even have time to pray. Almost instantly, the planes covering the convoy were on the *U-576*, with the *Unicoi* moving over to assist. Bombs struck all around the *U-576*, blowing it to the surface and cracking its pressure hull. And this time, there would be no shallow sandy bottom below. The *U-576* would go all the way down in 1,200 feet of water. There would be no survivors.[9]

It seemed to be happening everywhere. Earlier, on 3 July, the British trawlers had finally exacted their revenge on the U-boats. It had happened just outside the Eastern Sea Frontier boundary, approximately 175 miles off Boston, while the trawler *Le Tigre* was escorting a convoy. The *U-215*, a Type VIID commanded by Kapitänleutnant Fritz Hoeckner, torpedoed the Liberty ship *Alexander Macomb* at 0630. The *Macomb* was carrying explosives that were set off by the torpedo, and she went down quickly, with most of her crew jumping into the water and hanging on to pieces of wreckage. The *Le Tigre* ignored the seamen in the water and went on the attack. In twenty minutes, the U-boat had been definitely located. When the trawler got within 300 yards of the *U-215*, Hoeckner turned toward the *Le Tigre* and charged her at high speed. As the submerged U-boat passed down the starboard side of the trawler, the British skipper ordered a pattern of depth charges fired and then another. The *U-215* burst to the surface and then rolled over, disappearing forever into the deep water. The *Le Tigre* then calmly moved over and picked up the crew of the *Macomb*. It had been, the captain of the *Le Tigre* would later relate, "a most professional exercise."[10]

On the same day, a navy plane out of Cherry Point would spot another U-boat and summon the destroyer *Lansdowne* to the position. The *Lansdowne* had also made a professional attack, her depth charges puncturing one of the saddle tanks of the U-boat and sending her limping home. Ten days later, in the Bahamas, the *Lansdowne* would take her attack all the way, sinking the *U-153*. On 14 July, coast guard planes would spot the *U-402* off Cape Hatteras and batter it to the surface with bombs. Von Forstner and his crew survived, but they had no choice but to go home with no successes to report.[11]

The Gulf Sea Frontier had also benefited from Admiral Andrews's hard work to gain resources for all coastal forces. Late in the evening of 10 June 1942, a U-boat was definitely located moving west through the Old Bahama Channel. Admiral J. L. Kauffman, commander of the Gulf Sea Frontier, immediately ordered the concentration of "all available forces, both air and surface, in an attempt to hunt this submarine to exhaustion and destroy it . . ."[12]

The U-boat was the *U-157*, commanded by Korvettenkapitän Wolf Henne. If aware that he had been spotted, Henne made little attempt to hide. That same night, just 5 miles off the north coast of Cuba, he attacked and sank the *Hagan*, an American tanker loaded with blackstrap molasses. Six crew members were killed. Cuban gunboats rescued the survivors.[13] Before an hour had gone by after the sinking, a radar-equipped B-18 bomber was dispatched to look for the U-boat. Since Admiral Doenitz was still being assured by German scientists that such airborne radar was impossible, Henne suspected nothing and stayed on the surface. At first light the next morning, the B-18 found the *U-157* and attacked, sweeping over the heads of the startled crew on the conning tower. Luck, however, was with the Germans, as the bomber's bomb bays were not fully open on the first pass. After turning sharply, the bomber dropped four Mark XVII depth charges on the madly diving *U-157*. Henne managed to get his U-boat down, but he and his crew had been badly shaken. After the B-18 had to leave for fuel, three relief aircraft were immediately sent out for surveillance of the harried U-boat. Twelve coast guard patrol craft, including the coast guard cutters *Triton* and *Thetis*, were also sent out. The twelve were divided into two groups. The Key West Group was to search in and around the Nicholas Channel; the Miami Group was given the Santaren Channel. When the destroyer *Noa* arrived, she was given the Old Bahama Channel. The next day, the destroyer *Dahlgren* was ordered to proceed to a point off the eastern tip of Cay Sal Bank at the junction of the three channels in the hope she would catch the U-boat after it had been flushed by the others.[14]

On the morning of 11 June, a Pan-American Airways plane sighted the U-boat on the surface only about 4 miles from where it had been attacked by the B-18. More aircraft patrols were dispatched and a second B-18 placed on night patrol. Just before midnight, that B-18 made radar contact with the *U-157*, but could not call for help because of a faulty radio transmitter. It turned and raced back to Key West with the news. With that and other shreds of evidence, the naval intelligence officers determined that the U-boat had probably managed to get past the Nicholas Channel patrol and was trying to cross the Florida Straits during darkness, perhaps with the intention of fixing its position on Sand Key Light. On this assumption, another radar-equipped B-18 was dispatched on the morning of 12 June to the predicted position. Almost immediately upon arrival, the bomber received an excellent radar contact and then actually saw the U-boat crash-diving. More aircraft were dispatched to the area along with the *Dahlgren* and the *Noa* and the Key West Group of antisubmarine ships, including the cutter *Thetis*.[15]

On the afternoon of 12 June, an army A-29 on patrol saw what appeared to be a periscope in the Florida Straits and, upon closer inspection, sighted the clear shape of a submerged submarine. The Key West Group with the cutter *Thetis* was directed to proceed at best speed to the area the A-29 had reported. The captain of the *Thetis* seemed to know his business. As soon as he was in the area, he patiently set up a grid search pattern with the *PE 27*, the *Triton*, and three small PC boats and began to cover the bottom with sonar pings. In just over an hour, he found the *U-157*, his soundmen calling back a clear contact. The captain of the *Thetis* was not a man to hesitate or to ask for orders. When he found the U-boat too close to make an immediate run, he pushed the *Thetis* to 14 knots, passed over the U-boat, and then ordered full left rudder, steadying on a reverse course. Seven depth charges were released, five at five-second intervals from racks and two from the Y-gun. The captain of the *Thetis* had calculated it perfectly, bracketing the *U-157* with charges set at 200 and 300 feet. As the charges exploded below, the *Thetis* turned to starboard and reduced speed to observe the results. As soon as the turn was completed, an enormous "water slug" was observed smashing to the surface, a boil of water and air so huge that no depth charge could have done it.[16]

There was cheering aboard the *Thetis*, but her captain

stopped it immediately. The battle wasn't over for him until
he saw proof of it. He had apparently seen U-boats get away
before, even after he was certain he had them cornered. Ignoring the frantic signals from the other ships who wanted to
make a run on the same site, the *Thetis* stopped to pick up
pieces of freshly broken wood and articles of clothing. Then
two pairs of leather trousers were picked up and a spreading
oil slick sampled. There was no doubt. The *U-157* was dead. It
had, in fact, been the perfect attack and also was symbolic of
the end of German dominance in American waters. A harried
German U-boat and its crew had been destroyed in a single
pass by a confident, well-armed American ship and her well-
trained crew.[17]

When Admiral Andrews received the news of the *Thetis*'s
kill, it had to make him smile. The captain of the *Thetis* was an
Eastern Sea Frontier alumnus, one of Andrews's men who had
gone after the U-boats at the beginning of the battle, when the
U-boats ruled. Andrews and the captain of the *Thetis* had
learned together, Andrews on how to gather his forces and
then properly use them, the captain of the *Thetis* on more basic
but perhaps even more essential skills—such as how best to
drop a pattern of depth charges and how to stay afloat and
alive on an American sea owned by a ruthless foreign power.
Andrews recognized the name—he had to. At one time, the
man had commanded the ship that had dropped more depth
charges than any other in the Eastern Sea Frontier, the man
who had then been the executive officer of the same ship and
served under another man who brought more innovations to
the art and science of U-boat hunting and killing. The captain
of the *Thetis* was indeed well known in the halls of the Eastern
Sea Frontier Headquarters.

His name: Lieutenant Nelson G. McCormick of the *Thetis*,
once of the *Dione*.

After her week of repairs, the *Dione* continued alternating
her patrol and convoy escort duties throughout July and then
into August. Swede and the other men came back from their
leaves reluctantly, their time away making them doubly tired
of the daily toil of following the unofficial coast guard motto—

"You have to go out but you don't have to come back." For months, they had fought the U-boats and cleaned up after their bloody attacks. They had stayed with McCormick and then with Alger as the two commanders had kept the *Dione* constantly in the line of fire, days and nights in the sights of unseen periscopes. They had dodged torpedoes, been rammed by one of their own ships, escorted the first great American convoy in American waters, chased until exhaustion echoes and ghosts and real U-boats alike, expended depth charges by the hundreds. The sea was no longer the cold, dark winter sea of the Graveyard of the Atlantic, but it was still treacherous, quick to blow up around them, requiring the cutter to abandon all courses and turn head into the waves and wind, smashing through them, throwing men about, and lifting propellers high into the air, exposed, singing, smashing down. It was all very familiar and yet . . .

Over the summer sea of the Graveyard the *Dione* moved, just as she had done months before, but now she did not move alone. Overhead, constant airplane patrols moved past and on every horizon, big convoys worked their way north and south, dozens of escorts efficiently screening. At night, Alger and his men could look west and see nothing but darkness. The lights on shore had finally been shut off. There seemed to be only a smooth, efficient machine—finally developed, finally being applied against what had become a mismatched enemy, the still brave but obsolete Type VII and IX German U-boat. Up and down the east coast and in the Gulf, the freighters and tankers moved confidently. Their logs told the story. *Arrived*, they said. *Secure at pier. F W E.*

F W E—Finished With Engines . . . and safe.

By August, there was a quiet confidence not only aboard the *Dione* but in every American ship and every American airplane. If the enemy was still there, he was keeping his head down, aware that to show himself was to die. In fact, no U-boats were there. Admiral Doenitz had given up. He knew that the winds had turned, that only defeat and death awaited him along those far shores. In the *BdU War Log*, he had written:

In the sea area off Hatteras successes have dropped considerably. This is due [to the] formation of convoys and increased defense measures. Of the boats stationed there in the recent period only two, *U-754* and *U-701*, have had successes. On the other hand, *U-701* and *U-215* have apparently been lost, and *U-402* and *U-576* badly damaged by depth charges or bombs [author's note: the *U-576* had actually been sunk]. This state of things is not justified by the amount of success achieved.

It must have been very hard for Doenitz to write the final sentence, but he had no choice.

The two remaining boats (*U-574* and *U-458*) will therefore be removed.

It was finished. Admiral Doenitz would continue to occasionally send U-boats to the American coast until the war was over. In fact, the last U-boat to be sunk in World War II would be the *U-853*, blasted into remnants by several war-seasoned American destroyers and cutters off the coast of Rhode Island.[18] But Doenitz essentially ended the battle for American waters after the summer of 1942 and moved his U-boats elsewhere. A great naval victory had been won by an odd assortment of ships and planes operated by untried and untested men, somehow all scraped together by one, tireless man: Admiral Adolphus Andrews of the Eastern Sea Frontier.

It was a battle done and set aside, as the greatest war in history ground on. No campaign streamers or ribbons would ever be issued to the men of the American navy and coast guard and merchant marine or to the British in their tiny trawlers who suffered through this battle. Yet, their battle had to be won and finally it was, but only after much sweat and blood.

In the autumn of 1942, the *Dione* moved on what had become a different sea, a sea of peace and life. For Lieutenant Alger and his officers, there was much satisfaction when they heard of McCormick's success. He had deserved it. But it

served to remind them once again that the *Dione* still had not
caught a U-boat. Rescues, yes—many of those. What man
aboard would ever forget the *Naeco* and the sea of gasoline
Alger had taken them across to rescue the burned survivors of
that awful, charred hulk? "Wimble Willy" had seemed to have
been a success, but even it, Alger would come to realize, was
only a ghost. Allied intelligence was good enough to know
when a U-boat had died. The *Dione* had sunk nothing despite
all of her work.

She never would.

But Swede Larson would later remember the way he and
his fellow crewmen would realize what the *Dione*, through all
of her pain and sacrifice, had finally accomplished. They
would see it one day in October when the cook came back on
the stern with a sack of hard biscuits. Resting the sack beside
him, he took one of the biscuits and raised it toward the sky.
The *Dione*'s men, moving past on their duties, stopped and
watched. They had forgotten the gesture. Some minutes
passed and still the cook held his hand up, the men still watching, some of them shading their eyes and looking back and up
as if for a sign, as men must have done for thousands of years
while their priests held their hands out with offerings to the
gods.

And then the first one came. One lone seagull. And behind
this one brave gull came another and then another and another, pacing the *Dione*, rocking in the light breeze, calling
beseechingly at the cook, all but asking if it was safe. Would
the sea explode behind the *Dione* if they came near her? Would
the gulls die if they trusted?

The cook held his hand out. It was a simple gesture. But its
meaning was clear. Finally.

It was safe.

The first gull came down, too frightened to take the biscuit, so the cook broke it and threw it into the air. The gull
caught it, flipped its head back, gulped, and then wheeled off.
In its place, another gull came and fed, its cries of pleasure
exciting the other gulls to swoop in closer, to begin taking the
biscuit from the cook's hand. Swede and then others of the
crew slowly moved up beside the cook, taking biscuits from

the sack and holding them up. Soon, the sky was swarming with soaring gulls, laughing gulls, full flaps down to catch the biscuits then up to wheel and soar into the blue, sunlit sky. Lieutenant Alger was on the bridge and watched, bemused. He had never seen this ritual. It had last been seen before his arrival, when McCormick and the *Dione* had first begun to hunt the U-boat. Why now had the gulls returned?

There was a simple answer.

It was because of what he and the *Dione* had done.

It was safe.

Victory.

# Appendix

### Note of Explanation

The following tables list attacks on Allied shipping by German U-boats, and German U-boats sunk, from January 1942 to August 1942 in both American and Canadian waters. Locations of attacks listed in the tables are identified in the right-hand column by BdU quadrant as extracted from German records. BdU quadrants were a method of dividing the world's seas into letter and number groupings so that Admiral Doenitz could more precisely position his boats. U-boats also used this method to identify the position of their attacks for BdU and were so recorded. To simplify the preparation of the tables, BdU quadrant locaters were used instead of trying to convert them to longitude and latitude.

The maps on pages 306–313 are also shown using BdU quadrants so that the reader can locate any attack position by matching the number in the left-hand column of the table with the number on the appropriate map. Attacks in Canadian waters are those shown in the BdU quadrant column as BB—. "BB" locations are not shown on the maps, as that would have resulted in a map too small to show detail in the principal areas covered by the text of this book. Canadian attack locations can be found, however, by referring to any text showing the overall BdU quadrant map of North America, such as in *Axis Submarine Successes 1939–1945* by Jürgen Rohwer (please see the bibliography). The location of the U-boats sunk

by Allied forces are shown in longitude and latitude, as the
attacking ships and airplanes used these as position parame-
ters. Locations of U-boat wrecks are designated by a swastika
and the U-boat number on the appropriate map.

## U-boat Attacks in American/Canadian Waters: January–February 1942*

| No. | Date | Time (EWT) | U-Boat | U-Boat Captain | Ship | BdU Quadrant |
|---|---|---|---|---|---|---|
| 1. | 01/11/42 | 1949 | U-123 | Hardegen | *Cyclops* | CB2424 |
| 2. | 01/12/42 | 1918 | U-130 | Kals | *Frisco* | BB5800 |
| 3. | 01/13/42 | 0348 | U-130 | Kals | *Friar Rock* | BB5898 |
| 4. | 01/14/42 | 0235 | U-123 | Hardegen | *Norness* | CA3775 |
| 5. | 01/14/42 | 1938 | U-552 | Topp | *Dayrose* | BB6673 |
| 6. | 01/15/42 | 0341 | U-123 | Hardegen | *Coimbra* | CA2896 |
| 7. | 01/15/42 | 0534 | U-203 | Mützelburg | *Catalina* | BB6652 |
| 8. | 01/16/42 | 0758 | U-86 | Schug | *Toorak†* | BB6300 |
| 9. | 01/17/42 | 0521 | U-203 | Mützelburg | *Octavian* | BB6655 |
| 10. | 01/17/42 | 0704 | U-123 | Hardegen | *San José* | CA5756 |
| 11. | 01/18/42 | 0044 | U-552 | Topp | *Frances Salman* | BB6679 |
| 12. | 01/18/42 | 0233 | U-66 | Zapp | *Allan Jackson* | CA8779 |
| 13. | 01/18/42 | 1116 | U-123 | Hardegen | *Brazos* | CA7668 |
| 14. | 01/19/42 | 0024 | U-109 | Bleichrodt | *Empire Kingfisher* | BA9965 |
| 15. | 01/19/42 | 0143 | U-66 | Zapp | *Lady Hawkins* | CA8997 |
| 16. | 01/19/42 | 0309 | U-123 | Hardegen | *City of Atlanta* | CA7962 |
| 17. | 01/19/42 | 0501 | U-123 | Hardegen | *Ciltvaira* | CA7938 |
| 18. | 01/19/42 | 0644 | U-123 | Hardegen | *Malay†* | CA7938 |
| 19. | 01/21/42 | 1243 | U-203 | Mützelburg | *North Gaspe†* | BB6628 |
| 20. | 01/21/42 | 1322 | U-754 | Oestermann | *Belize* | BB6628 |
| 21. | 01/21/42 | 1543 | U-754 | Oestermann | *William Hansen* | BB6682 |
| 22. | 01/21/42 | 1621 | U-130 | Kals | *Alexandra Höegb* | CB1831 |
| 23. | 01/21/42 | 1916 | U-203 | Mützelburg | *Rosemonde* | BB6624 |
| 24. | 01/22/42 | 0639 | U-66 | Zapp | *Norvana* | DC1295 |
| 25. | 01/22/42 | 1643 | U-553 | Thurmann | *Inneröy* | CB3141 |
| 26. | 01/22/42 | | U-130 | Kals | *Olympic* | CA8400 |
| 27. | 01/23/42 | 0212 | U-109 | Bleichrodt | *Thirlby* | BA9956 |
| 28. | 01/23/42 | | U-82 | Rollmann | *Leisten* | BB8700 |
| 29. | 01/23/42 | 2040 | U-66 | Zapp | *Empire Gem* | CA7968 |
| 30. | 01/23/42 | 2043 | U-66 | Zapp | *Venore* | CA7968 |
| 31. | 01/24/42 | 2125 | U-754 | Oestermann | *Mount Kitheron* | BB6359 |
| 32. | 01/25/42 | 0402 | U-130 | Kals | *Varanger* | CA5435 |
| 33. | 01/25/42 | 1425 | U-125 | Folkers | *Olney‡* | CA8279 |
| 34. | 01/26/42 | 0004 | U-125 | Folkers | *West Ivis* | CA8883 |
| 35. | 01/26/42 | 1221 | U-754 | Oestermann | *Icarion* | BB6958 |
| 36. | 01/27/42 | 0343 | U-130 | Kals | *Francis E. Powell* | CA5743 |
| 37. | 01/27/42 | 0758 | U-130 | Kals | *Halo†* | CA7952 |
| 38. | 01/30/42 | 1205 | U-106 | Rasch | *Rochester* | CA8241 |
| 39. | 01/31/42 | | U-82 | Rollman | *Belmont* | BB8873 |

| | | | | |
|---|---|---|---|---|
| 40. 01/31/42 2130 | U-109 | Bleichrodt | *Tacoma Star* | CB4842 |
| 41. 02/01/42 0146 | U-751 | Bigalk | *Corilla*† | BB7356 |
| 42. 02/02/42 1340 | U-103 | Winter | *W. L. Steed* | CA5640 |
| 43. 02/02/42 2123 | U-106 | Rasch | *Amerikaland* | CA8458 |
| 44. 02/03/42 2227 | U-751 | Bigalk | *Silveray* | BB7488 |
| 45. 02/04/42 0000 | U-103 | Winter | *San Gil* | CA5764 |
| 46. 02/04/42 1953 | U-103 | Winter | *India Arrow* | CA5813 |
| 47. 02/05/42 1108 | U-103 | Winter | *China Arrow* | CA5813 |
| 48. 02/06/42 1008 | U-107 | Gelhaus | *Major Wheeler* | DC2134 |
| 49. 02/06/42 1152 | U-751 | Bigalk | *Empire Sun* | BB7494 |
| 50. 02/08/42 0435 | U-108 | Scholtz | *Ocean Venture* | CA8112 |
| 51. 02/09/42 1518 | U-108 | Scholtz | *Tolosa* | DC2118 |
| 52. 02/11/42 2041 | U-108 | Scholtz | *Blink* | DC2139 |
| 53. 02/13/42 2137 | U-576 | Heinicke | *Empire Spring* | BB8851 |
| 54. 02/14/42 2234 | U-566 | Borchert | *Meropi* | BB7544 |
| 55. 02/14/42 2243 | U-432 | Schultze | *Buarque* | CA8448 |
| 56. 02/16/42 1230 | U-564 | Suhren | *Opalia*† | CB4798 |
| 57. 02/18/42 1207 | U-432 | Schultze | *Olinda* | CA5817 |
| 58. 02/18/42 2118 | U-432 | Schultze | *Miraflores* | CA5288 |
| 59. 02/18/42 2145 | U-108 | Scholtz | *Flat ves.w/bridge* | CB1711 |
| 60. 02/19/42 1345 | U-128 | Heyse | *Pan Massachusetts* | DB9546 |
| 61. 02/19/42 1729 | U-96 | Lehmann-Willenbrock | *Empire Seal* | BB7753 |
| 62. 02/19/42 2253 | U-96 | Lehmann-Willenbrock | *Lake Osweya* | BB7884 |
| 63. 02/20/42 1923 | U-432 | Schultze | *Azalea City* | CA5867 |
| 64. 02/21/42 2044 | U-96 | Lehmann-Willenbrock | *Torungen* | BB7746 |
| 65. 02/21/42 2255 | U-504 | Poske | *Republic* | DB9765 |
| 66. 02/22/42 0551 | U-128 | Heyse | *Cities Svc. Empire* | DB9439 |
| 67. 02/22/42 1657 | U-96 | Lehmann-Willenbrock | *Kars* | BB7557 |
| 68. 02/22/42 1932 | U-504 | Poske | *W. D. Anderson* | DB9713 |
| 69. 02/26/42 1313 | U-504 | Poske | *Mamura* | DC7220 |
| 70. 02/27/42 0036 | U-578 | Rehwinkel | *R. P. Resor* | CA5221 |
| 71. 02/27/42 0100 | U-432 | Schultze | *Marore* | CA7936 |
| 72. 02/28/42 0244 | U-653 | Feiler | *Leif* | CA9971 |
| 73. 02/28/42 0500 | U-578 | Rehwinkel | *Jacob Jones* | CA5458 |
| 74. 02/28/42 1900 | U-588 | Vogel | *Carperby* | CB4110 |

* Please see map on page 339 for American wreck and attack locations.
† Damaged but not sunk.
‡ Attacked but not hit.

## U-boat Attacks in American/Canadian Waters: March–April 1942*

| No. | Date | Time (EWT) | U-Boat | U-Boat Captain | Ship | BdU Quadrant |
|---|---|---|---|---|---|---|
| 1. | 03/02/42 | | U-587 | Borcherdt | Unident. subchaser | BB8282 |
| 2. | 03/04/42 | | U-587 | Borcherdt | St. Johns Docks | BB6000 |
| 3. | 03/05/42 | 0535 | U-404 | V. Bülow | Collamer | BB7528 |
| 4. | 03/06/42 | | U-587 | Borcherdt | Hans Egede | BB6759 |
| 5. | 03/06/42 | 2150 | U-94 | Ites | APC Nort. Princess | CB4498 |
| 6. | 03/07/42 | 1510 | U-155 | Piening | Arabutan | CA8786 |
| 7. | 03/08/42 | 2025 | U-94 | Ites | Cayrú | CA5654 |
| 8. | 03/09/42 | 1509 | U-96 | Lehmann-Willenbrock | Tyr | BB7965 |
| 9. | 03/10/42 | 0032 | U-588 | Vogel | Gulftrade | CA5156 |
| 10. | 03/10/42 | 2116 | U-94 | Ites | Hvosleff | CA5489 |
| 11. | 03/11/42 | 0158 | U-158 | Rostin | Caribsea | DC1136 |
| 12. | 03/13/42 | 0005 | U-158 | Rostin | John D. Gill | DB3999 |
| 13. | 03/13/42 | 0043 | U-404 | V. Bülow | Tolten | CA5241 |
| 14. | 03/13/42 | 0120 | U-332 | Liebe | Albert F. Paul | CA8681 |
| 15. | 03/13/42 | 1147 | U-332 | Liebe | Trepca | CA8654 |
| 16. | 03/14/42 | 0158 | U-404 | V. Bülow | Lemuel Burrows | CA5176 |
| 17. | 03/14/42 | 2305 | U-158 | Rostin | Olean† | DC1164 |
| 18. | 03/15/42 | 0022 | U-158 | Rostin | Ario | DC1159 |
| 19. | 03/16/42 | 1355 | U-332 | Liebe | Australia | CA7959 |
| 20. | 03/16/42 | 2016 | U-404 | V. Bülow | San Demetrio | CA8163 |
| 21. | 03/16/42 | 2026 | U-124 | Mohr | Ceiba | CA8585 |
| 22. | 03/17/42 | 1258 | U-71 | Flachsenberg | Ranja | CB4941 |
| 23. | 03/17/42 | 1650 | U-124 | Mohr | Acmet | CA7966 |
| 24. | 03/17/42 | 1714 | U-124 | Mohr | Kassandra Louloudi | CA7993 |
| 25. | 03/18/42 | 0135 | U-124 | Mohr | E. M. Clark | CA7997 |
| 26. | 03/18/42 | 2231 | U-124 | Mohr | Papoose | DC1167 |
| 27. | 03/18/42 | 2338 | U-124 | Mohr | W. E. Hutton | DC1183 |
| 28. | 03/19/42 | 1319 | U-332 | Liebe | Liberator | CA7959 |
| 29. | 03/20/42 | 1539 | U-71 | Flachsenberg | Oakmar | CA9618 |
| 30. | 03/21/42 | 0025 | U-124 | Mohr | Esso Nashville† | DC1418 |
| 31. | 03/21/42 | 0405 | U-124 | Mohr | Atlantic Sun† | DC1441 |
| 32. | 03/21/42 | 2309 | U-373 | Loeser | Thursobank | CA6593 |
| 33. | 03/23/42 | 0315 | U-124 | Mohr | Naeco | DC1889 |
| 34. | 03/23/42 | 0931 | U-754 | Oestermann | British Prudence | BB8631 |
| 35. | 03/24/42 | 2213 | U-552 | Topp | Ocana | CB1363 |
| 36. | 03/25/42 | 0010 | U-105 | Schuch | Narragansett | CB7779 |
| 37. | 03/26/42 | 0858 | U-71 | Flachsenberg | Dixie Arrow | CA7995 |
| 38. | 03/26/42 | 2037 | U-123 | Hardegen | Atik (Carolyn) | CA9578 |

| | | | | |
|---|---|---|---|---|
| 39. 03/26/42 2038 | U-160 | Lassen | *Equipoise* | CA8400 |
| 40. 03/27/42 0320 | U-105 | Schuch | *Svenor* | CA9945 |
| 41. 03/29/42 1336 | U-160 | Lassen | *City of New York* | CA8781 |
| 42. 03/29/42 1458 | U-571 | Möhlmann | *Hertford* | CB2753 |
| 43. 03/31/42 | U-754 | Oestermann | *Menominee* | CA4997 |
| 44. 03/31/42 | U-754 | Oestermann | *Ontario†* | CA4997 |
| 45. 03/31/42 | U-754 | Oestermann | *Barnegat* | CA4997 |
| 46. 03/31/42 | U-754 | Oestermann | *Allegbeny* | CA4997 |
| 47. 03/31/42 1622 | U-71 | Flachsenberg | *San Gerardo* | CA6995 |
| 48. 03/31/42 2253 | U-71 | Flachsenberg | *Eastmoor* | CA6997 |
| 49. 04/01/42 0018 | U-754 | Oestermann | *Tiger* | CA7381 |
| 50. 04/01/42 1022 | U-160 | Lassen | *Rio Blanco* | CA8776 |
| 51. 04/02/42 0118 | U-123 | Hardegen | *Liebret* | DC1196 |
| 52. 04/02/42 2140 | U-552 | Topp | *David H. Atwater* | CA5714 |
| 53. 04/03/42 0549 | U-754 | Oestermann | *Otho* | CA8618 |
| 54. 04/03/42 1910 | U-572 | Hirsacker | *Ensis†* | CB7588 |
| 55. 04/04/42 2140 | U-552 | Topp | *Byron T. Benson* | CA7652 |
| 56. 04/06/42 0200 | U-160 | Lassen | *Bidwell†* | DC1246 |
| 57. 04/06/42 1100 | U-571 | Möhlmann | *Koll* | CA9922 |
| 58. 04/06/42 1458 | U-754 | Oestermann | *Kollskegg* | CA9986 |
| 59. 04/06/42 2217 | U-552 | Topp | *British Splendour* | CA7969 |
| 60. 04/07/42 0452 | U-552 | Topp | *Lancing* | CA7991 |
| 61. 04/07/42 2257 | U-84 | Uphoff | *Nemanja* | CB4269 |
| 62. 04/08/42 0152 | U-123 | Hardegen | *Oklahoma†* | DB6177 |
| 63. 04/08/42 0248 | U-123 | Hardegen | *Esso Baton Rouge†* | DB6177 |
| 64. 04/09/42 0250 | U-552 | Topp | *Atlas* | DC1163 |
| 65. 04/09/42 0116 | U-123 | Hardegen | *Esparta* | DB5663 |
| 66. 04/09/42 0258 | U-160 | Lassen | *Malcbace* | DC1227 |
| 67. 04/09/42 2147 | U-203 | Mützelburg | *San Delfino* | CA7965 |
| 68. 04/10/42 0127 | U-552 | Topp | *Tamaulipas* | DC1246 |
| 69. 04/10/42 | U-85 | Greger | *Cbr. Knudsen* | CA5500 |
| 70. 04/10/42 2222 | U-123 | Hardegen | *Gulfamerica* | DB5669 |
| 71. 04/11/42 0720 | U-203 | Mützelburg | *Harry F. Sinclair†* | DC1193 |
| 72. 04/11/42 1631 | U-160 | Lassen | *Ulysses* | DC1259 |
| 73. 04/12/42 0106 | U-203 | Mützelburg | *Stanvac Melbourne†* | DC1177 |
| 74. 04/12/42 2311 | U-123 | Hardegen | *Leslie* | DB9900 |
| 75. 04/13/42 0145 | U-123 | Hardegen | *Korsholm* | DB9150 |
| 76. 04/14/42 0915 | U-203 | Mützelburg | *Empire Tbrush* | CA7968 |
| 77. 04/14/42 1502 | U-571 | Möhlmann | *Margaret* | CA8754 |
| 78. 04/15/42 2138 | U-575 | Heydemann | *Robin Hood* | CB4400 |
| 79. 04/16/42 1200 | U-572 | Hirsacker | *Desert Light* | CA8915 |
| 80. 04/16/42 2323 | U-123 | Hardegen | *Alcoa Guide* | DC3179 |
| 81. 04/17/42 1846 | U-201 | Schnee | *Victoria†* | CA9375 |
| 82. 04/18/42 1834 | U-136 | Zimmermann | *Axtell J. Byles†* | CA7936 |
| 83. 04/19/42 2106 | U-572 | Hirsacker | *Empire Dryden* | DC3248 |

| | | | | |
|---|---|---|---|---|
| 84. 04/19/42 2228 | U-654 | Forster | *Steelmaker* | CA9800 |
| 85. 04/19/42 2324 | U-109 | Bleichrodt | *Harpagon* | DC3225 |
| 86. 04/20/42 1723 | U-654 | Forster | *Agra* | CA9892 |
| 87. 04/20/42 1830 | U-84 | Uphoff | *Chenango* | DC1314 |
| 88. 04/20/42 2036 | U-201 | Schnee | *Bris* | DC3456 |
| 89. 04/20/42 2248 | U-752 | Schroeter | *West Imboden* | CB1677 |
| 90. 04/21/42 1245 | U-576 | Heinicke | *Pipestone County* | CB4872 |
| 91. 04/21/42 2129 | U-201 | Schnee | *San Jacinto* | DC5631 |
| 92. 04/22/42 0305 | U-201 | Schnee | *Derrybeen* | DC6178 |
| 93. 04/23/42 0520 | U-752 | Schroeter | *Reinholt* | CA5394 |
| 94. 04/24/42 0809 | U-576 | Heinicke | *Tropic Star†* | CA3974 |
| 95. 04/24/42 1748 | U-136 | Zimmermann | *Empire Drum* | CA9521 |
| 96. 04/28/42 0935 | U-136 | Zimmermann | *Arundo* | CA2878 |
| 97. 04/29/42 2136 | U-402 | v. Forstner | *Ashkabad* | DC1221 |
| 98. 04/30/42 0137 | U-576 | Heinicke | *Taborfjell* | CA3357 |

\* Please see map on page 340 for American wreck and attack locations.
† Damaged but not sunk.

U-boat Attacks in American/Canadian Waters:
May–June 1942*

| No. | Date | Time (EWT) | U-Boat | U-Boat Captain | Ship | BdU Quadrant |
|---|---|---|---|---|---|---|
| 1. | 05/01/42 | 0043 | U-752 | Schroeter | *Bidevind* | CA5265 |
| 2. | 05/01/42 | 0536 | U-109 | Bleichrodt | *La Paz†* | DB9429 |
| 3. | 05/01/42 | | U-109 | Bleichrodt | *Worden* | DB9400 |
| 4. | 05/01/42 | 0940 | U-136 | Zimmermann | *Alcoa Leader* | CA5346 |
| 5. | 05/02/42 | 0041 | U-402 | v. Forstner | *Cythera* | DC1591 |
| 6. | 05/03/42 | 0212 | U-506 | Würdemann | *Sama* | DM2650 |
| 7. | 05/03/42 | 0224 | U-564 | Suhren | *Ocean Venus* | DB9434 |
| 8. | 05/03/42 | 0454 | U-109 | Bleichrodt | *Laertes* | DB9423 |
| 9. | 05/04/42 | 1142 | U-507 | Schacht | *Norlindo* | DM1739 |
| 10. | 05/04/42 | 1304 | U-564 | Surhen | *Eclipset* | DM2318 |
| 11. | 05/04/42 | 1932 | U-507 | Schacht | *Munger T. Ball* | DM1467 |
| 12. | 05/04/42 | 2215 | U-507 | Schacht | *Joseph M. Cudaby* | DM1433 |
| 13. | 05/04/42 | 2253 | U-564 | Suhren | *Delislet* | DB9762 |
| 14. | 05/05/42 | 2343 | U-333 | Cremer | *Java Arrow†* | DB9763 |
| 15. | 05/06/42 | 0335 | U-333 | Cremer | *Amazone* | DB9763 |
| 16. | 05/06/42 | 0525 | U-333 | Cremer | *Halsey* | DB9763 |
| 17. | 05/06/42 | 1343 | U-507 | Schacht | *Alcoa Puritan* | DA9393 |
| 18. | 05/07/42 | 2130 | U-507 | Schacht | *Ontario* | DB7426 |
| 19. | 05/08/42 | 0845 | U-507 | Schacht | *Torny* | DB7888 |
| 20. | 05/08/42 | 1212 | U-564 | Suhren | *Obioan* | DM2316 |
| 21. | 05/08/42 | 2127 | U-588 | Vogel | *Greylock†* | BB7500 |
| 22. | 05/09/42 | 0402 | U-564 | Suhren | *Lubrafol* | DM2343 |
| 23. | 05/09/42 | 2110 | U-588 | Vogel | *Kitty's Brock* | BB7810 |
| 24. | 05/10/42 | 0305 | U-333 | Cremer | *Clan Skene* | DC6111 |
| 25. | 05/10/42 | 0230 | U-506 | Würdemann | *Aurora* | DA9288 |
| 26. | 05/11/42 | 2340 | U-558 | Krech | *Bedfordsbire* | DC1183 |
| 27. | 05/11/42 | 2352 | U-553 | Thurmann | *Nicoya* | BB1485 |
| 28. | 05/12/42 | 0228 | U-553 | Thurmann | *Leto* | BB1476 |
| 29. | 05/12/42 | 1603 | U-507 | Schacht | *Virginia* | DA9347 |
| 30. | 05/13/42 | 1450 | U-506 | Würdemann | *Gulfpenn* | DA9536 |
| 31. | 05/13/42 | 2347 | U-506 | Würdemann | *David McKelvy* | DA9536 |
| 32. | 05/13/42 | 2355 | U-564 | Suhren | *Potrero del Llano* | DM2643 |
| 33. | 05/14/42 | 0557 | U-593 | Kelbling | *Stavros* | CA5344 |
| 34. | 05/15/42 | 1812 | U-507 | Schacht | *Amapala* | DL2211 |
| 35. | 05/15/42 | 2215 | U-751 | Bigalk | *Nicarao* | DN1656 |
| 36. | 05/16/42 | 0501 | U-506 | Würdemann | *Wm. C. McTarnaban* | DA9521 |
| 37. | 05/16/42 | 0510 | U-506 | Würdemann | *Sun* | DA9521 |
| 38. | 05/16/42 | 2254 | U-135 | Praetorius | *Fort Qu'Appelle* | CB5156 |

| | | | | |
|---|---|---|---|---|
| 39. 05/16/42 2334 | U-506 | Würdemann | *Gulf Oil* | DA9561 |
| 40. 05/17/42 | U-432 | Schultze | *Foam* | BB7800 |
| 41. 05/17/42 1301 | U-653 | Feiler | *Peisander* | CB7233 |
| 42. 05/19/42 0256 | U-506 | Würdemann | *Heredia* | DA9700 |
| 43. 05/19/42 1424 | U-103 | Winter | *Ogontz* | DL6271 |
| 44. 05/20/42 0158 | U-506 | Würdemann | *Halo* | DA9553 |
| 45. 05/20/42 2221 | U-106 | Rasch | *Faja de Oro* | DM4157 |
| 46. 05/21/42 1410 | U-588 | Vogel | *Plow City* | CA6650 |
| 47. 05/22/42 1824 | U-432 | Schultze | *Zurichmoor* | CB1928 |
| 48. 05/23/42 1503 | U-588 | Vogel | *Margot* | CB4750 |
| 49. 05/24/42 2216 | U-753 | v. Mannstein | *Haakon Hauan* | DA9200 |
| 50. 05/25/42 1458 | U-593 | Kelbling | *Persephone* | CA5165 |
| 51. 05/27/42 0503 | U-753 | v. Mannstein | *Hamlet* | DA9423 |
| 52. 05/28/42 | U-506 | Würdemann | *Yorkmoor* | DC5844 |
| 53. 05/30/42 0624 | U-404 | v. Bülow | *Alcoa Shipper* | CB4765 |
| 54. 06/01/42 | U-404 | v. Bülow | *West Notus* | DC3212 |
| 55. 06/02/42 0118 | U-553 | Thurmann | *Mattawin* | CB1895 |
| 56. 06/02/42 1427 | U-578 | Rehwinkel | *Berganger* | CA6287 |
| 57. 06/03/42 | U-404 | v. Bülow | *Anna* | DC2300 |
| 58. 06/??/42 | U- | | *Poseidon* | CA9400 |
| 59. 06/07/42 0142 | U-653 | Feiler | *Gannet* | CB7875 |
| 60. 06/07/42 | U-158 | Rostin | *Hermis* | DM4174 |
| 61. 06/07/42 2116 | U-135 | Praetorius | *Pleasantville* | DC3244 |
| 62. 06/09/42 0502 | U-432 | Schultze | *Kronprinsen* | CB1122 |
| 63. 06/11/42 | U-158 | Rostin | *Sheherazade* | DA9180 |
| 64. 06/12/42 | U-158 | Rostin | *Cities Svc. Toledo* | DA8368 |
| 65. 06/15/42 | U-701 | Degen | *Robert C. Tuttle*†‡ | CA7300 |
| 66. 06/15/42 | U-701 | Degen | *Esso Augusta*† | CA7300 |
| 67. 06/15/42 | U-701 | Degen | *Kingston Ceylonite*‡ | CA7300 |
| 68. 06/15/42 | U-701 | Degen | *Bainbridge*†‡ | CA7300 |
| 69. 06/15/42 2201 | U-67 | Müller-Stöckheim | *Managua* | DM5136 |
| 70. 06/15/42 2217 | U-87 | Berger | *Port Nicholson* | CA3268 |
| 71. 06/15/42 2221 | U-87 | Berger | *Cherokee* | CA3268 |
| 72. 06/17/42 | U-701 | Degen | *Santore*‡ | CA7300 |
| 73. 06/18/42 1703 | U-129 | Witt | *Millinocket* | DM5375 |
| 74. 06/19/42 0245 | U-701 | Degen | *YP 389* | CA7900 |
| 75. 06/20/42 0525 | U-67 | Müller-Stöckheim | *Nortind* | DA6700 |
| 76. 06/22/42 0634 | U-202 | Linder | *Rio Tercero* | CA5651 |
| 77. 06/23/42 0011 | U-67 | Müller-Stöckheim | *Rawleigh Warner* | DA9349 |
| 78. 06/24/42 0337 | U-404 | v. Bülow | *Ljubica Matkovic* | DC1223 |
| 79. 06/24/42 | U-373 | Loeser | *John R. Williams* | CA5400 |
| 80. 06/24/42 1316 | U-404 | v. Bülow | *Manuela* | DC1228 |

| 81. 06/24/42 1920 | U-404 | v. Bülow | *Nordal* | DC1228 |
| 82. 06/25/42 2010 | U-701 | Degen | *Tamesis*† | DC1231 |
| 83. 06/27/42 | U-701 | Degen | *British Freedom*† | DC1231 |
| 84. 06/27/42 1600 | U-404 | v. Bülow | *Moldanger* | CA6970 |
| 85. 06/28/42 1200 | U-701 | Degen | *William Rockefeller* | DC1246 |
| 86. 06/29/42 0150 | U-67 | Müller-Stöckheim | *Empire Mica* | DB4987 |
| 87. 06/29/42 | U-158 | Rostin | *Everalda* | DC5626 |

* Please see map on page 341 for American wreck and attack
locations.
† Damaged but not sunk.
‡ Mines.

# U-boat Attacks in American/Canadian Waters:
## July–August 1942*

| No. | Date | Time (EWT) | U-Boat | U-Boat Captain | Ship | BdU Quadrant |
|-----|------|------------|--------|----------------|------|--------------|
| 1. | 07/01/42 | 0027 | U-202 | Linder | *City of Birmingham* | CA9758 |
| 2. | 07/06/42 | | U-67 | Müller-Stöckheim | *Bayard* | DA9326 |
| 3. | 07/07/42 | 0302 | U-571 | Möhlmann | *Umtata* | DM2646 |
| 4. | 07/07/42 | 0416 | U-67 | Müller-Stöckheim | *Paul H. Harwood*† | DA6997 |
| 5. | 07/08/42 | 0216 | U-571 | Möhlmann | *J. A. Moffett, Jr.* | DM2824 |
| 6. | 07/08/42 | | U-571 | Möhlmann | *Nicholas Cuneo* | DM4328 |
| 7. | 07/10/42 | 0019 | U-67 | Müller-Stöckheim | *Benjamin Brewster* | DA9252 |
| 8. | 07/12/42 | 2208 | U-84 | Uphoff | *Andrew Jackson* | DM5283 |
| 9. | 07/13/42 | 0135 | U-67 | Müller-Stöckheim | *R. W. Gallagher* | DA9198 |
| 10. | 07/15/42 | 0149 | U-571 | Möhlmann | *Pennsylvania Sun*† | DM1976 |
| 11. | 07/15/42 | 1625 | U-576 | Heinicke | *J. A. Mowinckel*† | DC2100 |
| 12. | 07/15/42 | 1620 | U-576 | Heinicke | *Chilore* | CA7980 |
| 13. | 07/15/42 | 1625 | U-576 | Heinicke | *Bluefields* | CA7980 |
| 14. | 07/19/42 | 0045 | U-84 | Uphoff | *Baja California* | DM1651 |
| 15. | 07/19/42 | 1312 | U-129 | Witt | *Port Antonio* | DM4153 |
| 16. | 07/20/42 | 1239 | U-132 | Vogelsang | *Frederika Lensen* | BB1475 |
| 17. | 07/21/42 | 0307 | U-84 | Uphoff | *Wm. Cullen Bryant* | DM1994 |
| 18. | 07/25/42 | 0355 | U-89 | Lohmann | *Lucille M.* | CB1295 |
| 19. | 07/26/42 | | U-171 | Pfeffer | *Oaxaca* | DA7625 |
| 20. | 07/28/42 | | U-754 | Oestermann | *Ebb* | BB7768 |
| 21. | 07/29/42 | 1910 | U-132 | Vogelsang | *Pacific Pioneer* | BB8719 |
| 22. | 07/30/42 | | U-166 | Kuhlmann | *Robert E. Lee* | DA6900 |
| 23. | 08/05/42 | 1313 | U-458 | Diggins | *Draco* | BB8682 |
| 24. | 08/12/42 | 0555 | U-508 | Staats | *Santiago de Cuba* | DM2748 |
| 25. | 08/12/42 | 0555 | U-508 | Staats | *Manzanillo* | DM2748 |
| 26. | 08/13/42 | | U-171 | Pfeffer | *R. M. Parker* | DA9192 |

\* Please see map on page 342 for American wreck and attack
locations.
† Damaged but not sunk.

U-boats Sunk in American Waters:
January–August 1942*

| Date | U-Boat | Commander | Cause | Location |
|------|--------|-----------|-------|----------|
| 04/14/42 | U-85 | Greger | USS *Roper* | 35-55 N, 75-13 W |
| 05/09/42 | U-352 | Rathke | USCGC *Icarus* | 34-12 N, 76-35 W |
| 06/13/42 | U-157 | Henne | USCGC *Thetis* | 24-13 N, 82-03 W |
| 07/03/42 | U-215 | Hoeckner | HMS *Le Tigre* | 41-48 N, 66-38 W |
| 07/07/42 | U-701 | Degen | Aircraft | 34-50 N, 74-55 W |
| 07/17/42 | U-576 | Heinicke | Aircraft/ *Unicoi* | 34-51 N, 75-22 W |
| 08/01/42 | U-166 | Kuhlmann | Aircraft | 28-37 N, 90-45 W |

* Please see maps on pages 339–342 for wreck locations.

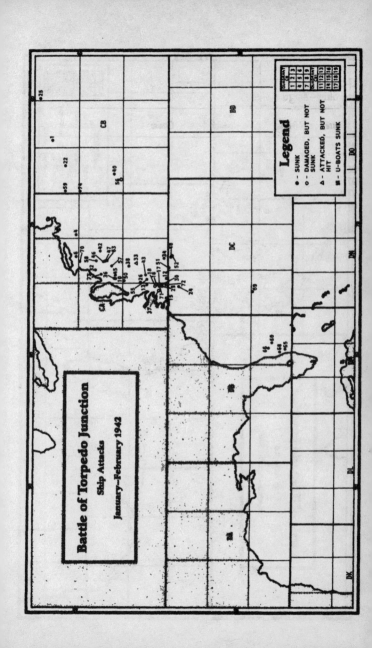

**Battle of Torpedo Junction**
Ship Attacks
January–February 1942

**Legend**

• – SUNK

○ – DAMAGED, BUT NOT SUNK

△ – ATTACKED, BUT NOT HIT

⊞ – U-BOATS SUNK

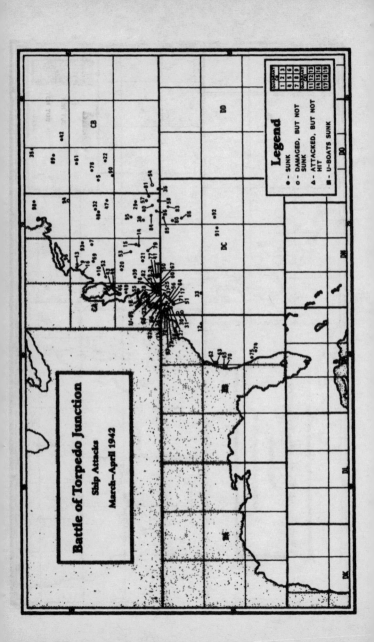

Battle of Torpedo Junction
Ship Attacks
March–April 1942

Legend

● – SUNK
○ – DAMAGED, BUT NOT SUNK
△ – ATTACKED, BUT NOT HIT
■ – U-BOATS SUNK

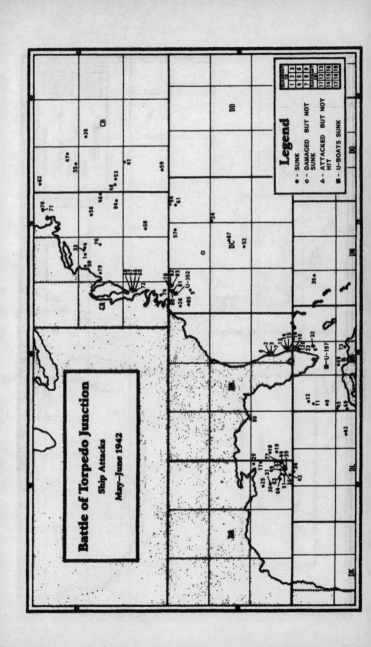

Battle of Torpedo Junction

Ship Attacks
May–June 1942

Legend

● – SUNK
○ – DAMAGED BUT NOT SUNK
△ – ATTACKED BUT NOT HIT
☒ – U-BOATS SUNK

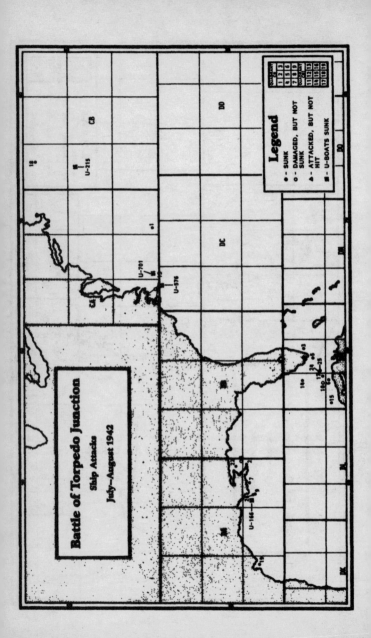

Battle of Torpedo Junction
Ship Attacks
July–August 1942

Legend

● - SUNK
○ - DAMAGED, BUT NOT SUNK
▲ - ATTACKED, BUT NOT HIT
■ - U-BOATS SUNK

# Notes

## Chapter One

1. Doenitz, *Memoirs*, 56–58.
2. Mason, *U-boat, The Secret Menace*, 23.
3. Ibid., 42–45.
4. Ibid., 49.
5. Doenitz, *Memoirs*, 58.
6. Ibid.
7. *War Diary, North Atlantic Naval Coastal Frontier*, December 1942, 10.
8. Ibid.

## Chapter Two

1. Doenitz, *Memoirs*, 58.
2. Frank, *The Sea Wolves*, 108.
3. *Report of Interrogation of Survivors of U-701 Sunk by U.S. Army Attack Bomber No. 9-29-322, Unit 296 B.S. On July 7, 1942*, IX.
4. Frank, *The Sea Wolves*, 108.
5. Ibid.
6. *Summary of Survivors' Statements, 1941–1945*, Office of the Chief of Naval Operations, NRS 1979-1.
7. Rohwer, *Axis Submarine Successes, 1939–1945*, 73.
8. Noli, *The Admiral's Wolf Pack*, 138.
9. Ibid.
10. Frank, *The Sea Wolves*, 109.
11. Noli, *The Admiral's Wolf Pack*, 139.
12. Rohwer, *Axis Submarine Successes, 1939–1945*, 74.
13. Noli, *The Admiral's Wolf Pack*, 141.
14. *War Diary, North Atlantic Naval Coastal Frontier*, December

1942, 11. Roscoe, *United States Destroyer Operations in World War II*, 73.

15. Letter, dated 2 May 1984, to the author from Lee A. O'Neill, Caracas, Venezuela.
16. *Kriegstagebuch* (War Diary), *U-66*.
17. Standard Oil Company of New Jersey, *Ships of the Esso Fleet in World War II*, 76. Norfolk *Virginian-Pilot*, 20 January 1942.
18. *Kriegstagebuch* (War Diary), *U-66*.
19. Standard Oil Company of New Jersey, *Ships of the Esso Fleet in World War II*, 76. Norfolk *Virginian-Pilot*, 20 January 1942.
20. *Summary of Survivors' Statements, 1941–1945*, Office of the Chief of Naval Operations, NRS 1979-1. Norfolk *Virginian-Pilot*, 29 January 1942 and 6 February 1942.
21. Rohwer, *Axis Submarine Successes, 1939–1945*, 74.
22. *War Diary, BdU*, 1 January 1942 through 31 March 1942, 11. Frank, *The Sea Wolves*, 70.
23. *Kriegstagebuch* (War Diary), *U-123*.
24. *Summary of Survivors' Statements, 1941–1945*, Office of the Chief of Naval Operations, NRS 1979-1. Norfolk *Virginian-Pilot*, 20, 22, 23 January 1942.
25. *Kriegstagebuch* (War Diary), *U-123*.
26. *Summary of Survivors' Statements, 1941–1945*, Office of the Chief of Naval Operations, NRS 1979-1. The *New York Times*, 22 January 1942. Norfolk *Virginian-Pilot*, 22, 29 January 1942, and 6 February 1942.
27. *Kriegstagebuch* (War Diary), *U-123*.
28. Frank, *The Sea Wolves*, 111.
29. Noli, *The Admiral's Wolf Pack*, 142.
30. Frank, *The Sea Wolves*, 111.
31. *Summary of Survivors' Statements, 1941–1945*, Office of the Chief of Naval Operations, NRS 1979-1. Norfolk *Virginian-Pilot*, 20, 21 January 1942.
32. *Summary of Survivors' Statements, 1941–1945*, Office of the Chief of Naval Operations, NRS 1979-1. The *New York Times*, 22 January 1942. Norfolk *Virginian-Pilot*, 22, 29 January 1942, and 6 February 1942.
33. *Kriegstagebuch* (War Diary), *U-123*. Rohwer, *Axis Submarine Successes, 1939–1945*, 76.
34. *War Diary, North Atlantic Naval Coastal Frontier*, January 1942, 3: 3. Taylor, *Fire on the Beaches*, 77–80.
35. Pfannes and Salamone, *The Great Admirals of World War II, Volume I: The Americans*, 38.
36. Analysis derived from letter, dated 12 December 1984, to the

author from Professor Elting E. Morison, Peterborough, New Hampshire, who compiled the *War Diary, North Atlantic Naval Coastal Frontier*, and the *War Diary, Eastern Sea Frontier, 1942*, and was on Admiral Andrews's Eastern Sea Frontier staff.

37. Moore, *A Careless Word, A Needless Sinking*, 205. *Kriegstagebuch* (War Diary), *U-66*. Rohwer, *Axis Submarine Successes, 1939–1945*, 75.

38. *War Diary, North Atlantic Naval Coastal Frontier*, January 1942, chap. 1. Norfolk *Virginian-Pilot*, 27 January 1942. *Kriegstagebuch* (War Diary), *U-66*.

39. Taylor, *Fire on the Beaches*, 65.

40. *Kriegstagebuch* (War Diary), *U-66*. *War Diary, North Atlantic Naval Coastal Frontier*, January 1942, chap. 1. Norfolk *Virginian-Pilot*, 27 January 1942.

41. Rohwer, *Axis Submarine Successes, 1939–1945*, 76. Norfolk *Virginian-Pilot*, 28 January 1942.

42. Rohwer, *Axis Submarine Successes, 1939–1945*, 76. *Summary of Survivors' Statements, 1941–1945*, Office of the Chief of Naval Operations, NRS 1979-1.

43. "Battle of Torpedo Junction, The," Fifth Naval District press release, 17 September 1945.

44. *War Diary, North Atlantic Naval Coastal Frontier*, January 1942, 3: 2.

45. *War Diary, North Atlantic Naval Coastal Frontier*, January 1942, 3: 3.

46. Noli, *The Admiral's Wolf Pack*, 144–45.

47. Mason, *U-boat, The Secret Menace*, 68.

## Chapter Three

1. War Log, USCGC *Dione* (WPC 107). Letters from and interviews with members of crew of the *Dione* (please see primary sources in the bibliography).

2. Stick, *Graveyard of the Atlantic*, 1.

3. Telephone interview with Commander Nelson C. McCormick, USCG (Ret.), April 1985.

4. Stick, *Graveyard of the Atlantic*, 209–12.

## Chapter Four

1. *War Diary, Eastern Sea Frontier*, February 1942, 1: 1.

2. Ibid., 2: 1, 2.

3. Ibid., 2: 2.
4. Rohwer, *Axis Submarine Successes, 1939–1945*, 74.
5. Rohwer, *Axis Submarine Successes, 1939–1945*, 76. Norfolk *Virginian-Pilot*, 7 February 1942.
6. *Summary of Survivors' Statements, 1941–1945*, Office of the Chief of Naval Operations, NRS 1979-1. Norfolk *Virginian-Pilot*, 8, 23 February 1942.
7. *Summary of Survivors' Statements, 1941–1945*, Office of the Chief of Naval Operations, NRS 1979-1. Norfolk *Virginian-Pilot*, 8, 23 February 1942.
8. *Kriegstagebuch* (War Diary), *U-103*.
9. Moore, *A Careless Word, A Needless Sinking*, 288. Standard Oil Company of New Jersey, *Ships of the Esso Fleet in World War II*, 83. Norfolk *Virginian-Pilot*, 12 February 1942. Taylor, *Fire on the Beaches*, 69–75.
10. Norfolk *Virginian-Pilot*, 5, 6 February 1942. *Summary of Survivors' Statements, 1941–1945*, Office of the Chief of Naval Operations, NRS 1979-1.
11. Norfolk *Virginian-Pilot*, 5, 6 February 1942. *Summary of Survivors' Statements, 1941–1945*, Office of the Chief of Naval Operations, NRS 1979-1.
12. *Kriegstagebuch* (War Diary), *U-123*. Moore, *A Careless Word, A Needless Sinking*, 134. Norfolk *Virginian-Pilot*, 7 February 1942. *Summary of Survivors' Statements, 1941–1945*, Office of the Chief of Naval Operations, NRS 1979-1. *War Diary, Eastern Sea Frontier*, February 1942, 5: 1–4.
13. Series of interviews and correspondence with Major Harold "Swede" Larson, USMC (Ret.), 1984–86.
14. Moore, *A Careless Word, A Needless Sinking*, 51. Norfolk *Virginian-Pilot*, 9 February 1942. *Summary of Survivors' Statements, 1941–1945*, Office of the Chief of Naval Operations, NRS 1979-1.
15. *Summary of Survivors' Statements, 1941–1945*, Office of the Chief of Naval Operations, NRS 1979-1.
16. Ibid.
17. Norfolk *Virginian-Pilot*, 26 February 1942. *Summary of Survivors' Statements, 1941–1945*, Office of the Chief of Naval Operations, NRS 1979-1.

## Chapter Five

1. Rohwer, *Axis Submarine Successes, 1939–1945*, 78. *War Diary, BdU*, 1 January 1942 through 31 March 1942, 74.

2. Norfolk *Virginian-Pilot*, 18, 19 February 1942. *Summary of Survivors' Statements, 1941–1945*, Office of the Chief of Naval Operations, NRS 1979-1.
3. Norfolk *Virginian-Pilot*, 21 February 1942. *Summary of Survivors' Statements, 1941–1945*, Office of the Chief of Naval Operations, NRS 1979-1.
4. Rohwer, *Axis Submarine Successes, 1939–1945*, 79.
5. Norfolk *Virginian-Pilot*, 22 February 1942. *Summary of Survivors' Statements, 1941–1945*, Office of the Chief of Naval Operations, NRS 1979-1.
6. Rohwer, *Axis Submarine Successes, 1939–1945*, 79. Norfolk *Virginian-Pilot*, 22 February 1942. *Summary of Survivors' Statements, 1941–1945*, Office of the Chief of Naval Operations, NRS 1979-1. Moore, *A Careless Word, A Needless Sinking*, 213.
7. Rohwer, *Axis Submarine Successes, 1939–1945*, 80. Norfolk *Virginian-Pilot*, 28 February 1942. *Summary of Survivors' Statements, 1941–1945*, Office of the Chief of Naval Operations, NRS 1979-1. Moore, *A Careless Word, A Needless Sinking*, 287. Frank, *The Sea Wolves*, 115.
8. Rohwer, *Axis Submarine Successes, 1939–1945*, 81.
9. Ibid., 81. Norfolk *Virginian-Pilot*, 28 February 1942. *Summary of Survivors' Statements, 1941–1945*, Office of the Chief of Naval Operations, NRS 1979-1. Moore, *A Careless Word, A Needless Sinking*, 230. Standard Oil Company of New Jersey, *Ships of the Esso Fleet in World War II*, 106.

### Chapter Six

1. Hughes and Costello, *The Battle of the Atlantic*, 196.
2. Farago, *The Tenth Fleet*, 42.
3. Ibid.
4. Pfannes and Salamone, *The Great Admirals of World War II, Vol. I: The Americans*, 48.
5. Hughes and Costello, *The Battle of the Atlantic*, 201.
6. Taylor, *Fire on the Beaches*, 79.
7. Ibid., 97–98. *War Diary, Eastern Sea Frontier*, February 1942, 7: 2.
8. *War Diary, Eastern Sea Frontier*, February 1942, 7: 1–2.
9. Ibid., 7: 1–7. Fourth Naval District, Report on USS *Jacob Jones*—Sinking of on 28 February 1942, dated 2 March 1942. Taylor, *Fire on the Beaches*, 97–100. Norfolk *Virginian-Pilot*, 4 March 1942.
10. Taylor, *Fire on the Beaches*, 99–100.

## Chapter Seven

1. *War Diary, Eastern Sea Frontier,* March 1942, 2: 1–9.
2. Rohwer, *Axis Submarine Successes, 1939–1945,* 82–83.
3. Norfolk *Virginian-Pilot,* 10 March 1942. *Summary of Survivors' Statements, 1941–1945,* Office of the Chief of Naval Operations, NRS 1979-1. Rohwer, *Axis Submarine Successes, 1939–1945,* 83. *War Diary, BdU,* 1 January 1942 through 31 March 1942, 122.
4. Rohwer, *Axis Submarine Successes, 1939–1945,* 84. *Summary of Survivors' Statements, 1941–1945,* Office of the Chief of Naval Operations, NRS 1979-1. Norfolk *Virginian-Pilot,* 11 March 1942.
5. Rohwer, *Axis Submarine Successes, 1939–1945,* 84. *Summary of Survivors' Statements, 1941–1945,* Office of the Chief of Naval Operations, NRS 1979-1. Norfolk *Virginian-Pilot,* 14 March 1942.
6. Rohwer, *Axis Submarine Successes, 1939–1945,* 84. *Summary of Survivors' Statements, 1941–1945,* Office of the Chief of Naval Operations, NRS 1979-1. Norfolk *Virginian-Pilot,* 15 March 1942.
7. Whedbee, *Legends of the Outer Banks and Tar Heel Tidewater,* 157–65. Stick, *Graveyard of the Atlantic,* 234.
8. Karig, Burton, and Freeland, *Battle Report—The Atlantic War,* 101.
9. Rohwer, *Axis Submarine Successes, 1939–1945,* 85. *Summary of Survivors' Statements, 1941–1945,* Office of the Chief of Naval Operations, NRS 1979-1. Norfolk *Virginian-Pilot,* 16 March 1942.
10. Rohwer, *Axis Submarine Successes, 1939–1945,* 26–82.
11. Rohwer, *Axis Submarine Successes, 1939–1945,* 85. Gasaway, *Grey Wolf, Grey Sea,* 195. *Summary of Survivors' Statements, 1941–1945,* Office of the Chief of Naval Operations, NRS 1979-1.
12. Rohwer, *Axis Submarine Successes, 1939–1945,* 85. *Summary of Survivors' Statements, 1941–1945,* Office of the Chief of Naval Operations, NRS 1979-1. Norfolk *Virginian-Pilot,* 19 March 1942. Moore, *A Careless Word, A Needless Sinking,* 377.
13. Rohwer, *Axis Submarine Successes, 1939–1945,* 85. *Summary of Survivors' Statements, 1941–1945,* Office of the Chief of Naval Operations, NRS 1979-1. Moore, *A Careless Word, A Needless Sinking,* 21.
14. Moore, *A Careless Word, A Needless Sinking,* 21, 377.
15. Rohwer, *Axis Submarine Successes, 1939–1945,* 85. *Summary of Survivors' Statements, 1941–1945,* Office of the Chief of Naval

Operations, NRS 1979-1. Moore, *A Careless Word, A Needless Sinking*, 26.

16. Rohwer, *Axis Submarine Successes, 1939–1945*, 85. *Summary of Survivors' Statements, 1941–1945*, Office of the Chief of Naval Operations, NRS 1979-1.

17. Rohwer, *Axis Submarine Successes, 1939–1945*, 86. *Summary of Survivors' Statements, 1941–1945*, Office of the Chief of Naval Operations, NRS 1979-1. Norfolk *Virginian-Pilot*, 22 March 1942. Gasaway, *Grey Wolf, Grey Sea*, 196.

18. Rohwer, *Axis Submarine Successes, 1939–1945*, 86. *Summary of Survivors' Statements, 1941–1945*, Office of the Chief of Naval Operations, NRS 1979-1.

19. Rohwer, *Axis Submarine Successes, 1939–1945*, 86. *Summary of Survivors' Statements, 1941–1945*, Office of the Chief of Naval Operations, NRS 1979-1. Norfolk *Virginian-Pilot*, 21, 23 March 1942. Gasaway, *Grey Wolf, Grey Sea*, 196–98. Moore, *A Careless Word, A Needless Sinking*, 336.

20. Rohwer, *Axis Submarine Successes, 1939–1945*, 86. *Summary of Survivors' Statements, 1941–1945*, Office of the Chief of Naval Operations, NRS 1979-1. Norfolk *Virginian-Pilot*, 22 March 1942. Moore, *A Careless Word, A Needless Sinking*, 79. Standard Oil Company of New Jersey, *Ships of the Esso Fleet in World War II*, 144.

21. Rohwer, *Axis Submarine Successes, 1939–1945*, 85–86.

## Chapter Eight

1. Letter from Lt. Victor M. Merchant, USN (Ret.), dated 2 July 1984, and several subsequent telephone interviews. Log Book of the USS *Dickerson*, DD 157.

2. Letter from Lt. Victor M. Merchant, USN (Ret.), dated 2 July 1984, and several subsequent telephone interviews. Log Book of the USS *Dickerson*, DD 157.

3. Rohwer, *Axis Submarine Successes, 1939–1945*, 83–85.

4. Frank, *The Sea Wolves*, 116.

5. Rohwer, *Axis Submarine Successes, 1939–1945*, 86. *Summary of Survivors' Statements, 1941–1945*, Office of the Chief of Naval Operations, NRS 1979-1. Norfolk *Virginian-Pilot*, 23 March 1942. Moore, *A Careless Word, A Needless Sinking*, 215.

6. Gasaway, *Grey Wolf, Grey Sea*, 199–200.

7. *Summary of Survivors' Statements, 1941–1945*, Office of the Chief of Naval Operations, NRS 1979-1. Norfolk *Virginian-Pilot*, 23 March 1942. Moore, *A Careless Word, A Needless Sinking*, 215.

Gasaway, *Grey Wolf, Grey Sea*, 199–200. Stick, *Graveyard of the Atlantic*, 234.

8. Letter from Lt. Victor M. Merchant, USN (Ret.), dated 2 July 1984, and several subsequent telephone interviews. Log Book of the USS *Dickerson*, DD 157. Action Report, Commanding Officer, USS *Dickerson*, DD 157, to Commander in Chief, U.S. Atlantic Fleet, 29 March 1942. *War Diary, Eastern Sea Frontier*, March 1942, 3: 1–3.

9. Action Report, Commanding Officer, USS *Dickerson*, DD 157, to Commander in Chief, U.S. Atlantic Fleet, 29 March 1942. *Summary of Survivors' Statements, 1941–1945*, Office of the Chief of Naval Operations, NRS 1979-1. Moore, *A Careless Word, A Needless Sinking*, 172.

## Chapter Nine

1. Mason, *U-Boat, The Secret Menace*, 72.
2. Gasaway, *Grey Wolf, Grey Sea*, 201.
3. Ibid., 202.
4. *Summary of Survivors' Statements, 1941–1945*, Office of the Chief of Naval Operations, NRS 1979-1. Norfolk *Virginian-Pilot*, 26 March 1942. Moore, *A Careless Word, A Needless Sinking*, 352. Gasaway, *Grey Wolf, Grey Sea*, 202. Stick, *Graveyard of the Atlantic*, 235–36. Standard Oil Company of New Jersey, *Ships of the Esso Fleet in World War II*, 155–63.
5. Moore, *A Careless Word, A Needless Sinking*, 24–25.
6. Standard Oil Company of New Jersey, *Ships of the Esso Fleet in World War II*, 155–63.
7. Rohwer, *Axis Submarine Successes, 1939–1945*, 87. Gasaway, *Grey Wolf, Grey Sea*, 205–7.
8. *Summary of Survivors' Statements, 1941–1945*, Office of the Chief of Naval Operations, NRS 1979-1. Norfolk *Virginian-Pilot*, 24 March 1942. Moore, *A Careless Word, A Needless Sinking*, 199. Gasaway, *Grey Wolf, Grey Sea*, 205–7.
9. Gasaway, *Grey Wolf, Grey Sea*, 208–9.
10. Norfolk *Virginian-Pilot*, 24 March 1942.
11. Moore, *A Careless Word, A Needless Sinking*, 199. Log Book of the USS *Roper*, DD 147. Series of interviews and correspondence with the *Roper* crew (please see primary sources in the bibliography). *Knoxville News Sentinel*, Van Gilder, 29 November and 6 December 1942.
12. Rohwer, *Axis Submarine Successes, 1939–1945*, 86. Moore, *A Careless Word, A Needless Sinking*, 205. *Summary of Survivors' State-*

*ments, 1941–1945*, Office of the Chief of Naval Operations, NRS 1979-1.

13. Rohwer, *Axis Submarine Successes, 1939–1945*, 87. Moore, *A Careless Word, A Needless Sinking*, 75. *Summary of Survivors' Statements, 1941–1945*, Office of the Chief of Naval Operations, NRS 1979-1. Norfolk *Virginian-Pilot*, 29 March 1942.

14. *War Diary, Eastern Sea Frontier*, March 1942, 1: 1. *War Diaries of the German Submarine Command*, 1939–1945, 129–50.

15. Norfolk *Virginian-Pilot*, 4 April 1942. Moore, *A Careless Word, A Needless Sinking*, 189–90. *Summary of Survivors' Statements, 1941–1945*, Office of the Chief of Naval Operations, NRS 1979-1.

## Chapter Ten

1. Moore, *A Careless Word, A Needless Sinking*, 198. Rohwer, *Axis Submarine Successes, 1939–1945*, 87.

2. Taylor, *Fire on the Beaches*, 130–35. Eds. of *Sea Classics* Magazine, *The Big War of the Little Ships*, 24–28.

3. Rohwer, *Axis Submarine Successes, 1939–1945*, 87. *Kriegstagebuch* (War Diary), *U-123*. Frank, *The Sea Wolves*, 116.

4. Frank, *The Sea Wolves*, 117.

5. Frank, *The Sea Wolves*, 117–19. Taylor, *Fire on the Beaches*, 136–38. *Kriegstagebuch* (War Diary), *U-123*.

6. Taylor, *Fire on the Beaches*, 139–40. Eds of *Sea Classics* Magazine, *The Big War of the Little Ships*, 24–28. *Kriegstagebuch* (War Diary), *U-123*.

## Chapter Eleven

1. Rohwer, *Axis Submarine Successes, 1939–1945*, 87. *War Diary, Eastern Sea Frontier*, March 1942, *Enemy Action Diary Appendix*.

2. Hoyt, *U-boats Offshore*, 107.

3. *War Diary, Eastern Sea Frontier*, March 1942, 2: 3.

4. *War Diary, Eastern Sea Frontier*, March 1942, 2: 6.

5. Showell, *U-Boats under the Swastika*, 48. Taylor, *German Warships of World War II*, 117, 136, 130, 132, 113, 118, 119, 115.

6. Rohwer, *Axis Submarine Successes, 1939–1945*, 88.

7. Ibid., 88. Moore, *A Careless Word, A Needless Sinking*, 280.

8. *War Diary, Eastern Sea Frontier*, April 1942, 2: 1–4. Roscoe, *United States Destroyer Operations in World War II*, 73. Morison, *The Battle of the Atlantic*, 134.

9. *Summary of Survivors' Statements, 1941–1945*, Office of the Chief of Naval Operations, NRS 1979-1.

10. Rohwer, *Axis Submarine Successes, 1939–1945*, 88.

11. Rohwer, *Axis Submarine Successes, 1939–1945*, 88. Moore, *A Careless Word, A Needless Sinking*, 369. Norfolk *Virginian-Pilot*, 7 April 1942.

12. *War Diary, Eastern Sea Frontier*, April 1942, 2: 4.

13. Ibid.

14. Rohwer, *Axis Submarine Successes, 1939–1945*, 88. Moore, *A Careless Word, A Needless Sinking*, 70.

15. Rohwer, *Axis Submarine Successes, 1939–1945*, 88. Moore, *A Careless Word, A Needless Sinking*, 212.

16. *War Diary, Eastern Sea Frontier*, April 1942, 2: 5.

17. Rohwer, *Axis Submarine Successes, 1939–1945*, 88. Moore, *A Careless Word, A Needless Sinking*, 36. *Summary of Survivors' Statements, 1941–1945*, Office of the Chief of Naval Operations, NRS 1979-1.

18. Rohwer, *Axis Submarine Successes, 1939–1945*, 88. Moore, *A Careless Word, A Needless Sinking*, 343. *Summary of Survivors' Statements, 1941–1945*, Office of the Chief of Naval Operations, NRS 1979-1. Norfolk *Virginian-Pilot*, 7 April 1942, *War Diary, Eastern Sea Frontier*, April 1942, 2: 5.

19. Rohwer, *Axis Submarine Successes, 1939–1945*, 88. *Summary of Survivors' Statements, 1941–1945*, Office of the Chief of Naval Operations, NRS 1979-1.

20. Rohwer, *Axis Submarine Successes, 1939–1945*, 89. *Summary of Survivors' Statements, 1941–1945*, Office of the Chief of Naval Operations, NRS 1979-1.

21. Rohwer, *Axis Submarine Successes, 1939–1945*, 89. *Summary of Survivors' Statements, 1941–1945*, Office of the Chief of Naval Operations, NRS 1979-1. Moore, *A Careless Word, A Needless Sinking*, 208. Norfolk *Virginian-Pilot*, 8 April 1942.

22. Rohwer, *Axis Submarine Successes, 1939–1945*, 89. *Summary of Survivors' Statements, 1941–1945*, Office of the Chief of Naval Operations, NRS 1979-1. Moore, *A Careless Word, A Needless Sinking*, 90. Norfolk *Virginian-Pilot*, 8 April 1942.

23. Moore, *A Careless Word, A Needless Sinking*, 90, 208.

24. Rohwer, *Axis Submarine Successes, 1939–1945*, 89. *Summary of Survivors' Statements, 1941–1945*, Office of the Chief of Naval Operations, NRS 1979-1. Moore, *A Careless Word, A Needless Sinking*, 25.

25. Rohwer, *Axis Submarine Successes, 1939–1945*, 89. *Summary of Survivors' Statements, 1941–1945*, Office of the Chief of Naval

Operations, NRS 1979-1. Moore, *A Careless Word, A Needless Sinking*, 89. Norfolk *Virginian-Pilot*, 10 April 1942.

26. Rohwer, *Axis Submarine Successes, 1939–1945*, 89. *Summary of Survivors' Statements, 1941–1945*, Office of the Chief of Naval Operations, NRS 1979-1. Moore, *A Careless Word, A Needless Sinking*, 89.

27. Rohwer, *Axis Submarine Successes, 1939–1945*, 89. *Summary of Survivors' Statements, 1941–1945*, Office of the Chief of Naval Operations, NRS 1979-1.

28. Rohwer, *Axis Submarine Successes, 1939–1945*, 89. *Summary of Survivors' Statements, 1941–1945*, Office of the Chief of Naval Operations, NRS 1979-1. Moore, *A Careless Word, A Needless Sinking*, 275. Norfolk *Virginian-Pilot*, 10 April 1942.

29. *War Diary, Eastern Sea Frontier*, April 1942, 2: 1–8.


## Chapter Twelve

1. Log Book of the USS *Roper*, DD 147. Series of interviews and correspondence with the *Roper* crew (please see primary sources in the bibliography). *Knoxville News Sentinel*, Van Gilder, 29 November and 6 December 1942.

2. *Dictionary of American Naval Fighting Ships, Vol. VI*, Naval History Div., Dept. of the Navy, 157. *History of the USS* Roper *(APD 20)(ex-DD 147)*, Office of Naval Records and History, Ships' Histories Branch, Navy Department.

3. Log Book of the USS *Roper*, DD 147. Series of interviews and correspondence with the *Roper* crew (please see primary sources in the bibliography). *Knoxville News Sentinel*, Van Gilder, 29 November and 6 December 1942. Letter from Commander Task Unit 4.1.2 to Commander Task Force Four, USS *Wilkes*, subject: Report of Escort Operations (EX169), 10–21 February 1942.

4. Log Book of the USS *Roper*, DD 147. Series of interviews and correspondence with the *Roper* crew (please see primary sources in the bibliography). *Knoxville News Sentinel*, Van Gilder, 29 November and 6 December 1942.

5. Log Book of the USS *Roper*, DD 147. Series of interviews and correspondence with the *Roper* crew (please see primary sources in the bibliography). *Knoxville News Sentinel*, Van Gilder, 29 November and 6 December 1942.

6. Office of Naval Intelligence report held under Navy Publications and Printing Service Office microfilm # AR-18-77. This document specifically holds the following: Lt. F. H. Williams,

USNR, Report of 17 April 42 on Disposition of Bodies and Effects; Diaries of *U-85* crewmen Erich Degenkolb and Eugen Ungenthum; and an Anonymous Draft History of the *U-85*.

7. Ibid.

8. Von Der Porten, *The German Navy in World War II*, 199. Mason, *U-boat, The Secret Menace*, 68.

9. Office of Naval Intelligence report held under Navy Publications and Printing Service Office microfilm # AR-18-77. This document specifically holds the following: Lt. F. H. Williams, USNR, Report of 17 April 42 on Disposition of Bodies and Effects; Diaries of *U-85* crewmen Erich Degenkolb and Eugen Ungenthum; and an Anonymous Draft History of the *U-85*.

10. Log Book of the USS *Roper*, DD 147. Series of interviews and correspondence with the *Roper* crew (please see primary sources in the bibliography). *Knoxville News Sentinel*, Van Gilder, 29 November and 6 December 1942. Norfolk *Virginian-Pilot*, 1 April 1942, 3 April 1942, 14 April 1942, and 28 July 1965.

11. Log Book of the USS *Roper*, DD 147. Series of interviews and correspondence with the *Roper* crew (please see primary sources in the bibliography). *Knoxville News Sentinel*, Van Gilder, 29 November and 6 December 1942. Norfolk *Virginian-Pilot*, 1 April 1942, 3 April 1942, 14 April 1942, and 28 July 1965.

12. Taylor, *German Warships of World War II*, 115.

13. Buchheim, *U-boat War*, chap. 6. Roessler, *The U-boat*, 102–9, 350.

14. Buchheim, *U-boat War*, chap. 6, 4th page.

15. Showell, *U-boats under the Swastika*, 99.

16. Office of Naval Intelligence report held under Navy Publications and Printing Service Office microfilm # AR-18-77. This document specifically holds the following: Lt. F. H. Williams, USNR, Report of 17 April 42 on Disposition of Bodies and Effects; Diaries of *U-85* crewmen Erich Degenkolb and Eugen Ungenthum; and an Anonymous Draft History of the *U-85*.

17. Rohwer, *Axis Submarine Successes, 1939–1945*, 89.

18. Besides the eyewitness accounts of the *Roper* crewmen listed in the primary sources, information concerning the sinking of the *U-85* is taken from Office of Naval Intelligence reports and documentation now held under Navy Publications and Printing Service Office microfilm # AR-18-77. This includes action reports, ship histories, recommendations for citations, and other official letters and documents pertaining to the

*Roper* and the *U-85*. The wreck of the *U-85* was also dived on and inspected by the author during 1981–82 to verify damage done to the U-boat, specifically the report by Harry Heyman and others aboard the *Roper* of the results of the hit by the gun crew. The *U-85* was found to have been hit by Heyman's shell with a penetration just abaft the conning tower.

19. Rohwer, *Axis Submarine Successes, 1939–1945*, 90.
20. Office of Naval Intelligence report held under Navy Publications of Printing Service Office microfilm # AR-18-77. This document specifically holds the following: Lt. F. H. Williams, USNR, Report of 17 April 42 on Disposition of Bodies and Effects; Diaries of *U-85* crewmen Erich Degenkolb and Eugen Ungenthum; and an Anonymous Draft History of the *U-85*.
21. A visit to the National Cemetery in Hampton was made by the author in 1984 to verify this.

## Chapter Thirteen

1. *War Diary, Eastern Sea Frontier*, April 1942, 2: 2.
2. Ibid., 7: 3.
3. Morison, *The Battle of the Atlantic*, 131.
4. Mellor, *Sank Same*, 25, 144–201. Hughes and Costello, *The Battle of the Atlantic*, 200. Morison, *The Two-Ocean War*, 131. Townsend, article in *The Big War of the Little Ships* by the editors of *Sea Classics* magazine, 79–83.
5. Mellor, *Sank Same*, 25–143.
6. Morison, *The Two-Ocean War*, 127.
7. Morison, *The Two-Ocean War*, 124–25. Hughes and Costello, *The Battle of the Atlantic*, 200.
8. Morison, *The Two-Ocean War*, 125–26. Hughes and Costello, *The Battle of the Atlantic*, 200. *War Diary, Eastern Sea Frontier*, May 1942, 2: 1–8.
9. *War Diary, Eastern Sea Frontier*, April 1942.
10. Ibid., 7: 4.
11. *War Diary, Eastern Sea Frontier*, April 1942, 7: 4. Letter of 10 April 1942 from Commander, Eastern Sea Frontier to the Secretary of the Navy, Subject: Submarine Activities on the Atlantic Coast.
12. *War Diary, Eastern Sea Frontier*, April 1942, vol. 3.
13. *War Diary, Eastern Sea Frontier*, April 1942, vol. 3. Karig, Burton, and Freeland, *Battle Report—The Atlantic War*, 92–93.
14. *War Diary, BdU*, 1–15 April 1942.
15. Rohwer, *Axis Submarine Successes, 1939–1945*, 89. *Summary of*

*Survivors' Statements, 1941–1945*, Office of the Chief of Naval Operations, NRS 1979-1. Moore, *A Careless Word, A Needless Sinking*, 112.

16. Rohwer, *Axis Submarine Successes, 1939–1945*, 89. *Summary of Survivors' Statements, 1941–1945*, Office of the Chief of Naval Operations, NRS 1979-1. Moore, *A Careless Word, A Needless Sinking*, 359.

17. *War Diary, Eastern Sea Frontier*, April 1942, 7: 1–2. Rohwer, *Axis Submarine Successes, 1939–1945*, 89. *Summary of Survivors' Statements, 1941–1945*, Office of the Chief of Naval Operations, NRS 1979-1. Norfolk *Virginian-Pilot*, 14 April 1942.

18. *Summary of Survivors' Statements, 1941–1945*, Office of the Chief of Naval Operations, NRS 1979-1.

19. Rohwer, *Axis Submarine Successes, 1939–1945*, 90. *Summary of Survivors' Statements, 1941–1945*, Office of the Chief of Naval Operations, NRS 1979-1.

20. Rohwer, *Axis Submarine Successes, 1939–1945*, 90. *Summary of Survivors' Statements, 1941–1945*, Office of the Chief of Naval Operations, NRS 1979-1. Moore, *A Careless Word, A Needless Sinking*, 171.

21. *War Diary, BdU*, 1–15 April 1942.

22. Rohwer, *Axis Submarine Successes, 1939–1945*, 90. *Summary of Survivors' Statements, 1941–1945*, Office of the Chief of Naval Operations, NRS 1979-1.

23. Rohwer, *Axis Submarine Successes, 1939–1945*, 90. *Summary of Survivors' Statements, 1941–1945*, Office of the Chief of Naval Operations, NRS 1979-1. Norfolk *Virginian-Pilot*, 28 April 1942.

24. Rohwer, *Axis Submarine Successes, 1939–1945*, 90. *Summary of Survivors' Statements, 1941–1945*, Office of the Chief of Naval Operations, NRS 1979-1. Norfolk *Virginian-Pilot*, 24 April 1942. Moore, *A Careless Word, A Needless Sinking*, 342.

## Chapter Fourteen

1. Rohwer, *Axis Submarine Successes, 1939–1945*, 90. Taylor, *German Warships of World War II*, 118.

2. Rohwer, *Axis Submarine Successes, 1939–1945*, 25, 27, 28, 50, 51, 62, 66, 68.

3. Botting, *The U-boats*, 120.

4. Botting, *The U-boats*, 162. Showell, *U-boats under the Swastika*, 113.

5. *War Diary, Eastern Sea Frontier*, April 1942, vol. 5. *Summary of*

*Survivors' Statements, 1941–1945,* Office of the Chief of Naval Operations, NRS 1979-1.

6. Doenitz, *Memoirs: Ten Years and Twenty Days,* 59.

7. Rohwer, *Axis Submarine Successes, 1939–1945,* 90–91. *Summary of Survivors' Statements, 1941–1945,* Office of the Chief of Naval Operations, NRS 1979-1. Moore, *A Careless Word, A Needless Sinking,* 265. Norfolk *Virginian-Pilot,* 3 May 1942.

8. Rohwer, *Axis Submarine Successes, 1939–1945,* 90–91. *Summary of Survivors' Statements, 1941–1945,* Office of the Chief of Naval Operations, NRS 1979-1. Moore, *A Careless Word, A Needless Sinking,* 265. Norfolk *Virginian-Pilot,* 3 May 1942.

9. Rohwer, *Axis Submarine Successes, 1939–1945,* 91. *Summary of Survivors' Statements, 1941–1945,* Office of the Chief of Naval Operations, NRS 1979-1.

10. Rohwer, *Axis Submarine Successes, 1939–1945,* 91. *Summary of Survivors' Statements, 1941–1945,* Office of the Chief of Naval Operations, NRS 1979-1.

11. Rohwer, *Axis Submarine Successes, 1939–1945,* 91. *Summary of Survivors' Statements, 1941–1945,* Office of the Chief of Naval Operations, NRS 1979-1. Norfolk *Virginian-Pilot,* 10 May 1942.

12. Rohwer, *Axis Submarine Successes. 1939–1945,* 91. *Summary of Survivors' Statements, 1941–1945,* Office of the Chief of Naval Operations, NRS 1979-1.

13. Rohwer, *Axis Submarine Successes, 1939–1945,* 91. Moore, *A Careless Word, A Needless Sinking,* 265. War Log of the USCG Cutter *Calypso* (WPC-104).

14. Rohwer, *Axis Submarine Successes, 1939–1945,* 91. *Summary of Survivors' Statements, 1941–1945,* Office of the Chief of Naval Operations, NRS 1979-1. Norfolk *Virginian-Pilot,* 26 April 1942. Moore, *A Careless Word, A Needless Sinking,* 252.

15. Rohwer, *Axis Submarine Successes, 1939–1945,* 92. *Summary of Survivors' Statements, 1941–1945,* Office of the Chief of Naval Operations, NRS 1979-1.

16. Waters, *Bloody Winter,* 269–70. Rohwer, *Axis Submarine Successes, 1939–1945,* 92.

17. *War Diary, Eastern Sea Frontier,* April 1942, 7: 5–6.

## Chapter Fifteen

1. Correspondence with Hellmut Rathke (please see primary sources in the bibliography). Office of Naval Intelligence interrogations of the *U-352*'s crew in the Navy Publications and Printing Office Diazo microfilm AR-35-77.

2. War Log, the United States Coast Guard Cutter *Icarus* (WPC 110). Correspondence and interviews with John G. Bruce (please see primary sources in the bibliography). *Life* Magazine, 14 December 1942.

3. Correspondence with Hellmut Rathke (please see primary sources in the bibliography). Navy Publications and Printing Office Diazo microfilm AR-35-77. Office of the Chief of Naval Operations, NRS 1979-1, Summary of Statements by the Master of SS *"Freden"*, Swedish cargo vessel of 1172 gross tons, A.N.D. Smith Co., Stockholm, owners.

4. Correspondence with Hellmut Rathke (please see primary sources in the bibliography). Navy Publications and Printing Office Diazo microfilm AR-35-77.

5. Series of interviews and correspondence with John Bruce (please see primary sources in the bibliography).

6. Correspondence and interviews with John Bruce and Hellmut Rathke (please see primary sources in the bibliography). Office of Naval Intelligence reports in the Navy Publications and Printing Office Diazo microfilm AR-35-77. Report on the sinking of the *U-352* from the Commandant, Sixth Naval District to the Chief of Naval Operations, 11 May 1942. *War Diary, Eastern Sea Frontier*, May 1942, 3: 8–14.

7. Correspondence and interviews with John Bruce and Hellmut Rathke (please see primary sources in the bibliography). Office of Naval Intelligence reports in the Navy Publications and Printing Office Diazo microfilm AR-35-77. Report on the sinking of the *U-352* from the Commandant, Sixth Naval District to the Chief of Naval Operations, 11 May 1942. *War Diary, Eastern Sea Frontier*, May 1942, 3: 8–14. Information on the sinking and the resulting condition of the *U-352* was confirmed by a series of dives by the author on the wreck in 1975–76.

8. Correspondence and interviews with John Bruce and Hellmut Rathke (please see primary sources in the bibliography). Office of Naval Intelligence reports in the Navy Publications and Printing Office Diazo microfilm AR-35-77. Report on the sinking of the *U-352* from the Commandant, Sixth Naval District to the Chief of Naval Operations, 11 May 1942. *War Diary, Eastern Sea Frontier*, May 1942, 3: 8–14.

9. Correspondence and interviews with John Bruce and Hellmut Rathke (please see primary sources in the bibliography). Office of Naval Intelligence reports in the Navy Publications and Printing Office Diazo microfilm AR-35-77. Report on the sink-

ing of the *U-352* from the Commandant, Sixth Naval District to the Chief of Naval Operations, 11 May 1942. *War Diary, Eastern Sea Frontier,* May 1942, 3: 8–14.

10. Correspondence and interviews with John Bruce and Hellmut Rathke (please see primary sources in the bibliography). Office of Naval Intelligence reports in the Navy Publications and Printing Office Diazo microfilm AR-35-77. Report on the sinking of the *U-352* from the Commandant, Sixth Naval District to the Chief of Naval Operations, 11 May 1942. *War Diary, Eastern Sea Frontier,* May 1942, 3: 8–14.

## Chapter Sixteen

1. Hughes and Costello, *The Battle of the Atlantic,* 196, 201.
2. Naisawald, *In Some Foreign Field,* 13.
3. Ibid., 17.
4. *Eastern Sea Frontier Enemy Action Diary,* 11 April 1942.
5. Action Report, USS SEMMES, Serial: 038, *Report of Collision Between SEMMES and HMS SENATEUR DUHAMEL on 6 May 1942,* 18 May 1942.
6. War Log, USCGC *Dione* (WPC 107). Correspondence and interviews with members of the crew of the *Dione* (please see primary sources in the bibliography).
7. Interview with Rear Admiral J. Alger, Jr. (Ret.), Pompano Beach, Florida, April 1985.
8. Naisawald, *In Some Foreign Field,* 19–20.
9. Ibid., 21–25.
10. Rohwer, *Axis Submarine Successes, 1939–1945,* 69.
11. Hoyt, *U-boats Offshore,* 120. Naisawald, *In Some Foreign Field,* 31, 35.
12. Hoyt, *U-boats Offshore,* 121–22. Naisawald, *In Some Foreign Field,* 36–39.
13. Naisawald, *In Some Foreign Field,* 41–43.
14. Ibid., 43–44.
15. Ibid., 45–47.
16. Naisawald, *In Some Foreign Field,* 47. *Eastern Sea Frontier Enemy Action Diary,* 16 May 1942.
17. Naisawald, *In Some Foreign Field,* 48–49.

## Chapter Seventeen

1. Doenitz, *Memoirs: Ten Years and Twenty Days,* 67–69.
2. Rohwer, *Axis Submarine Successes, 1939–1945,* 92. *Summary of*

*Survivors' Statements, 1941–1945,* Office of the Chief of Naval Operations, NRS 1979-1. Hoyt, *U-boats Offshore,* 127. *Eastern Sea Frontier Enemy Action Diary,* 1 May 1942. Hughes and Costello, *The Battle of the Atlantic,* 197.

3. Rohwer, *Axis Submarine Successes, 1939–1945,* 92. *Summary of Survivors' Statements, 1941–1945,* Office of the Chief of Naval Operations, NRS 1979-1.

4. Rohwer, *Axis Submarine Successes, 1939–1945,* 92. *Summary of Survivors' Statements, 1941–1945,* Office of the Chief of Naval Operations, NRS 1979-1. Norfolk *Virginian-Pilot,* 8 May 1942.

5. Rohwer, *Axis Submarine Successes, 1939–1945,* 92. *Summary of Survivors' Statements, 1941–1945,* Office of the Chief of Naval Operations, NRS 1979-1.

6. Rohwer, *Axis Submarine Successes, 1939–1945,* 92. *Summary of Survivors' Statements, 1941–1945,* Office of the Chief of Naval Operations, NRS 1979-1.

7. Rohwer, *Axis Submarine Successes, 1939–1945,* 93. *Summary of Survivors' Statements, 1941–1945,* Office of the Chief of Naval Operations, NRS 1979-1.

8. Rohwer, *Axis Submarine Successes, 1939–1945,* 93. *Summary of Survivors' Statements, 1941–1945,* Office of the Chief of Naval Operations, NRS 1979-1.

9. Cremer, *U-boat Commander,* xi–xii.

10. Ibid., 31.

11. Rohwer, *Axis Submarine Successes, 1939–1945,* 74–76.

12. Noli, *The Admiral's Wolf Pack,* 154–55.

13. Ibid., 157–59.

14. Cremer, *U-boat Commander,* 62.

15. Cremer, *U-boat Commander,* 63–65. Noli, *The Admiral's Wolf Pack,* 159–62.

16. Cremer, *U-boat Commander,* 65.

17. Ibid., 66.

18. Ibid., 68–69.

19. Rohwer, *Axis Submarine Successes, 1939–1945,* 93. *Summary of Survivors' Statements, 1941–1945,* Office of the Chief of Naval Operations, NRS 1979-1. Cremer, *U-boat Commander,* 70.

20. Rohwer, *Axis Submarine Successes, 1939–1945,* 93. *Summary of Survivors' Statements, 1941–1945,* Office of the Chief of Naval Operations, NRS 1979-1.

21. Rohwer, *Axis Submarine Successes, 1939–1945,* 93. *Summary of Survivors' Statements, 1941–1945,* Office of the Chief of Naval Operations, NRS 1979-1. Cremer, *U-boat Commander,* 71–72. Moore, *A Careless Word, A Needless Sinking,* 121.

22. Cremer, *U-boat Commander*, 72–74.
23. Cremer, *U-boat Commander*, 74. *Eastern Sea Frontier Patrol Log, Sixth Naval District*, 7 May 1942. Morison, *The Battle of the Atlantic*, 139.
24. Cremer, *U-boat Commander*, 75.
25. Mellor, *Sank Same*, 161–63.
26. Rohwer, *Axis Submarine Successes, 1939–1945*, 94. *Summary of Survivors' Statements, 1941–1945*, Office of the Chief of Naval Operations, NRS 1979-1. Cremer, *U-boat Commander*, 76.
27. Cremer, *U-boat Commander*, 82–213.
28. Rohwer, *Axis Submarine Successes, 1939–1945*, 94. *Summary of Survivors' Statements, 1941–1945*, Office of the Chief of Naval Operations, NRS 1979-1. Moore, *A Careless Word, A Needless Sinking*, 206–7.
29. Rohwer, *Axis Submarine Successes, 1939–1945*, 94. *Summary of Survivors' Statements, 1941–1945*, Office of the Chief of Naval Operations, NRS 1979-1.
30. Rohwer, *Axis Submarine Successes, 1939–1945*, 95. *Summary of Survivors' Statements, 1941–1945*, Office of the Chief of Naval Operations, NRS 1979-1.
31. Rohwer, *Axis Submarine Successes, 1939–1945*, 96. *Summary of Survivors' Statements, 1941–1945*, Office of the Chief of Naval Operations, NRS 1979-1. Norfolk *Virginian-Pilot*, 23 May 1942.
32. Morison, *The Two-Ocean War*, 113. Doenitz, *Memoirs: Ten Years and Twenty Days*, 69. Hughes and Costello, *The Battle of the Atlantic*, 202–3.

## Chapter Eighteen

1. *War Diary, BdU*, 6 May 1942.
2. Rohwer, *Axis Submarine Successes, 1939–1945*, 93. *Summary of Survivors' Statements, 1941–1945*, Office of the Chief of Naval Operations, NRS 1979-1. Moore, *A Careless Word, A Needless Sinking*, 204.
3. Rohwer, *Axis Submarine Successes, 1939–1945*, 93. *Summary of Survivors' Statements, 1941–1945*, Office of the Chief of Naval Operations, NRS 1979-1. Moore, *A Careless Word, A Needless Sinking*, 198.
4. Rohwer, *Axis Submarine Successes, 1939–1945*, 93. *Summary of Survivors' Statements, 1941–1945*, Office of the Chief of Naval Operations, NRS 1979-1. Moore, *A Careless Word, A Needless Sinking*, 161.
5. Rohwer, *Axis Submarine Successes, 1939–1945*, 93. *Summary of*

*Survivors' Statements, 1941–1945,* Office of the Chief of Naval Operations, NRS 1979-1. Moore, *A Careless Word, A Needless Sinking,* 10.

6. Rohwer, *Axis Submarine Successes, 1939–1945,* 93. *Summary of Survivors' Statements, 1941–1945,* Office of the Chief of Naval Operations, NRS 1979-1. Moore, *A Careless Word, A Needless Sinking,* 10.

7. Rohwer, *Axis Submarine Successes, 1939–1945,* 94. *Summary of Survivors' Statements, 1941–1945,* Office of the Chief of Naval Operations, NRS 1979-1.

8. Rohwer, *Axis Submarine Successes, 1939–1945,* 92. *Summary of Survivors' Statements, 1941–1945,* Office of the Chief of Naval Operations, NRS 1979-1.

9. Rohwer, *Axis Submarine Successes, 1939–1945,* 94. *Summary of Survivors' Statements, 1941–1945,* Office of the Chief of Naval Operations, NRS 1979-1. Moore, *A Careless Word, A Needless Sinking,* 342.

10. *War Diary, BdU,* 12 May 1942.

11. Rohwer, *Axis Submarine Successes, 1939–1945,* 95. *Summary of Survivors' Statements, 1941–1945,* Office of the Chief of Naval Operations, NRS 1979-1. Moore, *A Careless Word, A Needless Sinking,* 285. The *Virginian-Pilot,* 16 May 1942.

12. Rohwer, *Axis Submarine Successes, 1939–1945,* 95. *Summary of Survivors' Statements, 1941–1945,* Office of the Chief of Naval Operations, NRS 1979-1. Moore, *A Careless Word, A Needless Sinking,* 113–14.

13. Rohwer, *Axis Submarine Successes, 1939–1945,* 95. *Summary of Survivors' Statements, 1941–1945,* Office of the Chief of Naval Operations, NRS 1979-1. Moore, *A Careless Word, A Needless Sinking,* 70–71.

14. Rohwer, *Axis Submarine Successes, 1939–1945,* 96. *Summary of Survivors' Statements, 1941–1945,* Office of the Chief of Naval Operations, NRS 1979-1.

15. *War Diary, BdU,* 15 May 1942.

16. Rohwer, *Axis Submarine Successes, 1939–1945,* 96. *Summary of Survivors' Statements, 1941–1945,* Office of the Chief of Naval Operations, NRS 1979-1. Moore, *A Careless Word, A Needless Sinking,* 388.

17. Rohwer, *Axis Submarine Successes, 1939–1945,* 96. *Summary of Survivors' Statements, 1941–1945,* Office of the Chief of Naval Operations, NRS 1979-1. Moore, *A Careless Word, A Needless Sinking,* 385.

18. Rohwer, *Axis Submarine Successes, 1939–1945,* 96. *Summary of*

*Survivors' Statements, 1941–1945,* Office of the Chief of Naval Operations, NRS 1979-1. Moore, *A Careless Word, A Needless Sinking,* 113.

19. Rohwer, *Axis Submarine Successes, 1939–1945,* 97. *Summary of Survivors' Statements, 1941–1945,* Office of the Chief of Naval Operations, NRS 1979-1. Moore, *A Careless Word, A Needless Sinking,* 113. Norfolk *Virginian-Pilot,* 28 May 1942.

20. Rohwer, *Axis Submarine Successes, 1939–1945,* 97. *Summary of Survivors' Statements, 1941–1945,* Office of the Chief of Naval Operations, NRS 1979-1.

21. Rohwer, *Axis Submarine Successes, 1939–1945,* 96. *Summary of Survivors' Statements, 1941–1945,* Office of the Chief of Naval Operations, NRS 1979-1. Moore, *A Careless Word, A Needless Sinking,* 120.

22. *War Diary, BdU,* 16–31 May 1942.

## Chapter Nineteen

1. *War Diary, Eastern Sea Frontier,* May 1942, 3: 1–3.

2. Ibid., 3: 4–6.

3. Ibid., 3: 6–7.

4. Letter from Anthony Florence, officer, USS *Alabaster,* to the author dated 20 March 1985.

5. Rohwer, *Axis Submarine Successes, 1939–1945,* 95. *Summary of Survivors' Statements, 1941–1945,* Office of the Chief of Naval Operations, NRS 1979-1.

6. Rohwer, *Axis Submarine Successes, 1939–1945,* 96, 98. *Summary of Survivors' Statements, 1941–1945,* Office of the Chief of Naval Operations, NRS 1979-1.

7. Rohwer, *Axis Submarine Successes, 1939–1945,* 98. *Summary of Survivors' Statements, 1941–1945,* Office of the Chief of Naval Operations, NRS 1979-1.

8. Rohwer, *Axis Submarine Successes, 1939–1945,* 99. *Summary of Survivors' Statements, 1941–1945,* Office of the Chief of Naval Operations, NRS 1979-1. Standard Oil Company of New Jersey, *Ships of the Esso Fleet in World War II,* 221–25. *War Diary, BdU,* 26 May 1942.

9. *War Diary, Eastern Sea Frontier,* 4: 1–10.

10. Rawlings, *Saturday Evening Post,* 18 July 1942. Correspondence and interviews with the crew of the *Dione* (please see primary sources in the bibliography).

11. Rawlings, *Saturday Evening Post,* 18 July 1942. Correspondence

and interviews with the crew of the *Dione* (please see primary sources in the bibliography).

12. Rawlings, *Saturday Evening Post*, 18 July 1942. Correspondence and interviews with the crew of the *Dione* (please see primary sources in the bibliography).

13. Rawlings, *Saturday Evening Post*, 18 July 1942. Correspondence and interviews with the crew of the *Dione* (please see primary sources in the bibliography).

14. Rawlings, *Saturday Evening Post*, 18 July 1942 (in a bow to wartime censorship, *Diana* was Rawlings's name for the *Dione* in his story). Correspondence and interviews with the crew of the *Dione* (please see primary sources in the bibliography).

15. Rawlings, *Saturday Evening Post*, 18 July 1942. Correspondence and interviews with the crew of the *Dione* (please see primary sources in the bibliography).

16. *War Diary, Eastern Sea Frontier*, May 1942, 5: 1–2.

17. *War Diary, Eastern Sea Frontier*, May 1942, 5: 3–6. War Log of the USCGC *Dione* (WPC 107). Letters and interviews with members of the crew of the *Dione* (please see primary sources in the bibliography).

18. Rawlings, *Saturday Evening Post*, 18 July 1942. Correspondence and interviews with members of the crew of the *Dione* (please see primary sources in the bibliography).

## Chapter Twenty

1. *War Diary, Eastern Sea Frontier*, May 1942, 1: 1.

2. *War Diary, Eastern Sea Frontier*, May 1942, 1: 1. Doenitz, *Memoirs: Ten Years and Twenty Days*, 69.

3. Noli, *The Admiral's Wolf Pack*, 179. *War Diary, BdU*, 1 January 1942 through 31 March 1942, 145.

4. Noli, *The Admiral's Wolf Pack*, 129.

5. Ibid., 129–30.

6. Ibid., 130.

7. Ibid., 130.

8. Frank, *The Sea Wolves*, 64–66. Botting and the eds. of Time-Life, *The Sea Farers, The U-boats*, 111–12.

9. Frank, *The Sea Wolves*, 119–20, 126–30. Showell, *U-boats under the Swastika*, 85–91. Noli, *The Admiral's Wolf Pack*, 182–83.

10. Doenitz, *Memoirs: Ten Years and Twenty Days*, 68–69.

11. Offley, article in the *Ledger Star* of Norfolk, Portsmouth, Virginia Beach, Chesapeake, Suffolk, VA, 7 July 1982.

12. Taylor, *Fire on the Beaches*, 179. Rohwer, *Axis Submarine Successes, 1939–1945*, 73, 83–84.
13. Offley, article in the *Ledger Star* of Norfolk, Portsmouth, Virginia Beach, Chesapeake, Suffolk, VA, 7 July 1982.
14. Navy Department, Office of the Chief of Naval Operations, *Report of Interrogation of Survivors of U-701 Sunk by U.S. Army Attack Bomber No. 9-29-322, Unit 296 B.S. On July 7, 1942*, 22.
15. Rohwer, *Axis Submarine Successes, 1939–1945*, 100. *Summary of Survivors' Statements, 1941–1945*, Office of the Chief of Naval Operations, NRS 1979-1. Moore, *A Careless Word, A Needless Sinking*, 301. Norfolk *Virginian-Pilot*, 12 June 1942.
16. Rohwer, *Axis Submarine Successes, 1939–1945*, 100. *Summary of Survivors' Statements, 1941–1945*, Office of the Chief of Naval Operations, NRS 1979-1.
17. Rohwer, *Axis Submarine Successes, 1939–1945*, 100. *Summary of Survivors' Statements, 1941–1945*, Office of the Chief of Naval Operations, NRS 1979-1. Moore, *A Careless Word, A Needless Sinking*, 2, 30. Norfolk *Virginian-Pilot*, 11 June 1942.
18. Taylor, *Fire on the Beaches*, 177–78.
19. *War Diary, BdU*, 12 May 1942. Navy Department, Office of the Chief of Naval Operations, *Report of Interrogation of Survivors of U-701 Sunk by U.S. Army Attack Bomber No. 9-29-322, Unit 296 B.S. On July 7, 1942*, 9. Offley, article in the *Ledger Star* of Norfolk, Portsmouth, Virginia Beach, Chesapeake, Suffolk, VA, 7 July 1982.
20. Offley, article in the *Ledger Star* of Norfolk, Portsmouth, Virginia Beach, Chesapeake, Suffolk, VA, 7 July 1982.
21. Offley, article in the *Ledger Star* of Norfolk, Portsmouth, Virginia Beach, Chesapeake, Suffolk, VA, 8 July 1982.
22. Ibid.
23. Ibid.

## Chapter Twenty-one

1. *War Diary, Eastern Sea Frontier*, June 1942, 6: 1. *War Diary, BdU*, 26 May 1942 and 13 June 1942.
2. *War Diary, Eastern Sea Frontier*, June 1942, 6: 1–4.
3. Ibid., 5–6.
4. *War Diary, Eastern Sea Frontier*, June 1942, 6: 6. Hoyt, *U-boats Offshore*, 164.
5. *War Diary, Eastern Sea Frontier*, June 1942, 6: 6. Hoyt, *U-boats Offshore*, 164.

6. *War Diary, Eastern Sea Frontier*, June 1942, 6: 7. Hoyt, *U-boats Offshore*, 164.

7. *War Diary, Eastern Sea Frontier*, June 1942, 6: 7.

8. Ibid., 8–9.

9. Ibid., 10.

10. Hoyt, *U-boats Offshore*, 166–68.

11. Ibid.

12. Ibid.

## Chapter Twenty-two

1. War Log, USCGC *Dione* (WPC 107). Correspondence and interviews with members of the crew of the *Dione* (please see primary sources in the bibliography). *War Diary, Eastern Sea Frontier*, June 1942, 2: 3.

2. *War Diary, Eastern Sea Frontier*, June 1942, 4: 1–3. *Summary of Survivors' Statements, 1941–1945*, Office of the Chief of Naval Operations, NRS-1979-1. Moore, *A Careless Word, A Needless Sinking*, 112. Standard Oil Company of New Jersey, *Ships of the Esso Fleet in World War II*, 288–91.

3. War Log, USCGC *Dione* (WPC 107). Correspondence and interviews with members of the crew of the *Dione* (please see primary sources in the bibliography). *War Diary, Eastern Sea Frontier*, June 1942, 2: 3–6. *Summary of Survivors' Statements, 1941–1945*, Office of the Chief of Naval Operations, NRS 1979-1. Moore, *A Careless Word, A Needless Sinking*, 351–52, 381. Norfolk *Virginian-Pilot*, 17, 21 June 1942.

4. *War Diary, Eastern Sea Frontier*, June 1942, 2: 10–11.

5. *War Diary, Eastern Sea Frontier*, June 1942, 2: 11. *Summary of Survivors' Statements, 1941–1945*, Office of the Chief of Naval Operations, NRS 1979-1. Moore, *A Careless Word, A Needless Sinking*, 255. Norfolk *Virginian-Pilot*, 23 June 1942.

6. Mercey and Grove, *Sea, Surf and Hell, The U.S. Coast Guard in World War II*, 67.

7. Lodge, article in Norfolk *Virginian-Pilot*, 23 June 1942.

8. *War Diary, Eastern Sea Frontier*, June 1942, 2: 13–15.

9. Rohwer, *Axis Submarine Successes, 1939–1945*, 104. *War Diary, Eastern Sea Frontier*, June 1942, 4: 4–5. *Summary of Survivors' Statements, 1941–1945*, Office of the Chief of Naval Operations, NRS 1979-1. Moore, *A Careless Word, A Needless Sinking*, 50. Norfolk *Virginian-Pilot*, 24 June 1942.

10. Rohwer, *Axis Submarine Successes, 1939–1945*, 105. *War Diary, Eastern Sea Frontier*, June 1942, 4: 6. *Summary of Survivors' State-*

ments, *1941–1945,* Office of the Chief of Naval Operations, NRS 1979-1. Moore, *A Careless Word, A Needless Sinking,* 157.

11. Norfolk *Virginian-Pilot,* 5 June 1942.

12. Huges and Costello, *The Battle of the Atlantic,* 203–4; Morison, *The Two-Ocean War,* 135–36.

13. *War Diary, Eastern Sea Frontier,* June 1942, 3: 1–9.

## Chapter Twenty-three

1. *War Diary, Eastern Sea Frontier,* June 1942, 5: 1–6. Headquarters, Fifth Naval District *Report of Shellfire Attack on YP-389, 5–8 Miles N.E. of Buoy #4, Hatteras Mine Area, June 19, 1942, at 0220 EWT,* dated 30 June 1942.

2. *War Diary, Eastern Sea Frontier,* June 1942, 5: 1–6. Headquarters, Fifth Naval District *Report of Shellfire Attack on YP-389, 5–8 Miles N.E. of Buoy #4, Hatteras Mine Area, June 19, 1942, at 0220 EWT,* dated 30 June 1942.

3. *War Diary, Eastern Sea Frontier,* June 1942, 5: 1–6. Headquarters, Fifth Naval District *Report of Shellfire Attack on YP-389, 5–8 Miles N.E. of Buoy #4, Hatteras Mine Area, June 19, 1942, at 0220 EWT,* dated 30 June 1942.

4. *War Diary, Eastern Sea Frontier,* June 1942, 5: 1–6. Headquarters, Fifth Naval District *Report of Shellfire Attack on YP-389, 5–8 Miles N.E. of Buoy #4, Hatteras Mine Area, June 19, 1942, at 0220 EWT,* dated 30 June 1942.

5. Offley, article in the *Ledger-Star* of Norfolk, Portsmouth, Virginia Beach, Chesapeake, Suffolk, VA., 8 July 1982. Navy Department, Office of the Chief of Naval Operations, *Report of Interrogation of Survivors of U-701 Sunk by U.S. Army Attack Bomber No. 9-29-322, Unit 296 B.S. On July 7, 1942.*

6. Headquarters, Fifth Naval District, *Prisoners of War, Information Obtained From Seven Male German Prisoners of War Captured July 9, 1942,* 14 July 1942.

7. Offley, article in the *Ledger-Star* of Norfolk, Portsmouth, Virginia Beach, Chesapeake, Suffolk, VA., 8 July 1982. Navy Department, Office of the Chief of Naval Operations, *Report of Interrogation of Survivors of U-701 Sunk by U.S. Army Attack Bomber No. 9-29-322, Unit 296 B.S. On July 7, 1942. War Diary, Eastern Sea Frontier,* July 1942, vol. 9.

8. *War Diary, Eastern Sea Frontier,* June 1942, 5: 1–6. Headquarters, Fifth Naval District *Report of Shellfire Attack on YP-389, 5–8 Miles N.E. of Buoy #4, Hatteras Mine Area, June 19, 1942, at 0220 EWT,* dated 30 June 1942. Offley, article in the *Ledger-Star* of

Norfolk, Portsmouth, Virginia Beach, Chesapeake, Suffolk, VA., 8 July 1982. Navy Department, Office of the Chief of Naval Operations, *Report of Interrogation of Survivors of U-701 Sunk by U.S. Army Attack Bomber No. 9-29-322, Unit 296 B.S. On July 7, 1942. War Diary, Eastern Sea Frontier,* July 1942, vol. 9. Headquarters, Fifth Naval District, *Prisoners of War, Information Obtained From Seven Male German Prisoners of War Captured July 9, 1942,* 14 July 1942.

## Chapter Twenty-four

1. War Log, USCGC *Dione* (WPC 107). Correspondence and interviews with members of the crew of the *Dione* (please see primary sources in the bibliography).
2. Rohwer, *Axis Submarine Successes, 1939–1945,* 105. *Summary of Survivors' Statements, 1941–1945,* Office of the Chief of Naval Operations, NRS 1979-1. Norfolk *Virginian-Pilot,* 23, 24 June 1942.
3. Rohwer, *Axis Submarine Successes, 1939–1945,* 105.
4. War Log, USCGC *Dione* (WPC 107). Correspondence and interviews with members of the crew of the *Dione* (please see primary sources in the bibliography). Rohwer, *Axis Submarine Successes, 1939–1945,* 105. *Summary of Survivors' Statements, 1941–1945,* Office of the Chief of Naval Operations, NRS 1979-1.
5. War Log, USCGC *Dione* (WPC 107). Correspondence and interviews with members of the crew of the *Dione* (please see primary sources in the bibliography).

## Chapter Twenty-five

1. Rohwer, *Axis Submarine Successes, 1939–1945,* 106. *Summary of Survivors' Statements, 1941–1945,* Office of the Chief of Naval Operations, NRS 1979-1.
2. Offley, article in the *Ledger-Star* of Norfolk, Portsmouth, Virginia Beach, Chesapeake, Suffolk, VA., 8–10 July 1982. Navy Department, Office of the Chief of Naval Operations, *Report of Interrogation of Survivors of U-701 Sunk by U.S. Army Attack Bomber No. 9-29-322, Unit 296 B.S. On July 7, 1942.*
3. Offley, article in the *Ledger-Star* of Norfolk, Portsmouth, Virginia Beach, Chesapeake, Suffolk, VA., 8–10 July 1982. Navy Department, Office of the Chief of Naval Operations, *Report of*

*Interrogation of Survivors of U-701 Sunk by U.S. Army Attack Bomber No. 9-29-322, Unit 296 B.S. On July 7, 1942.*

4. Offley, article in the *Ledger-Star* of Norfolk, Portsmouth, Virginia Beach, Chesapeake, Suffolk, VA., 8–10 July 1982. Navy Department, Office of the Chief of Naval Operations, *Report of Interrogation of Survivors of U-701 Sunk by U.S. Army Attack Bomber No. 9-29-322, Unit 296 B.S. On July 7, 1942.* Rohwer, *Axis Submarine Successes, 1939–1945,* 106. *Summary of Survivors' Statements, 1941–1945,* Office of the Chief of Naval Operations, NRS 1979-1. *Eastern Sea Frontier Enemy Action and Distress Diary,* 27 June 1942.

5. Offley, article in the *Ledger-Star* of Norfolk, Portsmouth, Virginia Beach, Chesapeake, Suffolk, VA., 8 July 1982. Navy Department, Office of the Chief of Naval Operations, *Report of Interrogation of Survivors of U-701 Sunk by U.S. Army Attack Bomber No. 9-29-322, Unit 296 B.S. On July 7, 1942.*

6. Offley, article in the *Ledger-Star* of Norfolk, Portsmouth, Virginia Beach, Chesapeake, Suffolk, VA., 8 July 1982. Navy Department, Office of the Chief of Naval Operations, *Report of Interrogation of Survivors of U-701 Sunk by U.S. Army Attack Bomber No. 9-29-322, Unit 296 B.S. On July 7, 1942.* Rohwer, *Axis Submarine Successes, 1939–1945,* 106. *Summary of Survivors' Statements, 1941–1945,* Office of the Chief of Naval Operations, NRS 1979-1. *Eastern Sea Frontier Enemy Action and Distress Diary,* 28 June 1942. Standard Oil Company of New Jersey, *Ships of the Esso Fleet in World War II,* 320–23.

7. Navy Department, Office of the Chief of Naval Operations, *Report of Interrogation of Survivors of U-701 Sunk by U.S. Army Attack Bomber No. 9-29-322, Unit 296 B.S. On July 7, 1942.*

8. Offley, article in the *Ledger-Star* of Norfolk, Portsmouth, Virginia Beach, Chesapeake, Suffolk, VA., 8–10 July 1982.

9. Hoyt, *U-boats Offshore,* 181–83. *War Diary, Eastern Sea Frontier,* July 1942, vol. 4. Offley, article in the *Ledger-Star* of Norfolk, Portsmouth, Virginia Beach, Chesapeake, Suffolk, VA., 8–10 July 1982.

10. Offley, article in the *Ledger-Star* of Norfolk, Portsmouth, Virginia Beach, Chesapeake, Suffolk, VA., 8–10 July 1982.

11. Offley, article in the *Ledger-Star* of Norfolk, Portsmouth, Virginia Beach, Chesapeake, Suffolk, VA., 8 July 1982. Navy Department, Office of the Chief of Naval Operations, *Report of Interrogation of Survivors of U-701 Sunk by U.S. Army Attack Bomber No. 9-29-322, Unit 296 B.S. On July 7, 1942. War Diary, Eastern Sea Frontier,* July 1942, vol. 9. Headquarters, Fifth Na-

val District, *Prisoners of War, Information Obtained from Seven Male German Prisoners of War Captured July 9, 1942*, 14 July 1942.

12. Offley, article in the *Ledger-Star* of Norfolk, Portsmouth, Virginia Beach, Chesapeake, Suffolk, VA., 8–10 July 1982. *War Diary, Eastern Sea Frontier*, July 1942, vol. 9.

13. Offley, article in the *Ledger-Star* of Norfolk, Portsmouth, Virginia Beach, Chesapeake, Suffolk, VA., 8 July 1982. Navy Department, Office of the Chief of Naval Operations, *Report of Interrogation of Survivors of U-701 Sunk by U.S. Army Attack Bomber No. 9-29-322, Unit 296 B.S. On July 7, 1942. War Diary, Eastern Sea Frontier*, July 1942, vol. 9. Headquarters, Fifth Naval District, *Prisoners of War, Information Obtained From Seven Male German Prisoners of War Captured July 9, 1942*, 14 July 1942.

14. Offley, article in the *Ledger-Star* of Norfolk, Portsmouth, Virginia Beach, Chesapeake, Suffolk, VA., 8–10 July 1982. *War Diary, Eastern Sea Frontier*, July 1942, vol. 9.

15. Offley, article in the *Ledger-Star* of Norfolk, Portsmouth, Virginia Beach, Chesapeake, Suffolk, VA., 8 July 1982. Navy Department, Office of the Chief of Naval Operations, *Report of Interrogation of Survivors of U-701 Sunk by U.S. Army Attack Bomber No. 9-29-322, Unit 296 B.S. On July 7, 1942. War Diary, Eastern Sea Frontier*, July 1942, vol. 9. Headquarters, Fifth Naval District, *Prisoners of War, Information Obtained From Seven Male German Prisoners of War Captured July 9, 1942*, 14 July 1942.

16. Offley, article in the *Ledger-Star* of Norfolk, Portsmouth, Virginia Beach, Chesapeake, Suffolk, VA., 8 July 1982. Navy Department, Office of the Chief of Naval Operations, *Report of Interrogation of Survivors of U-701 Sunk by U.S. Army Attack Bomber No. 9-29-322, Unit 296 B.S. On July 7, 1942. War Diary, Eastern Sea Frontier*, July 1942, vol. 9. Headquarters, Fifth Naval District, *Prisoners of War, Information Obtained From Seven Male German Prisoners of War Captured July 9, 1942*, 14 July 1942.

17. Offley, article in the *Ledger-Star* of Norfolk, Portsmouth, Virginia Beach, Chesapeake, Suffolk, VA., 8 July 1982. Navy Department, Office of the Chief of Naval Operations, *Report of Interrogation of Survivors of U-701 Sunk by U.S. Army Attack Bomber No. 9-29-322, Unit 296 B.S. On July 7, 1942. War Diary, Eastern Sea Frontier*, July 1942, vol. 9. Headquarters, Fifth Naval District, *Prisoners of War, Information Obtained From Seven Male German Prisoners of War Captured July 9, 1942*, 14 July 1942.

18. Offley, article in the *Ledger-Star* of Norfolk, Portsmouth, Virginia Beach, Chesapeake, Suffolk, VA., 8 July 1982. Navy Department, Office of the Chief of Naval Operations, *Report of*

*Interrogation of Survivors of U-701 Sunk by U.S. Army Attack Bomber No. 9-29-322, Unit 296 B.S. On July 7, 1942. War Diary, Eastern Sea Frontier,* July 1942, vol. 9. Headquarters, Fifth Naval District, *Prisoners of War, Information Obtained From Seven Male German Prisoners of War Captured July 9, 1942,* 14 July 1942.

19. Offley, article in the *Ledger-Star* of Norfolk, Portsmouth, Virginia Beach, Chesapeake, Suffolk, VA., 8 July 1982. Navy Department, Office of the Chief of Naval Operations, *Report of Interrogation of Survivors of U-701 Sunk by U.S. Army Attack Bomber No. 9-29-322, Unit 296 B.S. On July 7, 1942. War Diary, Eastern Sea Frontier,* July 1942, vol. 9. Headquarters, Fifth Naval District, *Prisoners of War, Information Obtained From Seven Male German Prisoners of War Captured July 9, 1942,* 14 July 1942.

20. Offley, article in the *Ledger-Star* of Norfolk, Portsmouth, Virginia Beach, Chesapeake, Suffolk, VA., 8 July 1982. Navy Department, Office of the Chief of Naval Operations, *Report of Interrogation of Survivors of U-701 Sunk by U.S. Army Attack Bomber No. 9-29-322, Unit 296 B.S. On July 7, 1942. War Diary, Eastern Sea Frontier,* July 1942, vol. 9. Headquarters, Fifth Naval District, *Prisoners of War, Information Obtained From Seven Male German Prisoners of War Captured July 9, 1942,* 14 July 1942.

21. Offley, article in the *Ledger-Star* of Norfolk, Portsmouth, Virginia Beach, Chesapeake, Suffolk, VA., 8 July 1982. Navy Department, Office of the Chief of Naval Operations, *Report of Interrogation of Survivors of U-701 Sunk by U.S. Army Attack Bomber No. 9-29-322, Unit 296 B.S. On July 7, 1942. War Diary, Eastern Sea Frontier,* July 1942, vol. 9. Headquarters, Fifth Naval District, *Prisoners of War, Information Obtained From Seven Male German Prisoners of War Captured July 9, 1942,* 14 July 1942.

22. Offley, article in the *Ledger-Star* of Norfolk, Portsmouth, Virginia Beach, Chesapeake, Suffolk, VA., 8 July 1982. Navy Department, Office of the Chief of Naval Operations, *Report of Interrogation of Survivors of U-701 Sunk by U.S. Army Attack Bomber No. 9-29-322, Unit 296 B.S. On July 7, 1942. War Diary, Eastern Sea Frontier,* July 1942, vol. 9. Headquarters, Fifth Naval District, *Prisoners of War, Information Obtained From Seven Male German Prisoners of War Captured July 9, 1942,* 14 July 1942.

23. Offley, article in the *Ledger-Star* of Norfolk, Portsmouth, Virginia Beach, Chesapeake, Suffolk, VA., 8 July 1982. Navy Department, Office of the Chief of Naval Operations, *Report of Interrogation of Survivors of U-701 Sunk by U.S. Army Attack Bomber No. 9-29-322, Unit 296 B.S. On July 7, 1942. War Diary, Eastern Sea Frontier,* July 1942, vol. 9. Headquarters, Fifth Na-

val District, *Prisoners of War, Information Obtained From Seven Male German Prisoners of War Captured July 9, 1942*, 14 July 1942.

24. Offley, article in the *Ledger-Star* of Norfolk, Portsmouth, Virginia Beach, Chesapeake, Suffolk, VA., 8 July 1982. Navy Department, Office of the Chief of Naval Operations, *Report of Interrogation of Survivors of U-701 Sunk by U.S. Army Attack Bomber No. 9-29-322, Unit 296 B.S. On July 7, 1942. War Diary, Eastern Sea Frontier*, July 1942, vol. 9. Headquarters, Fifth Naval District, *Prisoners of War, Information Obtained From Seven Male German Prisoners of War Captured July 9, 1942*, 14 July 1942.

25. Offley, article in the *Ledger-Star* of Norfolk, Portsmouth, Virginia Beach, Chesapeake, Suffolk, VA., 8 July 1982. Navy Department, Office of the Chief of Naval Operations, *Report of Interrogation of Survivors of U-701 Sunk by U.S. Army Attack Bomber No. 9-29-322, Unit 296 B.S. On July 7, 1942. War Diary, Eastern Sea Frontier*, July 1942, vol. 9. Headquarters, Fifth Naval District, *Prisoners of War, Information Obtained From Seven Male German Prisoners of War Captured July 9, 1942*, 14 July 1942.

26. The story is told that after landing, one of Burke's aircrew was assigned to guard the prisoners with a Thompson submachine gun. When more help was needed to get the last men on board, the "guard" handed his gun to a German and jumped into the ocean to help out. For a while, the German was the only armed man aboard!

27. Offley, article in the *Ledger-Star* of Norfolk, Portsmouth, Virginia Beach, Chesapeake, Suffolk, VA., 8–10 July 1982.

28. Ibid.

## Chapter Twenty-six

1. War Diary, Eastern Sea Frontier, July 1942, vols. 1, 5, 6.

2. Ibid., 6: 1.

3. War Diary, Eastern Sea Frontier, July 1942, vol. 7. Rohwer, *Axis Submarine Successes, 1939–1945*, 109.

4. Rohwer, *Axis Submarine Successes, 1939–1945*, 91–92. *War Diary, BdU*, 15–30 April 1942.

5. *War Diary, BdU*, 1–15 July 1942.

6. Submarine Attack at 1442 (E.W.T.) July 14, 1942, Report On, by Scouting Squadron Nine, USMC Air Station, Cherry Point, N.C., 16 July 1942.

7. *War Diary, BdU*, 16–31 July 1942.

8. War Diary, Eastern Sea Frontier, July 1942, vol. 7. Rohwer, *Axis Submarine Successes, 1939–1945*, 109.

9. National Archives microfilm NRS 1973-109, *U-576.*
10. War Diary, Eastern Sea Frontier, July 1942, vol. 6. Rohwer, *Axis Submarine Successes, 1939–1945,* 107. Taylor, *German Warships of World War II,* 119.
11. War Diary, Eastern Sea Frontier, July 1942, vol. 6. *War Diary, BdU,* 1–15 July 1942, 25.
12. Letters and reports concerning the sinking of *U-157* can be found in the National Archives and include correspondence from Headquarters Seventh Naval District; Commander Gulf Sea Frontier; United States Atlantic Fleet Anti-Submarine Warfare Unit; Commanding Officer, Atlantic Fleet Anti-Submarine Warfare Unit; Commanding Officer, USS *Noa* (DD 343); Commander, Service Squadron Nine; Commanding Officer, USS *PC 519;* Commanding Officer, USS *PE 27;* Commanding Officer, USCGC *Thetis;* Commanding Officer, USCGC *Triton;* Commanding Officer, First Sea-Search Attack Group, Langley Field, Virginia.
13. Rohwer, *Axis Submarine Successes, 1939–1945,* 102. Moore, *A Careless Word, A Needless Sinking,* 119.
14. Letter, Headquarters Seventh Naval District, Subject: "Killer Hunt" for Enemy Submarine, 10–14 June; preliminary report on, from Commander Gulf Sea Frontier to Commander in Chief, United States Fleets, 18 June 1942.
15. Ibid.
16. Letters and reports concerning the sinking of *U-157* can be found in the National Archives and include correspondence from Headquarters Seventh Naval District; Commander Gulf Sea Frontier; United States Atlantic Fleet Anti-Submarine Warfare Unit; Commanding Officer, Atlantic Fleet Anti-Submarine Warfare Unit; Commanding Officer, USS *Noa* (DD 343); Commander, Service Squadron NINE; Commanding Officer, USS *PC 519;* Commanding Officer, USS *PE 27;* Commanding Officer, *Thetis;* Commanding Officer, *Triton;* Commanding Officer, First Sea-Search Attack Group, Langley Field, Virginia.
17. Morison, *The Battle of the Atlantic,* 142–44.
18. Taylor, *German Warships of World War II,* 140. United States Naval Institute *Proceedings,* December 1960.

# Bibliography

## Primary Sources

1. Insight on the activities of the staff of the Eastern Sea Frontier was derived from an interview with, and a letter, dated 12 December 1984, from Professor Elting E. Morison, Peterborough, New Hampshire. Professor Morison compiled the *War Diary, North Atlantic Naval Coastal Frontier*, and the *War Diary, Eastern Sea Frontier, 1942* and was on Admiral Andrews's Eastern Sea Frontier staff.

2. Information concerning the United States Coast Guard Cutter *Dione* (WPC 107) was gained in a series of correspondence and interviews with members of the ship's crew from 1981–1988, including Rear Admiral James Alger, Jr., USCG (Ret.), Pompano Beach, Florida; Mr. R. E. Bacchus, Jr., Greensboro, NC; Captain David Oliver, USCG (Ret.), Wilmington, NC; Mr. J. V. B. Metts, Jr., Wilmington, NC; Major Harold "Swede" Larson, USMC (Ret.), McAllen, TX; Dr. John J. Fleming, Erie, PA; Mr. Richard Welton III, Virginia Beach, VA; Mr. Frederick G. Swink (who served aboard the *Dione*'s sister cutter, the *Calypso*); Kenneth A. Bastholm, D.D.S., Miami, Florida (who served on Cape Hatteras as a radioman during the battle and recalled the *Dione*'s ship-to-shore traffic); and Commander Nelson C. McCormick, USCG (Ret.), New London, CT. Members of the *Dione*'s crew also vividly remembered the famous writer, Charles Rawlings, and his photographer, Jack Manning, and helped fill in details Rawlings did not include in his article.

3. Information concerning the USS *Dickerson* (DD 157) and her ill-fated encounter with the *Liberator* was gained from a letter from Lieutenant Victor M. Merchant, USN (Ret.), dated 2 July 1984, and several subsequent telephone interviews.

4. Information concerning the USS *Roper* (DD 147) was gained by

a series of interviews and correspondence with the ship's crew in 1981–1985, including Rear Admiral Hamilton W. Howe, USN (Ret.), Winston-Salem, NC; Mr. Pen Shiflett, Richmond, VA; Commander W. F. DeLong, USN (Ret.), Belleair, FL; Mr. W. H. Mouquin, Miami, FL; Mr. Harry Heyman, Lakewood, NJ; Mr. Kenneth Tebo, Falls Church, VA; Dr. Winton H. Johnson, Sparta, NJ; Mr. Jesse W. Wozniak, Wilmington, DE; and Mr. Joe Hitzemann, Darien, WI.

5. The wreck of the *U-85* was dived on and inspected by the author during 1981–82 to verify damage done to the U-boat, specifically the report by Harry Heyman and others aboard the *Roper* of the results of the hit by the gun crew.

6. Information concerning shipboard life aboard the United States Coast Guard Cutter *Icarus* (WPC 110) and the sinking of the *U-352* was gained by a series of correspondence and interviews with former crewman Mr. John G. Bruce, Coupeville, WA, in 1975–1978.

7. Information concerning shipboard life aboard the *U-352* and her sinking was gained by correspondence and interviews with former commander Hellmut Rathke, Flensberg, FRG, during 1975–1979.

8. Information on the sinking of the *U-352* was confirmed by a series of dives by the author on the wreck of the *U-352* in 1975–76.

## Selected Secondary Sources

Botting, Douglas, and the eds. of Time-Life Books. *The U-boats*. Alexandria: Time-Life Books, 1979.

Buchheim, Lothar-Günter. *Das Boot*. New York: Alfred A. Knopf, 1975.

Buchheim, Lothar-Günter. *U-boat War*. New York: Alfred A. Knopf, 1978.

Cremer, Peter. *U-boat Commander*. Annapolis: Naval Institute Press, 1984.

Doenitz, Admiral Karl. *Memoirs: Ten Years and Twenty Days*. New York: Leisure Books, 1959.

*Sea Classics Magazine. Big War of the Little Ships*. Canoga Park, CA: Challenge Publications, 1985.

Farago, Ladislad. *The Tenth Fleet*. New York: Ivan Obolensky, 1982.

Frank, Wolfgang. *The Sea Wolves*. New York: Holt, Rinehart and Winston, 1955.

Gasaway, E. B. *Grey Wolf, Grey Sea*. New York: Ballantine Books, 1970.

Hadley, Michael L. *U-Boats Against Canada*. Montreal: McGill-Queen's University Press, 1985.

Hoyt, Edwin P. *U-boats Offshore*. New York: Stei & Day, 1978.

Hughes, Terry, and Costello, John. *The Battle of the Atlantic*. New York; Dial Press, 1977.

Karig, Commander Walter (USNR), Burton, Lieutenant Earl (USNR), and Freeland, Lieutenant Stephen L. (USNR). *Battle Report—The Atlantic War*. New York: Farrar & Rinehart, 1946.

Mason. *U-boat, The Secret Menace*. New York: Ballantine Books, 1969.

McCoy, Samuel Duff. *Nor Death Dismay*. New York: Macmillan Co., 1944.

Mellor, William B., Jr. *Sank Same*. New York: Howell, Soskin Publishers, 1944.

Mercey, Commander Arch A. (USCGR), and Grove, C. Sp. Lee (USCGR). *Sea, Surf, and Hell, The U.S. Coast Guard in World War II*. New York: Prentice-Hall, 1945.

Morrison, Samuel E. *History of U.S. Naval Operations in World War II*. Boston: Little, Brown & Co., 1947.

Morison, Samuel E. *The Battle of the Atlantic, September 1939–May 1943*. Boston: Little, Brown & Co., 1962.

Morison, Samuel E. *The Two-Ocean War*. Boston: Little, Brown & Co., 1963.

Naisawald, L. Van Loan. *In Some Foreign Field*. Winston-Salem: John F. Blair, 1972.

Newton, J. G., Pilkey, O. H., and Blanton, J. O. *Oceanographic Atlas of the Carolina Continental Margin*. Durham: Duke University Marine Laboratory, 1971.

Noli, Jean. *The Admiral's Wolf Pack*. New York: Doubleday & Co., 1974.

Ott, Wolfgang. *Sharks and Little Fish*. New York: Ballantine Books, 1966.

Pfannes, Charles E., and Salamone, Victor A. *The Great Admirals of World War II, Vol. I: The Americans*. New York: Kensington Publishing Corp., 1983.

Preston, Anthony. *U-boats*. London: Bison Books, 1978.

Rawlings, Charles. *We Saw the Battle of the Atlantic: Diana, of Periscope Lane, Torpedo Junction*. New York: Pickwick Ltd., 1942.

Rohwer, Jürgen. *Axis Submarine Successes, 1939–1945*. Annapolis: Naval Institute Press, 1983.

Rohwer, Jürgen. *Profile Warship Kriegsmarine U-107/Submarine.* Windsor, England; Profile Publications Ltd., 1971.

Roessler, Eberhard. *The U-boat.* Annapolis: Naval Institute Press, 1984.

Roscoe, Theodore. *United States Destroyer Operations in World War II.* Annapolis: U.S. Naval Institute, 1953.

Roskill, Stephen. *Churchill and the Admirals.* New York: William Morrow & Co., 1977.

Schaeffer, Heinz. *U-boat 977.* New York: Bantam Books, 1987.

Scheina, Robert. *U.S. Coast Guard Cutters & Craft of World War II.* Annapolis: Naval Institute Press, 1982.

Schofield, William G. *Eastward the Convoys.* New York: Rand McNally & Co., 1965.

Showell, J. P. Mallmann. *U-boats under the Swastika.* Annapolis, Maryland: Naval Institute Press, 1987.

Standard Oil Company. *Ships of the ESSO Fleet in World War II.* New Jersey: Standard Oil Co. of New Jersey, 1946.

Stick, David. *Graveyard of the Atlantic.* Chapel Hill: University of North Carolina Press, 1952.

Stick, David. *Outer Banks of North Carolina.* Chapel Hill: University of North Carolina Press, 1958.

Taylor, J. C. *German Warships of World War II.* New York: Doubleday & Co., 1966.

Taylor, Theodore. *Fire on the Beaches.* New York: Norton, 1958.

Von Der Porten, Edward P. *The German Navy in World War Two.* New York: Ballantine Books, 1974.

Waters, Captain John M., USCG (Ret.). *Bloody Winter.* Annapolis: Naval Institute Press, 1984.

Werner, Herbert A. *Iron Coffins.* New York: Holt, Rinehart & Winston, 1969.

Whedbee, John F. *Legends of the Outer Banks.* Winston-Salem: John F. Blair, 1966.

# Index

The Naval Institute Press is the book-publishing arm of the U.S. Naval Institute, a private, nonprofit professional society for members of the sea services and civilians who share an interest in naval and maritime affairs. Established in 1873 at the U.S. Naval Academy in Annapolis, Maryland, where its offices remain today, the Naval Institute has more than 100,000 members worldwide.

Members of the Naval Institute receive the influential monthly naval magazine *Proceedings* and substantial discounts on fine nautical prints, ship and aircraft photos, and subscriptions to the Institute's recently inaugurated quarterly, *Naval History*. They also have access to the transcripts of the Institute's Oral History Program and may attend any of the Institute-sponsored seminars regularly offered around the country.

The book-publishing program, begun in 1898 with basic guides to naval practices, has broadened its scope in recent years to include books of more general interest. Now the Naval Institute Press publishes more than forty new titles each year, ranging from how-to books on boating and navigation to battle histories, biographies, ship guides, and novels. Institute members receive discounts on the Press's more than 300 books.

For a free catalog describing books currently available and

for further information about U.S. Naval Institute membership, please write to:

Membership Department
U.S. Naval Institute
Annapolis, Maryland 21402

or call, toll-free, 800–233–USNI.